SACRAMENTO PUBLIC LIBRARY

STREET

5814

8/2011

D0380391

PRAISE FOR *THE END (*

"No collection better demonstrates how taki[...]
too-human origin. This superb, often witty, an[...]n
explains how early Christianity is only a pale resemblance of any or the [...]s-
tian sects today. As well, the authors reveal how vastly improbable Christian dogmas
are, such as the notion that a god designed the universe, that life replete with personal
identity continues after death, that hell represents divine justice; and that morality is
exclusively Christian. Overall, very sobering for Christians, and so wonderfully
delightful for the rest of us."

> —Malcolm Murray, PhD, associate professor of philosophy,
> University of Prince Edward Island;
> author of *The Atheist's Primer*

"*The End of Christianity* reads like a family reunion that brings together the family of
disbelieving intellectuals we've grown to love and respect. The stories that form the
great narrative of the history of unbelief find in this book fresh voices with new and
exciting angles. Loftus and his friends annihilate the Christian Goliath with their dis-
putatious slingshots. The reader will probably hope that believers will not shy away
from this text if only so that Loftus will soon publish yet another exciting anthology."

> —Johnnie Terry, instructor in philosophy, Sierra College

"This fascinating book's beefy arguments as well as its tasty tidbits of information are
all geared to show that when it comes to 'God talk' and the 'revealed religion' known
as Christianity, the questions outnumber the certainties. And though Christianity and
religion in general will certainly endure long enough for John Loftus to edit additional
works, that sort of blessing does not appear to be one for which some Christians will
be eager to thank God."

> —Edward T. Babinski, editor of *Leaving the Fold:*
> *Testimonies of Former Fundamentalists*

"*The Christian Delusion* is the first book I give to anyone who wants to understand why
I am no longer a Christian. Loftus and company have returned with *The End of Christianity*, which will now be the *second* book I give to anyone who wants to read a substantive case against Christian faith."

> —Luke Meuhlhauser, owner of the popular blog
> *Common Sense Atheism*, which named
> Loftus's *Why I Became an Atheist* as the
> Best Atheism Book of the Decade (2000–2009)

THE END OF

Christianity

THE END OF
Christianity

EDITED BY JOHN W. LOFTUS

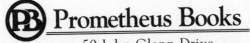

Prometheus Books

59 John Glenn Drive
Amherst, New York 14228–2119

Published 2011 by Prometheus Books

The End of Christianity. Copyright © 2011 by John W. Loftus. All rights reserved. No part of this publication may be reproduced, stored in a retrieval system, or transmitted in any form or by any means, digital, electronic, mechanical, photocopying, recording, or otherwise, or conveyed via the Internet or a website without prior written permission of the publisher, except in the case of brief quotations embodied in critical articles and reviews.

Cover image © 2011 Media Bakery
Cover design by Jacqueline Nasso Cooke

Inquiries should be addressed to

Prometheus Books
59 John Glenn Drive
Amherst, New York 14228–2119
VOICE: 716–691–0133
FAX: 716–691–0137
WWW.PROMETHEUSBOOKS.COM

15 14 13 12 11   5 4 3 2 1

Library of Congress Cataloging-in-Publication Data

The end of Christianity / edited by John Loftus.
    p. cm.
Includes bibliographical references.
ISBN 978–1–61614–413–5 (pbk.)
ISBN 978–1–61614–414–2 (e-book)
1. Christianity—Controversial literature. I. Loftus, John W.

BL2775.3.E53 2011
230—dc22

2011009827

Printed in the United States of America

Dedicated to the memory of Ken Pulliam.
He was a good husband, father, friend, and scholar.

CONTENTS

INTRODUCTION

This present anthology is now what I call the third book in a series—the first of which I consider my magnum opus, *Why I Became an Atheist* (2008), followed by the anthology *The Christian Delusion* (2010), titled after Richard Dawkins's bestselling book, *The God Delusion*. *The End of Christianity* is titled after Sam Harris's bestseller, *The End of Faith*, which started the so-called New Atheist movement. Unlike Harris, who called for an end to religious faith as a whole, we're calling for an end to a specific kind of religious faith: Christianity. I honestly think that with this book (and certainly the series) Christianity has been debunked. The jury has returned its verdict. The gavel has come down. The case is now closed.

I think the chapters in this anthology speak for themselves, so I'll not introduce them except to say I'm very pleased and honored to be a part of this work, which includes several leading atheists, agnostics, and religious critics of our day. Once again I thank each contributor and especially Richard Carrier for the yeomen job he did with editing and peer review of nearly all the chapters.

GETTING ON BOARD WITH THE OTF

My signature argument is the *Outsider Test for Faith* (OTF), which I defended in my earlier books. It plays an important role in this series, so I want to say more about it here. Who would have thought that such a simple and obvious argument would be so hotly contested that I would have to revisit it again? But it is contested, probably because it can and does undermine religious faith so well.

We are all raised as believers by our parents in our respective cultures. If our parents said something was true, then we believed it as children. We didn't know not to do so. One of the most important things our parents told us to believe is that their particular religion is true. And so, fundamentalists will raise fundamentalists. Snake handlers will raise snake handlers. Polygamists will raise polygamists. Catholics will raise Catholics. Militant Muslims will raise militant Muslims. Mormons will raise Mormons. Orthodox Jews will raise Orthodox Jews. Scientologists will raise Scientologists. And so on and so forth. We can even locate specific geological boundary lines of religious faiths around the globe. If we were raised in Thailand, we would probably be Buddhists. If we were raised in India, we'd probably be Hindus. If we were raised in Mexico, we'd probably be Catholics. Even if we revised our religion upon further reflection, we'd still be found doing so from the inside within that same tradition. And if we switch religions as adults, usually we still adopt a religion very similar to the one we were already taught.

As we grow older, however, we learn to question what we were taught. Skepticism is therefore a learned virtue. We must learn to question. As we do, we eventually become adults. But the strange thing is that even as adults we do not usually question our religious beliefs. They just seem too obvious to us. They have become too ingrained within us. They are part of the culture we live in. We usually see no need to question them. They are such a part of who we are that for many of us, like me, it takes a personal crisis to do what we should have been doing all along: critically examining the religion that was handed down to us. But given the proliferation of religions around the globe, they cannot all be correct. So how can we test whether our inherited religious faith is the correct one? That's where the OTF comes in.

The OTF asks believers to test their own inherited religious faith from the perspective of an outsider with the same level of skepticism they use to evaluate other religious faiths. The OTF asks believers to abandon the double standard they have about religious faiths, nothing more. The process should be fair; no one should place a thumb on the weighing scales. If we merely asked believers to evaluate their faith objectively, most of them will claim they have already done so. But ask them to evaluate their own religious faith with the same level of skepticism they use to evaluate the other religious faiths they reject, and *that* will get their attention. Hopefully I have their attention now.

Believers who object to the OTF must show why the anthropological, psychological, and sociological data that necessitates the test is erroneous (all of which I've laid out in the previous books in this series), or show that the test is faulty or unfair in some important way. So far, they have emphatically not succeeded at doing either.

IS THE OTF TOO EXTREME?

One objection to the OTF is that it unreasonably asks believers to do something no one can be expected to do: to give up their whole worldview—including their lifestyle. From a practical standpoint it's very hard to give up one's religious faith all at once. Still, believers should use the OTF to critically examine each and every tenet of their faith, one at a time, thus resolving this difficulty. Nonetheless, this objection confuses a set of religious beliefs with a total worldview. Former believers only had to give up a particular set of religious beliefs and a few closely interrelated moral and sociopolitical ideals. We did not have to give up our whole worldview. When I left the faith, I didn't leave my culture, my language, or most of the rest of what my culture leads me to think about history, democracy, geography, love, friendship, work, or what makes me happy. The OTF isn't asking anyone to do the impossible. In America, for instance, the religious right is conservative both religiously and socially. But just subtract the religion from these conservatives, and they usually become liberals, and their worldview then becomes skeptical or naturalistic. While doing this can be a bit painful, it isn't asking believers to do something that many former believers aren't already doing on a daily basis.

DOES THE OTF UNDERMINE MORALITY?

Another objection to the OTF is that it should equally be applied to morality, and any sociopolitical ideals based on it, otherwise the test unfairly targets only "religious faith" for criticism. But this misses the mark, as illustrated by a sharp disagreement in this book between Richard Carrier and David Eller. Carrier argues in the last chapter that moral facts exist and that science can find them, while Eller, a cultural anthropologist, has argued instead in favor of cultural relativism.[1] In neither case do their views on morality undercut the OTF, although they are both antithetical to a faith-based morality. If Carrier is right, then all discovered moral facts will *pass* the OTF, because they will be found by science. If Eller is right, then the claim that there is *an* absolute, unchanging, universal, cross-cultural morality simply fails the OTF. The one argues morality can pass the test, while the other says it fails the test. Thus both of them are using the standard of the OTF to assess morality. And regardless of their disagreement, as outsiders they both reject Christian morality.[2] Try to show people like them otherwise, okay? You'll need the OTF to do it.

I personally find it very difficult to argue against cultural relativism once we grant evolution. Yet at the same time there seems to be some moral values that human beings all share irrespective of their religious beliefs. Political freedom seems to be one of these values, best seen in the fall of the Berlin Wall in November 1989 and in the Muslim world with the ousting of Egyptian president Hosni Mubarak in February 2011. These shared moral values, if that's what they are, might not undercut cultural relativism, but we still share them.

Nonetheless, one problem in subjecting moral values to the same skepticism demanded of religious faiths is that *we need common shared moral values to live our lives in our respective cultures*, whereas religious faiths are irrelevant and unnecessary, and can even be harmful. So even though we should be skeptical of our moral values, we still need them in order to live our lives in our respective cultures (which is arguably one way they do in fact pass the OTF, whereas we do not need religious faiths at all.

One thing we can all agree upon is that we want to be happy. The need for happiness drives all our moral values (regardless of what others claim). That we want happiness is an empirical fact. It cannot be denied. It passes the skepticism of an outsider's test because it is indeed a fact. It is, as Aristotle argued, always desired in and of itself and never as a means to something else. He was speaking about holistic happiness and not merely about a pig who is satisfied. What that means is up for debate, of course. But whatever it is, it's the thing we do everything else *for*. And it's precisely because we want to be happy in this way that we also want the people close to us to be happy, and in turn we want the people close to them to be happy, and so on. This then, if anything, is the basis for our choosing which moral values produce the most good for the most people, and the basis for our caring about that in the first place. And if the sciences can't find what makes us happy as human beings, then nothing else can.

The bottom line is that no matter what we think is the case, and no matter what we think about morality, or how we justify it, we all know what it is to doubt something. I'm asking believers to doubt their own inherited religious faith. Just their faith. One thing at a time. You can question the validity of your inherited *morals* later, which, when you do, will help you see morality better without being hamstrung by a religion that cannot be defended. I see no reason why someone cannot do this. As I said, many of us have done just that. My contention is that one of the main reasons there is moral diversity is because there is religious diversity. So as religions are debunked by the OTF, there will be a greater potential for achieving a global moral consensus.

DOES THE OTF UNDERMINE ATHEISM?

Another objection to the OTF is that it should equally be applied to the atheist position, otherwise the test unfairly targets religious faith for criticism. But the truth is that atheists are almost always nontheists or nonbelievers because they are, first and foremost, skeptics. Skepticism is an adult attitude for arriving at the truth. Consequently, atheists do not technically have a "viewpoint" to subject their nonbeliefs to except the evidence itself. Atheists are skeptics who do not believe in supernatural beings or forces because we conclude the evidence is not there. We are nonbelievers. That's all there is to it. We came to disbelieve because there just wasn't enough evidence to convince us otherwise. We can't subject these nonbeliefs to any further testing! They are tested only by the facts. Atheism is simply what we have left when all religious beliefs fail the OTF. Just present us with facts that pass the OTF, and we'll believe.

So when Christians ask if I have taken the outsider test for my own "belief system," I simply say, "Yes, I have; that's why I'm a nonbeliever." Then they'll ask if I am equally skeptical of my skepticism, or whether I have subjected my nonbelief to nonbelief, or my disbelief to disbelief. These questions express double negatives. When retranslated, they are asking me to abandon skepticism in favor of a gullible faith. For *that's* the opposite of skepticism— something no thinker should do. Doubt is, again, an adult attitude.

The bottom line is that *skepticism* is a word used to describe doubt or disbelief. It doesn't by itself represent any ideas we've arrived at. It's merely a filter we use to strain out the bad ideas, leaving us with the good ones. We cannot be skeptical of that filter because there is no alternative except gullibly accepting anything and everything, which is so self-evidently a recipe for failure it's clear that it is skepticism, and not gullibility, that passes the OTF.

Christian thinkers, in a desperate attempt to defend their faith with Orwellian double-speak, will claim that they are *more* skeptical than I am because they are skeptical of skeptical arguments—a "full-blown skepticism." (Yep, just ask Christian scholar Thomas Talbott). Their claim is that a true skeptic is an open-minded one who is open to the miraculous, which in turn is supposed to leave room for their faith. They will even claim not to know what an extraordinary event is (something I call *definitional apologetics*, that is, defining a problem away in the face of a concrete example like the virgin birth or a bodily resurrection). But when we truly consider what must be believed to be a Christian, we find here a prime example of what I mean when I say Christianity is a delusion. If this contorted epistemology is embraced, then "skepticism" becomes an utterly unjustified open-mindedness, leaving us with no way to test what to believe. Then other religionists can use this same epistemology to defend their own faiths, and so every claim that a witch flew through the night to have sex with the devil would be, technically speaking, on the boards. *No*, I am not open to that extraordinary claim without a *lot* of evidence to support it. With such an epistemology, we would have no way to determine which faith—or which wildly improbable claim—is true.

On top of this, if nonbelievers are to take the OTF, then Christians need to tell us what an outsider perspective for us would be. Is it the perspective of Catholicism or Protestant Fundamentalism? Is it the perspective of snake handlers, holy rollers, or the obnoxious and racist KKK? Is it that of a Satanist, a Scientologist, a Shintoist, or a Sikh? What about that of a Mormon, a militant Muslim, or a Moonie? How about a Jew, a Jain, or a Jehovah's Witness? The problem is that there just isn't a worthy religious contender from out of the myriad number of religions that can be considered an outsider perspective for nonbelievers. This is not a fault with the OTF. It's the fault of religion.

In desperation to avoid facing the OTF themselves, Christians have actually asked me if I have ever examined modernism from a nonmodernist point of view. Believers will even go so far as to say that they don't even know what the scientific method is (yep, just ask Christian scholar Randal Rauser, another case of *definitional apologetics*). Perhaps they might try explaining why science continues to advance without one, because I'm all ears. We might as well return to the prescientific, superstitious era of ancient peoples. While philosophers debate the minutia of what makes science science, science proceeds to deliver the goods in chemistry, astronomy, geology, medicine, physics, biology, meteorology, and so on, and so forth. Christians themselves accept the results of science in a vast majority of areas except in those rare ones that go against what some prescientific "agency-detectors" wrote in a collection of ancient superstitious biblical texts. There is a reason why atheist groups state that they promote science and reason. And there is a reason why faith-based groups sneer at them both.

We simply cannot turn back the hands of time and become Amish. We can only go forward with the sciences. To the outsider, the sciences are the paragon of knowledge. That's why they replaced our former ways of knowing. Scientific knowledge has so decisively passed an outsider test that we must examine all religious faiths in light of it. Show me the math, and we agree. Show me the experiment, and the argument is over. Show me the scientific poll, and the case is closed. Show me what we learn from brain science, and there can be no dispute. The sciences, then, are the only way to keep us all from deluding ourselves. So for a religious faith to pass the OTF it must be detectable by the sciences. Period. If believers want to claim that the sciences cannot detect God, then that means we cannot objectively know God at all. For the sciences are based on the evidence of the senses. If they reject the sciences, then let them propose a better alternative. What is that alternative?

The only true outsider position is agnosticism, which I've called the default position—as such, it is the neutral point of view. An agnostic as defined here in this instance is one who is skeptical of all metaphysical claims, and this is a true skepticism. I see no reason why we shouldn't start by looking at the world as agnostics, for it helps us determine fact from fantasy. All metaphysical claims must pass the OTF before we should believe them. Atheists and agnostics share this skeptical common ground. It's just that atheists are willing to conclude there are no supernatural beings or forces with enough assurance to say so. That's pretty much all there is to it.

In short, the OTF merely asks believers to test their own culturally inherited religious faith from the perspective of an outsider *with the same level of skepticism* they use to evaluate other religious faiths. It does *not* matter what level of skepticism they might apply, only that they *test all beliefs the same*, privileging none. Again, the OTF simply asks that believers take whatever level of skepticism they would use when examining religious faiths they reject and use that same level of skepticism when testing their own religious faith. Nothing more. Liberals, for instance, should be as skeptical of their own faith as they already are of fundamentalism, and vice versa. This isn't a radical doubt. It's the same doubt believers already embrace—just not when it comes to their own "faith." And I'm saying that's wrong. Fatally wrong.

This dispels once again the wrongheaded objection that if the OTF asks believers to be skeptical as outsiders of their own religious faith, then why not be skeptical as outsiders that there is even a material world? That's like rejecting the OTF because it's not skeptical *enough*, and then using that as an excuse to not be skeptical *at all*. The OTF does not entail such radical skepticism. We have more than enough evidence to conclude that the existence of the material world is far more probable than any proposed alternative—which is why we think it exists.[3]

WHY THE OTF FRIGHTENS CHRISTIANS SO

The whole reason Christians object to the OTF is because they intuitively know their faith will not pass the test, even though this tacitly concedes the whole argument. If their faith passed the test, they would be the first ones embracing the OTF and pushing it on everyone else. Instead, they argue against it. This tells us there is something very wrong with the Christian faith. In effect, what they're doing is like arguing against the need for a fair and impartial ruling coming from a fair and impartial judge in a court case. Why would anyone interested in the truth want that? No fair-minded person would ever want this, much less publicly argue for it. Believers will retort that it is impossible *not* to be biased, but this is the very thing I admit that causes me to propose the OTF in the first place. Again, what is the alternative?

Now, it didn't have to turn out that the Christian faith would fail the OTF. If God exists, he could have made the Christian faith pass it. He didn't do this, even though he should have done so, for it only takes a moment's thought to realize that if Christianity is true, it *should* pass the OTF. Otherwise there are billions of rational non-Christians who were raised in different cultures who could not believe by virtue of the fact that they were born as outsiders and will subsequently be condemned to hell. So, if Christians want to continue objecting to the OTF because of fears that their faith cannot pass it, let them admit that God is allowing people born into non-Christian cultures to be condemned to hell merely by virtue of the fact that they were born as outsiders into different religious cultures. And let Christians stop all cross-cultural, missionary-evangelist work, too, for if Christianity was not created to pass the OTF, then there could be no hope such efforts would succeed.

THE CONSEQUENCES OF ACCEPTING THE OTF

Christians might finally admit the OTF is neither faulty nor unfair and then bite the bullet by asserting their faith passes the test. But once they make this claim, they have just agreed that the skepticism of the OTF is a consistent, fair, and justified standard for evaluating one's own religious faith. At that point, Christians can no longer continually punt to faith when critically evaluating the grounds for their own particular Christian sect, since that is not how they critically evaluate the many other religions they reject. They don't let other religions get away with that, so they can't let themselves get away with it, either. What we're left with is an agreed-upon standardized test in assessing the grounds for any religion based in reason and evidence. At that point, the debate can really begin. Prior to this, there wasn't a debate at all but rather two opposing sides talking past one another. Afterward, believers should welcome the skeptic's point of view and even seek us out.

From then on, there can be no more quoting the Bible as a final authority without examining the reasons and the evidence for doing so all over again. No more repeatedly using what I call the "Omniscience Escape Clause," which is invoked whenever there is an intractable difficulty, such as that found in passages like Isaiah 55:8: "'My thoughts are not your thoughts, neither are your ways my ways,' declares the Lord." Why? Because we must be able to understand enough of God's ways to know that he exists, that he knows what he's doing, and that his ways are good. Most importantly, the problem of who has the burden of proof will have been resolved as well. For then it's agreed that the person with the burden of proof is the one making an extraordinary claim about supernatural beings and forces. All these things are good, and I welcome them if this argument achieves nothing else.

I would proceed to argue from here that Christians who bite this bullet are not actually testing their religion fairly. The impact of the OTF disallows a person from assuming faith in the religion under scrutiny. Having faith in a religion while assessing it will unfairly exempt that religion from an objective critical evaluation. Believers cannot claim to critically evaluate their own faith in a fair manner if when doing so they have their thumbs on the weight scales.

I would further argue that Christians are just fooling themselves when faced with the facts *apart from their faith*. Fooling themselves? Could that be? Yep. This is exactly what cognitive dissonance theory predicts. According to conclusive scientific studies in this area of research, we believe what we prefer to be true. Once our minds are made up, it is very hard to change them.[4] We seek to justify our decisions, especially the costly ones in terms of commitment, money, effort, time, and inconvenience. Almost shockingly, these studies have shown us that reading information that goes against our point of view can actually make us convinced we are right. We will even take the lack of evidence as evidence for what we believe. Social psychologists Carol Tavris and Elliot Aronson document these types of things in their book *Mistakes Were Made (But Not By Me): Why We Justify Foolish Beliefs, Bad Decisions, and Hurtful Acts*. They tell us: "Most people, when directly confronted with proof that they are wrong, do not change their point of view or course of action but justify it even more tenaciously."[5]

This is backed up by the conclusion derived from a series of studies in 2005 and 2006 by researchers at the University of Michigan:

> Facts don't necessarily have the power to change our minds. In fact, quite the opposite . . . when misinformed people, particularly political partisans, were exposed to corrected facts in news stories, they rarely changed their minds. In fact, they often became even more strongly set in their beliefs. Facts . . . were not curing misinformation. Like an underpowered antibiotic, facts could actually make misinformation even stronger.[6]

Christian, the mental pain you may feel as you read this book is called cognitive dissonance. To reduce it you must make a choice, and cognitive dissonance theory predicts you will almost always dig your feet in deeper—depending on how important your faith is to you. It also predicts that for us to overcome your objections, we must make a completely overwhelming case that leaves you nowhere else to run before you will change your mind—a demand that is largely unrealistic, because the kind of evidence required seems unavailable.

Since a completely overwhelming case seems elusive, Christians confronted with this scientific data usually proceed with the all too familiar "You Too" (*tu quoque*) informal fallacy, saying, "Hey, cognitive dissonance theory applies to you, too." Christians will then use it to sidestep what this data does to their own faith, but this blatantly ignores the implications of this scientific data, which shows us we're all in the same boat, epistemologically speaking. Again, for emphasis: *We are all in the same boat.* That's how human beings like us think, all of us, with the exception that people who understand these things will be better critical thinkers than others. Because these thinkers are aware of their errors and biases, they're much more prone to compensate for them. To be in the same boat means we should all be skeptics who trust the sciences, knowing how easily the mind is swayed by nonrational cultural factors. We should be more demanding of hard, cold evidence before concluding much of anything. We will, in the end, be skeptics who base what we know on valid logic and the facts established by the sciences.

Don't get me wrong here. I grant that a religion could pass the OTF. It's just that I don't think any so-called revealed religion can do so, and I'm doubtful any religion can pass it. If it turns out no religion can pass the test, keep in mind it's not the fault of the test. It's the fault of religion. It simply means none of them can be justified, because this test is an entirely fair one that has not been shown to be faulty in any way.

THE LIBERAL BELIEVER AND
THE END OF CHRISTIANITY

There are professing Christians who will read the books in this series and feel as if some of their particular beliefs have escaped our criticism. They believe differently precisely because there are just too many ways to be a Christian, as David Eller argues in chapter 1 of this book. Since Christianity is a culturally evolving thing, skeptics are chasing down a greased pig. All is not lost, though. Christians in opposing camps can take up where we leave off, and they do. When it comes to Christianity, I agree with the Protestant criticisms of the Catholics as well as the Catholic criticisms of the Protestants. I agree with the fundamentalist criticisms of the liberals as well as the liberal criticisms of the fundamentalists. In addition, I agree with the Hindu, Muslim, and Jewish criticisms of Christianity, as well as the Christian criticisms of their religions. When they criticize each other, I think they're all right. What's left is the demise of religion and Christianity as a whole.

For instance, I don't say much by way of criticizing liberalism because I don't have to do so. Christian fundamentalists do that for me. Their criticism of the liberals is my criticism, which centers on one question: Why do they even bother with the Bible at all? Why not the Koran, the Bhagavad Gita, or Mary Baker Eddy's *Science and Health with Key to the Scriptures*? Or, why not just receive direct inspiration from God? Or "listen to their heart"? The liberal deconstruction of the Bible has put an end to biblical studies, as argued most effectively by professor Hector Avalos in chapter 4 of this book. If believers no longer accept the historical underpinnings of their faith, they should look for a different one or none at all. It's the intellectually honest thing to do. To me, liberalism *is a pretend game* much like M. Night Shyamalan's movie *The Village*. In my opinion, liberals should stop pretending.

Liberals should openly recognize they did not come to their conclusions without a fight against the goads. They were forced against their preferences into accepting what science and biblical criticism led them to think. Now all they do is pick and choose what parts of the Bible to believe with no solid criteria for distinguishing the believable parts from the unbelievable parts except their shared evolving consensus—and, since it's an evolved consensus, they don't need the Bible to inform it. Liberals don't accept anything the Bible says just because it says it. So they can quite easily dispense with it altogether as irrelevant for their lives.

My hope is that this series of books helps honest Christians know the truth about their faith. Christian, is your faith true? Only if it passes the OTF will you ever know. If, however, you're reading this book with no other purpose than to find fault with it, then shame on you. Let this indicator serve as a forewarning that you are probably not being honest with your faith. What other indicator will do if that one doesn't?

Finally, if Christians can end their books with a call for a commitment, I can too. If after reading and thinking through this book you no longer believe, don't forget the last page, the commitment page. After filling that page out, you might find yourself experiencing what psychologist Marlene Winell calls "shattered faith syndrome." If so, I highly recommend reading her book, *Leaving the Fold*.[7]

As with our last book, there is a companion website for this one. It can be found at https://sites.google.com/site/theendofchristianity. We will respond to important criticisms there when they appear.

—John W. Loftus

Part 1

WHY TWO THOUSAND YEARS ARE ENOUGH

Chapter 1

CHRISTIANITY EVOLVING
On the Origin of Christian Species

Dr. David Eller

[T]he paramount, vital doctrine[s] of Western Christianity such as the trinity, the Incarnation, and the Redemption and other details of dogma connected with them are all cultural creations. . . . At the beginning even the name "Christian" was not known to it, and it developed itself historically until its particular traits and characteristics and attributes took form and became fixed and clarified and refined and recognizable as the religion of a culture and civilization known to the world as Christianity. . . . Hence Christianity, by the virtue of its being created by man, gradually developed its system of rituals by assimilation from other cultures and traditions as well as originating its own fabrications; and through successive stages clarified its creeds such as those at Nicaea, Constantinople, and Chalcedon. Since it had no revealed law it had to assimilate Roman laws; and since it had no coherent world view projected by revelation, it had to borrow from Greco-Roman thought and later to construct out of it an elaborate theology and metaphysics. Gradually it created its own specifically Christian cosmology, and its arts and sciences developed. . . .[1]

The end of Christianity is not some far-off dream, nor is it on the verge of occurring. Instead, it happened two thousand years ago—in fact, Christianity never even began; it was stillborn. According to the words above, there is no such thing as the religion of Christianity; at best it is a multitude of related but distinct and often-enough opposed traditions, shifting and swaying with the winds of local culture and passing history. And who is the author of these words? Some angry atheist out to destroy religion? No, it is Muhammad al Naquib al-Attas, a devout Muslim and staunch enemy of secularization, who firmly attests that Christianity is and always has been secular, worldly, changing, and evolving to adapt to its social circumstances. And al-Attas is correct: Christianity *has* always been secular, worldly, changing, and evolving to adapt to its social circumstances—but so has Islam and every other human-made religion (why else would there be Sunni and Shi'ite Islam, as well as numerous Muslim schools of interpretation and jurisprudence?).

Many contemporary Christians see "evolution" as the antithesis and nemesis they must oppose and refute. Yet, as al-Attas and even the merest acquaintance with Christian history or modern global Christianity clearly prove, Christianity not only fails to refute evolution but actually *illustrates* evolution. Evolution is the process by which some entity changes and adjusts and develops in response to its environment. There is no disputing that life-forms and social-forms evolve over time: humans are not what we were millions of years ago, nor is an institution like government or language or marriage what it was "in the beginning" (in fact, none of these existed "in the beginning" at all). Likewise, there is no disputing that Christianity has evolved over time: Christianity today is not what it was 500 or 1,000 or certainly not 2,000 years ago (and there was no such thing as Christianity more than 2,000 years ago), nor will it be the same thing 100 or 200 years in the future. To be honest, it is not even the same thing in every country and congregation in the world right now.

Like every other product of evolution, Christianity is a bushy tree of sundry and squabbling species—or in the case of religions, "sects" and "denominations." One very reputable count estimated there are over 33,000 of these Christian species in the world, and that was a decade ago; doubtless there are many more today, with more appearing every day.[2] There are some fifty sects of Methodism alone, which the Association of Religion Data Archives arranges into a literal Methodist "family tree" as scientists would organize any set of related species.[3] What this means is that every Christian denomination hangs on one branch of a rambling bush of Christian churches, the commonalities and differences between which belie their evolutionary origin and history just as surely as any biological species. Even more, the evolution of Christianity follows exactly the same processes as biological evolution such as speciation, radiation, competition, extinction, and so on.

This chapter reveals three historical epochs of Christian speciation: (1) the early period, from the first centuries to the Reformation; (2) the American period, with many new, uniquely American adaptations; and (3) the twenty-first-century global period with new Christianities emerging in Africa, Latin

America, Asia, and elsewhere. Christianity will be exposed as a thicket of bickering religions, absorbing local influences and reinventing themselves over and over again—which does undermine any possible claim of uniqueness or truth in Christianity.

THE INVENTION OF TRADITIONS (LIKE RELIGION)

Every tradition, no matter how old, was once new. Worse still, when a new tradition first appears, it is obviously not yet "traditional"; it is novel, often even unconventional or heretical. Keen and honest observers have known this for a long time, but the historians Eric Hobsbawm and Terence Ranger made it explicit in their book *The Invention of Tradition*, where they explain that traditions seek to inculcate certain values and norms of behavior by repetition, which automatically implies continuity with the past. In fact, where possible, new traditions normally attempt to establish continuity with a suitable historic past. However, insofar as there is such reference to a historic past, the peculiarity of "invented" traditions is that the continuity with it is largely factitious. In short, they are responses to novel situations that take the form of reference to old situations or that establish their own past by quasi-obligatory repetition.[4]

That is, traditions often claim a certain kind of antiquity, and often base their authenticity on that alleged antiquity, when they are not old at all; indeed, the newest (would-be) traditions have the biggest authenticity problems and therefore frequently go to the greatest extremes to disguise their novelty and to link themselves to some venerable history.

Humans invent traditions regularly, but two further facts are true. First, most traditions are not so much invented as *fabricated* or *compiled over time*; a tradition seldom pops up in the world out of nothing, nor does it arise fully formed. A new tradition cannot help but grow out of the preexisting social milieu of prior traditions, ideas, values, and vocabulary; that is why every new invented tradition, no matter how radical, always shows the signs of its pedigree. Like any new species, it is an incremental change from the species before. Also, the newly minted tradition is born incomplete, embryonic, and continues to develop and grow after its birth so that the tradition a century or a millennium later will hardly resemble its original form. In fact, it may have branched off several times over the ages, giving birth to additional new traditions.

Second, some social contexts tend to be more fertile for the production of new traditions than others. In particular, occasions of social crisis are breeding grounds for new traditions, which we should regard as social movements or as what anthropologist Anthony Wallace called "revitalization movements," defined as "a deliberate, organized, conscious effort by members of a society to construct a more satisfying culture."[5] The preconditions for the movement typically involve some circumstances that upset the previous satisfactory culture, including natural disaster, contact with another society, war and conquest, and so on. At first only a few individuals, those closest to the problems, feel the effects, but over time the situation can lead to a "cultural distortion" in which people's understanding of their world and their existing traditions no longer function.

What can occur next is both very common and highly predictable. Out of the chaos of failing understandings and declining fortunes steps a man or woman with an idea; this person is the "prophet." Usually this future leader has had a troubled life, involving personal and professional disappointments, ill health, and/or proclivities toward altered states of consciousness (dreams, visions, hallucinations, possessions, and the like). Indeed, the answer that the "prophet" brings is purportedly not his or her own but something received from a higher or prior power. The innovator now begins to communicate the message, professing it on every occasion as well as performing wonders and entering into trancelike states. Sometimes, he or she attracts an audience or a group of followers, and, if lucky, the movement starts to grow. As it grows, it must necessarily organize, the first and most primitive form of organization being a direct one-on-one relationship between master and disciple based on the master's charisma. However, even in the master's lifetime there may be adaptation—changes to the original message due to expansion of the membership, resistance from outsiders, altered circumstances, or differing interpretations. Here the movement adjusts to the needs and understandings of members and to the challenges and pressures of the wider society; one frequent adjustment is militarization and violence. And when the founder dies, the movement experiences the crisis of succession: Who will lead the followers now? This is often a moment for institutionalization, for establishing rules and structures for the group including qualifications for membership and a canon of acceptable beliefs and behaviors. If the movement is successful, its effect can be felt by the entire society and even beyond to other societies. Finally, a "cultural transformation" occurs, and the movement becomes part, maybe the defining part, of the culture; the innovation becomes a tradition. Having presumably solved the problem that spawned it in the first place, the movement settles into its role as the new norm and becomes "routine."

Wallace goes on to describe the finite variety of revitalization movements. Any particular movement may emphasize old, new, or foreign elements. It may first attempt or profess to revive some or all of the precrisis culture on the premise that life was good then and what we need now is to be *more* traditional, to strengthen and recommit to our long-standing norms and values; Wallace calls these revivalistic or nativistic movements. Other efforts may import some or all parts of a foreign culture, typically because that culture is seen as superior; such movements Wallace dubs vitalistic, or we might call them "modernizing." A third kind of movement introduces original content from the mind of the prophet. In reality, any actual movement combines aspects of any or all of these styles, including the millenarian style that anticipates (and generally welcomes) an immediate and apocalyptic end to this existence and the coming of a better existence in the future. Wallace also adds that movements vary in the extent to which they pursue secular versus religious means. Secular means refer to human relationships like politics, while religious means involve relationships between humans and supernatural beings. "No revitalization movement can, by definition, be truly nonsecular, but some can be relatively less religious than others."[6] In other words, if a social movement is to change the world in some way, it must include some worldly changes to the economy or family or political system; still, these transformations are often made at the suggestion of, with the assistance of, and on the authority of the spirits. Here as everywhere, secular and supernatural cannot be rigidly separated.

The result is the key process of *syncretism*, by which elements of culture can be added, subtracted, and reassembled in an infinite number of ways that, nonetheless, belie their historical descent. Just as one gene may mutate in a living species while other genes remain untouched, or a foreign gene may be introduced into the species, so the parts of a culture can and easily do fragment, fission, flow, and fuse in new yet not exceptional forms. The outcome is a kind of "speciation," the process by which a new kind emerges from an old kind— not totally unlike the former species but not totally like it, either. Sometimes the product is two species where once there was one; they may go in different directions or coexist or compete. Eventually the first species may die out com-

pletely, or it may speciate again at a later time, just as the new species may further speciate. This gives living things and social ideas and institutions their
"bushy" quality.

THE INVENTION(S) OF CHRISTIANITY

Christianity sprouted as a social/revitalization movement precisely like so
many movements before and since, and it has followed an absolutely standard
growth process. It was born in a moment of cultural crisis, a moment that bred
many other, often quite similar responses—the conquest of Palestine by the
Romans, and before that the introduction of Greek or Hellenistic culture. The
experience was profoundly disorienting for the ancient Jews: foreign people,
foreign power, foreign ideas, foreign gods abounded. As in any such situation,
there were simultaneous and diverse reactions. Already in the century before
Jesus, the political-military movement of the Maccabees organized an army to
liberate the homeland in the 160s BCE and reconquered Jerusalem in 164 (this
event, by the way, is the origin of the "tradition" of Hanukkah). But the Maccabees' success was short-lived, and under Roman authority a number of Jewish
adaptations appeared together. The so-called Sadducees were the religious
"conservatives" or "elitists" who sought to maintain traditional priestly power,
even if that meant collaborating with the Romans. The Pharisees were comparative innovators who aimed to protect the religion by changing it: their goal
was "to make the faith of Israel relevant to everyday situations and to new circumstances under Roman rule and Hellenizing threats. Besides this, they held
some doctrines, such as the final resurrection and the existence of angels, which
the more conservative Jews declared to be mere innovations"[7] (positions now
"traditional" in Christianity). Outside of the "establishment," other independent movements flared, spread, and faded. One was the Essenes, a sort of
separatist group that withdrew into the wilderness to escape the hated alien
influence. Another was the politically engaged Zealots who advocated armed
rebellion; while the Sicarii carried out daring daytime assassinations of Roman
officials and Jewish collaborators.

It was in this environment that Christianity first evolved. Or, more accurately, what first evolved was not "Christianity" but a typically tiny revitalization movement that has rightly been called the Jesus Movement; in their book

titled *The Jesus Movement*, Ekkehard and Wolfgang Stegemann define it as "the Jerusalem primitive church and the 'churches of Judea' mentioned by Paul."[8] Gerd Theissen, New Testament scholar, dates the period of the Jesus Movement from about 30 CE until about 70 CE.[9]

There are several senses in which "Christianity" did not appear in those years or for many more years to come. The first is that the members "had no intentions of founding a new 'church'" and instead "remained wholly within the framework of Judaism."[10] Justo Gonzalez concurs: "The early Christians did not believe that they were founding a new religion. They were Jews, and . . . the Christian message to Jews was not that they should abandon their Jewishness. On the contrary, now that the Messianic age had begun, they were to be better Jews."[11] Accordingly, the Jesus Movement preserved most of the elements of Judaism it inherited (elements that themselves had coalesced over millennia of history—especially the Messianic idea), just like the other movements and prophets who shared the field such as Judas, Theudas, and Jonathan.[12]

A second sense in which "Christianity" failed to materialize in that early period is the Gospels themselves. Christianity was a "multiple birth," its origins being told in four different (official) versions that are not entirely compatible. Worse, as the scriptures of the movement *gradually* came into shape, many candidates for inclusion were voted out, such as the "infancy" Gospels of James and Thomas; the so-called Jewish Christian Gospels of the Hebrews, the Nazarenes, and the Ebionites; the Gospels of Thomas, Peter, Nicodemus, Mary, Philip, Judas, and Bartholomew; the "Gnostic" Gospels; and any number of other writings like Dialogue of the Savior, Apocalypse of Peter, Apocryphon of John, Coptic Gospel of the Egyptians, and on and on. The New Testament (or Testaments, for there are multiple versions of the official canon in different Christian traditions) is (are) a classic example of history being written, or assembled, by the victor. Worse yet, Elaine Pagels makes a compelling case for each canonical Gospel being a product of its particular moment and perspective of composition; each reflects the politics of its day by depicting Mark conciliating the Romans, Matthew railing against the Pharisees, Luke (the only non-Jewish Gospeller) writing to "those Gentile converts to Christianity who consider themselves the true heirs to Israel," and John distancing himself from the entire corrupt Jewish community.[13]

A third and final problem—which has remained the defining problem for unified Christianity—was the diversity of opinion and activity in the various local early Christian communities. This is the point of Paul's Epistles as well as his travels, for the disjointed movement took different directions in different locations. Paul struggled to impose a certain standardization, a certain ortho-doxy on the disparate congregations. This is especially significant for the future of Christianity because Paul had never met or heard Jesus, and Paul's letters and preaching efforts took place *before* the composition of the Gospels. That is to say, Paul's Epistles are actually the earliest writings of the movement, so in many ways he shaped the Jesus Movement as much as or more than Jesus. Perhaps most significantly, as Theissen reminds us, Paul hardly ever quotes Jesus, because he never knew Jesus and because Jesus' quotes had not been recorded yet.[14] Paul's main contribution was the creation of what Robert Wright in a cagey recent article called "a good Jesus," a gentle teacher whose only "doctrine" was "love"—an opportunistic view that emerged "from the interplay between Paul's driving ambitions and his social environment."[15] In short, Paul was crafting a message that would appeal to, and include, a wider audience, Jew and Gentile alike, "giving pragmatism priority over scriptural principle" (except that there was no scripture yet!).

If the first stage of eventual Christianity was the Jesus Movement, then the next stage was the Hellenistic church, of which Paul was a major architect, him-self a *Hellenized* (Greek-influenced) Jew. The Jesus Movement utterly failed at its original task to reform Judaism and effect any actual change in the political and spiritual fortunes of the Jews. The Jesus Movement essentially disappeared in Israel, moving on to the more urban and cosmopolitan centers in the Middle East and in the Roman Empire—and, according to Gonzalez, it survives partly *because* it moved on to these locations and by no longer being nor claiming to be a specifically Jewish phenomenon. Outside the parochial world of Judaism, the developing church encountered three important and intertwined influ-ences. The first was a Roman social system that explicitly practiced religious syncretism, tolerating and even incorporating all sorts of religious practices and notions. The second was a whole world of quite similar "mystery religions," many of them featuring god-men who died and returned to life as saviors; there is nothing unique or original to Christianity about this motif. The third was the dominant Greek-Hellenistic culture with its powerful intellectual and philo-sophical traditions. It was in this milieu that "Christianity" evolved from the simple Jesus Movement, and it was to such people that the reins of Christianity were passed with inevitable and indelible consequences.

Christianity only really began to evolve when the Jesus Movement cross-bred with Hellenistic culture; Christianity is at least as much a Greco-Roman religion as a Judaic one. The emerging church found two particular allies in the Hellenistic world: the thought-system of Plato and the later philosophy of Stoicism. As Gonzalez aptly notes, Platonism had already questioned the pagan pantheon and posited a "higher realm" of ultimate truth, as well as an immortal soul that was superior to the inferior body. Stoicism was itself an adaptation of Greek thinking to the urban and fractured quality of contemporary life, holding up the idea of a universal natural law to which humans must adjust and submit; the point of life was overcoming passion and cultivating "moral insight, courage, self-control, and justice."[16] "All this many early Christians found attractive and useful," and "although at first these philosophical traditions were used for interpreting the faith to outsiders, eventually they began influencing the manner in which Christians understood their own faith."[17]

Under the gravitational forces of Roman society and law and of Greek philosophy, an unavoidable problem arose: What exactly *were* the beliefs and practices of the new religion? These questions had never been settled, partly because there was no need to settle them—the church being relatively small and the end of time being supposedly nigh—and partly because the intellectual tradition of asking such questions did not exist until Christianity imbibed the Greek philosophical spirit. Now came the first great age of Christian disputation and, predictably, dissent. One issue was the relationship between Christian and non-Christian culture: some, like Tertullian, were opposed to "pagan" influences and yet evinced those influences by engaging in debates and written battles with nonbelievers, as in Tertullian's own *Prescription against Heretics*. Others like Tatian and Justin admired Greco-Roman culture and saw value, as well as the roots of Judeo-Christian belief, in it.

Another and more troubling issue was the precise meaning and interpretation of Christian beliefs: Jesus himself had written nothing and said many enigmatic things, and Paul had developed only certain aspects of doctrine—and those in only certain directions. There was much to settle and many different possible and available settlements. Many of these questions centered around the identity of Jesus and the correct reading of (recently amassed and obviously human-authored) scripture. One of the oldest and most persistent views was Gnosticism, which held that privileged people (the Gnostics themselves, naturally) had a deeper esoteric knowledge (*gnosis* is Greek for "knowledge," often implying wisdom or profound understanding) not available to others. Gnosticism itself was a congeries of positions and movements, but all shared a dualistic notion of matter versus mind/spirit and of progress toward pure spirit through secret (i.e., nonscriptural) knowledge. Two main nonorthodox claims of Gnosticism were that God had a number of "emanations" or "sons," including a daughter Sophia (wisdom), and that Jesus, being a pure and perfect spirit, did not have a human body and thus was never really incarnated. The developing "orthodox" opinion was that Jesus was both body and spirit, both man and God.

This business about the humanity and divinity of Jesus was one of the most vexing problems for early Christians and a source of many, if not most, of its heresies. Sabellius in the second century taught that Jesus, as well as the Father and the Holy Ghost, were three "modes" of the one God, making him completely divine and not human, and if Jesus was not also (and equally?) human, then he did not suffer and die, which contradicted the orthodox understanding of salvation. Docetism (from the Greek *dokesis* for "to seem") insisted that Jesus only seemed to be human but that his physical body was an illusion; at the other end of the spectrum, "adoptionism" held that Jesus was a mere human who was adopted by God, either at conception or at baptism. Marcion's heresy was both more extreme and more effective, for he actually conceived of the biblical God Yahweh/Jehovah as a flawed or perhaps evil being who was not the Supreme Father; the God above Yahweh/Jehovah was all-good and the father of Jesus. Therefore, Marcion assembled his own scripture (before the "official" New Testament was established) that included only Luke and the letters of Paul. Most threateningly of all, Marcion organized his own church with its own leadership as a serious alternative to the budding "catholic" church.

The list of early heresies could continue and has been well researched. Montanus offered a form of Christianity encouraging ecstatic states and prophesying and, of course, placing Montanist prophecies above biblical ones or even above the life and sayings of Jesus. Praxeas maintained a position sometimes called *patripassianism*, that God as father suffered crucifixion, since God sometimes took the form of father, sometimes son, sometimes ghost. Pelagius suggested that original sin did not forever stain human nature (so humans could be good without a god), while the Euchites or Messalians argued that the essence of the Trinity was perceptible to the senses and that salvation could be obtained by prayer alone, without the church or its rituals and sacraments. Extreme dualisms like Manichaeism and Mandaeism opposed the light (usually spirit) against the dark (usually the body and the material world). However, one of the most stubborn heresies was Arianism, proposed by Arius in the early fourth century, which asserted a particularly strict sort of monotheism such that Jesus could not be divine (only God was divine) and that Jesus had not existed eternally with God but had been created later by God.

Christological controversies of this sort are irrelevant, even silly, to non-Christians, but these were the subjects that tried men's souls in the Hellenistic church. The questions were supposedly answered in the third species of Christianity, the imperial church. When Roman emperor Constantine converted to the new faith and appointed himself its chief spokesman and mediator, many of these disputes were allegedly ended by decree or majority vote. The Council of Nicaea in 325, for instance, adopted a creed or statement of faith that was deemed authoritative—Jesus was "begotten, not made" and "of one substance" (the technical term is *homoousia*, for "same-substance")—and anyone who continued to believe that Jesus was "of a different substance" or that "before being begotten He was not" (i.e., Jesus did not exist "in the beginning" alongside God) was "anathematized" by the official church.

The church doctors, of course, failed to arrest the evolution of Christianity, even as imperial adoption itself contributed to further evolution. For one thing, Constantine illustrated that Christianity did not so much replace previous religions as piggyback them: the emperor never abandoned his pagan religion, remaining high priest of the Roman cult and instituting the first day of the week, the pagan day to honor the Unconquered Sun—or "Sunday"—as the Sabbath of Christianity. The elevation of Christianity to official status ended the persecutions and thus the subculture of martyrdom, which had thrived under the oppression; Tertullian, among others, insisted that there was no way to achieve salvation except through the shedding of one's own Christian blood. Once in power, Christians soon dropped that attitude. Another attitude they dropped was opposition to military service: early Christians had often refused (or been forbidden) to serve in the army on the political premise that such duty required veneration of the emperor as much as on the spiritual premise that killing was wrong. But the Christian objection to war was soon overcome when the religion attained political primacy; indeed, "[t]he practice of early Christianity was so far reversed by the early fifth century that under

Theodosius II those polluted by pagan rites were excluded from the army—only Christians could serve."[18] The Christian embrace of war would reach its climax in the Crusades ("wars of the cross") in the eleventh and twelfth centuries, with literally battalions of warrior-monks like the Knights Templar wreaking havoc on the Holy Land because *Deus lo volt*—"God wants it."

In the imperial church period, if orthodoxy was not firmly established, at least many of the styles of what would evolve into the Catholic Church were instituted: "Christian worship began to be influenced by imperial protocol,"[19] from luxurious clerical robes to ornate cathedrals and intricate rituals. Christianity not only borrowed forms from the political-secular realm but also contributed to the stability of the latter: the religion "became more and more the social cement of the totalitarian state of late antiquity."[20] This included censuring the enemies of the state-church, and these enemies included not only rival empires and barbarian bands but heretics who challenged state-church unity and orthodoxy. The Council of Chalcedon (380) made heterodoxy a crime punishable by the state (the church often palmed its dirty work off on secular authorities). Subsequently, "[r]eligious intolerance soon became a Christian principle":

> Within fifteen years of 380, imperial edicts deprived all heretics and pagans of the right to worship, banned them from civil offices, and exposed them to heavy fines, confiscation of property, banishment, and, in certain cases, death. By 435, there were sixty-six laws against Christian heretics plus many others against pagans. The purpose of persecution was to convert the heretics and heathen, thus establishing uniformity.[21]

But even the execution of Bishop Priscillian of Spain and six others in 385 could not prevent the continuing evolution of Christianity.

When the empire ended, the imperial church did not; rather, in a way it was set free, but it was also mutated by the influx of "barbarians" and its ascension to real political power. Many non-Roman tribes (Goths, Vandals, etc.) were Christianized, but Christianity was also barbarized: shock doctrines like hell were emphasized to appeal to less urbane minds. The Catholic Church also considered itself a king-maker, empowering itself to crown heads of state like Charlemagne. And the "papacy," from some perspectives nothing more than the bishopric of Rome, came to see itself as *the* embodiment of Jesus on earth, the "vicar of Christ," the seat of global Christian authority.

However, other bishops did not necessarily see things that way. For some, each bishop was equal, and the assertions of preeminence only added to the divisions between the Catholic or "Western" or "Latin" church and other "Eastern" churches. The Egyptian and Ethiopian churches had long maintained a distinct local identity, and the church in Constantine's old capital (Constantinople or Byzantium) found itself at growing odds with Rome over various issues, from papal authority to the use of icons in worship to priestly celibacy. The Byzantine (or Eastern or Orthodox) church also conducted its own missionary activities, including to the realm of Russia and eastern Europe. In 1054 the Roman church excommunicated the Byzantine church, creating the first enduring schism or speciation in European Christianity. Of course, then and today the "Orthodox" church is in reality a family of "national" churches (Greek Orthodox, Russian Orthodox, Latvian Orthodox, etc.), a permanent set of subspecies of Christianity.

As the imperial church gave way to the medieval church, there was no church but only *churches*. The situation would never revert but only extend, as additional sects, schisms, movements, and heresies ebbed and flowed. Among the challengers to Western-Christian unity were

- Peter Waldo and the Waldensians (1100s–1340s)
- The Cathars or Albigensians (1000s–1300s), against whom the Holy Inquisition was largely directed
- John Wycliffe and the Lollards (1300s)
- The Brethren of the Free Spirit (1300s)
- Jan Huss and the Hussites (1400s), who fought a long and costly war with the Catholic church
- The Huguenots (1500s)
- The Protestants, especially the Lutherans who followed Martin Luther (1518) and then the Calvinists of John Calvin, soon followed by George Fox and the Quakers or Society of Friends, King Henry VIII and the Anglicans or Church of England, and many, many other colorful groups like the Ranters, the Levellers, the Anabaptists, *ad infinitum*—these groups often splitting into subgroups and sub-subgroups.

CHRISTIAN DIVERSITY COMES TO AMERICA

> Here and there throughout American society you meet men filled with an
> enthusiastic, almost fierce spirituality such as cannot be found in Europe.
> From time to time strange sects arise which strive to open extraordinary roads
> to eternal happiness. Forms of religious madness are very common there.[22]

It has often been repeated that the United States is a Christian country. It
would be more accurate to say that the United States is a remarkably, even daz-
zlingly, diverse country and a creative country when it comes to religion. While
the United States undeniably has a deep streak of Christian influence in its culture, that streak has taken many forms, included many sects and denominations, and has spawned many new local Christianities, quasi-Christianities, and
pseudo-Christianities.

From the first European footstep on American soil, there were multiple
and often mutually hostile Christianities jostling for space. Puritans (seven-
teenth-century Protestant "fundamentalists") settled Massachusetts and
turned into Congregationalists; Maryland was settled by Catholics, Virginia
by Anglicans, and Pennsylvania by Quakers. Once Christianity was let loose
upon the new land, like any newly introduced species, it adapted to local conditions and radiated out into a plethora of novel species and sometimes whole
new genera, mixing with each other and the native flora and fauna in the most
unprecedented hybrids.

The carriers of this new virus of religion, resulting in what is called the
First Great Awakening (around 1720–1750), were men of passion, if not
learning, like Jonathan Edwards, George Whitefield, James Davenport,
Charles Woodmason, Devereux Jarratt, and Samuel Morris. They were the first
"circuit-riders" of Christianity, itinerant preachers who traveled from village to
farm to hamlet, spreading the Gospel in open-air or tent "revivals" wherever
they could find an audience. Not only did they circulate among the masses, but
they delivered the message in a style and language that the masses could digest,
with all the excitement and crudity that frontier settlers wanted: "Trance
states, ecstatic whirling, automatic utterances, falling down in the spirit, joyful
exuberance, and spiritual happiness were all common occurrences."[23]

After the relative calm of almost a century, the Second Great Awakening
broke out in the mid-1800s. By this time some of the formerly innovative
churches had institutionalized: Methodism had grown from fewer than five

thousand members to more than two hundred thousand. The decades from about 1840 to about 1870 then saw another explosion of enthusiasm and inventiveness, producing some uniquely American Christianities.

One of the first signs was the emergence of a "primitive Christianity" movement. In the early 1800s, Elias Smith had called for a simpler, more egalitarian kind of Christianity, one in which the masses could interpret the Bible for themselves; his camp rejected any name and merely called themselves "Christians" or "Disciples of Christ." Barton Stone and Alexander Campbell led other segments of the primitivist movement, and their members combined in 1830 to form the fifth-largest Protestant denomination by the end of the era.

A distinct element of the first half of the 1800s was a sort of reverence of nature known as transcendentalism. The latter was characterized by the recurrent American attitude, as expressed by Ralph Waldo Emerson, that "religion must have feeling, must *be* feeling."[24] Transcendentalists like Emerson not only demoted but actually rejected old, literalist "religion" in favor of spiritual intuition flowing from contact with nature; religion as usually performed was little more than "the dead forms of our forefathers."[25] They literally asked Americans to "forget historical Christianity." Another important influence on nineteenth-century thought was the "spiritualism" of figures like Emanuel Swedenborg, who took Christianity in new directions in writings such as *The Worship and the Love of God* and his eight-volume *Arcana Coelestia*. His main claim was that the Christian Bible was not to be taken as a literal, historical document but as a spiritual code or allegory.

That Americans were capable of and committed to inventing new forms of Christianity was imminently clear in the proliferation of new Christianities in the mid-nineteenth century. The most successful of these, claiming over twelve million members by the early twenty-first century, was Mormonism or the Church of Jesus Christ of Latter-Day Saints; it perhaps deserves the title of the first truly American Christianity since its dogmas assert that Jesus made an appearance and conducted a mission on American soil long before the Europeans set foot on the continent. The New World was the site of an ancient flourishing Judeo–Christian civilization, according to the Book of Mormon, the unique Mormon scripture Joseph Smith discovered transcribed on golden plates revealed by the angel Moroni at Hill Cumorah in upstate New York in the 1820s.

Out of the apocalyptic fervor of that era (and many Christian eras before and since), an end-of-the-world movement gathered around William Miller in the 1830s, also from upstate New York (a region so rife with Christian enthusiasm that it has been called "the burned-over district"). Several dates in the 1830s and 1840s were announced as the apocalypse, but none materialized, which is remembered as the Great Disappointment. Some Millerites drifted away from the movement, but others hung on, pushing the expected date into the future or developing a clever "shut-door theology" in which the world as we know it really *had* ended: while the earth still existed, heaven had closed its gates and only those who were already saved would be saved (i.e., the door to heaven was shut). Adherents of this position were called Shut-door Adventists. Another more enduring sprout from the Millerite branch was the Seventh-Day Adventists, largely based on the post-Millerite revelations of Ellen White.

Two final trends in the 1800s were the utopian (communitarian or "dropout") style and the "mentalist" or mind-over-matter style. The first is part of a larger tradition in American culture, including non-Christian efforts like the Oneida Community, often with generally socialist aspirations; a Christian example is the United Society of Believers, better known as the "Shakers," founded as early as the end of the 1700s by "Mother Ann" Lee. It became a separatist colony demanding common property, strict discipline, unitarianism, material simplicity, spiritual perfection, and absolute celibacy. Mentalism is also a strong American current, seen even today in think-yourself-healthy/rich/popular programs as disparate as Norman Vincent Peale, Deepak Chopra, and *The Secret*. The best illustration from nineteenth-century Christianity is the Church of Christ, Scientist (aka Christian Science) formally inaugurated in 1879 by Mary Baker Eddy as a "health conscious" movement syncretizing religion and science around the notion of "mind cure" and "spiritual medicine." Henry Wood's 1893 *Ideal Suggestion through Mental Photography* argued that neither illness nor healing is a purely physical process but a psychological/spiritual one, too: recovery occurs when the patient opens his or her heart and mind to the "great light" of God, achieved through specific "meditations" and ideal thoughts, such as "God is here," "I am not this body," and "I will be healed."

Obviously, then, orthodox Christianity has never had a monopoly on the American mind; rather, it has shared the religious field with many other forces (religious and otherwise) and affected and been affected by those forces. In addition to the spiritualism and transcendentalism and mentalism of the age—

all of which continue to exert their pull on society and Christianity today—the late 1800s added influences from Eastern religions and the occult, producing what could rightly be called the first "New Age." Uriah Clark, for instance, published a guide for séance procedures in 1863 called *Plain Guide to Spiritualism*. Equally if not more significantly, Americans were discovering Asian scriptures, and archaeological discoveries in Egypt and Mesopotamia, India, and Central and South America also provided fodder for religious creativity. One example was Theosophy (from the Greek for "god-wisdom"). The Theosophical Society was founded in 1875–1876 by "Madame" Helena Blavatsky and Henry Olcott. Blavatsky's 1877 *Isis Unveiled* elaborated her occult system received from "ascended masters" who revealed the knowledge to her. In 1879 she and Olcott moved the Theosophical Society to India, where it absorbed more Hindu content and practice (and where Hinduism absorbed it). Yoga and meditation were discovered and transmitted to the American public; Hindu terms and concepts like *samadhi* and *guru* were popularized. In 1888 she compiled her teachings into the "Bible" of Theosophy, *The Secret Doctrine*.

The "esoteric boom" of the early 1900s had many forms and faces. Some of its leading figures were Aleister Crowley, Edgar Cayce, and H. P. Lovecraft, and its accomplishments included Levi H. Dowling's 1907 *The Aquarian Gospel of Jesus the Christ*, Baird T. Spalding's 1924–1925 five-volume *Life and Teachings of the Masters of the Far East*, Ian Ferguson's 1924 *The Philosophy of Witchcraft*, and Manly Hall's 1928 *Encyclopedic Outline of Masonic, Hermetic, Qabalistic, and Rosicrucian Symbolical Philosophy*. Institutionally, in 1915 H. Spencer Lewis founded the Ancient and Mystical Order Rosae Crucis; in 1920 Paul Foster Case introduced a mystical order called Builders of the Adytum; and in 1924 Alice Bailey opened the Arcane School in New York. There was also a revival of mystical/gnostic/witchcraft interest in the form of the Ku Klux Klan's use of titles like Hydra and Giant and Great Titan and Exalted Cyclops, not to mention the invention of the "Wiccan" religion, which purports to be a continuation of pagan pre-Christian beliefs and practices but which is largely the creation of Gerald Gardner in such writings as *A Goddess Arrives* (1948), *Witchcraft Today* (1954), and *The Meaning of Witchcraft* (1959).

In reaction to these heresies and other threats like evolutionary theory and modernism, as well as more mainstream movements within Christianity (such as the "social gospel," which sought to apply Christian thought and energy to social problems like poverty, racism, alcoholism, child labor, and war; or the "prosperity gospel," which combines Christianity with New Age mentalism of the think-yourself-healthy/rich/popular variety), there emerged a movement that explicitly called itself "fundamentalism." Fundamentalism is neither a uniquely Christian nor uniquely modern phenomenon, but wherever and whenever it is seen, it is relatively self-conscious and militant about "tradition," even if it partly *invents* its tradition. At any rate, American fundamentalism arose from a series of documents published in 1910 and 1915 titled *The Fundamentals: A Testimony to the Truth*. These writings led to an organization, the World's Christian Fundamentals Association, founded by William B. Riley in 1919. While the specifics of these and other similar efforts differed, on some general points they were in substantial agreement. All invoked the purity and perfection of scripture, whether old or new. Each looked upon not just a physical world but a spiritual world that had "gone wrong" somehow (which is a very old tradition in American Christianity: a century earlier Alexander Campbell wrote, "The stream of Christianity has become polluted").[26] And each saw itself as representing authentic Christianity; each imagined itself— and *only* itself—as the *restoration* of religion.

While the first generation of fundamentalism was discredited by foolish activities like the Scopes "monkey" trial in 1925, it reemerged in the mid-twentieth century in two new and effective guises: Evangelicalism and Pentecostalism. Evangelicalism, perhaps represented best by Billy Graham, is the "good news" wing of contemporary American Christianity. An evangelical is a "born again" Christian, one who has made the personal commitment to Jesus and become a messenger of the Gospel. Pentecostalism goes a step further, stressing the "gifts" of faith like speaking in tongues, laying on hands for healing, and what would be regarded in any other religion as possession or trance experiences. Both of these trends were mostly nonpolitical through the 1950s and 1960s, a period that also saw the "Jesus freak" phenomenon and, more ominously for the mainstream, the rise of feminism, the hippie counterculture, and the atheist movement. By most accounts, the final straw was the legalization of abortion in the *Roe v. Wade* decision in 1973. From that time, Christianity began to become more politically mobilized in such forms as the Moral Majority and the Christian Coalition and behind such leaders as Jerry Falwell, Pat Robertson, and Ralph Reed. Of course, American Christianity had never been entirely nonpolitical: the essentially Christian KKK had been politically active for a century and had been energized by the civil rights struggles of the 1950s and 1960s. But now, as Robertson expressly stated, Christians were going to exert their political power: "We have together with the Protestants and Catholics enough votes to run this country. And when the people say, 'We've had enough,' we are going to take over."[27]

Christian fundamentalism gets much (deserved) attention in the United States, but few people probably realize how diverse it is. At one extreme are the peaceful fundamentalists, folks who take their religion exceptionally seriously but merely wish to be left alone, like the Amish. At the other extreme are the "reconstructionists" or "dominionists," folks who want to impose their brand of Christianity on everyone else. Christian Reconstructionism as expressed by R. J. Rushdoony and his organization, the Chalcedon Foundation, seeks to institute Old Testament law to the tune of banning all non-Christian (and other Christian) religions; rolling women's status back to ancient times; setting the death penalty for adultery, blasphemy, witchcraft, abortion, and homosexuality; and eliminating the prison system (since most of the criminals will be dead anyhow). In between are more or less fanatical groups, from the Christian Identity, who promote an exclusively Caucasian identity of Christianity, to the Christian Exodus movement, which has given up on "mainstream" America and started the process of creating its own society somewhere on American soil.

Finally, American Christianity has never been shy (although it has often been ambivalent) about borrowing whatever the popular culture has to offer. Ever since there was radio, there was Christian radio. The advent of television led to the advent of televangelism (people are watching TV anyhow, so why not give them Christian TV?); the fruits of this labor have included Jimmy Swaggart, Oral Roberts, Jim and Tammy Bakker, Benny Hinn, and many more. Christians now offer whole television stations and networks, from Robertson's *700 Club* to Eternal Word Television Network (EWTN) to the Trinity Broadcasting Network to the Daystar Television Network, to name but a very few, each with its own website.[28] These are joined by an incalculable number of others, including many private and local sites, blogs, YouTube videos, and such. Beyond appropriating the media of modern culture, American Christianity also unavoidably appropriates its content. The result is Christian rock, Christian rap, Christian dating services, Christian movies, Christian popular literature (the *Left Behind* series being only one small example), and Christian computer games (including a "Left Behind" PC game[29]).

Finally, Christianity cannot help but adjust to its constituency, providing them the kind of experience that makes sense and appeals to them—black churches, Hispanic churches, rural churches, suburban churches, urban churches, and so on. For middle-class corporate Americans, the "megachurch" phenomenon, pioneered by the Willow Creek Community Church, makes Christianity feel like another day at the office. The style of the various churches suits the "consumers" of the religious "product," and what do Americans want more than success? Hence, the "prosperity gospel" represents perhaps the apex of American Christianity: God wants you to be rich, God wants you to have a big house and a fancy car; in fact, God will arrange for it to be paid for if you can't afford it.

How could American Christianity be anything but diverse, syncretic, ersatz, unorthodox, and frankly contradictory, since Americans are all those things? American Christianity is, in the final analysis, less Christian than American—and Americans are a diverse, creative, and cantankerous people.

CHRISTIANITY GOES GLOBAL

Christianity started out in Palestine as a fellowship; it moved to Greece and became a philosophy; it moved to Italy and became an institution; it moved to Europe and became a culture; it came to America and became an enterprise.[30]

The original species of Christianity evolved as one of many mutations of Judaism in the fermented environment of Roman-dominated Jerusalem. Christianity quickly ceased to be a Jewish reform movement and quickly became a Hellenistic "new religion," eventually being elevated to a Roman imperial religion. As it spread into Europe, it became largely a European religion, with medieval and Renaissance components, and it picked up whatever was there as it moved, from pine trees and Yule logs to "Easter" (originally the name of the Nordic goddess of spring). Each of these phases and influences left an indelible mark on the religion(s) so that the Christianity inherited by the United States was a distinctly European, even British, Christianity, which met some Spanish and French Christianities on the continent—not to mention Native American, African, and, later, Eastern religions.

In other words, although like any "world religion" Christianity has claimed and aimed to own the world, it has been for most of its history showing its local origins very conspicuously; it has been essentially a European religion carried around the world. However, just as it continued to morph and mutate as it passed north from Palestine to Rome to Western Europe and then west to North America, so it would inevitably adapt and transform as it encountered other lands and other peoples. The result would be another generation of Christian evolution.

Global Christianity as an early-modern European phenomenon cannot be separated from colonialism: like a virus (and like literal viruses) it was spread by explorers, settlers, soldiers, traders, and administrators as much as by missionaries, and it left as permanent a mark. The first substantial contact between Europeans and native peoples occurred in the Americas, and this was naturally the site of the first crossbreeding between Christian species and local religious species, producing a sort of "native Christianity." An early manifestation of indigenous Christianity was the "Lady of Guadalupe," an apparition of a home-grown Virgin Mary experienced by a Nahuatl (Mexican) man in December 1531. By that date Christianity had been in Mexico for twelve years, and the conquistador Hernan Cortes had done all he could to transplant the Mary meme in the New World: "in Spanish chronicles of the conquest he leaves a trail of Marian images in native temples as he marches on Tenochtitlan, the most famous of which is the statue known as La Conquistadora [the female conqueror]," while his crowning achievement was "his ejection of the image of Huitzilopochtli from the Mexica's Great Temple and its replacement by a crucifix and a statue of Mary."[31] Soon a spectral Indian Mary appeared, a "beautiful girl with tan complexion" who spoke in the Nahuatl language, according to the legend—a legend that was not fully invented and disseminated until more than a century later, in a 1649 book written by a Creole priest named Luis Laso de la Vega. The indigenization of Mary culminated only in 1999 when Pope John Paul II declared the Lady of Guadalupe the patron saint of the Americas, yet in another way this incident can be taken as a (rather typical) case of the identification and integration of a native god with a Christian character, namely the Aztec goddess Tonantzin, also known as "Our Revered Mother" and upon whose former temple the Basilica of Guadalupe was built.

The pattern of reformulating Christianity into a local shape, and/or blending it with other non-Christian elements to generate some hybrid Christianity, has been repeated in the Americas and beyond. Often the processes that moved Christianity in new directions were intimately linked to processes that moved people to new locations, especially the transfer of Africans to American soil already occupied by native societies. Among these Afro-American religions is Candomblé, an African-Brazilian mix with components from Yoruba, Fon, and Bantu belief: African gods called orishas or orixas with names like Ogun and Obatala and Shango operate through specific Christian saints and human (especially female) priestesses or spirit mediums (*maes de santo*, or "mothers of the saint/deity" and *filhas de santo*, or "daughters of the saint/deity") to intervene against sin and to aid with salvation. Umbanda is another Afro-Brazilian cult, one that not only practices possession rituals along with baptisms, consecrations, and weddings and believes in a supreme god called Zambi or Zambiapongo but also features Buddhist symbols and images alongside Christian ones. Probably the best known of the Afro-Caribbean religions is Vodun, popularly called "voodoo," which includes a supreme being (Olurun) and a lesser god (Obatala) in perpetual struggle, as well as many minor spirits and saints (*loa* and *rada*) and guardian angels (*bon ange*).

More recently, Jamaica has witnessed the appearance of the Rastafarian movement, bringing together a number of quite disparate influences such as Marcus Garvey's early-twentieth-century black nationalism, Russian Orthodox Christianity, East Indies Hinduism, a reverence for the Ethiopian leader Haile Selassie (who was named Ras Tafari before his coronation), and a focus on the Abrahamic or Old Testament side of Christianity. For good measure, Rasta culture adds in a distinctive hairstyle (dreadlocks); the red, gold, and green colors; and the use of marijuana.

While Mexican *curanderismo* (spiritual curing) is not an entire religion, it is definitely an amalgamation of Christian aspects (prayer to God, Jesus, and Catholic saints) and pre-Christian facets like trance and possession and the use of herbs, all sometimes channeled through the spirits of famous dead healers. Most recently, in response to the social and racial injustices in Latin America, a movement known as "liberation theology" emerged. For many inside and outside the Catholic Church, the dominant Latin American Christianity was often perceived as in collusion with political and economic leaders to exploit the weak and the poor, especially indigenous peoples. Religious thinkers like Gustavo Gutierrez, Juan Luis Segundo, and Lucio Gera in the Catholic tradition, and Emilio Castro and Julio de Santa Ana in the Protestant tradition began to propose ways to marshal Christian sources for the purpose of effecting real social change, ending oppression, and achieving equality and liberation.

The Americas have hardly been the only site of Christian evolution. Asia and the Pacific have also been active areas for religious development and speciation, yielding unique results because of unique historical encounters and the strong local religious traditions. The Taiping "rebellion" or movement in 1850s and 1860s China is a fine example of religious syncretism—not only of the confluence of religions but of the confluence of religion with nonreligious bits and pieces. In this case, a man named Hung Xiuquan had a vision in which he met his true mother and father, namely God and God's wife, making Hung God's other son and Jesus' younger brother. Hung soon organized the *Bai Shangdi Hui* or God-Worshipping Society, instituted a number of rules for members, and formed his followers into military units to conduct their war against the evil powers of Confucianism, the Chinese government, and foreign (European) invaders. In 1851 Hung decreed the era of the Taiping Heavenly Kingdom, an era that died in 1864 after his death, the defeat of his godly army, and the loss of tens of millions of lives.

In colonial Vietnam a similar, although locally specific, Christian-related religion formed, known as Cao Dai. The founding prophet was Ngo Minh Chieu, who began receiving revelations from the high god Duc Cao Dai in 1920. The faith that coalesced had much in common with Catholicism, including a "pope" and a church structure with a "college" of church officials and administrators, "archbishops," and "priests." However, Christianity is not Cao Dai's only source: it also draws from, and claims to draw together, the major Eastern religions of Buddhism, Confucianism, and Daoism. Each of the historical founders of these religions is seen as an emissary of the great god, bringing a local message to a particular people. Cao Dai, though, is the final unification of Eastern and Western religions alike under the watchful left eye of god and celebrated through the three key personages or saints of Trang Trinh (a fifteenth-century Vietnamese nationalist poet), Sun Yat-sen (leader of the 1911 Chinese revolution), and French novelist Victor Hugo.

Speaking of unification, Asia also spawned the Unification Church of Reverend Sun Myung Moon (whose followers are often dubbed "Moonies"). Officially called the Holy Spirit Association for the Unification of World Christianity and formed in 1954 in Seoul, South Korea, it sprang from a vision of Jesus received by Moon in 1935 at age fifteen. In 1959 Moon moved his church to the United States, that land of overgrown religion. When a predicted apocalypse failed to materialize, the church began its institutionalization, much like the Seventh-Day Adventists and Jehovah's Witnesses before it. True to its name, the Unification Church sees itself as the one religion that joins and fulfills all previous religions (Moon has even stated that Jesus, Muhammad, the Buddha, and other religious and secular figures have conceded this point). Even so, its Christian roots are obvious, though like all mutations it develops those roots in new and sometimes heretical directions: the church rejects the Trinity, gives its God both male and female aspects (the Holy Spirit in particular is a feminine energy), believes that Eve had a sexual affair with Lucifer, and places its hopes on the "third Adam" (Adam being the first Adam and Jesus the second Adam), who was born in Korea before 1930—conveniently, around the time Moon was born.

Of all the Christian, pseudo-Christian, and crypto-Christian movements in Asia and Oceania, none is more colorful than the so-called cargo cults throughout New Guinea and the Pacific islands. Many of these regions were spared much foreign contact until the twentieth century, when war brought huge numbers of outsiders and their vast hauls of materiel to the islands. The problem for the natives was to determine where all this "cargo" came from and how they themselves might get some. There were actually many diverse local cargo cults, but the Vailala "madness" is typical. Sometime after 1910, a native man named Evara began to have visions and physical symptoms, including dizziness, upset stomach, trance, and dissociation. In his revelations, he saw a steamship coming, bearing the dead ancestors as well as stashes of cargo; when the ships arrived, the invading white people would be driven away and the indigenous people restored to independence. Over time, Evara's movement developed a more elaborate doctrine with a visibly Christian aspect. Many members referred to themselves as "Jesus Christ men," and garbled notions of heaven and God emerged. God was called *Ihova*, and heaven was named *Ihova kekere*, or Jehovah's land. Other beings sharing heaven with *Ihova* included *Noa* (Noah), *Atamu* (Adam), *Eva*, and *Mari* (*Atamu's* daughter). An old picture of King George V was offered as the likeness of *Ihova Yesu-nu-ovaki*; that is, Jehovah, the younger brother of Jesus.

For some final examples, we can turn to Africa, which was the last continent to be integrated into the European-Christian colonial project. Christianity was a crucial part of the colonial enterprise in Africa; among the Tshidi of South Africa, for instance, "evangelical Methodism was to prove an efficient teacher of the values and predispositions of the industrial workplace."[32] The goal was to substitute one way of life (Christian) for another way of life (traditional/animistic). However, the reality was more complex and more hybrid: Christian teachings necessarily "became embroiled in local histories, in local appropriations and transpositions, and were deflected in the process—often in surprising, sometimes in subversive, always in culturally meaningful, ways."[33]

The Catholic missions to the Pogoro of Tanzania got involved in many aspects of tribal life, from employment and transportation to radio access and food distribution; they even became intermediaries in the traditional marriage system, secluding the young marriageable girls and intervening in marriage choices and the transfer of wealth between families. In fact, so interested in material/financial matters were the Catholics that the local people referred to Christianity "as *'dini ya biashara,'* 'the religion of business.'"[34] Meanwhile, the natives filtered Catholicism through their own cultural notions: they called church offerings *sadaka*, the same term they used for traditional offerings to the dead ancestors (which was how they understood the Catholic mass), and they viewed the priests like traditional ritual specialists who could fight evil spirits and witches with their words of power and their potions like holy water and anointing oils (*dawa ya kikristo*, or "Christian medicines").

In Budjga country (Zimbabwe/Mozambique), multiple Christianities competed for the souls of the natives, including Catholicism, Methodism, Seventh-Day Adventism, and Canadian Pentecostalism. Each accommodated native religion in various ways while challenging it in others: Methodism, for instance, adopted a local term for God (*mwari*) and perpetuated certain customs like ecstatic experiences but denounced others like the cult of the ancestor-spirits; Catholicism was more tolerant of the ancestor cult and included more ritual as in keeping with pre-Christian belief.[35] The diversity of Christianity was not limited to introduced species; local African Christianities also evolved and spread, including Vapostori, a sect based on the revelations of Muchabaya Ngamerume in the 1930s. This movement featured a structure with offices including baptizer, evangelist, prophet, and healer, and its doctrines and practices mixed Christian (a Sabbath day on Friday, moral instruction, Bible reading, and Methodist hymns) with traditional or novel (witchcraft trials, polygamy, white robes for all members) elements.

Across the continent many other Christian species developed, sometimes referred to as African Initiated Churches or African Independent Churches or African Indigenous Churches. A famous example is Aladura, a Nigerian sect whose name means "owners of prayer." Many Aladura members practice faith healing and disparage all medicine (both modern and traditional), and they believe that God speaks to them through dreams and visions. In 1920 Joseph Sadare founded the Precious Stone Society, also in Nigeria; an offshoot of this movement became the Christ Apostolic Church in 1941, stressing Bible study and education and even leading to the opening of a teacher-training school. Moses Orimolade started the Cherubim and Seraphim Society in 1925 as a branch of the Anglican Church, and this new group eventually split into over fifty different sects. Other examples from a long list of new African Christian-ities are the Kimbanguist Church, or the Church of Jesus Christ on Earth, Jamaa (a Catholic-Franciscan-inspired church with a sort of Pentecostal feel); and Kitawala (a more socially radical sect originating from Jehovah's Witness activity in central Africa). Speaking of radicalism, some Christian groups have taken a decidedly nasty turn in Africa (as elsewhere), like the Lord's Resistance Army in Uganda, led by Joseph Kony, a self-proclaimed spirit medium and prophet who seeks to form a religious state by kidnapping children to fight in his holy army. An apocalyptic Ugandan church called the Movement for the Restoration of the Ten Commandments of God, a splinter group originated by excommunicated Catholic priests, apparently committed either mass suicide or mass murder of approximately one thousand members.

THE FUTURES OF CHRISTIANITIES

Some have said that the ultimate test of Christianity will come if and when we discover intelligent life on another planet: supposedly Christianity will then be debunked once and for all, since humans will no longer be a unique species in the universe, their God's special creation. However, the religion has proven highly resilient in the past and will continue to be resilient in the future. When Christians first encountered Native Americans, they were compelled to do some heavy thinking and interpreting in order to integrate those societies into the Christian worldview (Were they human at all? Were they descendants of Adam and Eve? Did they have souls? Were they capable of religion?), but Christians managed to adjust. Whenever we finally meet the extraterrestrials, Christians will be equally resourceful. Some will conclude that only humans are godly and qualified to be Christians, while the ETs are godless, even dumb animals. Others will entertain the notion that their God created the extraterrestrials, too; some will go so far as to suggest that Jesus died for the outerspace beings, too, or even that their God may have had a son with some space woman and arranged their species-specific salvation. And at least a few ambitious congregations will send missionaries to the distant planet, as in the novel *The Sparrow* by Mary Doria Russell (probably with the same tragic results). You can be sure that if the space natives have their own culture and religion, Christianity will crossbreed with it and yield some interplanetary Christian cults.

For the moment, we must leave our speculations on Planet Earth, where there is more than enough opportunity for—and evidence for—Christian evolution. Christianity first appeared in the world as a small religious movement in the Middle East, quickly jumped the fence to become a Hellenistic mystery religion, then got swept up in the Roman Empire and transformed into an imperial religion, diffused into Europe and morphed into a European religion, and subsequently was carried to North America and every other part of the world, where it assimilated local features while it accommodated itself to those local features. Now Christianity is truly a world religion—or a loose association of religious species with only a passing family resemblance between them. There is truly no such thing as Christianity but only *Christianities*, and more and more of them—more and more different from each other and from the ancestral species, the Jesus Movement—every day.

Worst of all for contemporary Western Christians, the globalization of Christianity not only promises to change the world but to change Christianity, too. Already, the familiar old Western/Caucasian Christianities are giving way to non-Western and non-Caucasian Christianities, which are feeding back onto the parental species and sects that sired them: as Philip Jenkins has put it, "Christianity as a whole is growing and mutating in ways that observers in the West tend not to see."[36] In 2002, Jenkins estimated that almost half of the population of Africa was Christian, and by 2025 more than half of all Christians in the world will live in Africa or Latin America, with another 17 percent in Asia; that would mean that Western or European Christians, formerly the dominant group and the ones who have given the religion its recent complexion (in both senses of the term), will be a distinct minority. Indeed, there may already be more Anglicans in Nigeria than in England.

The effects of this change will be, and to an extent already are, a profound modification of Christianity, something like the end of the era of the dinosaurs and the beginning of the era of mammals. Catholic writer Walbert Buhlmann has gone so far as to envision a new Reformation, a "Third Church" different from all previous Catholic, Orthodox, and Protestant Christianities (which would actually make it a fourth church, but who's counting?). Not only will the center of gravity of global Christianities shift (there might someday be a Latin or Asian or African pope!), but the contents of local non-Western Christianities are and will continue to be different from the comfortable Western styles and will impact back on those comfortable Western styles. Predicts Jenkins:

> The revolution taking place in Africa, Asia, and Latin America is far more sweeping in its implications than any current shifts in North American religion, whether Catholic or Protestant. There is increasing tension between what one might call a liberal Northern Reformation and the surging Southern religious revolution, which one might equate with the Counter-Reformation, the internal Catholic reforms that took place at the same time as the Reformation. . . . No matter what the terminology, however, an enormous rift seems inevitable.[37]

This rift will not only be geographical but also deeply cultural: because of the religious traditions in those places as well as their often intense conservatism, "[w]orldwide, Christianity is actually moving toward supernaturalism and neoorthodoxy, and in many ways toward the ancient world view expressed in the New Testament."[38] Of course, some Western and American religious conservatives may endorse this trend, but even they will find that the new Christian traditionalism is not their grandfather's Christian traditionalism. For liberal and mainstream Christians (and of course for non-Christians), these developments are unwelcome and even menacing. For instance, the Anglican archbishop of Nigeria, Peter Jasper Akinola, has not only taken a strong stand in his country against homosexuality and the ordination of gay priests but has also pressured his British and American brethren to block such behavior, which he has called "an attack on the Church of God—a Satanic attack on God's Church."[39]

Whether or not figures like Akinola represent the future of Christianity—or one local future of one local Christianity—the ultimate lesson is the same. Christianity is not and never has been one single unified religion with a monolithic dogma and morality. Christianity, like every other religion and every other culture, is an organism. Once its initial ancestor is loose on the world, it absorbs nutrients from its environments, adapts to local conditions, mutates, and interbreeds with other nearby species. The new species formed in these matings multiply, migrating to new lands even as they feed back into the ancestral population. The final result is many locally unique species, with a few extinctions along the way, each related closely or remotely to its ancient ancestor, but none identical to it and none more or less "true" than any other. The "original" ancestor (the Jesus Movement) long since disappeared, never to be revived, and—as with every evolutionary tree—it was no more true or authentic or special than any of its descendants anyhow.

Chapter 2

CHRISTIANITY'S SUCCESS WAS NOT INCREDIBLE

by Dr. Richard Carrier

It's often claimed that Christianity could never have begun or succeeded unless the people of its first three centuries had overwhelming evidence that it was true. Therefore we should conclude there was overwhelming evidence it was true, even if that evidence doesn't survive for us to see it now, and since we should believe anything for which there is overwhelming evidence, we should believe Christianity is true. But when we look at the actual facts of that time and place, we find Christianity's conception and growth were not remarkable at all. In fact, what happened is quite the contrary of what we should expect if it really did have the backing of a benevolent miracle-working God. This evidence thus actually *disconfirms* Christianity. Since I have already surveyed and analyzed all the evidence elsewhere, most extensively in my book *Not the Impossible Faith*, I will only summarize the facts and cite where each is established.[1]

A WHOLLY UNREMARKABLE GROWTH

It will often be claimed or assumed that Christianity, right out of the gate, was as successful as sex in the sixties, winning over millions of people in just two or three generations. But it was exactly the opposite.[2] All evidence and scholarship confirms Christianity was for a long time a tiny fringe cult that was so socially invisible that the most experienced Roman legal expert of his generation, Pliny the Younger, a Roman senator who had held the positions equivalent to chief of police in Rome, attorney general for the whole empire, copresident of all the provinces, and state governor (multiple times), had never in his life even seen any Christians. He had no idea what they believed, why it was illegal to be one, or even what the punishments were supposed to be until some troublemakers started in on them in his jurisdiction... in 110 CE.[3] That's eighty years after the movement is supposed to have begun, the equivalent then of nearly two entire lifetimes and more than four generations. The number of Christians must have been exceedingly small for a very long time, of no greater account than any lunatic fringe.

A full analysis of all the reliable evidence available indicates the rate of growth of Christianity as a whole, from its very beginning and throughout its entire history, was less than 4 percent a year, the same as that of any other aggressively evangelistic religion (such as the Mormon Church). It can therefore claim no supernatural success in winning converts. Its rate of development and success was entirely natural. Since that rate was natural, we should expect its cause was natural, which alone closes the book on Christianity having any supernatural evidence or guidance. Had it had such, its rate of success would reflect that. It does not.

Even after nearly three centuries of that entirely ordinary growth, only when Christianity acquired absolute despotic power (first in the hands of Emperor Constantine, and then by all his subsequent family and imperial heirs thereafter) did its growth begin even to approach a majority—and even then, only after the collapse of many of the Roman Empire's social institutions following fifty years of constant civil war and a ghastly collapse of the economy were people thrown into the arms of escapist movements exactly like Christianity. That it would then come to dominate the Western world after such a sequence of perfectly natural events is likewise perfectly natural.[4]

All of this does mean that the claim that the rise of Christianity caused the fall of the Roman Empire is a myth. It was the other way around: the fall of the Roman Empire caused the triumph of Christianity. Its success was a symptom of a decaying age of anxiety and despotism. The accompanying chart (see fig. 1) shows the maximum possible rate of growth conforming to known data. Notice how Christianity is practically insignificant (even at its very height, barely a few percent of the population were Christian) until a fifty-year civil war began destroying the social system (starting in the 230s CE), followed by a catastrophic economic depression (in the 270s CE). All of this came over a generation before Constantine, the first Christian emperor, seized power by force. Even after that, it took over a century for Christians to fully take over, just as it

FIGURE 1.

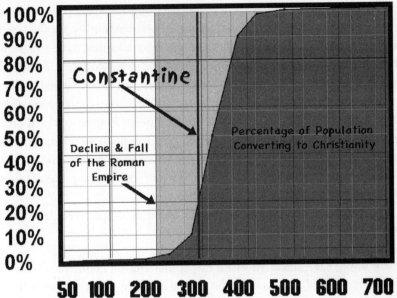

became increasingly difficult or even outright illegal to practice any other religion (paganism was outlawed in 395 CE along with Jewish evangelism).

Accordingly, scholars have only ever found natural causes for the growth and success of Christianity, its behavior conforming entirely to known sociological models.[5]

AN INORDINATE FONDNESS FOR
HUMILIATED GODS AND HEROES

Nevertheless, you'll hear the befuddled question "But who on earth would believe a religion centered on a crucified man?"

Well, the Sumerians, perhaps. One of their top goddesses, Inanna (the Babylonian Ishtar, "Queen of Heaven"), was stripped naked and crucified, yet she rose from the dead and, triumphant, condemned to hell her lover, the shepherd-god Dumuzi (the Babylonian Tammuz).[6] This became the center of a major Sumerian sacred story, preserved in clay tablets that date back over a thousand years before Christ.

The Romans might have believed such a thing. One of their most revered gods, Romulus, suckled a wolf and murdered his own brother. Or the Greeks, whose most beloved hero, Hercules, was briefly condemned to be a stable boy shoveling cow-flop. Even full-blooded Greek gods were forced, on occasion, to endure menial lives: like Apollo, who was condemned to be enslaved as a shepherd; or Poseidon, a bricklayer. Or the Anatolians, whose most popular religion, with priests and followers all over the Roman Empire, centered on the worship of a lowly eunuch (the castrated Attis), and whose priests as a result castrated themselves in honor of their god. This despite the fact that the emasculating act of castration was among the worst of embarrassing disgraces to the snobbish elite of the time, worse even than crucifixion.

Seneca wrote of this practice of castration and comparable acts of mutilation promoted by other popular cults:

> If anyone has leisure to view what they do and what they suffer, he will find practices so indecent for honorable men, so unworthy of free men, so unlike those of sane men, that if their number were fewer no one would have any doubt they were demented. As it is, the only support for a plea of sanity is found in the number of the mad throng.[7]

Thus, even something so foul and repugnant to an educated man like Seneca nevertheless commanded a large following. There can be no ground for claiming Christianity was any different than the cult of Cybele and Attis in this regard. One man's disgrace was apparently another man's holy salvation. Clearly, the most repugnant beliefs could command large followings—all the more so among the powerless, oppressed, and disenfranchised, for whom humiliated heroes sometimes became a rallying point for opposition to an unjust imperial order. Hence, being unjustly crucified could even be a point in someone's favor.[8] Indeed, contrary to what's often claimed, many Jews *expected* a humiliated Messiah who would be unjustly executed shortly before the end of the world.[9] Among pagans, murdered gods who came back from the dead were wildly popular, not shockingly novel (more on that in a moment).

There is no evidence that a crucified god was an obstacle to converting— for anyone who actually converted. Especially considering hardly anyone converted until Christians had so magnified and exalted their God-man that he was exactly to everyone's liking. This change is evident even in the behavior and treatment of Jesus on the cross (and his march to it) from the earlier Gospel of Mark (15:15–37) to the later Gospel of John (19:16–30). Thus, the story could be changed to suit any audience, from the subversively humiliated hero to the triumphant divine dignitary who's always in charge and needs no one's help. There's certainly nothing supernatural about rewriting history to market your product.

HOW'D A STUPID, WORKING-CLASS HICK FROM GALILEE GET SO POPULAR?

Well, OK, weirdly humiliated gods were popular. But surely no one would have flocked to a cult claiming an uneducated rural construction worker from some inglorious town in the middle of nowhere was now God of the Universe! Well, why not? Where demigods came from was rarely of much concern to anyone. They all had obscure origins in small rural towns. That didn't stop their popularity one bit, and if you're actually marketing your cult to working-class hicks, what better God to have than a working-class hick? Among the lower and middle classes in antiquity, there was actually a strong disdain for the elite and aristocratic and their lofty ideas, and a strong reverence for respectable men of their own class. This is indisputably evident among the ancient Jews and just as much among their pagan contemporaries.[10]

There were many popular working-class gods, from Hephaestus the blacksmith to Orpheus the musician. The resurrected demigod Pollux was a professional boxer. Romulus started out as a poor orphan herding sheep. Of course, they were all revealed to be supernaturally awesome. But then, in his own myth, so was Jesus. Such a rise from humble origins to supreme glory actually made him *typical*, not unusual, and what's typically successful needs no further explanation for its success. This is especially true since what Jesus did while on earth was irrelevant to what he could do for you now that he was exalted to the highest throne in heaven, and it was the heavenly Jesus that was sold to the masses, not just some dead carpenter from Galilee.

WAIT . . . YOU'RE NOT JEWISH, ARE YOU?

But why would a world filled with anti-Semites ever flock to a Jewish demigod? The ancient world wasn't really that anti-Semitic. Jews weren't uniformly popular, but neither was it Nazi Germany. We already know that many Gentiles were flocking to Judaism even before Christians came along, either converting to it, supporting it, or holding it in high esteem.[11] Judaism was at that time evangelistic—converts were actively sought, and anyone who entered the covenant by circumcising themselves and holding themselves bound by God's law was considered fully Jewish (exactly as God had commanded: Exodus 12:48). And Jews of the Diaspora (meaning outside of Palestine) were more liberal and culturally integrated, speaking the same languages as their pagan neighbors; they also often had much more in common culturally with those pagan neighbors than with conservative Palestinian Jews. We know Christianity was most successful in its first hundred years within exactly those groups: Diaspora Jews and their Gentile converts and sympathizers.[12]

Once Christianity had saturated that market apparently as far as it could, it began de-Judaizing the religion in order to make it palatable to more Gentiles. We see this process begin in the early second century CE, and some scholars claim to see it beginning already in the Gospels or even with Paul. But this move had become increasingly necessary after two failed Jewish wars against Rome (in the 60s and 130s) had lost the Jews a lot of their earlier public support and sympathy.

Those early Christians who began to make their religion more philosophical, more Hellenistic, and less Jewish (all the while claiming to have rendered Judaism obsolete) then had the most marketable version of Christianity, which is why it is only *that* version that continued to grow. Thus, even when its Jewishness really did become a problem, Christianity just got rid of it. Had Christianity remained obstinately Jewish, it would have failed—and as a matter of fact, the original Jewish sects of Christianity did fail.

Even in its first century, although Christianity was still the most successful among Diaspora Jews and their pagan sympathizers, it *also* made some early inroads into groups outside that category for the simple reason that Christianity made it easier to convert. A large deterrent against conversion to Judaism was its intense list of arduous social and personal restrictions and its requirement for an incredibly painful and rather dangerous procedure of bodily mutilation: circumcision (in a world with limited anesthetics and anti-septics). Once the Christian evangelist Paul abandoned those requirements for entry (barely a decade after the movement had begun), he had on his hands a sect of Judaism that was guaranteed to be more popular than any previous form of it. Thus, far from Christianity's increased success being impossible, it was now guaranteed. The already significant inflow of Gentiles toward the Jewish religion was certain to become significantly greater for its Christian sect. Meanwhile, Christians continued poaching the entire market once targeted by Jewish evangelization with a much cheaper product. Just like flooding the market with twenty-dollar iPhone knockoffs, their market dominance was a sure thing. No miracles needed.

FOR WE SO LOVED OUR DYING-AND-RISING GODS

Meanwhile, among pagans, genuine sons of god who had to be murdered, buried, and then miraculously resurrected from the dead in order to judge and rule from heaven on high as our divine saviors were actually a common fad of the time, not a shocking novelty at all. Osiris and Romulus were widely worshipped to the tune of such sacred stories demonstrably *before* the rise of Christianity, and similar stories surrounded other dying-and-rising gods long before such as Zalmoxis, Adonis, and Inanna.[13] And there were probably others (of whom evidence only barely survives).

Indeed, resurrection was wildly popular among the pagans. Of course, it was already a common Jewish staple, with past resurrections in its sacred stories and future resurrections in its imagined plan of salvation. But the claim that all pagans scoffed at the idea is simply false. The idea of a future resurrection for all the saved actually derives from pagan Zoroastrianism, then the Persian state religion, which had influenced many popular cults in the Roman Empire (including Mithraism and religious Stoicism). Indeed, it's from them that the Jews got the idea in the first place, having picked it up when they were in captivity in Persia several centuries before Christianity began.

But that wasn't the limit of it. Besides the many popular resurrected savior gods already mentioned, pagan tales of other resurrected heroes, gods, saints, and just-plain-lucky lads were incredibly common.[14] One very popular example at the time: not only was "the savior" Asclepius a resurrected and deified son of god, but he was also the preeminent "resurrector of the dead," which was in fact a prominent reason pagans held him in such esteem. Since the ancient Christian apologist Justin could not deny this, he was forced to insist "the devil" must have introduced "Asclepius as the raiser of the dead" in order to undermine the Christian message in advance.[15]

Clearly, pagans would have no problem with one more dying-and-rising son of god and savior. That notion was actually conspicuously *popular* at the time, *which is why Christians thought of it* and why it was at all successful. Even the claim that Jews would never have bought the idea of a singular resurrection before the general resurrection of all Jews is false: such special resurrections already appeared in their own Bible and were readily believed to still be occurring.[16] Even the future resurrection was often imagined as occurring in stages, which could include singular individuals (Adam, for example, was often thought to be the first to rise), and the earliest Christians taught that Jesus was indeed only the *first stage* of that general resurrection.[17] So Christian teaching was already right in line with popular Jewish thinking, and it was quite suspiciously tailor-made to fit right in with popular pagan belief, too. As the same Justin said (emphasis mine):

> When we say that the Word, who is our teacher, Jesus Christ the firstborn of God, was produced without sexual union, and that he was crucified and died, and rose again, and ascended to heaven, we propound *nothing new or different from what you believe* regarding those whom you consider sons of God.[18]

Nothing new or different. Translation: we packed our religion with every popular fad we could. Obviously, this is a natural recipe for success, not failure.

IT WAS NEW, IT WAS MORAL, IT WAS RADICAL (IN OTHER WORDS, IT WAS TYPICAL)

You'll sometimes hear that the ancient mindset was openly hostile to "novelty" and new ideas, and that pagans were all drunken, orgy-loving rapscallions who would never deign to embrace an austere cult of high moral standards. But such claims have more to do with Hollywood than history.

In reality, Romans were often prudes by modern standards, and cults and philosophies promoting austere morals were commonplace. Judaism, as already noted, was far more austere than Christianity yet still won converts, and Christianity only made it easier. Indeed, Christians were practically party animals by comparison. Secular moral cults like Stoicism were fashionable, too. All the major evangelistic religions of the day promoted systems of morality that were just as restrictive as Christianity (even if in different ways). Moral doctrines were components of all the mystery cults like Mithraism and Isidism.[19]

Even by the standards of popular fables and customs, Christian morality was not so far removed from what was already widely regarded as admirable and right, and the extent to which it went beyond, other non-Christian sects and philosophies had gone there, too. Indeed, for many the morals of Christian communities could even be attractive. At any rate, it was competing in a market already successfully mined by the same business model: morals and rules in exchange for eternal salvation. Christianity had tons of customers just waiting to be sold on the idea.

Ancient hostility to novelty, on the other hand, was more facade than fact.[20] In reality, novelty was popular and common—and ceaseless. New ideas, new philosophies, and new religions always spread like wildfire, never hindered at all by any supposed hostility to novelty. In part, this is because any new idea could be sold as an old one: just show how some revered ancient sages or texts already support or point the way to what's being sold now, and you no longer had a new idea but instead the perfection of an old one.

That's exactly how Christianity marketed itself. Even from the very beginning in the letters of Paul, and for centuries thereafter, every Christian text aimed at persuasion connects Christianity intimately and profoundly with the Jewish scriptures, regarded even by pagans as among the most ancient oracles of man. Christianity was never claimed to have been "founded" by Jesus—it was always claimed Jesus was merely the culmination of a divine plan that had been written down for millennia (Romans 16:25–26) by an ancient God whose worship many Romans respected precisely because the Jewish religion could claim such great antiquity.

It was in just this same way that the Romans so frequently found ways to paint the new as old that an endless stream of novel cults and philosophies came to permeate every inch of the empire, even despite resistance from some among the elite who found the unstoppable popularity of these novelties appalling. But unstoppable they were. No appeal to a Roman resistance to the "new" can argue against the natural success of Christianity. If dozens of other new cults and philosophies could succeed in spite of this, then so could Christianity. Especially since the most conspicuous elements of innovation in Christianity were already its most popular features: as already noted, it took the religion of Judaism, which was already winning converts from among the pagans, and made it even more attractive by making it far less onerous (in other words, making it far more *pagan*); and like modern Marxism (also once wildly popular despite stalwart elite hostility), it promised to subvert the most despised of elite values and produce an egalitarian utopia of justice for the common man, already a popular idea. Thus, even what really was new about Christianity was nevertheless exactly what would contribute to its success.

And then there's the fact that many of Christianity's supposed "innovations" were actually rip-offs of already popular ideas, such as a ritual ceremony of symbolically dying-and-rising and thus being "born again." Such a ceremony and concept was already an established part of Isis cult. Likewise, faith healing and exorcism were already commonly practiced by Jewish holy men and pagan sorcerers and keepers of holy shrines; incarnate gods were a dime a dozen, as were gods who magically impregnated women and had sons by them. Even many Jews accepted the notion of God having sons and spiritually possessing them.[21] Again, incorporating already popular features in a new religion (especially when you could then sell this as the perfection of an old one) was a perfectly natural road to success.

YOU DON'T NEED EVIDENCE, YOU JUST NEED FAITH

Wouldn't it have been so easy to check and discover their claims were false? Actually, no. It would have been neither easy nor common. When we pore over all the documents that survive, we find no evidence that any Christian convert did any fact-checking before converting or even would have done so. We can rarely even establish that they *could* have, had they wanted to. There *were* people in antiquity who could and would, but curiously we have no evidence that any of those people converted. Instead, every Christian who actually tells us what convinced him explicitly says he *didn't* check any facts but merely believed upon hearing the story and reading the scriptures and just "feeling" it was right. Every third-person account of conversions we have tells the same story.[22] Likewise, every early discussion we have from Christians regarding their methodology for testing claims either omits, rejects, or even denigrates rational, empirical methods and promotes instead faith-based methods of finding secrets hidden in scripture and relying on spiritual inspirations and revelations, and then verifying all this by whether their psychosomatic "miracles" worked and their leaders were willing to suffer for the cause. Skepticism and doubt were belittled; faith without evidence was praised and rewarded.[23] It's no surprise such an approach would be "successful" because such an approach is purely psychological—it does not depend on any *actual* evidence.

Hence, when we look closely, we discover that all the actual evidence that Jesus rose from the dead consisted of unconfirmable hearsay, just like every other incredible claim made by ancient religions of the day.[24] Christian apologists make six-figure careers out of denying this, but their elaborate attempts always collapse on inspection. There just wasn't any evidence Jesus really rose from the dead other than the word of a few fanatics and a church community demonstrably full of regular hallucinators and fabricators. The only miracles Christians themselves could perform in public were some faith-healings and exorcisms and unremarkable bouts of prophesy—in other words, quite suspiciously, *only things that we know have natural causes* (being entirely cultural and psychosomatic phenomena).[25]

Even if every public, checkable claim made by Christian missionaries were entirely true, it still cannot be concluded that their private, uncheckable claims were true as well; yet only the latter had any plausible claim to being supernatural. In the long run, once Christianity became centuries old, it was just one more religion packed with incredible claims no one could verify. And just as (once upon a time) all *those* cults could go on succeeding, often by exploiting social and political advantages that made joining them attractive, so did Christianity. Indeed, when it gained the despotic power to compel conversion and monopolize the society's wealth and education, its triumph was all but assured.

AND BLOOD IS OFTEN SEED

Surely the fact that the Romans tortured and killed Christians and ruthlessly hunted them all down would have made their success impossible but for divine intervention. Right? Wrong.

First, in actual fact, the Romans didn't "hunt them all down." All reliable evidence confirms that persecution of Christians was limited, occasional, and sporadic at best. Most pagans didn't care about Christians or even aided and harbored them.[26] They are essentially just like the persecuted Jews throughout history. Hitler's regime alone killed far more Jews than Romans ever killed of Christians, yet Judaism thrives worldwide—so should we now all convert to Judaism? Medieval Christian pogroms against Jews were likewise as ruthless and horrifying as any pagan oppression of Christians had ever been (arguably, in some cases, even more so). Sporadic persecution just doesn't stop religions from growing and surviving. That's why Hitler had to dream up a Final Solution—the Interim Solution hadn't succeeded even after thousands of years of earnest effort. And yet, alas, even his Final Solution was really just the Final Failure to Have Any Effect at All. In the long haul, when it comes to zealous people and their devoted murderers, the villains tend to lose.

Second, the fact that believers are willing to die for their belief does not confirm their belief is true, since there have been willing martyrs for Judiasm, Islam, Buddhism, Marxism, even paganism, and many other religions and ideologies throughout history. In the right social conditions, such martyrdom doesn't even slow recruitment because such willingness to die is *normal* for such movements, not unusual. As W. H. C. Frend says of that time, "there was a living pagan tradition of self-sacrifice for a cause, a preparedness if necessary to defy an unjust ruler, that existed alongside the developing Christian concept of martyrdom inherited from Judaism."[27] Christian martyrdom particularly made sense from a cultural and sociological perspective. Many sociologists studying world martyrdom movements have found they have a common social underpinning throughout history, from aboriginal movements in the New World to Islamic movements in the Middle East. For example, Alan Segal says that in every well-documented case a widespread inclination to martyrdom "is an oblique attack by the powerless against the power of oppressors," in effect "canceling the power of an oppressor through moral claims to higher ground and to a resolute claim to the afterlife, as the better" and only "permanent" reward. "From modern examples," Segal concludes, "we can see that what produces martyrdom," besides the corresponding "exaltation of the afterlife," is "a colonial and imperial situation, a conquering power, and a subject people whose religion does not easily account for the conquest." Some of these subjects are "predisposed to understand events in a religious context," and are suffering from some "political or economic" deprivation, or even a social or cultural deprivation (as when the most heartfelt morals of the subgroup are not recognized or realized by the dominating power structure).[28]

The Roman Empire was tailor-made to breed exactly such resentment and deprivation. There were enough people disenfranchised, abused, exploited, callously ignored, or all too often denied justice and the means to live, to feed the ranks of suicidal Christians.[29] Such people basically had only two options: they could just "take it," or they could decide not to take it anymore. Those who preferred the latter option are the segment of the population from which Christianity successfully recruited—until it had enough money to attract people for other reasons, and then enough power to find armed protectors, and then of course to control the entire apparatus of the state. After that point, persecution was no longer an obstacle. But until then, the resulting selection bias had significant ramifications for the attitudes and behavior of early Christians, who inevitably differed markedly from non-Christians precisely because they already differed from their peers, in attitude and behavior, before converting.[30] They also would have differed in exactly the respect relating to martyrdom and sacrifice that Segal describes. Christians represented those who weren't going to take it anymore. The behavior of Christians, and the attractiveness of Christianity as a movement, can only be understood within this context.

Indeed, the logic of Christian ideology (as with all other comparable movements in history) is impeccable: if sinners go to hell or oblivion, and the faithful go to eternal heavenly bliss, then nothing else matters, for everything else is temporary and insignificant compared to the eternal future. The Christians promised that the faithful will even inherit the earth itself, gaining all the power and plenty they always longed for while watching their oppressors and exploiters suffer utter downfall and defeat. In other words, "everyone gets what they deserve." Anyone convinced of this will suffer anything. They will endure any death, any torture, any discomfort, any indignity; all the while they will smile inside, knowing their abusers will "get it" in the end while they themselves will get twice the reward. In human history there has never been so powerful a motivator as this—a point well-taken by Islamic authorities who found a way to exploit it en masse to command entire armies and mollify oppressed and exploited populations. The very same motivation led Buddhists to set themselves on fire to protest the Vietnam War. Yet this doesn't mean there has ever been "irrefutable proof" that Islam and Buddhism are true.

Combine the Christian eschatological ideology with the scale of deprivation endured by many of the subjects of Rome, and all you'll get is a powder keg. Had Christianity not arisen of its own, it would have been necessary to invent it—or something like it—for such an apocalyptic movement was all but inevitable under the sociocultural conditions of the Roman Empire. It's human nature to long for peace, love, justice, and the control of your own life. Take all that away from millions of people, and it's just a matter of time before rebellions break out. Within a system like that of the Roman Empire, which lacked real democracy or even a sufficient scale of freedom of speech, there could only be two kinds of rebellion: the violent or the cultural. Violent revolution is always an economic contest of military resources, which Rome would always win—and Rome always did. Therefore, the only rebellion that could succeed was a cultural revolution, which meant a war of ideas—and that was a war the rebels could win, so long as they had the more popular ideas and employed the right tactics on the battlefield of the mind. Such a war still had casualties (martyrs) and hardships (persecution), but it was still a war, and like all well-motivated wars, soldiers didn't give up simply because of the prospect of dying or suffering. Indeed, as in any righteous war, dying and suffering is exactly what soldiers are willing to pay for victory.[31]

Clearly the sociocultural conditions of the early Christian willingness to endure persecution and martyrdom fit exactly those of every other comparable movement in history, matching every element of the above analysis perfectly. Yet it follows, since it holds in every other case known, that their motivation was not some particular historical claim or esoteric dogma. As in every other case, their motivation was rebellion against a corrupt social order in defense of a superior vision of society. Their motive was a moral system, a view of the way society should function and structure itself. That was what attracted recruits to the Christian movement, that is what they suffered and died for—not "proof" that Jesus stepped out of a tomb, or any other such claim. In none of the mass movements throughout history involving a willingness to suffer and sacrifice has the motive ever been anything like that, but always a socio-moral ideal. Christianity was surely no different. Indeed, its social program was the one truly tangible thing it had to offer. It should not surprise us that many were willing to die for it.

Once the battle lines were drawn in this culture-war of compassion against insolence, brotherhood against exploitation, justice against corruption, and equality against inequity, there would surely be plenty of volunteer soldiers fighting for the Christian side. And like all volunteers for every just war in history, they would be fully prepared to assume the burdens of battle with all its attendant miseries, sacrifices, and risks. That's simply human nature; nothing supernatural about it. The shame is that the Christian church eventually succumbed to the very same corruption, villainy, and injustice it began its faith fighting against.

HEY, SMART RECRUITMENT TACTICS REALLY DO WORK!

Several other claims you might hear from time to time are simply false. One such claim is that having women as witnesses to important faith-claims (such as the "empty tomb") would have impeded Christianity's growth "because no one trusted the testimony of women." This is flat-out false—both socially and as a matter of law.[32] The claim that no one would believe in a god who didn't know everything is equally false.[33] But some claims are true and in fact reveal how Christianity's success was indeed a product of entirely natural sociological causes, such as the claim that ancient cultures were subject to certain kinds of groupthink. The mindset of that period was strongly oriented toward collectivist psychology—not quite to the extent of Asian cultures but certainly more so than modern Western individualism. This meant that it was difficult to just pick off recruits from within families and towns and subgroups. People more easily yielded to pressures to conform and more ardently pressured others to conform. But Christians didn't succeed against the grain of these facts but actually exploited these facts to maximize their growth.[34]

All evidence indicates that Christian missionaries, especially in the first two centuries, routinely targeted heads of household and then used that collectivist authority to pressure or motivate the rest of their extended family to convert (medieval missionaries used the same tactic by first converting kings, chieftains, or other heads of state, and thus inspiring or compelling the rest of their nation or tribe to follow suit). At the same time they also harvested the disaffected, those who had already been separated from their families (such as migrant workers or widows and orphans), who were already in search of a new "family" they could belong to.[35] They also recruited new members by exploiting established channels of social authority to which they already belonged and whose vernacular they had mastered, like synagogues. Many of their methods resembled those of Christian missionaries in later periods of history, such as retooling Christianity to resemble what their target audience already accepted (a tactic explicitly described in 1 Corinthians 9:19–23), or asking at first very little and offering attractive benefits, and then once the recruit has become integrated and invested, asking for more and more commitment until they are then committed to the faith with the same full weight of groupthink as they had been to their former lives.[36] There are a number of complex ways the Christian message was constructed to be particularly successful in its ancient cultural matrix (which I further discuss in *Not the Impossible Faith*), and we can expect this from the lessons of natural selection: other Christian sects failed while those that picked up the right tools succeeded. This is exactly as we should expect if Christianity's success was merely a natural phenomenon like that of any other religion. Thus, for this and every other reason surveyed in this chapter, Christianity's purely ordinary growth rate has purely ordinary explanations.

WHY UNREMARKABLE = FALSE

The same analysis will follow for any other indicator or claim we examine. The conclusion is always the same: Christianity's origin, growth, and success look entirely natural and not supernatural at all. If they're not supernatural, we should wonder how they can even be true—and rightly so. A sound application of Bayes' theorem proves that Christianity's being unremarkable entails that, in fact, it is false.

I explain the basic mechanics of Bayes' theorem in another chapter (see chapter 12, "Neither Life nor the Universe Appear Intelligently Designed"). Here I'll only reiterate that when the premises in Bayes' theorem cannot be denied, then the conclusion cannot be denied because that conclusion follows necessarily as a matter of inviolable logic.

Bayes' theorem has four premises: (1) the prior probability that a given claim (say, CHRISTIANITY) is true; (2) the prior probability that it's false (~CHRISTIANITY); (3) the consequent probability that we would have all the specific evidence we do if that claim is true (or C); and (4) the consequent probability that we would have all that same evidence even if that claim is false (or D). All these probabilities are conditional on our total background knowledge (everything we know with reasonable certainty is true about history, science, and everything else). What matters for the present analysis is that when the prior probabilities are equal, then the probability that the claim is true equals C / (C + D). This is necessarily the case and cannot be denied.[37]

I believe the prior probability that Christianity just happens to be the one true religion among all the worldviews embraced across the world—which means the probability *before* looking at any specific evidence for Christianity—is exceedingly small. But I won't argue that here.[38] Instead, just for the sake of argument, I'll say its prior probability is flat-out even money: 50-50. The prior probability that Christianity is true (that is, again, *prior* to considering any specific evidence for it) certainly can't be any greater than that. That leaves how likely the evidence we have would be if Christianity is true, and how likely that evidence would be if Christianity is false. What I've shown in this chapter (and support even further in *Not the Impossible Faith* and *The Christian Delusion*) is that there is nothing about the rise and success of Christianity that is at all unexpected on the hypothesis that it is false. If Christianity is just one more false religion, like Islam or Buddhism or Mithraism or anything else, then the evidence would be exactly like what we have: a movement founded on little verifiable evidence but instead exploiting known natural psychological and sociological processes to leverage its success in the marketplace of ideas, growing at a normal expected rate, and then capitalizing on historical opportunities that would have benefited any other religion in the same position just as much.[39] The consequent probability of the evidence on the hypothesis that Christianity is false, in other words, is essentially 100 percent (or as near to it as makes all odds).

Is that exactly the same evidence we should expect, however, if Christianity is *true*? If it were, then we'd have to agree there is no evidence whatever that Christianity is true—because then all the evidence we have is exactly the same evidence we'd have if it were false. To argue that Christianity is true, we'd have to have evidence that's unlikely unless Christianity were true. But we have none. Even the "feeling" that Christ now speaks to us or lives in our hearts is not such, because people of completely different religions have exactly the same feelings and experiences, only of their own gods and spirits and forces, so we know the odds of such feelings and experiences being had even by believers in false religions is 100 percent. Christians experiencing such feelings, too, proves nothing precisely because this is already expected even if their religion is false.[40]

In contrast, when we seriously consider what evidence we would likely have if Christianity really *were* true, we find the evidence that we actually have looks nothing like that.[41] If Christianity is false, we should expect exactly this: (a) reported revelations of a newly risen Jesus would occur only to die-hard believers, only for a very brief time, only in one single geographic location, and only exceedingly rarely to anyone else—and even they will be closely connected to the cult and thus (we can expect) in some way inspired by it to "see Jesus" too. Only if Christianity were *true* would it be at all likely that (b) Jesus would genuinely appear, and not only to die-hard believers but just as clearly and powerfully to a great many outsiders, all over the world, in every generation ever after. Outcome (a) is exactly what we expect if Christianity is false. Yet (a) is exactly what we observe. Outcome (b) is what we should expect if Christianity is true. Yet (b) is *not* what we observe. Thus the actual evidence is *less probable* if Christianity is true than if it's false. Therefore, C < D. And when C < D, the product of C / (C + D) will be less than 50 percent. And if it's less than 50 percent, the probability that Christianity is true is less than 50 percent. In other words, it probably isn't true.[42]

Elsewhere I've put this in more visceral terms:

> If God Himself were really appearing to people, and really was on a compassionate mission to reform and save the world, there is hardly any credible reason he would appear to only one persecutor rather than to all of them. But if [the persecutor] Paul's experience was entirely natural, and not at all divine, then we should expect such an event to be rare, possibly even unique—and, lo and behold, that appears to be the case. Paul's conversion thus supports the conclusion that Christianity originated from natural phenomena, and not from any encounter with a walking corpse. A walking corpse—indeed a flying corpse (Luke 24:51 and Acts 1:9–11) or a teleporting corpse (Luke 24:31–37 and John 20:19–26)—could have visited Pilate, Herod, the Sanhedrin, the masses of Jerusalem, the Roman legions, even the emperor and senate of Rome. He could even have flown to America (as the Mormons actually believe he did), and even China, preaching in all the temples and courts of Asia. In fact, being God, he could have appeared to everyone on earth. He could visit me right now. Or you! And yet, instead, besides his already-fanatical followers, just one odd fellow ever saw him.
>
> If Jesus was a God and really wanted to save the world, he would have appeared and delivered his Gospel personally to the whole world. He would not appear only to one small group of believers and one lone outsider, in one

tiny place, just one time, two thousand years ago, and then give up. But if Christianity originated as a natural movement inspired by ordinary hallucinations (real or pretended), then we would expect it to arise in only one small group, in one small place and time, and especially where, as in antiquity, regular hallucinators were often respected as holy and their hallucinations believed to be divine communications. And that's exactly when and where it began. The ordinary explanation thus predicts all we see, whereas the extraordinary explanation predicts things we don't see at all.[43]

We should also expect that a compassionate god who wanted us to know his message of salvation would not allow any errors or alterations to be made to the book containing that message (we would be supernaturally incapable of making such changes, and thus all Bibles ever made from antiquity to the present would be identical—they are not), which would verify that his message was the true message (whereas otherwise it looks exactly like just one more human-made message purporting to be from God, such as every other religion produces); or faithful Christians (then and still) could have miraculous powers that *aren't* natural phenomena, such as the ability to regenerate destroyed limbs and organs or verifiably resurrect the genuinely dead.[44]

Of course that such things didn't happen is 100 percent expected if Christianity is false. But that none of them, not even anything else like them, would happen is certainly not 100 percent expected if Christianity is true. Surely the odds are *something* less than that. Thus, C < D. Any such evidence, or anything else instead that was at all like them (in being very unexpected unless Christianity were true), would also have generated a rate of growth for the movement far greater than natural phenomena are already known to produce. Instead, Christianity grew at the same rate as every other aggressively evangelistic religion in history—despite those religions being, one must suppose, false. Hence we expect that rate if it's false; we don't expect it if it's true. Thus, again, C < D. Even Christianity itself predicted that, if it were true, Jesus would have stuck around or very soon returned and remained on earth to judge and rule all peoples by now. This is explicitly predicted by Jesus. His prediction didn't come true.[45] We surely can't say that his prediction not coming true by now was 100 percent certain. To the contrary, it must necessarily have been less likely than that. Yet that it wouldn't come true is 100 percent certain if Christianity is *false*. Thus, again, C < D.

We can extend this observation all the way back in human time: given its importance and (we're to suppose) fitness and elegance, the Gospel should have been revealed, preached, and known to every shaman and tribe of the human race from the dawn of history to now, not *never* heard of, by anyone, anywhere, ever before, until ten thousand years of civilization had gone by, and then heard of in only one place and time and thereafter spread merely by humankind and solely by word of mouth. That Jesus revealed "the true Gospel" only once and only to Palestinians (and only after thousands of years of religious soul-searching there) is exactly what we expect if this was just a human-made religion. The odds of this being the case are then 100 percent. But the odds of this being the case if Jesus was God and cared about all humankind are surely not 100 percent, as if we could predict with absolute certainty from that premise ("Jesus is God and cares about all humankind") that Jesus would never reveal himself at the same time to Asians and Indians and Celts and Australians and Persians and Native Americans and all other peoples (in other words, all humankind). No, the odds of *none* of the latter happening cannot possibly be 100 percent. It must be *something* less than that. Which entails, again, C < D.

Finally, we have all the bizarre facts of Christianity, which make little sense if it's true but perfect sense if it was just a natural product of its time and place like every other religion. For example, why does God bother bearing a son? He could send an angel, the holy spirit, or reveal himself directly or through any other means. Why does he need to actually impregnate a woman and wait decades while the resulting child grows up and then wanders around preaching with all the illogical limitations of a mere mortal? We can explain this *culturally*. Because that was then the fashionable thing: gods were routinely believed to impregnate women and their sons to walk the earth telling tales and founding kingdoms and suffering until ascending to their celestial glory. That's a weird thing to believe *now*. It's no longer a peculiarity of our culture. But back then, it was. That Christianity would begin with such an idea is 100 percent exactly the sort of thing we expect if it's merely a product of its culture. But as an idea of a universal god who is not bound by any fleeting fashions and cultural expectations like that—a god to whom such ideas should surely seem as quaintly silly as they now do to us—it's certainly *not* 100 percent exactly what we expect. Thus, again, C < D.

Likewise, a son of god who has to be killed, then rise from the dead, then ascend to heaven. That was, as we saw, a fashionable idea in that culture at that very time. There were lots of gods like that. Then, it seemed natural; now, it seems ridiculous. As Captain Kirk said in *Star Trek V*, "What need does God have of a starship?" we, too, must ask, "What need does God have of a dying-and-rising demigod?" It's not as if this is in any way what we would expect a universal god needs to forgive our sins. Quite the contrary. Except for that bizarrely peculiar and entirely parochial cultural fad for dying-and-rising divine sons, it's not even remotely what we would ever expect at all. Thus, again, C < D.

The same goes for the notions of blood sacrifice and vicarious atonement—which were commonplace then and very much in the mindset of the time, but which are now seen for what they are: silly. That someone can accept the punishment for someone else is hardly believed to be just or appropriate anymore (if it were, we'd allow criminals to walk free if they can find anyone to volunteer to do their time for them).[46] That God "likes" the smell of burning flesh (Ephesians 5:2, referencing Exodus 29:25) or "needs blood" to effect atonement, or that God blood has "more magical power" than animal blood (Hebrews 9:13–14 and 9:22), is all primitive superstitious hokum no one takes seriously anymore. Back then, it was taken very seriously indeed. But God is not a primitive slave of ancient culture. Only men were. Thus that Christianity would be founded on a primitive superstition of atonement magic is 100 percent exactly the sort of thing we should expect if Christianity is false (as then it will have as its core ideas just what was culturally assumed it should then have), but certainly not 100 percent what we'd expect if it's true, as if a cosmic God who made the universe fourteen billion years ago is still hung up on blood magic. Thus, again, C < D.

It doesn't matter what excuses you try to make for why the evidence looks *exactly* like it would look if Christianity is false. Either you must concede there is no evidence that Christianity is true—because only then would all the evidence we have be exactly the same as it would be if it were false (which is all you end up with if you make excuses for every single thing)—or you must concede *something* about the evidence we have is unexpected on the hypothesis that Christianity is true. In other words, either you must concede D = C (and, therefore, there is no evidence for Christianity, and Christianity is no more likely than its own prior probability), or you must concede C < D (and therefore Christianity is probably false). You must pick one or the other. Even the first option (conceding there is no evidence for Christianity) falls against the horns of every argument there is that the *prior* probability that Christianity is true is certainly not as high as 50 percent. And if it's less, then Christianity is still false *even if you insist* D = C.

CONCLUSION

All attempts to argue that Christianity's origin and success were supernaturally special only end up exposing how not special it is and how not supernatural its origins and growth were. Because a close look at the actual facts fully undermines the claim that Christianity ever had the backing of God. Such backing entails we should see a very different set of historical facts than we do. That Christians need to believe Christianity was supernaturally remarkable when it really isn't is a sign that they don't really believe in Christianity because it's true; they desperately need to massage or even doctor the facts to convince themselves it's true. Anyone who analyzes this argument for Christianity rationally will discover both facts: that the evidence actually disconfirms the supernatural claims of Christianity, and that Christians can only deny this by ignoring or altering those facts. Once we *all* realize this, Christianity will come to an end.

Chapter 3

CHRISTIANITY IS WILDLY IMPROBABLE

by John W. Loftus

> I now regard "the case for theism" as a fraud, and
> I can no longer take it seriously enough to present
> it to a class as a respectable philosophical posi-
> tion—no more than I could present intelligent
> design as a legitimate biological theory. . . . I just
> cannot take their arguments seriously anymore, and
> if you cannot take something seriously, you should
> not try to devote serious academic attention to it.
> I've turned the philosophy of religion courses over
> to a colleague. . . . So, with the exception of things
> I am finishing now, I am calling it quits with the
> philosophy of religion.[1]
> —*PROFESSOR KEITH PARSONS.*

There are many religions in the world we don't take seriously enough to
pay attention to them. There are also many dead religions of the past
that we ignore in today's world, including several dead Christianities. They do
not merit our thought or discussion. They are dead. They have no relevance for
our lives. Unless we're interested in the history of these religions, we simply
ignore them. We ignore their scriptures, their prophets, their religious duties,
their rituals, and their threats of punishment in the afterlife. They no longer
matter to us.

When it comes to Christianity, two thousand years are enough. It's time
this ancient myth was put to rest. This book calls for the same end of Christianity as the other religions we reject as dead to us. Just as we ignore other

faiths, our hope is that someday we can ignore the Christian faith because its future adherents will live in cultural backwaters—like the Amish people, who pose no threat to the peace of the world. Bob Price makes such a case for Evangelicalism in the afterword of this book. The decision of Keith Parsons quoted above probably shows we're making some progress, for one of the reasons he tells us he's calling it quits with the philosophy of religion is because several atheists have "produced works of enormous sophistication that devastate the theistic arguments in their classical and most recent formulations" and as such, "presented powerful, and, in my view, unanswerable atheological arguments." The case is therefore closed. There's nothing much more to add. Christianity is living on borrowed time. In the end, science ends Christianity.

THE CHRISTIAN FAITH IS PREPOSTEROUS

In this chapter I'll use a smorgasbord of arguments to show that Christianity, especially Protestant Evangelicalism, is wildly improbable. Evangelical Christian beliefs are so wildly improbable to me that they are ridiculous, preposterous, absurd, and bizarre. I'll show this by first placing evangelical beliefs out on the periphery of the Christian faith and then in turn by placing the Christian faith as a whole out on the periphery of religion itself. I'll also show this in its many bizarre derivative beliefs. Next I'll show that the contortionist ways Christian apologists defend their faith make otherwise intelligent people look stupid. Then I'll close with a reality check, a wakeup call, for Christians to consider. Christianity is just way too improbable to be believed or defended by any thoughtful, scientifically minded person in today's world.

First, consider the following ten creedal affirmations:[2]

1) There exists an eternal, all-powerful, all-knowing creator God, who, though of one essence, exists as three distinct, but not separate, persons: Father, Son, and Holy Spirit.
2) There exists a devil, Satan, and numerous other demonic beings as well as angels, archangels, cherubim, seraphim, and other types of supernatural beings.
3) The earth is not billions of years in age, but created by God six to ten thousand years ago.

4) There was an actual Adam and Eve in a literal Garden of Eden who sinned and brought upon this world the horrible suffering it contains; as such, organic evolution is false.

5) God has a morally sufficient reason for permitting all the evil that ever has or ever will occur.

6) A first-century Galilean Jew, Jesus of Nazareth, was born of a virgin as an incarnate God in the flesh and performed numerous miracles during his life, including walking on water, turning water into wine, and feeding thousands with a small serving of bread and fish.

7) This Jesus was crucified by the Roman authorities according to specific prophecies in the Old Testament as a divine sacrifice to atone for the past, present, and future sins of the world.

8) This same Jesus bodily arose from the dead on the third day, and after forty days of additional earthly presence, during which he performed more miracles, he bodily ascended off the earth into the sky to go to heaven.

9) A collection of sixty-six ancient texts, composed by numerous persons, nearly all unknown, over a period of over a thousand years, in their original versions, contained no inconsistencies, absurdities, or errors of fact or morality.

10) There is life after death, and only people who have accepted a legitimate form of Christian belief will go to eternal bliss in heaven, while all others, with a few rare exceptions, will suffer an eternity of torment in hell.

The Christianities that embrace fewer of these creedal affirmations are less improbable than those that embrace more of them. Any professing Christian who interprets all these creeds mythically is a religionist who simply believes in a higher power of some kind, or a cultural Christian, who likes studying the Bible as literature in the social grouping of the church, something that I find completely unnecessary.[3] Any professing Christian who goes beyond that and literally believes only one of these affirmations has an improbable faith, since each one of them alone is highly disputable with respect to its truth or intelligibility. Any professing Christian who literally believes more than five of them has a wildly improbable faith (and that's being very generous). And any professing Christian who literally believes them all has an incredibly bizarre faith.[4]

Christians who accept these ten creedal affirmations must show that the biblically described events actually happened. This task is fatally hamstrung by virtue of the fact that such efforts are based upon the poor quality of historical evidence that survives from the ancient superstitious past.[5] Usually, the farther we go back in the past the harder it is to reconstruct exactly what happened. Sometimes the evidence leading to a different conclusion has been lost or destroyed. Other times it was hidden away only to be discovered much later. In most circumstances historians can at best say only what did not happen as they falsify one historical supposition after another. When we factor in claims of miracles, it gets even worse, for extraordinary claims of miracles demand a greater deal of solid evidence for them (e.g., if a person tells us he levitated, we would need more than just his testimony to believe him).[6]

So, expecting this kind of solid evidence for miracles in the past is asking more of history than it's possible to show from historical study (e.g., unlike a person who personally tells us he levitated, we cannot interrogate an ancient text that says a certain person levitated). But we're not done yet. Christians must also show that the doctrines they derive from the supposed biblical events are true. However, this task is fatally hamstrung by virtue of the fact that their interpretations of the biblical texts are historically situated and culturally conditioned, as is evident from the number of Christianities that have existed and exist today.[7] If this isn't enough of an impossible barrier to belief, Christians have the additional task of trying to show, if they can, how the doctrines they arrive at are supported by the evidence from the sciences (i.e., creationism, the Exodus, the virgin birth, the ascension of Jesus, the efficacy of petitionary prayer, etc.). Lastly, Christians have the task of showing how philosophy can make coherent sense of their doctrines (like Trinitarianism, the incarnation, atonement, personal identity after death, and the goodness of an omnipotent God in the presence of massive and ubiquitous human and animal suffering). Accomplishing all these Herculean tasks is needed to defend what they believe. It cannot be done.

Yet many Christians talk as if they are certain Christianity is true. When I first converted to the Christian faith, I attended a youth group of a Pentecostal church where John Lloyd was my first youth pastor. Not that long before this book went to press I met with him, and he said to me, "John, I know that I know that I know that what I believe is true." And when he said this he closed his eyes as if he was experiencing God. He means what he says. But what he says cannot be true. Many other people in different religions would all say the same thing. Neurologist Robert Burton describes this "delusion of certainty" in his book *On Being Certain: Believing You Are Right Even When You're Not*: "Despite how certainty feels, it is neither a conscious choice nor even a thought process. Certainty and similar states of 'knowing what we know' arise out of involuntary brain mechanisms that, like love or anger, function independently of reason."[8] There is simply no way anyone can claim what my friend Lloyd does. How can he? His faith is based on a historical claim, a much disputed extraordinary one about a man who came back to life in the ancient superstitious world. Many ordinary historical reconstructions are weakly justified because that's the best historians can do with the paucity of evidence for them, so how much the worse for an extraordinary one? Why won't evangelicals admit this?

When it comes to extraordinary miraculous claims, yesterday's evidence has lost all its power to convince. In order to see yesterday's evidence as convincing evidence for a miracle, we must already believe in an interpretive framework that allows us to see it as such. In the case of Christianity, the raw uninterpreted data of the past will not be enough for us to believe a miracle took place without first having a Christian interpretive framework for that raw data. This is a circular catch-22 for faith.

Where does the Christian interpretive framework come from, then? It doesn't come from philosophical analysis, or from any "background knowledge" or any "priors," for there are no relevant "priors" prior to establishing the Christian interpretive framework. Christians must first independently establish that the miraculous resurrection of Jesus took place from the uninterpreted raw historical data. Not until then can they place such a miraculous belief into their bag of "priors" in the first place! This problem is fatal for anyone who wishes to believe Jesus bodily arose from the dead.

In my world, miracles do not happen. What world are *you* living in? The odds of a resurrection, from my experience, are at 0 percent. No Bayesian analysis can multiply a virtual zero probability with any other likely number and get very much higher than zero. That's what the probabilities are. I am skeptical of the extraordinary claim that Jesus resurrected because I cannot dismiss my present experience. I must judge the past from my present. I cannot do otherwise. Christians cannot believe based on the raw uninterpreted historical evidence, and yet they must approach said evidence from our present-day perspective where miracles, like virgin births and resurrections, do not happen. The only way they can reach their faithful conclusions is by assuming what needs to be shown based on their upbringing in a Christian culture, and that's it. If in our world miracles do not happen, then they did not happen in first-century Palestine, either. And that should be the end of it.

We can even grant the existence of Yahweh, or a creator god, along with the possibility of miracles, and it changes very little. What needs to be shown is that Yahweh did such a miracle here in this particular case. After all, over-whelming numbers of Jews in the days of Jesus did not believe Jesus arose from the dead even though they believed in Yahweh and the Old Testament. And they were there! They didn't think there was sufficient evidence to believe, and yet two thousand years later I'm supposed to? If they didn't, why should I? In fact, even if God exists and raised Jesus from the dead, there is simply no way *we* can know that he did this with the historical tools available to us. And these tools are all we've got.

All we have is hearsay testimonial evidence coming from the ancient past, containing inconsistencies and improbabilities, on behalf of the resurrection of Jesus. We do not know who wrote the Gospels. We do know they were written decades or more after the alleged facts supposedly occurred. How reliable of a testimony can that be? We also know there were many forgeries written by Christians, some of them accepted into the canonical New Testament. Can we really say all four canonical Gospels are genuine? Can we say they represent four separate testimonies when later Gospels borrowed from and expanded on the Gospel of Mark, a Gospel where the resurrected Jesus does not appear to the disciples at all? We don't even know whether all the characters in them are real people. Much less can we claim to know what they actually said and did. We cannot interview them or the Gospel writers themselves. Even if we were to grant that the Gospel writers reported some things correctly, there are things in them we simply cannot believe. After all, we're told that at the death of Jesus the tombs of the dead saints opened, and they walked around Jerusalem (Matthew 27:52–53). Why should we believe anything they said at that point? There is a reason why hearsay evidence is not admissible in court: it cannot be substantiated or cross-examined. This problem is even more exacerbated when it comes to the ancient superstitious past.[9]

People who claim otherwise are just fooling themselves. *The tools of the historian are inadequate for the task of detecting miracles.* The historian must be skeptical, must seek independent corroboration, must assume a natural cause for events in history, and must never claim more than the evidence allows. Historians qua historians cannot use faith to establish their historical reconstructions, otherwise they could be easily duped by claims that witches flew through the night, or that the sun really did stop dead in its tracks for Joshua. In this manner, the historian is a model outsider when it comes to Christianity. He or she sets faith aside as irrelevant, just as a scientist does, in the interests of getting at the truth. Such a method has produced the goods so many times it makes our heads spin, whereas faith can only get lucky with hunches at best.

Plenty of natural explanations have been suggested for the claim that Jesus miraculously resurrected from the grave, too. The visionary basis for the view that Jesus arose from the dead beginning with Peter (or Mary Magdalene) works just fine, as I suggested in my book *Why I Became an Atheist*. Bob Price offers a natural alternative in a later chapter for this book. But nonbelievers do not have to propose an alternative scenario at all, just as historians don't have to do so. One historian can look at another historian's reconstruction of what happened at Custer's Last Stand and say such a scenario is improbable without having to suggest a better alternative. It could well be that after showing such a reconstruction is improbable there just isn't enough evidence to say what actually took place.

WHO HAS THE MOST EXTRAORDINARY CLAIMS?

The improbability of Christianity becomes even more pronounced when we consider the nature and number of extraordinary claims it makes compared to other religious viewpoints. An extraordinary claim is a claim about an alleged event considered improbable because it's outside the realm of the ordinary, something we wouldn't expect to happen. The only kinds of out of the ordinary or extraordinary claims I can accept are those that meet two criteria: (1) they are within the range of what science considers naturally possible; and (2) there are good reasons based on good evidence to think these claims are about events that actually took place.[10] The most improbable kinds of extraordinary claims are about alleged events that cannot be explained within nature and thereby require supernatural being(s) or forces to explain them. If someone claimed he or she levitated, that would be an extraordinary claim of this sort because it would be something against what is expected in the natural course of events—something like the Transfiguration of Jesus told by the Gospel writers (e.g., Mark 9:1–8). If that same person also claimed he or she vanished, that would be an additional extraordinary claim. If that person then claimed to have rematerialized in a remote part of the globe, that would be a third extraordinary claim. The important point is that these are three independent extraordinary claims. People might come to believe the first one happened but not the second or the third, or come to believe the second claim but reject the first or the third ones, and so on. So I see no reason why we must believe them all if we come to believe in one of them. Even believing in one of them doesn't seem reasonable without a ton of evidence.

Protestant evangelicalism is a wildly improbable faith inside a Christian faith that is already more improbable than others because of the number of extraordinary claims being made. The following chart shows the major religious and nonreligious viewpoints based on the number of extraordinary claims they each make. The more extraordinary claims they make, the farther to the right these positions are placed:

Greater Extraordinary Claims Scale

$$\longrightarrow$$

A T H E I S T	P A N T H E I S T	D E I S T	J E W	M U S L I M	C H R I S T I A N

This scale shows us which viewpoints make the most extraordinary claims. On the left side is the atheist (or agnostic) who makes no extraordinary claims about supernatural beings or forces at all. I know such an assertion is contested by believers, but it's the only familiar and consistent way to explain what an atheist is when contrasting the atheist position to those who believe in supernatural beings and forces. Atheists are nontheists and by extension nonbelievers. We do not believe in supernatural beings or forces and hence do not make any extraordinary claims about nonnatural entities that are beyond what we can or should expect. We simply have no religious beliefs in that sense.[11]

As we move off to the right, the pantheist claims all is *one*. While this is a hard claim to wrap one's head around, it is a simple one. The pantheist makes only one extraordinary claim, even though it's a huge one that denies everything we experience every single day of our lives as an illusion (*maya*).

With deism we see an additional extraordinary claim is being made. Deists only accept what reason leads them to, and for most of them this means there is only a creator God. Their claim is more extraordinary than pantheism since they affirm a spiritual reality that exists in addition to the reality we experience, inhabited by a creator God (which is a kind of dualism as opposed to a monism).

The Orthodox Jew accepts the existence of a creator God but in addition also believes the Old Testament is the revealed word of God. The Muslim accepts some of the early portions of the Old Testament but in addition believes the Koran is additionally revealed by God (i.e., Allah) and that Jesus was his prophet.

See a trend here?

Unlike the Jews and the Muslims, Christians believe in a creator God, the Old Testament, and also the New Testament as the revealed word of God. Christians also believe there is a Trinitarian God, an incarnation, a supernatural atonement for sins, a resurrection of Jesus, and all the other miracle claims in the New Testament. There are mutual beliefs shared with these other religions, but the point is that Christians add many *more* to them.

Now when we look at these positions based on who makes the greater number of extraordinary claims, then isn't it quite obvious Christians do—especially those who accept all ten creedal affirmations? If we step back and ask how many extraordinary claims each of the monotheisms have, then Christianity has more by far. While all theisms are improbable, it sure would look *to an outsider* that Christianity is preposterous precisely because of the number of extraordinary claims being made.[12] If we rightly define the larger viewpoint as the one having the greater number of extraordinary claims chained together as a cluster, where the whole cluster can only be as probable as the weakest link, then Christianity is the most improbable viewpoint of them all. For any two extraordinary claims, if each has a chance of being true of 1 in 100, the odds of *both* being true are 1 in 10,000; add a third, and those odds drop to one in a million, and so on down the line. Christians must defend too many beliefs, any one of which, if false, would be fatal to their whole faith. Therefore Christianity is by far more preposterous than Pantheism, or Deism, or Islam, or Orthodox Judaism, while evangelicalism is the most wildly improbable faith of them all.[13]

I am so sure of this that I'm willing to risk Pascal's Wager on it. His "you should believe or you risk hell if you're wrong when you die" gambit has no more force on me than someone who runs around town crying "wolf" all the time or someone who screams that "the sky is falling." You would think that if I'm willing to risk going to hell for what I think then I must be pretty sure, right? I am. I have to be. Just keep in mind that Christians are not bothered in the least that they are risking Allah's hell by not being Muslims. We all risk the hells of other religions. All I'm doing is risking one more hell than others do. Once I've risked one of them, they all look like nothing but the exact same empty threat, just repeated over and over. Because that's what they are. And if God wants our true heartfelt obedience at all, then why does he threaten us with eternal punishment if we disobey—is this any reasonable way to gain what he wants from us?

In fact, as far as I'm concerned, Christian theism has no more credibility than Scientology, Mormonism, Haitian Voodoo, or the southwest Pacific Ocean cargo cults, because they are all based on faith.[14] It has no more credibility than the many different dead ancient religions of the past, including the faith of ancient Israel and several of the other early Christianities that didn't survive, or the many other resurrected savior cults that preceded it (such as those of Zalmoxis, Romulus, and Osiris).[15]

Skeptics reject all these religious faiths because none of them offers satisfactory answers to basic questions—nor do they present sufficient evidence to accept them. So it is not the case that we single Christianity out for rejection, and therefore it's not the case we do so because we have hardened, sinful, selfish, prideful, rebellious hearts, or that we had poor father figures, or any such nonsense.[16] All such attempts to dismiss our rejection of Christianity tacitly admit that the Christian faith does not offer good reasons to believe based on sufficient evidence. For you would never see a serious scientist dismissing another scientist in the same manner by saying: "That guy had a poor father figure, so that's why he rejects my new theory!"

Since I'm a thinking person, I cannot accept just any claim at all. Given the number of false beliefs that have been propagated down through history and in today's world, I am right to require reasonable answers to basic questions, and I am right to require sufficient evidence commensurate with the claims being made before I will accept them. I can see no reasonable objection to this requirement at all.[17] Even if there is a god, he supposedly created me this way, as a thinking person. So the existence of a god changes nothing, for it would be duplicitous and counterproductive of a deity to create me as a thinking person and not also provide me with the answers and the evidence that a thinking person needs to accept the Christian claims.

There are Christians who object that we should not trust our intellect. But it seems utterly contradictory for them to appeal to our intelligence when arguing for why we cannot trust our intelligence. There are Christians who object that our thinking about such matters is unreliably clouded because our minds are fallen. But that means thinking people are hopelessly condemned because we don't know any other way to search for the truth but by using our minds. There are Christians who object that it doesn't matter if thinking people can't understand the truth because all of us deserve to be condemned for the sin of our first human parents in a Garden of Eden anyway. But isn't it obvious that only if some of us would *not* have sinned under the same initial conditions can such a test be considered a fair one rather than a sham? But if some of us would not have sinned in the Garden of Eden under the same "ideal" conditions, then there are people who are being punished for something they never would've done in the first place. There are Christians who object that we are in a cosmic war where thinking people are just unfortunately being deceived by Satan. But since humans are no match for Satan's supposed intellect and power, then God is to be blamed for allowing Satan's continued existence or for not successfully helping us to know the truth. It just seems unreasonable for God to demand that deceived people should ask for his help when they don't even know that they are deceived enough to ask for his help in the first place.

Bertrand Russell was asked what he would tell God on judgment day as to why he did not believe. Russell reportedly said: "Not enough evidence, God, not enough evidence." That's what I would say. If a good omnipotent God existed, there would not be so much massive suffering in the natural world. In fact, the probability that such a God exists is inversely proportional to the amount of suffering there is in the world (i.e., the more suffering there is, then the less probable it is that God exists), and there is way too much suffering to suppose that he does. If there is a God who wants us to believe in him, there would not be so much religious diversity spread around the globe. The probability that the Christian God exists is also inversely proportional to the amount of religious diversity that exists (i.e., the more religious diversity there is, then the less probable it is that God exists), and there is way too much religious diversity to suppose that he does.

If the "God did it" explanation is to be taken seriously, modern science should not be able to offer much in the way of alternatives to that explanation. Either believers argue from the gaps in scientific knowledge to their God or they don't. If they do, then they are arguing from ignorance, which is a well-known informal fallacy that believers use in each new generation as science closes previous gaps only to open up new ones. If believers don't argue from the gaps and instead claim God is merely the sustaining creator of the universe, then our universe ends up being indistinguishable from one without God at all. The probability that the Christian God exists is thus inversely proportional to the amount of reasonable alternative scientific explanations there are for religious claims (i.e., the more science can explain without God, then the less probable it is that God exists), and there are way too many scientific explanations to suppose that he does.[18]

Even if the Christian faith ends up being true, there is still no reason thinking people should accept it. We can only accept claims that can be reasonably justified. That means we have to reject a lot of true claims because they have not met their own burden of proof. This is both obvious and noncontroversial. Aliens from space might have abducted someone, but without sufficient evidence commensurate with such a claim there is no reason why anyone should believe the person who asserts it. There are surely cases in which someone murdered another person, but no one suspects he did the evil deed because there is just no evidence to lead anyone to think he did. There are many hundreds of claims that we should never believe, even if they are true. That's the case when it comes to Christianity. Even if it's true, thinking people cannot accept it because it's wildly improbable.

DERIVATIVE BIZARRE BELIEFS

Most Christians have not thought deeply about their faith. Most of them just believe in God and the resurrection of Jesus. Based upon these twin beliefs, they accept the whole Bible, and so ends most of their attempts to understand what they believe. But behind these beliefs are a quagmire of others that can best be described *by an outsider* to be nothing short of bizarre. So in the interests of showing just how preposterous their beliefs are, I'll share some of them here that will seem bizarre precisely because Christians will be unfamiliar with them and the problems they entail.

First, the Trinity. Christian scholars wrestle with trying to make sense of the Trinity. There are social Trinitarians and antisocial Trinitarians. Both sides accuse the other side of abandoning the Chalcedon creed, either in the direction of tritheism (i.e., the Godhead is three separate beings forming three separate Gods), or in the direction of unitarianism (i.e., denying there are three distinct persons in the Godhead). There are Christians who maintain the Father eternally created the Son and the Holy Spirit, while others argue such a view is tantamount to the Son being a creature created ex nihilo (out of nothing). Yet an eternally existing Trinity is inexplicable; there just happened to be three divine beings who all shared the same nature.[19] It's hard enough to conceive of one person who is an eternally uncaused God, much less a Godhead composed of three eternally uncaused persons who have always shared a divine nature and who therefore never learned anything new, never took a risk, never made a decision, never disagreed within the Godhead, and never had a prior moment to freely choose his own nature.

This Godhead is also conceived of as a timeless being that was somehow able to create the first moment of time. How a timeless being could actually do this is extremely problematic. How does one make a decision when there is no time in which to make a decision? Even if God's decision to create a first moment of time is an "eternal" one (whatever that's supposed to mean), there is still no temporal gap between his decision to create the first moment of time and the actual first moment of time. Even then, God's first act is located in time—it happens at the first moment of time. In other words, a timeless God could not eternally decide to create something at some "future" time since there is no future time for him. His decision to create would be simultaneous with the act of him creating. Therefore if God created at all, he can *never* be outside of time.

There is also the problem of what it means to say God is a spirit and how a spiritual being can create the physical universe. How does something that is spirit create something material, or interact with it, unless there is some point of contact between them that they both share? For instance, how can God speak audibly and be heard by sound waves to our ears, unless he can move sound waves? Logically they cannot interact, unless they share some kind of quality. Are spirit and matter two poles of the same reality? Then welcome to *panentheism*, or process theology. Are they one and the same? Then welcome to pantheism (all is "spirit") or metaphysical naturalism (all is matter). If a spiritual God can create this universe, then Christians need to show how it is possible for God to create the physical universe if he is a spirit.[20]

From here it only gets worse.

We are told that the Logos, the second person of the Trinity, became a man, Jesus. No conception of this God-man in the flesh has yet been able to stand scrutiny. How, for instance, can such a being be 100 percent God and 100 percent man with nothing left over? The Bible itself tells us that ancient superstitious people believed sons of god walked the earth (Acts 14:11–12; 28:6), so why should I believe Jesus was any more a son of God than they were? All attempts to solve this problem have failed. Jesus began to exist while God did not. Jesus had a specific location on earth in a body, while God is everywhere. Jesus died and stayed dead for three days, while God has always been alive. Jesus was not omniscient (Mark 13:32), while God supposedly knows all true propositions. Jesus was tempted to sin, while God cannot be tempted to sin against himself.

But we're not done, for there is a question about when the second person of the trinity became a man. If the eternal Logos was always 100 percent god and 100 percent man before creation and before his birth on earth, then we have the inexplicable problem of an eternally existing human being. How could the Logos be a human being before God created humanity? Humanity then existed as God did: without a beginning. Is a human being therefore divine like God? What, then, is the difference between deity and humanity? If, however, Jesus the God-man was a unique, never-before-existing being who is described in the creeds as being one unified person, then the Logos became forever united with the flesh of the man Jesus in first-century Palestine. So when Jesus died on the cross, why didn't the Logos also cease to exist? Otherwise, what sense can be made of the claim that the Logos was united in the man Jesus? If united as one being then when Jesus died, so also the Logos should have died. Or conversely, if the Logos can't die, then Jesus could not have died.

There is an additional question about where the human side of this God-man is right now. Since the human side of the God-man is believed to be sinless, then the human side of the God-man can't be destroyed by a good God in hell, nor can he be separated from the Logos, since such a being is considered to be one unified person according to the creeds. Theologians have concluded the Trinity now includes an embodied Logos (if he wasn't already embodied before the incarnation). Now we have a Trinity who will forever exist with an embodied human being attached to the Logos, the human side of Jesus. If conceiving the Trinity isn't hard enough to swallow, *picture that three-headed monster* with a *human head* attached to one part of it! Just step back for a moment and ask yourself if this isn't indeed a *very* bizarre set of beliefs.

Consider what kind of evidence could possibly convince you if a trusted friend said that last week he met a person in India who was God incarnate. I daresay nothing would convince you of this. Think about it. Now, when it comes to Jesus, we don't personally know anyone who claims to have met him, nor do we know the authors of the Gospels, nor can we adequately judge their honesty (honest writing can easily be faked). But we do know these authors lived in an era when people believed sons of gods walked the earth and that they had virgin births. So if we wouldn't believe such an extraordinary claim today, how much more should we not believe one in the superstitious era of the first-century CE? Since this is obviously the case, Christians don't believe because of the evidence. No. Rather, they believe because they were raised to believe in a Christian culture, and now they defend what they prefer to be true.[21]

Stepping forward a bit, there is the question of a resurrected body for believers. Many human bodies have been eaten by cannibals, bears, sharks, and parasites. Others have been lost at sea or cremated. How can there be a bodily resurrection for these bodies if they no longer exist? If eaten by parasites, are those bodies still human? If decomposed into the ground as fertilizer for weeds, are those bodies still human? Is a resurrected body therefore a replica of the one on earth? How can it be said the replica is the same as the original? If the resurrected body is a replica, then what do believers say about such a replica being created *before* we die, or even a multiple number of them? Is it possible for a person to be one and the same with a multiple number of persons in heaven? Which body of ours is the basis for the replica one that gets resurrected—the one we had when we were ten years old, forty years old, or the one we died with while suffering from Alzheimer's disease? Would we even want a replica body in the resurrection since most of our bodies are flawed to some degree? And if we are instead given perfect bodies, then what does a perfect body look like? Does it even make sense to say resurrected people will all receive perfect bodies? If perfect, will they all look exactly the same—or not, and if not, will some of them have imperfections precisely because of these differences? If believers are rewarded differently in heaven with better, more perfect bodies depending on how they lived their lives, then what becomes of the claim that God in Jesus forgave them for all their sins? Either he did or he didn't. There can therefore be no different rewards for people in heaven; otherwise, God doesn't forgive all sins after all, for the failure to obey God perfectly would be a sin not forgiven, a sin of omission, which is punished with a less perfect body or a less perfect mansion in the sky.

We're also told by Christian apologists that sinners who are sent to hell will retain their free will. They have a great difficulty in thinking a good God would punish people so cruelly unless sinners continue to rebel (and rightly so). But then these same apologists will turn around and claim the saved who enter heaven will have their free will taken away, in order to guarantee there will be no future rebellion in heaven. Hey, why not? But if free will is such a great gift, why reward people by taking it away from them and punish people by having them retain it? That makes little sense to me. If that's the kind of people God eventually wants in heaven, then why even bother creating this world in the first place? Why not skip a step and just create people in heaven without any free will?

Then finally the God who created time must forever be subject to time in a sequence of events. He cannot become timeless again (if it ever made sense for him to be timeless in the first place), for to do so would destroy everything that took place in human history. If God became timeless again then time itself never existed, and hence neither did we.

So in the end an inexplicably triune, timeless God will forever exist inside time with a human being connected at the hip to the Logos in a heaven where the saved are not free to disobey him and the damned in hell are free to obey but never change their rebellious ways, even knowing that their ways put them there in the first place. Why does this *not* sound like an utterly absurd myth?

A one-worded question cries out to be answered: *Why?* Why did a completely fulfilled, triune supreme being, who neither needed nor wanted anything, bother creating at all? Why would he do it knowing this world would have so much ubiquitous suffering in it and knowing he would inexplicably have to suffer an atoning death on the cross for us? He knew billions of people would suffer eternally for his decision. For Christians to respond that God did this because it was his gift of grace utterly misses the point of the question. How is it a gracious gift to create such a world, knowing in advance that all this suffering would have to take place, just so that people who no longer have free will could be with him in heaven? If this is actually what God did, then thinking Christians themselves should all rise up and demand an answer for why God created this world at all. If I was a Christian, I would protest God for creating this world even if I were to end up in heaven. I would rather that God never created anything at all than for him to create this world if my friends and family members were to wind up in hell, along with billions of other people. If I were a selfless, "agape" loving Christian, I would gladly have preferred nonexistence to an enslaved existence in heaven for me and along with it the eternal sufferings of so many others in hell.

Who in their right mind would embrace Christianity if he or she heard about all these and all the other weird beliefs when first being challenged to believe? Very, very few people. In their book *Sway: The Irresistible Pull of Irrational Behavior*, Ori and Rom Brafman document that human beings have irrational biases that blind us to all evidence that contradicts our initial assessment of a person or situation. In order to counteract these biases, they suggest asking a simple question: "If I were just arriving on the scene and were given the choice to either jump into this project as it stands now or pass on it, would I choose to jump in?"[22] Similarly, believers must ask themselves if they knew what they know now, would they ever make the decision to convert in the first place? What evidence was initially presented? Usually none at all. Usually what produces a conversion to faith is the gospel story itself and the divine hope and love it promises. There is no discussion about how Jesus was 100 percent God and 100 percent man, or how the death of Jesus atones for sins, or even what to think about the millions of people who will wind up in hell. So, if you were arriving on the scene when you were first presented the gospel, would you believe, knowing what you do now? That's a great question to ask!

DEFENDING THE FAITH MAKES
BRILLIANT PEOPLE LOOK STUPID

If Christianity is wildly improbable, then defending it can make even brilliant people look stupid. I mean no offense here. In fact, I think it takes a great deal of intelligence to defend Christian theism, because Christianity cannot be defended without a great deal of mental contortionism. To see this, we'll just look briefly at three arguments by the three men admired most by evangelicals in our generation: Alvin Plantinga, William Lane Craig, and Richard G. Swinburne.

Alvin Plantinga is the author of a number of very important books, which include *God and Other Minds* (1967), *The Nature of Necessity* (1974), *God, Freedom, and Evil* (1974), and *Warranted Christian Belief* (2000). He delivered the prestigious Gifford Lectures and was described by *Time* magazine in 1980 as "America's leading orthodox Protestant philosopher of God."[23] Plantinga served as president of the American Philosophical Association, and president of the Society of Christian Philosophers. He retired in 2010 from being the John A. O'Brien Professor of Philosophy at the University of Notre Dame. Now read what he has to say in reference to Marx and Freud's critiques of religion:

> To show that there are natural processes that produce religious belief does nothing, so far, to discredit it; perhaps God designed us in such a way that it is by virtue of those processes that we come to have knowledge of him. Suppose it could be demonstrated that a certain kind of complex neural stimulation could produce theistic belief. This would have no tendency to discredit religious belief. . . . Clearly, it is possible both that there is an explanation in terms of natural processes of religious belief, and that these beliefs have a perfectly respectable epistemic status.[24]

Why do I highlight this argument of his? Because time after time, in order to defend what they believe, Christians must continually retreat to what is possible rather than what is probable. So, let's assume in this scenario by Plantinga that there are natural processes that produce religious beliefs, and that neurologists have natural explanations for why people have them. That is, science can explain the brain processes that produce religious faith. (Actually, I think neurology *has* already gone a long way toward explaining religious/paranormal beliefs).[25] Plantinga claims that even if this should prove to be the case, his religious faith could still possibly be true. What should we say to this? We say what is obvious. Yes, it is still *possible*, Alvin. But what has he gained? Nothing at all. For what we want to know is what would be *probable* given an explanation of religious faith in brain processes, not what is possible. If all we had to be concerned about was what is possible, then maybe the Loch Ness Monster exists but is smart enough to escape being detected by us, too. Get the point? But there's more. If Plantinga can say this in defense of his Christian faith, then a Mormon or a Muslim could say the exact same things he did in defense of their faiths, that their religious faiths could still be true despite neurological science. And where does that get us? Nowhere. My claim is that at crucial places in defense of religious faith, believers must punt over and over to what is possible rather than what is probable. My claim is that the more believers must do this to defend what they believe, then the less likely their faith is true.[26] It is utterly unreasonable for apologists like Plantinga to demand that skeptics must prove the Christian faith is *impossible* before they will consider that it's *improbable*. Just think if his banker told him that investing all his money in a particular fund will *probably* bring upon him financial ruin. Can anyone imagine Plantinga investing his money anyway because his banker didn't say it's not possible to invest all his money in that fund without being financially ruined?

If, as Plantinga allows, the evidence from psychology, anthropology, and brain science could explain why Muslims and Hindus and Buddhists believe what they do, then Plantinga is conceding that they believe what they do for exactly the same reasons Christians believe what they do. This, then, would confirm that whatever causes Christians to believe what they do is *verifiably incapable* of reliably causing a true belief at all. Those same causes would just as easily generate one different religious faith as another one, faiths that in many cases believe mutually contradictory things. In fact, given that those same causes cause *thousands* of sects and religions, which must all be false (as at most only one of them can be true), we would here have indisputable proof that these causes are *maximally likely* to produce false beliefs. In the light of this evidence, Plantinga's excuse that "maybe I'm the exception" is simply foolish. The odds against him actually being that exception are thousands to one.

William Lane Craig is a research professor of philosophy at Talbot School of Theology in La Mirada after having earned two doctorates. He was my former professor at Trinity Evangelical Divinity School, where half of the hours I took for my Master of Theology degree in the Philosophy of Religion were under him. He has impressive evangelical credentials, being known as the foremost Christian debater of our generation who has debated everyone from John Dominic Crossan and Gerd Lüdemann to Antony Flew, Walter Sinnott-Armstrong, Christopher Hitchens, and five of the contributors to this book. Many evangelicals describe him as the leading apologist of our generation. He has authored or edited over thirty works, including *The Kalam Cosmological Argument* (1979), *Reasonable Faith* (3rd ed. 2008), *Philosophical Foundations for a Christian Worldview* (with J. P. Moreland, 2003), *The Blackwell Companion to Natural Theology* (with J. P. Moreland, 2009), and numerous articles.

Now let's consider William Lane Craig's explanation for why there is global religious diversity if there is a hell to pay for people who die outside the Christian faith. He claims, "It is possible that God has created a world having an optimal balance between saved and lost and that God has so providentially ordered the world that those who fail to hear the Gospel and be saved would not have freely responded affirmatively to it even if they had heard it." Craig argues that if this scenario is even possible, "it proves that it is entirely consistent to affirm that God is all-powerful and all-loving and yet that some people never hear the Gospel and are lost."[27]

Again, there are many things that might be possible, but apologists like Craig and Plantinga seem to resort to that standard escape too many times. Contrary to Craig, when we look at the billions of people who have never been given a chance to be "saved" because of "when and where they were born," his scenario seems extremely implausible, to say the least. Surely there exists at least one more person among them who would believe if presented with the Gospel. No wonder he only wants to talk about what is possible. When it comes to foreknowing our future, Craig argues that God has *Middle Knowledge* such that he knows "what every possible creature would do under any possible circumstances," and he would know this "prior to any determination of the divine will."[28] So despite his protestations to the contrary, isn't it obvious that if Craig's God has this kind of foreknowledge, he could simply foreknow who would not accept his offered salvation before they were even created, and then never create them in the first place so "hotel hell" would never have even one occupant? Why not?

Richard G. Swinburne retired in 2002 as the emeritus professor of the philosophy of the Christian religion at the University of Oxford. Over the past forty years he has written more than a dozen major books, including *The Concept of Miracle* (1970), *The Coherence of Theism* (1977), *The Existence of God*

(2nd ed. 2004), *Providence and the Problem of Evil* (1998), and *The Resurrection of God Incarnate* (2003), along with hundreds of articles. He is one of the foremost Christian apologists of our era, clearly the best of the best when it comes to providing an intellectual defense of Christianity, so I'll focus a bit more on him.

In his 2007 book *Revelation*, Swinburne attempts to defend the Christian revelation claim as the one and only true revelation from the one true God.[29] There is so much I'd like to say about his book because a good deal of it is very painful to read. In it we see him being ignorant of his own ignorance, specializing in special pleading, and begging the question too many times for him not to look ignorant. To see this, all we have to do is look at just one of his main arguments. In chapter 5, he argues that if God exists he needed to give human beings a propositional (or spoken) revelation. God needed to do this, Swinburne argues, to reveal to us exactly who he is, to explain why the world has so much suffering in it, to tell us what he has done about it, what he expects from us, and to warn us that we will be rewarded and punished based on our response to him. We need this revelation because this is the kind of important information we couldn't learn on our own, he opines.

What Swinburne has done in arguing for this needed revelation is to do what all Christian apologists do (to some degree). He simply takes for granted his particular view of God and this presently existing world to make his case. Then based on what he takes for granted, and with a little sleight of hand, Swinburne goes on to argue that God would need to provide us with a propositional revelation. And, surprise of surprises, Swinburne happily announces in triumph, this is exactly what God did. Did you catch this? Let me explain the trick he just pulled.

What Swinburne has done is nothing less than special pleading with regard to his God and question begging with regard to this present world. The truth is there is little to be surprised about once we grant Swinburne these things for his argument to work. Like all Christian apologists, Swinburne ultimately lacks even a child's imagination. His imagination is stunted by his faith and the need to defend what he believes. So let's backtrack a bit with a better imagination for a minute.

First off, I can easily imagine a different kind of god, one that is much more reasonable to accept than the one Swinburne prays to, who does not need to give us any propositional revelation at all. Swinburne thinks he can successfully defend some of the classical arguments for God's existence.[30] But at best all he ends up doing is showing that the god of his reasoning is consistent with the God of his faith. But just showing that the god of the philosophers is *consistent* with the God of his faith does not show that the God of his faith probably exists. The arguments leading Swinburne to affirm that a god of some kind exists are also consistent with a deistic god who out of boundless love will save everyone in the end regardless of what they believe, or who instead created this world as but nothing more than a scientific experiment and who thinks of us as rats in a maze, wondering what we will conclude about it all and how we will live our lives. The philosophers' god is also consistent with a divine tinkerer who is learning as he goes by creating one successive universe after another. Alonzo Fyfe conjectured on such a god in these words:

> Perhaps I was created by a god who got bored and who was seeking some way to entertain himself. He came up with the idea of creating a planet and populating it with people who[m] he [programmed to] have a strong disposition to accept religious teachings without question. He then went to different groups and said, "You are God's chosen children. You have a right and a duty to rule over the world. All others are infidels who should be either converted or killed." When he was done, he sat back in [h]is heavenly recliner with his heavenly beer and potato chips and watched the unfolding drama of Survivor Earth, and he saw that it was good. Or, at least, he was entertained.[31]

We're not done yet, for the philosophers' god is also consistent with a deity who created the quantum wave fluctuation that produced this universe as his last act before committing suicide. Or a god who *had* to die in order to create the world.[32] Such a god is also consistent with a creator god who guides the universe ultimately toward an evil purpose, but who has chosen to maliciously present himself as benevolent to trick us. If such a trickster god exists, then all the evidence leading Swinburne to conclude his good God exists was simply planted there to deceive us by that very same God. Based on this alternative god hypothesis alone, the best any believer can claim is agnosticism in the sense of being skeptical of *all* metaphysical affirmations.[33] Never mind all the others! And yet they're just as possible. I can see no reasonable objection to these other god hypotheses once we allow them into our equations. They are just as possible as *his* god hypothesis. That's why scientists cannot posit god explanations for answers to the origin of the universe. For once we allow supernatural explanations into our equations, any god will do, since there seems to be no way to exclude any.

So much for God. But I can just as easily imagine a different kind of *world* than the present one, which wouldn't require any divine propositional revelation if an omnipotent god created it. By using at least as much imagination as a child's, this is easy to do. If the god that exists is less complicated to understand (as any of the non-triune deities mentioned above would be, or countless others I can imagine), and if he had created us with a greater level of intelligence to understand more of that which god understands, then we would have less trouble believing that he exists and less trouble understanding who he is. At the very minimum, we would be able to understand everything that is important to understand. He could even create us so that this information is automatically imprinted in our brains at birth. Even if not, all god had to do was provide us with sufficient evidence to think he exists in the created world. Then we would at least know he exists, since that's so very important to him (but for what reason escapes me). I have previously suggested the kind of evidence that would convince me that god exists[34] along with several different ways he could've created the world that would all but eliminate both human[35] and animal[36] suffering (sorry, no room to revisit this here—after all, this *is* the third book in a series). In the end, a miracle-working God could do perpetual miracles that could alleviate this suffering, if for some reason God didn't create the world correctly in the first place. But if god had created the world in any of these ways, there would be no need of a propositional revelation since there would be little, or nothing, that needed an explanation.

Furthermore, if god created us with the propensity for being good and/or if there were some good consequences when we behaved well and some bad consequences if we behaved badly, then we wouldn't need to be told by god what we should do. An ethics based in natural law would be sufficient for us. We wouldn't need a Bible, just logic and the scientific method (yet neither of which are taught to us in the Bible). And if there was no eternal punishment, there would be no need for any divinely revealed warnings about a hell in the afterlife, either. For even if we did disobey this god, then such a deity could simply forgive us without any need for an incarnation or an atonement, which lack any rationally acceptable explanation anyway.[37] With no incarnation or need for an atonement, there would be no need of a resurrection either. It's precisely because of these additional and unnecessary extraordinary claims of divine redemptive acts that most nonbelievers don't accept the supposed propositional revelation in the Bible anyway. If this is what God did to redeem us, then he simply did not sufficiently explain why these acts were needed or how they are even possible. Nor did he provide enough evidence to believe that they took place in the historical past. Hence Swinburne's religion simply looks ridiculous on any mature reflection.

In fairness to Swinburne, he'll claim to have defended his view of god and why this particular world exists as we find it, elsewhere in his writings. But whenever I chase that rabbit called "elsewhere" down the apologist's rabbit hole, all I ever find is more ignorance coupled with more special pleading and more question begging. There is no "elsewhere" that accomplishes what he needs to do, even though he is one of the most prolific professional apologists for Christianity in our generation. If that's the best apologists can do, that alone proves Christianity is absurd.

I would think that if the Christian faith is reasonable at all, then Christian apologists like Swinburne would not be required to be so unimaginative about the kind of god that might exist and the kind of world an omnipotent god could have created. But they must be, because they were taught in our Christian culture to believe what some ancient, barbaric, prescientific, superstitious agency-detectors wrote down and claimed was the word of God. Today's apologists have killed their imagination and buried it away because they cannot defend their god against these other god hypotheses and they cannot defend the existence of this present world if their particular god exists. They were raised to believe that their kind of god exists and that therefore this kind of world must be the best one for such a god to create, and that's all there is to it. So ends their quest to understand it, and so begins their attempt to defend it. That's all there is to it. This is what it takes for them to defend their inherited Christian faith, and as such, it makes these otherwise brilliant people look, well, dumb. But then, that's what it takes to be a Christian apologist. Again, no offense, but that's the way it really is. They have to be this way in order to defend what cannot reasonably be defended at all.

A REALITY CHECK FOR BELIEVERS

I'm ending this chapter with a reality check for Christians—especially evangelicals. Following are fifteen additional items they believe and why each one of them involves double standards, non sequiturs, special pleading, begging the question, or just plain ignorance. This is my attempt at throwing a cold cup of water in the face of believers to wake them up from their dogmatic slumbers. Wake up, Christians! Your faith is wildly improbable.

The evidence is simply not there to believe in a three-headed, eternally existing god who became one of us to die on a cross for our sins in one lone part of the ancient world; a god who bodily resurrected from the grave but was only seen by a small number of people, which forces the rest of us to take their word on it or else spend an eternity in hell because we were not there to see it for ourselves. People around the world are raised in different cultures to believe in their particular god(s) and cannot see things any other way, and yet Christians still claim there is only one god who will judge all people based upon what they believe even though what they believe does not pass the Outsider Test for Faith! This divine plan does not look like an intelligent one coming from a perfectly good, all-powerful god. Given the fact that countless contradictory sects of religious faiths believe and defend what they were raised or taught to believe, and that most of them are certain about their faith, I must demand evidence—hard evidence, positive evidence—before I'll accept what any of them believe. Until one of them steps up to the plate and offers something more by way of evidence than the other faiths, I cannot believe in any of them.

Here, then, in summary fashion, is what it takes to believe and defend Christianity:[38]

1) That there exists a perfectly good, omnipotent God, who created a perfectly good universe even though there is no cogent theodicy that can explain why there is such ubiquitous and massive human and animal suffering in it. How do you think human beings first learned that venomous creatures like certain kinds of spiders, snakes, ants, or scorpions could kill us? People, frequently children, had to die, lots of them. How do you think human beings first learned that polluted water or lead poisoning could kill us? Again, people, frequently children, had to die, lots of them. It was inevitable, since God never told us what to avoid in order to stay alive. We had to learn these kinds of things firsthand. He didn't even tell us how to discover penicillin or a vaccine for polio or tuberculosis.

2) That Christianity is a faith that must dismiss the tragedy of death. It

does not matter who dies, or how many, or what the circumstances are when people die. It could be the death of a mother whose baby depends upon her for milk. It could be a pandemic like cholera that decimated parts of the world in 1918, or the more than 23,000 children who die every single day from starvation. These deaths could be by suffocation, drowning, a drive-by shooting, or being burned to death. It doesn't matter. God is good. Death doesn't matter. People die all the time. In order to justify God's goodness, Christianity minimizes the value of human life. Despite all its rhetoric to the contrary, it is actually a pro-death faith, plain and simple. Because all of this horrible death is just God's perfect plan, he can kill or let die whomever he wants, and by letting it all happen can do no wrong. Believers even praise him for it.

3) That the highest created being, known as Satan or the Devil, led an angelic rebellion against an omnipotent, omniscient, omnibenevolent, omnipresent God . . . and expected to win. This makes Satan out to be suicidal, inexplicably evil, and dumber than a box of rocks. Yet he still defies God's power by supposedly meddling in the world without God stopping him even though he could.

4) That when it comes to verifiable matters of historical fact (like the Exodus, the extent of David's rule, Luke's reported worldwide census, the darkening of the sun at Christ's death, etc.), the biblical stories are disconfirmed by evidence to the contrary as fairy tales, but when it comes to supernatural claims of miracles that cannot be tested against external facts, like a virgin birth and resurrection from the grave, the Bible reports true historical facts.

5) That although a great number of miracles were claimed to have happened in the different superstitious cultures of the ancient world, only the ones in the Bible actually happened as claimed. Likewise, that although in the ancient world there were false virgin birth claims about famous people (like Plato and Alexander the Great) and mythical heroes (like Perseus and Romulus), Jesus was the only one truly born of a virgin. There are many other similar mythological stories told in ancient Near Eastern literature that predate what we read in the Bible at every step of the way, so why should we think the stories in the *Bible* involve a real God concerning real events and real people?

6) That an omniscient God could not foresee that his revealed will in the Bible would lead believers to commit atrocities against other believers that included the Inquisition, the witch hunts, and the Thirty Years' War (1618–1648), in which eight million Christians killed each other over correct doctrine. This leads reasonable people to conclude there is no divine mind behind the Bible. I now call this *The Problem of Divine Miscommunication*.[39]

Instead of *suppressing* religious freedom and expression in the Bible (Exod. 20:3; 22:18; Deut. 7; 13:1–16, 17:2–5; I Kings 18:40; II Kings 23), God could have permitted the ancient Israelites what the heathen nations had by granting them first amendment–type liberties.[40] Then boatloads of people would not have been killed by the Jews or later by the historic church for what they believed or said. It's that simple.

Christians might try to argue that by granting religious freedom, the Israelites would have strayed completely away from Yahweh, their tribal deity. But this argument presupposes the evidence was not there for them to believe in the first place, for if there was enough evidence to believe, there would be no reason to suppress religious freedom. Either the evidence was there to believe or it wasn't. If it was, then there was no reason to prohibit religious freedom of thought or expression. If it wasn't, then their God should have provided more of it. With a few extra prophets and a little more evidence, the Israelites would freely choose to believe without any command prohibiting people from freely choosing their religion. Consequently, down through the centuries there would be no precedent for the Inquisitional rallying cry of "Convert or Die" that rang in Europe's dungeons for two hundred years, nor for the witch hunts that lasted for three hundred years, nor for the Thirty Years' War.

7) That Jesus fulfilled Old Testament prophecy even though there is not one passage in the Old Testament that is specifically fulfilled in his life, death, and resurrection that can legitimately be understood as a prophecy and that singularly points to Jesus as the Messiah by any objective method. My friend Dan Lewandowski said it to me this way: the Christian must believe "the Jewish people, who like any ethnic and cultural group know their own language, history, and tra-

ditions better than anyone, and who have been studying them with reverential diligence for millennia, have always been completely wrong about the most important meanings of their own most sacred scriptures—even as communicated to them by their own God."

8) That miracles took place even though believing in them demands a near impossible double burden of proof. What believers must show is that an alleged biblical miracle could not have happened within the natural world because it was impossible (or else it's not considered miraculous). Then they must turn right around and claim such an impossible event probably took place anyway. The probability that an alleged miracle took place is directly proportional to the probability that such an event could take place (i.e., the less probable it is that a miracle could take place, then the less probable it is that it did take place), so the improbability of a miracle claim defeats any attempt to show that it probably happened. That's why miraculous claims in the Bible can never be proof for the existence of that God, for in order to accept such a claim by a writer in the prescientific past, a person must already believe in a miracle-working God who did *these particular kinds of miracles.*

9) That their faith is true even though the textual evidence in the New Testament shows that at best the founder of the Jesus cult was a failed apocalyptic prophet who prophesied that the end of the world would take place in *his* generation and would involve a total cosmic catastrophe, after which God would inaugurate a literal kingdom on earth with the "Son of Man" reigning from Jerusalem over all the world's nations. This *still* has never happened.[41]

10) That their faith is true even though, apart from the author of Revelation, the Apostle Paul is the *only* New Testament author to claim he saw the risen Jesus, and Paul reportedly said he merely saw a vision of Jesus on the Damascus Road rather than Jesus himself. Yep, just see Acts 26:9: "So then, King Agrippa, I (Paul) was not disobedient to the vision (i.e., ὀπτασίᾳ) from heaven." In fact, he himself insists he saw Jesus in no other way (in Gal. 1:11–12, 16). The author of Revelation (John of Patmos) likewise clearly states he saw Jesus only in a vision (Rev. 1:1–2, 9–10). Christians must convince themselves that this is to be considered not only evidence but *conclusive* evidence,

even though the same kind of evidence would confirm the claims of Joseph Smith, Muhammad, Jim Jones, and almost every other religious leader who claimed to have had personal and private revelations from their God.

11) That even though God's supposed revelation in the canonical Bible is indistinguishable from the musings of an ancient, barbaric, superstitious people, the Bible is the word of God anyway. As my friend George Yorgo Veenhuyzen once put it:

> The lord doesn't work in mysterious ways, but in ways that are indistinguishable from his nonexistence. It seems to me that there is nothing in the Christian scriptures, no sentence, paragraph, or idea, that couldn't be anything more than the product of the humans alive at the time the apparently divinely inspired scriptures and ideas were "revealed." Sure, it's possible for a god to reveal himself in an inspired book, and throughout history, in ways that are indistinguishable from the work of human minds and human minds alone. But how probable does that seem to you? The available evidence shows that the Bible is nothing but the cultural byproduct of human invention. There is no divine mind behind it.[42]

12) That although it's claimed God got the attention of Abraham, Moses, the Egyptian Pharaoh, Gideon, Mary the mother of Jesus, Joseph, doubting Thomas, and Saul on the Damascus Road (who became Paul), there is no objective evidence he's trying to get the attention of the billions of people who don't believe. Doing so did not abrogate their freedom, so why doesn't he do this more often? In fact, Christians are much more concerned than God is that nonbelievers are converted. Just compare the lengths to which Christians will go in order to convert nonbelievers, with a God who has the means to convert anyone and yet does nothing detectable to help them. I don't even have to say in advance what it would take for me to believe. God should already know. But he just doesn't do it. If nothing else, God could snap his fingers and simply take away enough of my critical thinking skills so that I wouldn't need evidence to believe. He could make me gullible enough so I would believe just like others do.

13) That God's punishments are good, right, and just, even though it

means sinners are thrust into a surprisingly dangerous world, and in death will be blindsided by an eternal punishment in hell, which is Christianity's most damnable doctrine. Modern societies use humane punishments rather than the barbaric ones of the past, which were the basis for human conceptions of God's punishments. People do not really know their choices will send them to an eternal punishment in hell. For to the degree we knew this, we wouldn't sin. The probability that we would not "sin" is inversely proportional to the evidence that there is an eternal punishment in hell when we die (i.e., the more evidence there is a hell, then the less we would "sin"), and there just isn't enough of it to make us refrain from doing so, as the whole world proves daily.

14) That the God of the Bible is real and good, even though the Bible contains things that democratic, free, loving people would all abhor, like slavery (Lev. 25:44–46), the denigration of women (Gen. 3:16), capital punishment for adultery, homosexuality, cursing a parent, or working on the Sabbath day (Exod. 21; Lev. 20; Deut. 22), and the utter denial of religious freedom and speech (Exod. 20:3–11).[43] What we find in the Bible is simply not something we would expect from a perfectly good, intelligent God.[44]

15) That ex-Christians like me were never Christians, even though we believed and trusted in God for salvation. Let me get this straight, okay? God supposedly promised that if we believe we'll be saved, and yet he never kept his promise—that he never saved us even though we believed? Such logic as this is the logic of a delusion, as is Christianity itself.

There is no doubt in my mind. Christianity is wildly improbable.

Part 2

PUTTING AN ANCIENT MYTH TO REST

Chapter 4

WHY BIBLICAL STUDIES MUST END

by Dr. Hector Avalos[1]

The only mission of biblical studies should be to end biblical studies as we know them. This chapter will explain why I have come to such a conclusion. For our purposes, we can summarize our plea to end biblical studies as we know them with two main premises:

1. Modern biblical scholarship has demonstrated that the Bible is the product of cultures whose values and beliefs about the origin, nature, and purpose of our world are no longer held to be relevant, even by most Christians and Jews.
2. Paradoxically, despite the recognition of such irrelevance, the profession of academic biblical studies still centers on maintaining the illusion of relevance by a variety of scholarly disciplines whose methods and conclusions are often philosophically flawed (e.g., translation, textual criticism, archaeology, history, and biblical theology).

The first premise acknowledges that we have indeed discovered much new information about the Bible. The Dead Sea Scrolls and the enormous archaeological treasures found in the ancient Near East in the last 150 years or so have set the Bible more firmly in its original cultural context. However, it is those very discoveries that show that the Bible is irrelevant insofar as it is part of a world radically dissimilar to ours in its conception of the cosmos, the supernatural, and the human sense of morality.

"Irrelevant" here refers to a biblical concept or practice that is no longer viewed as valuable, applicable, and/or ethical. Thus, whereas most Americans today regard genocide as contemptible, that was not the case in many biblical

107

texts. In fact, Michael Coogan, a widely respected biblical scholar, admits that some biblical practices are so objectionable today that churches try to hide parts of the Bible from their members. As Coogan phrases it:

> Conspicuously absent from lectionaries are most or all of such books as Joshua, with its violent extermination of the inhabitants of the land of Canaan at divine command, or Judges, with its horrifying narratives of patriarchy and sexual assault in chapters 11 and 19—to say nothing of the Song of Solomon, with its charged eroticism, or of Job, with its radical challenge to the dominant biblical view of a just and caring God.[2]

Likewise, our modern medical establishment has discarded the supernatural explanations for illness found in the Bible, rendering such explanations irrelevant. Here are some more examples of scientific and scholarly "discoveries" that provide further evidence of the Bible's irrelevance:

- Though modern science has demonstrated otherwise, some biblical authors held that the universe was created in only six days.[3]
- Despite the weight that theologians place on the words and deeds of the great figures in the Bible (Abraham, Moses, and David), research indicates that these figures are not as "historical" as once thought.[4]
- There is no independent evidence for the life or teachings of Jesus in the first century CE, which means that most modern Christians are not even following Jesus' teachings.[5]
- Biblical authors generally believed that women were subordinate to men.[6]

Even when many persons in the modern world still hold to biblical ideas (e.g., creationism), it is partly because academic biblical scholars are not sufficiently vocal about undermining outdated biblical beliefs. Instead, such scholars concentrate on maintaining the value of the biblical text in modern society.

A case in point is an article written by Daniel J. Estes in *Bibliotheca Sacra*, a prestigious evangelical Christian journal.[7] Estes, too, is worried about irrelevancy; he has even developed a "scale" to measure the relevance of biblical teachings. Something close to the zero side would be considered obsolete, whereas something at ten would be considered a directive that Christians must still follow.

He then provides the example of the law of first fruits in Deuteronomy 26:1–11, which commands Israelites to go to a location chosen by Yahweh to provide the priest with the first yields of their agricultural season. Estes would rank this close to the zero side of the scale (obsolete precepts) because, among other things, most modern Christians no longer are farmers, nor do they recognize a central location that Yahweh has chosen.

Estes recognizes that "[n]one of these specific items has a precise equivalent in the identity and experience of Christian believers today.... Many of the Old Testament legal prescriptions are in this category, including, for example, the dietary regulations."[8] When pressed to find examples of "total continuity" between the original biblical audience and today's Christian audience, Estes admits that "[i]ndisputable examples of total continuity between the two audiences are relatively rare."[9]

John Bright, regarded as one of the most outstanding American biblical scholars of the last century, reflected a similar sentiment regarding the sabbatical and jubilee years in Leviticus 25, when he remarked that "the regulations described therein are obviously so little applicable to the modern situation that a preacher might be pardoned if he told himself that the passage contains no relevant message for his people whatever."[10] In fact, if we were to go verse by verse, I suspect that 99 percent of the Bible would not even be missed, as it reflects many practices, injunctions, and ideas not much more applicable than Leviticus 25.

Our second major premise is that despite this admission of irrelevance, the profession of academic biblical scholarship paradoxically and self-servingly promotes the illusion of relevance. The maintenance of this illusion is intended to make believers think that they have "the Bible" when all they really have is a book constructed by modern elite scholars. So even if 99.9 percent of modern Christians said that the Bible was relevant to them, such relevance is based on their illusory assumption that modern versions do reflect the original "Bible" to some extent.[11] Promoting the illusion of relevance serves to justify the very existence of the profession of biblical scholarship, and not much more.

Our argument is that there is really nothing in the entire book Christians call "the Bible" that is any more relevant than anything else written in the ancient world. Mine is a frank secular humanist view of biblical studies. Biblical studies as we know them should end. We should now treat the Bible as the alien document it is, with no more importance than the other works of literature we ignore every day. Biblical studies should be geared toward helping humanity wean itself off of the Bible and toward terminating its authority completely in the modern world. Focus then could shift to the thousands of other ancient texts still untranslated and unread. One day, the Bible might even be viewed as one of the curiosities of a tragic bibliolatrous age, when dependence on a text brought untold misery and stood as an obstacle to human progress. We might then study the Bible as a lesson in why human beings should never again privilege any book to this extent.

I maintain that the main subdisciplines of biblical studies have succeeded in demonstrating that the Bible is the product of cultures whose values and beliefs about the origin, nature, and purpose of our world are no longer held to be relevant, even by most Christians and Jews. These subdisciplines include translation, textual criticism, biblical history and archaeology, historical Jesus studies, literary criticism, and biblical theology.

TRANSLATIONS

Insofar as the general public is concerned, nothing maintains the relevance of the Bible more than translations. According to one estimate, by the year 2000, the Bible had been translated into more than two thousand languages.[12] If it were not for the translations that made the Bible accessible to countless millions of people over the centuries, it would probably have been forgotten.

Indeed, the Bible is such a foreign text that translators and scholars become assistants to the reader. The preface to the *New Century Bible* says: "Ancient customs are often unfamiliar to modern readers . . . so these are clarified either in the text or in a footnote."[13] But even more surprising is the assumption that the relevance of the Bible is best maintained by using translation to hide and distort the original meaning of the text in order to provide the illusion that the information and values conveyed by biblical authors are compatible with those of the modern world.[14]

There are clear cases where the translators should know that the translation does not correspond to what is found in the biblical texts being translated. This may also mean that significant words are omitted or added, not just mistranslated. In short, Bible translations "lie" to keep the Bible alive.

According to the ethicist Sissela Bok, a lie is "an intentionally deceptive message in the form of a statement."[15] We may say that Bible translations lie when they misrepresent what is actually in an underlying text. Commenting on students who ask why they are often not told of all of the violent and objectionable passages in the Bible, Michael Coogan responds, "In part, the answer is that they [students] could not be trusted to read the Bible: It is a dangerous, even subversive collection."[16] Although Bible translations do not lie in every instance, translators distort scripture with passages they deem to hold meanings that might be considered objectionable. Overall, translators know that the Bible is the product of cultures whose modes of life and thought were very different from ours. In some cases, the Bible's philosophy is so barbaric and violent that it defies explaining why anyone would consider it sacred at all.[17] Let me offer just three examples.

Example 1: Politically Correct Polytheism

Our first example deals with polytheism, which most modern Christian readers of the Bible would disdain as idolatry. Most modern readers probably expect that the Bible does not endorse polytheism. Consider the following translation of Deuteronomy 32:8–9 in the New American Bible (NAB), an American Catholic translation:

> When the Most High assigned the nations their heritage, when he parceled out the descendants of Adam, He set up the boundaries of the peoples after the number of the sons of God; While the LORD's own portion was Jacob, his hereditary share was Israel.

Most readers will miss the fact that "the Most High" and "the LORD" are two different gods, among many other gods, here. The term translated as "the Most High" is probably the name of a god, pronounced as Elyon, and the term translated as "LORD" corresponds to the Hebrew name we pronounce as Yahweh, ancient Israel's main god. There is evidence these were recognized as two different gods in surrounding cultures, so some scholars have argued that in this passage "the Most High" probably refers to the god "Elyon," who is here being represented as superior to, and separate from, Yahweh. Yahweh appears to be Elyon's son. Elyon divided up the earth, and Elyon's son, Yahweh (Lord), received the portion of the earth that came to be known as Israel.[18]

The more obvious case of polytheism is the reference to what the NAB translates as "the sons of God." In most pantheons of the ancient Near East, the gods were believed to have divine fathers and mothers. The Dead Sea Scrolls, which are the oldest manuscripts of the Hebrew Bible, still preserve the (probably older) reading of "sons of El" or "sons of Elohim." The "sons of El" would be the gods fathered by the god named El. The fact that ancient editors recognized the polytheistic nature of this expression ("sons of El") probably led the editors of the standard text (called the Masoretic text) of the Hebrew Bible to change "gods" to "sons of Israel." Some Greek translations have "angels of God" instead of "sons of El" or "gods."[19]

The New Revised Standard Version (NRSV), an American multidenominational translation, does adopt the more original polytheistic expression, "according to the number of the gods," reflected in the Dead Sea Scrolls. However, other modern translations still do not fully reflect the polytheism of the passage. Note the following examples from the Revised English Bible (REB), a British ecumenical version, and the New Jerusalem Bible (NJB), a British Catholic translation.

> **REB**: "according to the number of the sons of God."
> **NJB**: "according to the number of the children of God."

Note that the NJB bears a gender-neutral rendition ("children") instead of the more culturally proper "sons," who were the main inheritors of land in biblical cultures. Political correctness in the NJB, therefore, also obscures the patriarchal nature of land inheritance in the Bible.

Such distortions are not limited to the Old Testament. Christianity often markets itself as more inclusive and loving than the religion of the Old Testament and Judaism. However, this has required using mistranslations to hide or suppress some of the starker discontinuities between what Jesus taught and what current versions of Christianity want their audiences to think Jesus taught.

Example 2: Endorsement of Genital Mutilation

The Contemporary English Version (CEV) sanitizes Jesus' seeming endorsement of genital mutilation with this translation of Matthew 19:12:

Some people are unable to marry because of birth defects or because of what someone has done to their bodies. Others stay single for the sake of the kingdom of heaven. Anyone who can accept this teaching should do so.

Compare this translation to that of the older Revised Standard Version:

For there are eunuchs who have been so from birth, and there are eunuchs who have been made eunuchs by men, and there are eunuchs who have made themselves eunuchs for the sake of the kingdom of heaven. He who is able to receive this, let him receive it.

In other words, the RSV conveys much more accurately the idea that people can make themselves eunuchs, which might literally involve castration, for the sake of the kingdom of heaven. Jesus does not seem to object, and, in fact, he can be interpreted to endorse the idea of self-mutilation. That this passage could be so understood is shown by the fact that Origen, the famous church father, is reported to have castrated himself in light of this verse.[20]

The rendition of "stay single" seems most disingenuous in light of how the CEV is portrayed by its advocates: "The CEV is not a paraphrase. It is an accurate and faithful translation of the original manuscripts."[21] Yet, commenting on the CEV's "stay single" translation, Stanley Porter, the New Testament scholar, remarked: "Is it possible, in light of the overtly evangelistic purpose of the CEV, that the New Testament has been toned down in some places so that it does not scare off those attracted to Christianity?"[22]

Example 3: Anti-Semitism

The Holocaust generated a lot of self-critical analysis on the part of many Christians, and rightly so. Some Christian scholars have acknowledged the anti-Judaism in their history, while others have claimed that any anti-Judaism has been the result of misunderstanding crucial passages.[23] But one of the methods used to atone for a long Christian history of anti-Judaism centers on hiding the anti-Jewish statements in the New Testament.[24] According to the proposal by Irvin J. Borowsky in *Removing the Anti-Judaism from the New Testament*:

The solution to erasing this hatred is for bible societies and religious publishers to produce two editions, one for the public similar to the *Contempo-*

rary English Version which reduces significantly this anti-Judaic potential, and the other edition for scholars taken from the Greek text.[25]

Orwellian doublespeak could not be celebrated more fervently. The proposal is paternalistic because it assumes that readers need to be protected from their own Bible. Borowsky adds, "[T]he stakes are high. People have been murdered because of these words."[26] Similar and no less satisfactory attempts to address anti-Judaism have also been outlined by Norman A. Beck, a Lutheran biblical theologian.[27] Such efforts only expose the fact that scholars themselves know that "the Bible" is a violent document that must be sanitized to keep it alive.

TEXTUAL CRITICISM

Textual criticism is the scholarly discipline that seeks to reconstruct the most original text possible for any particular written work.[28] Such a discipline, therefore, is not restricted to the Bible. Most of the famous works of antiquity were not preserved intact. Unlike most works of antiquity, however, the textual criticism of the Bible carries crucial theological and moral consequences for those who believe they must have an accurate record of God's word to guide the conduct of their lives.[29]

Yet in the past few decades, there have been some prominent textual critics who have worried whether this field will survive. In 1977, Eldon J. Epp, a prominent New Testament textual critic and the 2003 president of the Society of Biblical Literature, wrote:

> The reasons for this recent and rapid erosion of the field of [New Testament] textual criticism are elusive. Most of it has taken place in a little more than a decade. Whether the disappearance of opportunities for graduate study in the field is a cause or a symptom of the erosion is not clear, though certainly the discipline would seem to have no bright future in America and little hope of survival here without opportunities.[30]

The findings of textual critics devastate any claim that the Bible has been transmitted faithfully from any original text.[31] Powerful computers have made the task of sorting through variations easier, though there are still major problems with determining even how many variant readings there are. Yet it is those very advances and new discoveries that have made the whole goal of textual criticism—if that means finding the original text or providing believers with some intact record of God's word—all but obsolete. Textual criticism, in fact, has helped destroy any notion that there was ever a stable entity called "the Bible."

The most important fact to consider in trying to reconstruct an "original" is that we do not possess the autograph of any biblical writing (i.e., the very first text that the author himself/herself wrote), and this much is admitted by the staunchest religionist apologists. This means all we have are copies of the originals, so we usually cannot reconstruct an ancient autograph that is no longer available—nor could we recognize the autograph even if we found it. The "original text" proves to be a mirage unless we have access to the entire transmission process from inception to current copy. Such access is something we don't have, and probably never will have in the case of the Bible.

We can illustrate the problem quite simply. Let's suppose that we have six surviving manuscripts labeled A, B, C, D, E, and F, which are related to a hypothetical original X. X could be *the autograph*, the text from an original author's own hand, and from which all subsequent copies derive. Perhaps, we might plausibly conclude that A, B, and C derive from the same source because their wording is very similar. For example, only those three share some hypothetical expression ("seal of God") as opposed to D, E, and F, which have "lamb of God" at the equivalent slot in the text. Thus, we can reasonably conclude that A, B, and C must have a common *antigraph* (i.e., the presumed written source behind any copy) with the words "seal of God." Likewise, we might plausibly conclude that copies D, E, and F must go back to a different antigraph that has the wording "lamb of God."

However, since both antigraphs are different in at least one reading ("lamb of God" versus "seal of God"), then it would be difficult to decide which one of them was "the original." In fact, their variants tell us they must have been copied from a still-earlier antigraph from which subsequent copies diverged. Even if one reconstructed X as the source behind both presumed antigraphs, it does not show that the X manuscript is the autograph. Why? Because X itself could be a copy of another antigraph that was not derived from "the original." How would we know?

Textual criticism has made important contributions to our understanding of the Bible. However, those contributions have spelled the end of textual criticism. Historically, the primary goal of biblical textual criticism was to reconstruct the original text. Textual criticism has shown that this is impossible. Thus, textual criticism has ended in that sense. Textual criticism of the Bible becomes more than ever an elite leisure pursuit that will have difficulty asking taxpayers and churchgoers to continue funding an endeavor that brings joys akin to solving Sudoku puzzles but provides little benefit to anyone else.

BIBLICAL ARCHAEOLOGY

Biblical archaeology lies in ruins, be it literally, socially, or metaphorically.[32] Biblical archaeology once was a premier and even glamorous field within biblical studies, and now even some of its most famous practitioners are proclaiming its death. In 1995, William G. Dever, a doyen of the archaeology of ancient Israel, declared that "American Syro–Palestinian and [b]iblical archeology are moribund disciplines; and archaeologists like me who have spent a lifetime in the profession, feel like the last members of an endangered species."[33] In 2006, Ronald Hendel, a professor of the Hebrew Bible at the University of California at Berkeley, remarked, "Biblical Archaeology doesn't really exist today in the way it once did."[34]

To be fair, Dever and Hendel are speaking of "biblical" archaeology in the sense of archaeology focused on supporting the historicity of the Bible. Dever himself once advocated the broader term "Syro–Palestinian" archaeology, though now his terminology is more varied. Nonetheless, part of the problem lies in the fact that the study of biblical history, which has been intimately tied to biblical archaeology, is itself increasingly under attack. As Dever phrases it, "If the actual *history* of the biblical world no longer matters, then archaeology is clearly irrelevant."[35]

There was probably an entity called "Israel" by the Egyptians at the time of Merneptah (ca. 1210 BCE), but whether "Israel" was a self-designation at that point is not clear. A location for this group or territory in the steppes of Transjordan is just as plausible as in the highlands west of the Jordan River. Whether "Israel" saw itself as part of Canaan or as part of some larger Canaanite group is unclear at that point. "Israelite" is no more an appropriate designation for the people occupying the hill country in the so-called Iron I period than "Canaanite" or the designation for any other people living in those highlands according to the biblical texts.

There is no independent evidence for a kingdom headed by Solomon either, so that is where we have to leave that claim—inconclusive. The gates at Gezer, Hazor, and Megiddo speak nothing about Solomon. In terms of illuminating the religion of the "Israelites," Dever had it right when in 1983 he wrote, "[A]rchaeology of either the 'biblical' or the 'secular' persuasion has scarcely augmented our understanding of the actual cult in ancient Israel in any fundamental way."[36]

Within the Deuteronomistic History, it is reasonable to believe in the existence of the following kings based on independent corroboration in Assyrian and Babylonian documents:[37]

Northern Kingdom (Israel)	Southern Kingdom (Judah)
Omri (ca. 885–874 BCE)	
Ahab (ca. 874–853 BCE)	
Jehu (ca. 841–790 BCE)	
Joash (ca. 805–790 BCE)	
Menahem (ca. 740 BCE)	Hezekiah (725–696 BCE)
Pekah (ca. 735 BCE)	Manasseh (696–642 BCE)
Hoshea (ca. 730–722 BCE)	Jehoiachin (605–562 BCE)

Overall, this is a very impoverished yield for any sort of "biblical history" when one compares it to many of its Near Eastern neighbors.

Biblical archaeology has helped to bury the Bible, and archaeologists know it. Ronald Hendel was exactly right when he said, "Archaeological research has—against the intentions of most of its practitioners—secured the nonhistoricity of much of the Bible before the era of kings."[38] We can now expand Hendel's observation and affirm that there is not much history to be found in the era of kings either.

So does biblical archaeology matter anymore? Since archaeology has failed to reveal much biblical history that matters, biblical archaeology not only has ceased to be relevant, but it has ceased to exist as we knew it. Instead of revealing biblical history, archaeology has provided a fundamental argument to move beyond the Bible itself. If biblical archaeology has to serve theology once more to be relevant, its days as a secular academic field are numbered. Either way, biblical archaeology ended in ruins—literally, socially, and metaphorically.

THE UNHISTORICAL JESUS

While the search for Abraham, Jacob, and Moses is now dead in academia, the search for the "historical" Jesus seems to be even more vibrant than at the time of Hermann Samuel Reimarus (1694–1768), who is credited with initiating the modern scholarly search for the historical Jesus. According to Tom Wright, by the late twentieth century we had arrived at a so-called Third Quest for the historical Jesus.[39] While we have accumulated much information about first-century Palestine, there is a terminus in the amount of knowledge that we can extract about Jesus in the first century.

In the case of the liberal Jesus, we shall concentrate on the project known as the Jesus Seminar and its members in order to show that while the supernatural has been eliminated from the reconstruction of the historical Jesus, the portrayals that have resulted are so inconclusive that we still cannot say with any confidence what Jesus said or did.[40]

Even John Dominic Crossan, one of the most recognized members of the Jesus Seminar, admits to the chaos that is historical Jesus scholarship today. Note his remarks, which also serve as a historical summary of historical Jesus research in the last four decades:

> There is a Jesus as a political revolutionary by S. G. F. Brandon (1967), as a magician by Morton Smith (1978), as a Galilean charismatic by Geza Vermes (1981, 1984), as a Galilean Rabbi by Bruce Chilton (1984), as Hillelite or proto-Pharisee by Harvey Falk (1985), as an Essene by Harvey Falk (1985), and as an eschatological prophet by E. P. Sanders (1985) ... But that stunning diversity is an academic embarrassment. It is impossible to avoid the suspicion that historical Jesus research is a very safe place to do theology and call it history, to do autobiography and call it biography.[41]

The Jesus Seminar bears all the features identified as part of the third quest, and so it is reasonable to see how successful their criteria and results have been. Briefly, the Jesus Seminar began in 1985 under the auspices of the Westar Institute. It was founded by Robert Funk, who served as president of the *Society of Biblical Literature* in 1975. Thirty scholars met in the initial year, but eventually some two hundred members, called "fellows," became part of the seminar. The epistemology follows in the positivist tradition, judging by this statement:

The Fellows of the Seminar are critical scholars. To be a critical scholar means to make empirical, factual evidence—evidence open to confirmation by independent neutral observers—the controlling factor in historical judgment.[42]

For more specifics on the criteria of historicity used by the Jesus Seminar, we turn to one of their primary publications, the Five Gospels. Note this statement:

> In sorting out the sayings and parables attributed to Jesus, Gospel scholars are guided by this fundamental axiom: Only sayings and parables that can be traced back to the oral period, 30–50 CE, can possibly have originated with Jesus. Words that can be demonstrated to have been first formulated by the Gospel writers are eliminated from contention. Scholars search for two different kinds of proof. They look for evidence that particular formulations are characteristic of individual evangelists or can only be understood in the social context of the emerging Christian movement. Or they search for evidence that sayings and parables antedate the written Gospels.[43]

However, it does not take long to see that these criteria used by the Jesus Seminar are fundamentally flawed.[44] They simply have traded one sort of dogmatism for another. Note, for example, that the above general criteria are supported by three "rules of attestation," the first of which is "[s]ayings or parables that are attested in two or more independent sources are older than the sources in which they are embedded."[45] The false assumption here parallels that of the search for an "original text" in that it assumes that by reconstructing some earlier source behind later ones, one has come closer to the "original" Jesus. In fact, in such a case one has simply uncovered an earlier tradition about Jesus, but that earlier tradition is not necessarily "less invented" (or "more authentic") than some later source.

Second, even attestation by two "independent" sources really proves nothing more than the existence of a "tradition," rather than the existence of the actual words or deeds of Jesus. That is to say, if Source X and Source Y agreed that Jesus said Z, then all you have proved is that two independent sources agree that there was a tradition that "Jesus said Z." This does not mean that Jesus actually said Z.

All this is dependent, in turn, on the seminar's premise that there was "an oral period" that spanned from 30 CE to 50 CE, before the first texts about

Jesus were supposedly written. Of course, this would mean that any written tradition reconstructed still has at least a twenty-year gap to fill with sources whose veracity cannot be verified by us, and probably not by any of the persons who were recording events at which they were not present.

If we look at specific texts, we start seeing the subjectivity of specific judgments. Consider Matthew 5:38–41 in the Jesus Seminar's translation:

> 38. As you know, we once were told, "An eye for an eye," and "A tooth for a tooth." 39. But I tell you: Don't react violently against the one who is evil: when someone slaps you on the right cheek, turn the other as well. 40. When someone wants to sue you for your shirt, let that person have your coat along with it. 41. Further, when anyone conscripts you for one mile, go an extra mile. 42. Give to the one who begs from you; and don't turn away the one who tries to borrow from you.[46]

According to the editors, Jesus did not say what is in verse 38. However, he did say everything (except "But I tell you") in verses 39–41. In verse 42, only the first clause is certain according to the Jesus Seminar, and the second one ("and don't . . .") is less so. And how were these degrees of certainty decided? The editors tell us that

> [t]he aphorisms in 5:38–41 are case parodies with a very narrow range of application. In contrast, the aphorisms in 5:42 are universal injunctions: give to everyone who begs and lend to all who want to borrow—everywhere, at all times. These sayings are short and pithy, they cut against the social grain, and they indulge in humor and paradox. The person who followed them literally would soon be destitute. It is inconceivable that the primitive Christian community would have made them up, and they appear not to have been part of the common lore of the time.[47]

All this is quite confusing. The instructions in 5:38–41 are described as having a "very narrow range of application" in contrast to the instructions in 5:42, which are universal injunctions. But what "narrowness" and "universality" have to do with any decision seems irrelevant because it is not clear that the injunctions in 5:38–41 are not universal. Why doesn't the injunction about turning the cheek in verse 39 apply "everywhere, at all times" just as much as the one about giving to the one who begs in verse 42? And why is the last clause of verse 42 given a lesser degree of certainty even though it seems just as universal as the first clause in that same verse? Moreover, the entire exercise is premised on having a very clear psychological and personality profile of Jesus. But how do we know what Jesus might have been thinking in the first place except through the texts that the Jesus Seminar has predetermined to derive from Jesus? After all, one reason given is that it is "inconceivable" that the primitive church would have made these sayings up. But we have no information on what the early Church members, who might have penned these words, could conceive or not. So what data is being used to judge the "conceivability" of any idea for these church members?

Consider also Mark 2:1–12, which relates the famous case of a paralytic who had to be lowered through a roof of the house where Jesus was staying because the crowds outside the house were so large. According to the Jesus Seminar translation, Jesus' first words to the paralytic were (verse 5) "Child, your sins are forgiven."[48] Jewish scholars present were said to have been astounded by such a pronouncement, as they believed only God had the power to forgive sins. But Jesus responded in verse 10 that he had said this "so that you may realize that [on earth] the son of Adam has authority to forgive sins."[49]

The Jesus Seminar judges that Jesus did not use a term such as "Son of Adam" or say anything about forgiving sins. Actually, they have a contradictory conclusion. On the one hand, Jesus' claim seems bold enough that "it is just possible that Mark 2:10 preserves early tradition."[50] On the other hand, the editors ultimately decided that

> [t]he early church was in the process of claiming for itself the right to forgive sins and so would have been inclined to claim that its authorization came directly from Jesus as the Messianic figure, "the son of Adam." In that case, v. 10 would be the product of the Christian storyteller, who is reading the convictions of the later community back into an incident in Jesus' life.[51]

There are problems with the reasoning leading to both conclusions. First, the idea of a healer forgiving sins is not as bold as the seminar suggests. In fact, in the DSS we find a text called "The Prayer of Nabonidus," which is named for a Babylonian king of the sixth century BCE. In that text, an exorcist heals Nabonidus, and the latter may be interpreted to say that "an exorcist forgave my sin. He was a J[ew]. . . ."[52]

Second, the reasoning used to reject the authenticity of the saying is also based on numerous and circular suppositions. For instance, what sources are used to evaluate what the church was "in the process of claiming" between 30 and 50 CE? More importantly, why can't we use this same rationale to evict from the Gospels almost any saying of Jesus? That is to say, anything Jesus said could have been the product of a Christian storyteller who wanted to bolster particular creeds that his faith community was "in the process of claiming."

It would be futile to multiply examples because they are all based on similar principles. The Jesus Seminar has predetermined what Jesus or the early church thought, and then they have simply selected those verses that accord with what the Jesus Seminar thinks that Jesus thought.[53] So despite no supernaturalism in their assumptions, the members of the Jesus Seminar are no different from fundamentalists who pick and choose proof texts to bolster their image of Jesus. All they have done is create a Jesus in their own image, as Robert Price, and Albert Schweitzer before him, acutely argued.[54]

But there's more to consider, because the existence of other Gospels changes everything. Charles W. Hedrick, who discovered a "lost Gospel," placed the number of Gospels at thirty-four in 2002.[55] According to him, we have four canonical Gospels, four complete noncanonical Gospels, seven fragmentary Gospels, four Gospels known only from early quotations, two hypothetical Gospels (Q and the Signs Gospels), and thirteen known only by a name mentioned in some ancient source.

In any case, and without rehearsing the contents and debates about each of the noncanonical Gospels counted by Hedrick, we can make the following brief comments about their implications for the end of biblical studies. First, these "lost" Gospels confirm that early Christianity was so diverse and chaotic that we can no longer speak of "Christianity" but now must talk of "Christianities," a point made by, among others, Bart Ehrman in his book *Lost Christianities*.[56] What these "Christianities" have in common is their claimed connection with a "Christ," who is portrayed in astoundingly variegated fashion.

Second, we can no longer privilege just the canonical Gospels as the earliest or best sources for depicting early Christianity. This, of course, is a fundamental principle of the Jesus Seminar, and John Dominic Crossan's study of the Historical Jesus already places the Gospel of Thomas and the Egerton Gospel in the earliest stratum of his sources (alongside 1 Thess., Gal., 1 Cor., and Rom.).[57]

The fact remains that the earliest dated manuscript of any Gospel is a tiny fragment known as P[52], which contains only a few verses from John 18. That fragment cannot tell us if the unpreserved part of that manuscript bears a Gospel of John much like ours. The other three Gospels do not have manuscripts dated before the third century, and the complete ones come from the fourth. However, such dates for canonical materials overlap with at least some of the dates for noncanonical Gospels. The Greek fragments of the Gospel of Thomas as well as the Egerton Gospel have been dated to the second century, and the Greek manuscripts of the Gospel of Mary have been dated to the third century (as well as one manuscript of the Gospel of Judas, which is also attested even earlier—like many noncanonical Gospels, in the second century).[58]

Thus, we cannot say that these Gospels have less "authentic" or "historical" material than the canonical Gospels—if they have any authentic or historical material at all. And if we dismiss noncanonical Gospels as forgeries because they were probably not written by the claimed authors, then the same must be said for many books in the canon, ranging from Moses's "books" to 2 Peter.[59] The point remains that we cannot verify or falsify many claims in these noncanonical Gospels any more than we can verify or falsify claims in the canonical ones.

If we identify biblical studies with the study of only the canonical materials, then it is clear that "biblical studies" actually ended decades ago. After all, we have been studying many of the noncanonical works in the Dead Sea Scrolls for decades. But as the shift to noncanonical Gospels accelerates, so, too, will the final death of biblical studies.

The quest for the historical Jesus is an abject failure. Further progress is futile because we simply don't have *any* preserved accounts of Jesus from his time or from any proven eyewitnesses. And even if we were to discover lots of new material mentioning Jesus in his supposed lifetime, such material still would not render us much surer of anything. After all, we possess an abundance of contemporary material about Mary at Medjugorje, but most Protestant apologists easily dismiss it. Contemporaneity means very little, after all, if we cannot verify the information in any contemporary reports.

We can dismiss the conservative scholars as motivated by religious agendas, but what propels the more liberal academic scholars to invest in such futile searches for the historical Jesus? The answer is that both the conservative and liberal historical Jesus scholars still share religionist and bibliolatrous bonds. They believe that Jesus' words matter or should matter. But who is the audience for historical Jesus studies? The audience consists mostly of believers who think that Jesus' words and deeds are preserved in the Bible, or that at least some of them are recoverable. Intellectual honesty should compel at least the liberal scholars to announce aggressively to the world that Jesus cannot be found, and that any notion of following actual words or deeds of Jesus is vacuous.[60]

LITERARY CRITICISM

As it relates to biblical studies, literary criticism is the discipline devoted to elucidating the literary artistry of biblical authors. For our purposes, we use literary criticism to describe a suite of approaches unified by the idea that biblical texts are constructed artfully and have artistic merit. As David J. A. Clines and J. Cheryl Exum, two of its most influential current practitioners, observe in their own survey of literary criticism, "its primary concern is the text as an object, a product, not as a window upon historical actuality."[61] Such a description reflects what is called "New Criticism" in broader secular literary studies. The New Criticism focuses on a work of art as an autonomous object whose beauty is not dependent on its historical context. A Rembrandt painting retains its beauty no matter what historical forces brought it about.[62]

One need not excavate deeply to find the motives for literary analysis of the Bible among virtuosos such as Robert Alter, Meir Sternberg, and Frank Kermode.[63] In fact, the apologetic intent is sometimes quite frank, as in the case of Robert Alter's comment on how ancient and modern readers have approached the Hebrew Bible:

> Subsequent religious tradition has by and large encouraged us to take the Bible seriously rather than enjoy it, but the paradoxical truth of the matter may well be that by learning to enjoy the biblical stories more fully as stories, we shall also come to see more clearly what they mean to tell us about God, man, and the perilously momentous realm of history.[64]

Literary criticism of the Bible is suffering from a crisis that is besetting all of literature. On the one hand, the old rationales for studying literature no longer seem self-evident. For example, it is not clear that literature enhances "mental discipline," a rationale used in the famous Yale Report, which desperately sought to justify requiring the study of the classics in a modern university.[65]

The question of the canon has become much more polarized, with other voices clamoring to be part of the canon.[66] Nonetheless, justifying literary studies of the Bible still poses a special set of problems. First, biblical scholars have failed to provide a coherent rationale for why biblical literature is better than that of many other cultures. When asked what differentiated the Bible from Shakespeare, Phyllis Trible, a feminist apologist for the Bible, and the president of the Society of Biblical Literature in 1994, could only reply, "I ask myself that question, and if I had a clear answer, I would give it to you."[67]

Second, the Bible has been studied far longer than any other text. So why invest any more time in this text when there are so many others that have yet to be studied? If the Bible is kept because of its supposed moral lessons, then why not allow that the many ancient texts that are still unknown to the modern world might also have worthy lessons? Likewise, aesthetic worth can be found in many ancient texts, and so the Bible cannot be privileged on those grounds either.

Third, the question of relevance is particularly acute for ancient texts such as the Bible. How does knowing anything about biblical characters or biblical poetic structures help us to become better people or to solve any practical problems in the modern world? That is why the notion that the Bible must be studied for its "intrinsic value" also fails as yet another meaningless and indefinable feature meant only to maintain the privilege of that text.[68]

But let us say that literature is a beneficial part of our human experience, which should be celebrated along with the humanities.[69] The problem is that such a rationale overlooks how the Bible also has been detrimental to human beings. For every page of *Hamlet* that we might enjoy innocently, there is a passage of the Bible that prompted someone to kill another human being. One can't say that about *Hamlet*. The differential in detrimental effect is also a main argument for ending a privileged status for the Bible in any modern canon.

Suffice it to say that literary beauty is subjective; one could argue that many biblical texts are actually ugly; the Bible fails to satisfy the standards of beauty set by scholars themselves; other texts could also satisfy or surpass the Bible when the same criteria of beauty are applied; ethics can be invoked to judge some biblical texts as aesthetically defective. In sum, the current emphasis on literary analysis and aesthetics becomes simply another apologetic device to maintain the value of the Bible in modern society.[70]

BIBLICAL THEOLOGY

Like other disciplines within biblical studies, biblical theology has a complex and contested history.[71] Krister Stendahl, the former dean of the Harvard Divinity School, in a much-cited article in *The Interpreter's Dictionary of the Bible*, argued that scholars should distinguish "what it meant and what it means."[72] The background of such a claim was Stendahl's realization that the Bible is so alien to our culture that only reinterpretation could keep it alive.

Jon Levenson also champions the legitimacy of "recontextualization" and "reappropriation," which claims that a text can and should mean whatever a faith community needs it to mean to keep the community alive. For Levenson, recontextualization is legitimate even when it might contradict what an author originally meant. And both Levenson and Stendahl argue that since faith communities do apply other meanings to the Bible, it is legitimate for them to do so. This rationale may be expressed more schematically as "People do X = People ought to be allowed to do X."

But upon closer inspection, Levenson's own reappropriation program carries the seeds of the destruction of biblical studies. When considering the meaning of a biblical text for faith communities, two positions can be identified for those who believe there is even such a thing as authorial intent:

A: Authorial intent is the only one that matters

B: Authorial intent is not the only one that matters

If one chooses A, then biblical studies has been highly unsuccessful. We often do not possess enough information to determine what an author meant, even if we believe that authorial intent matters and should be the primary goal of interpretation. If one chooses B, then the only result is chaos and relativism that renders scholarly biblical studies moot and superfluous. Faith communities do not need academic biblical scholars to inform them about any original context in order to keep the Bible alive for themselves. So what is the purpose of academic biblical studies in such a case? The answer is that there is no purpose, except perhaps to preserve the employment and status of biblical scholars.

However, it is not usually the case that a modern faith community acknowledges that Text A has original meaning B, but that meaning B will be disregarded or contradicted so that Text A can take on modern meaning C. Rather, most members of faith communities assert that Text A means C, *but not because it is recontextualized*. For them, B = C. Academic scholars might call that "recontextualization" because they have concluded on empirico-rationalist grounds that the meaning attributed to a text by faith communities today is not original, even when faith communities might be claiming *not a reinterpretation* but rather *a continuity in interpretation*.

But once an equation is made between a modern sense and an original sense, it is not a case of scholars allowing "another sense" but rather a case where simple empirico-rationalism comes into play. As such, a secular biblical scholar is perfectly right in concluding that a modern community is falsely claiming that "the modern sense = the original author's sense." Followers of the historical-critical method would be no more monopolistic or fundamentalistic in this case than if they were correcting someone who claimed that 1 = 3.

Even if we suppose that all authorial intention is irrelevant or indeterminate, Levenson's position would also lead to the argument that biblical studies should end.[73] The consequences of Levenson's position differs not in the least from ejecting that ancient text from modern life altogether. If Text A can mean both B and Not-B, then how is Not-B any different from regarding meaning B as irrelevant in modern life? And how does regarding meaning B as irrelevant in modern life differ from simply ejecting Text A and its meaning B from modern life altogether? More importantly, why are we expending any energy in determining the history or original meaning of a text in the first place?

John J. Collins, the president of the Society of Biblical Literature in 2002, once remarked: "The Bible was written long ago and in another culture, vastly different from our own."[74] In the end, Levenson's pleas for the legitimacy of recontextualization only expose the fact that the Bible is so foreign to modern life that it can survive only if people pretend that it is something other than it is. The fact that people reappropriate scripture is not an argument that they should do so. Levenson never answers the question of why we should bother to reappropriate such texts at all, given that there are many other texts whose voices are still silent and silenced by scholars who could resurrect them just as well.

Despite the claims of academic rigor and increasing self-criticism, all biblical theologies have one thing in common: bibliolatry. They may not agree on what the central concept of the Bible is or how many concepts there are, but they all agree that the Bible is valuable enough to have its concepts receive exhaustive analysis for the purpose of helping readers. Never is there an Old Testament or biblical theology centered on completely deprivileging the biblical text and on helping move human beings beyond its antiquated, opprobrious sections. Instead, biblical theologians endeavor to rescue the Bible from itself, while providing the illusion that biblical theology should matter. If this is the best biblical theology has to offer, then it deserves to come to a most ignominious end.[75]

CONCLUSION

Biblical studies as we know them should end. Biblical scholars all agree the Bible is a product of another age and culture, whose norms, practices, and conception of the world were very different from ours. Yet these very same scholars paradoxically keep the general public under the illusion that the Bible does matter or should matter. We have argued that whether they intend it or not, their validation of the Bible as a text for the modern world serves to validate their own employment and relevance in the modern world.

We have seen how translations, rather than exposing the alien and more opprobrious concepts of biblical authors, instead conceal them. We have seen how textual critics, even after knowing that the original text is probably irrecoverable, do not announce to most churches that their Bibles are at best constructs that cannot be traced earlier than the second century for the New Testament and the third century BCE for the Hebrew Bible. In our look at biblical history and archaeology, we learned that "biblical history" has not so much been erased as it has been exposed as not being there in the first place. The supposed superior artistic merit of the Bible has also been unmasked for what it is—another bibliolatrous apologetic device.

Why do we need an ancient book that endorses everything from genocide to slavery to be a prime authority on our public or private morality? Why do we need any ancient text at all, regardless of what morality it espouses? "The Bible" is mostly a construct of the last two thousand years of human history. Modern human beings have existed for tens of thousands of years without the Bible, and they don't seem to have been the worse for it. There are modern secularized societies in Europe that seem to get along just fine without the Bible.

From my perspective, there are really only three alternatives for what is now called biblical studies.

1. Eliminate biblical studies completely from the modern world.
2. Retain biblical studies as is, but admit that it is a religionist enterprise.
3. Retain biblical studies, but redefine its purpose so that it is tasked with eliminating completely the influence of the Bible in the modern world.

I do not advocate the first option, at least for the moment, because I do believe that the Bible should be studied, if only as a lesson in why human beings should not privilege such books again. My objection has been to the religionist and bibliolatrous purpose for which it is studied. The second option is actually what is found in most seminaries, but we must advertise that scholars in all of academia are doing the same thing, though they are not being very open and honest about it.

I prefer the third option. The sole purpose of biblical studies, under this option, would be to help people move toward a postscriptural society. It may be paternalistic to "help people," but no more so than when translators hide the truth or when scholars don't aggressively disclose the truth for fear of upsetting believers. All of education is to some extent paternalistic, since an elite professoriate is there to provide information that uneducated people lack. The third option is also the most logical position, given the discovery of the Bible's alien character.

Mine would also be the less self-interested option because it would not have my own employment as an ultimate goal, and it would allow thousands of other texts that have not yet been given a voice to also speak about the possible wisdom, beauty, and lessons they might contain. Indeed, thousands of Mesopotamian texts continue to lie untranslated. So even those who believe that literature does matter should be advocating that we bring to light more of the as-yet unread ancient texts.

What I seek is liberation from the very idea that *any* sacred text should be an authority for modern human existence. Abolishing human reliance on sacred texts is imperative when those sacred texts imperil the existence of human civilization as it is currently configured. Thus, total abolition of biblical authority becomes a moral obligation and a key to this world's survival. The letter can kill. That is why the only mission of biblical studies should be to end biblical studies as we know them.

Chapter 5

CAN GOD EXIST IF YAHWEH DOESN'T?

by Dr. Jaco Gericke[1]

> In former times, one sought to prove that there is
> no God—today one indicates how the belief that
> there is a God arose and how this belief acquired
> its weight and importance: a counter-proof that
> there is no God thereby becomes superfluous. . . .
> When in former times one had refuted the "proofs
> of the existence of God" put forward, there always
> remained the doubt whether better proofs might
> not be adduced than those just refuted: in those
> days atheists did not know how to make a clean
> sweep.
> —*FRIEDRICH NIETZSCHE, DAYBREAK*[2]

INTRODUCTION

To this day, many atheist philosophers of religion still tend to try to disprove the alleged reality of the Christian God by pointing out the logical problems in divine attributes or by trying to argue via science or philosophy why "God" as first cause or cosmic designer or benevolent providence does not or cannot exist. This is all fine and well, but what is often overlooked is the fact that there will be no end to apologists' reinterpretations of the concept of "God," no end to their error theories to account for why they seem irrational and others remain skeptical, and no end to their labors to make their pseudoscientific speculations and ad hoc hypotheses appear intellectually respectable. This means that any disproof merits only a relative efficiency value at best when it tackles the god of the philosophers.

In my view, there is a far more devastating way of showing why what most people call "God" does not and cannot exist. It involves philosophers of religion instead focusing on the God of Abraham, Isaac, and Jacob and actually taking the Bible seriously (more seriously than the fundamentalists do). It involves exposing the fact that the clothes have no emperor in the Christian philosophy of religion by looking at the emperor with no clothes in the repressed history of Israelite religion from which it originated. Then one lets common sense do the rest—most people can add two and two without needing the answer spelled out for them. Eating from the tree of knowledge will always make one aware of one's nakedness and is a guaranteed one-way ticket out of the fool's paradise.

WHO IS "GOD"?

What the Western world means when it refers fuzzily to "God" is not some untouchable, ineffable ultimate reality beyond the grasp of human rational faculties that will one day catch up with unbelievers, making them realize their cognitive blindness. Rather, the entity most readers refer to when they speak of "God" is actually an upgraded, mysteriously anonymous version of what actually used to be a relatively young, quite particular, and oddly hybrid Middle Eastern tribal deity called Yahweh. The trick was done when "God" got lost in translation—in the Bible the word "God" can, in the Hebrew of the Old Testament, be both a personal name and a generic term. A nice illusion of conceptual dignity is created in English Bible translations where the Hebrew word "god" in the generic sense is capitalized, even when it does not function as a personal name but as the name of a species or natural kind (i.e., a god). Of course, translators only do this when it's used of the "god of Israel," who promptly becomes the "God of Israel."

In philosophical monotheism since Thomas Aquinas, God is considered as not belonging to a genus, despite the biblical assumption to the contrary, assuring us that we are dealing with a particular kind of god among others. Often other gods are also lost in translation when rendering the Hebrew plural term for divinity as "mighty ones," "angels," or "heavenly beings," and so on.

Many people don't know that the expression "sons of God/the gods" in Genesis 6:1–4 just means "male gods" (as the expression "daughters of man" just means "female humans"). References to a "divine council" like those in 1 Kings 22:19–22, Psalm 82, and Isaiah 6:14 also presuppose the reality of other "gods." Only later in the history of Israelite religion are these "gods" turned into semidivine "messengers." Yet even the word "angel" is misleading since these beings were nothing like what Christians today popularly associate with them. In the Hebrew Bible they are fierce humanoid male demigods or animal-type functionaries (cherubs/seraphs). They are also to be distinguished from the divine beings in Yahweh's divine council (and just for the record, there are no kind women or cute baby cupid angels in the Old Testament, except for the one reference to women in a late passage in Zechariah).

To be sure, many texts in the Old Testament do not assume polytheism. However, many others assume monolatrism rather than monotheism—that is, the belief that one god should be *worshipped*, not that only one god exists. People who read the English Bibles seldom notice this, but one need not know Hebrew to recognize monolatrist assumptions. Take the Ten Commandments, for example. If there were no other gods assumed, readers never bother to ask why Yahweh was called a god (and not something else) in the first place, or of whom he was supposed to be jealous as the first command assumes. How is one—a god no less—jealous of something that does not exist?

I am not denying monotheistic beliefs in the Old Testament, but the beliefs of one biblical author on this matter often contradicted those of another. The translations obscure this, and I offer a literal rendering of the Hebrew:

"On all the gods of Egypt I will execute judgments: I am Yahweh" (Exod. 12:12).

"When Elyon gave to the nations their inheritance, when he separated the sons of men, he fixed the bounds of the peoples according to the number of the sons of El. But Yahweh's portion is his people; Jacob his measured out inheritance" (Deut. 32:8–9, about which see Hector Avalos's preceding chapter).

"Will you not possess what Chemosh your god gives you to possess? And all that Yahweh our god has dispossessed before us, we will possess" (Judg. 11:24).

"God stands up in the council of the gods, he judges in the midst of the gods; I have said myself, you are all gods, and you are sons of the most high (god)" (Ps. 82:6).

"For who is like Yahweh among the sons of the gods" (Ps. 89:7).

"For Yahweh is a great god and a great king over all the gods" (Ps. 95:3).

"All the gods bow down before him" (Ps. 97:7).

"Then he will act, with the aid of a foreign god" (Dan. 11:39).

These texts make sense only on the assumption that they (in contrast to other texts) assume there are other gods. It is no credit to Yahweh if he is fighting against, king of, jealous of, judging, or greater than entities that do not exist. Of course, many reinterpretations of these passages are available in apologetic literature, but these are motivated by dogma more than the need to accept the Bible on its own terms.

In the Old Testament taken as a whole, not only Yahweh but other national gods are called gods. Also, spirits of the dead, heavenly messengers or counselors, kings, and even demons can be called a "god" (see 1 Sam. 28; Deut. 32; Ps. 45; etc.). Add to the capitalization of the generic term the fact that the highly specific Hebrew(!) personal name for this god—"Yahweh"—is recast with the generic term "Lord" (following the Jewish tradition), and you avoid the scandal of peculiarity altogether. "The Lord your God" sounds somewhat more respectable and intimidating than "Yahweh your god." So what is often overlooked in debating the existence of "God," if by "God" is understood anything with any relation to biblical theism, is the fact that the entity as known today is in fact the product of a complex conceptual evolution from the variable conceptions of the god Yahweh to "God," a panel-beaten hybrid that can be made into what can seem like philosophically respectable proportions.

So what? Well, this little bit of information is more atheologically potent and philosophically significant than it seems at first sight. For it means that, in trying to prove "God" does not exist, so long as "God" is in any way related to the entity worshipped in modern (or postmodern) biblically derived forms of theism (no matter how sophisticated), the only thing needed is to show that representations of Yahweh in ancient Israelite religion do not refer to any ultimate reality outside the text. It's not unlike trying to prove there is no Zeus. Not even Christians can do it, but you can demonstrate belief in Zeus to be absurd by pointing out the ridiculously superstitious nature of the representations of the entity in question (i.e., his human appearance, his less than scientifically informed mind, and his nonexistent divine world), thus exposing his artificial origins. Well, the same can be done with "God," aka Yahweh.

TAKING THE NATURE OF THE BIBLE SERIOUSLY

The Bible is a text, a literary artefact. The question is the relation between Yahweh as depicted therein and the world outside the text in which we live. On this matter, many biblical scholars are still theists of sorts.

First, there are still some fundamentalists (naive realists). This is your average committed conservative (often "evangelical") Christian scholar who thinks one is warranted to believe in a correspondence between representations of Yahweh in the biblical text and an alleged extratextual reality to which they supposedly refer. The text and language are assumed to function like a *window* through which you see reality as it really is. The Bible is literally the Word of God.

Second, the majority of mainstream biblical scholars are theists but critical realists. They believe the Old Testament contains Israel's fallible human perspectives on God in their beliefs about Yahweh, who is assumed, nevertheless, as really existing. According to this view, the biblical text is like a *painting*, an attempted semirealist representation of the reality it seeks to describe. The text is God's Word in human speech or human words about God.

Third, there are those of us who realize that what we have in the text is the character Yahweh who, as depicted, can for various reasons not possibly exist outside the stories in which he acts. Yahweh is like Donald Duck, who is real in some fictionalist sense. He does not exist outside the cartoons about his character (except people in costumes, I suppose). We are the nonrealists who believe that the text is neither a window to some divine reality nor a painting of it. It is simply a house of concave and convex mirrors which in a warped manner reflects to us only human ideals, beliefs, desires, fears, and values. For us the text is just human words, period. As Robert Carroll noted, "The biblical God is a character in Hebrew narrative and therefore is, in a very real sense, a figure of fiction."[3]

The same idea was reiterated by David Clines, ex-president of the Society of Biblical Literature, who realized that a biblical scholar needs to believe as little in Yahweh as a classical scholar in Zeus or an Egyptologist in Ra. In his view, when it comes to the representation of God in the Pentateuch, "God in the Pentateuch is a character in a novel. God in the Pentateuch is not a 'person'; he is a character in a book. And there are no people in books, no real people, only fictions; for books are made, not procreated...."[4]

Moreover, even a populist crypto-fundamentalist like the postliberal Old

Testament theologian Walter Brueggemann had no problem admitting this when he wrote in the fashion of what William Harwood rightly implied is nothing but "faculty-of-mythology doubletalk": "even with reference to God, the imaginative generative power of rhetoric offers to the hearer of this text a God who is not otherwise known or available or even—dare one say—not otherwise 'there.'"[5]

In general, these Old Testament scholars are reluctant to engage in philosophy of religion. As a result, they have not attempted to spell out why they believe that Yahweh as represented in the biblical texts does not really exist. But the Bible itself offers a mandate for challenging any claim to divinity. Thus we find that the God of the Old Testament could at times rant and rave and even challenge the reality of foreign gods, claiming them to be human-made idols; for example, Isaiah 41:21–24 (NRSV):

Set forth your case, says the LORD; bring your proofs, says the King of Jacob. Let them bring them, and tell us what is to happen. Tell us the former things, what they are, so that we may consider them, and that we may know their outcome; or declare to us the things to come. Tell us what is to come hereafter, that we may know that you are gods; do good, or do harm, that we may be afraid and terrified. You, indeed, are nothing and your work is nothing at all; whoever chooses you is an abomination.

One would like to put the same request to Yahweh, if only to be fair. If only the writers of this text applied the same criteria to themselves. But let us not tempt this god—we shall let his alleged divine revelation speak for itself. For of all the arguments that show why a claim to divinity is false, none seems as devastating as the argument from the projection of all-too-human qualities onto an alleged superhuman entity. What is ironic is that taking the Old Testament seriously will reveal that using the same line of reasoning against representations of Yahweh in that text has devastating consequences.

Before we begin, it should be noted that we are not trying to be difficult or blasphemous—there is no pleasure in destroying the beliefs of others. We just want to make known the truth about the Bible, to show why the Bible (which is just a book) is itself the most subtle of idolatrous agents. Our critical approach is demanded by the polemics of many a biblical prophet himself and certainly seems prudent. After all, no god appeared to us to tell us that this book is true. No god will appear to you as you read this chapter to inform you that it is wrong. But humans calling themselves Christians will just keep quoting from the Bible or referring to their religious experience or some philosophical position to convince you it is. But even the character Yahweh himself taught us that one should not trust in humans—if there is a god, let him fend for himself (see Judg. 6 on Baal). And we need to be critical, since biblical religion makes too important claims about reality not to have it scrutinized as though one's life depended on it. The fact is that many of those writing in this book were committed "biblical" Christians ourselves. So was the author of this chapter. Yet in trying to be even more biblical, we all discovered what the Bible actually says and as a result lost our faith.

Taking the Bible seriously does that. If you read the scriptures and are not shocked out of all your religious beliefs, you have not understood them. If you don't believe me (and you don't have to), just keep reading. The novelty and fatality of the arguments lie in the way they will combine philosophy of religion with the history of Israelite religion—and we shall never have to appeal to anything but what is in the Bible itself. The focus will be on the Old Testament, and if the discussion to follow does not open your eyes to the Bible as fantasy literature, and the God of the Bible as nothing more than a memorable old monster, nothing will.

YAHWEH'S BODY

Most believers might think of "God" as incorporeal and spiritual. But if this is the case, they do not believe in Yahweh as depicted in many biblical texts. Many don't, and do not appreciate the truth expressed in the popular joke suggesting that, in the beginning, God created man in his own image and that man, in response, promptly returned the favor. In this regard, theologians, both biblical and systematic, have endlessly debated what it could possibly mean when, for example, Genesis 1:26–27 speaks of man being created in "the image of God." They have insisted that the obvious meaning of the words—that God was believed to look like a male human because it was thought that God created humans to look like himself (see Gen. 5:1–3; 9:6)—cannot possibly be what was intended. Sophisticated apologetics notwithstanding, this is what Genesis 1 seems to be saying, and I wish to take it seriously.[6]

Most references to Yahweh are not symbolic. It cannot be denied that there are a number of textual references to the body (and body parts) of Yahweh that, in the context of biblical narratives, seem to have functioned as nonmetaphorical descriptions of what the deity supposedly actually looks like. Thus, in the book of Exodus, we find literal references to Yahweh's face (Exod. 33:20); his backside (Exod. 33:23); his hands and fingers (Exod. 31:18); his feet (Exod. 24:10–11); and so on. There are other texts implying that Yahweh literally has a nose with which to smell the pleasant aromas of sacrifices (Gen. 8:21; Lev. 1:9, 13, 17; 26:31). The presence of some literalism in the Old Testament texts is therefore to be acknowledged: we all need to take the Bible seriously. When Christian scholars try to tone down the problem with the concept of anthropomorphism (i.e., speaking as if Yahweh appeared only in human form but does not look like a human), it's because they, too, realize the absurdity in such a belief.

One justification for taking seriously the Old Testament's religious language can be found in the recognition that nonmetaphorical elements tend to spill over into those depictions of Yahweh that make sense only if the limitations of embodiment are assumed to be of constraining effect on him. Thus we find him needing to rest in order to be refreshed (Gen. 2:1; Exod. 31:17); having to travel to obtain information and to verify reports (Gen. 3:8–11; 11:5–7; 18:17); needing to test people to discern their beliefs, intentions, and motives (Gen. 22; Deut. 8:2; 2 Chron. 32:31; etc.); being forced to act based on a fear of human potential (Gen. 3:22; 11:5–7); being of insufficient power so that his people could not defeat the enemy because it had iron chariots during the battle (Judg. 1:21) and desiring assistance in some matters (Judg. 5:23; 1 Kings 22:20–23; Isa. 63:3–5); etc.[7]

Having a male body, Yahweh was believed to have male body parts. This also means sexual organs (i.e., "loins," Ezek. 1:27–28). Texts such as Genesis 6:4, where the gods come to have intercourse with female humans, assume as much, as does the New Testament discreet divine visitation of the teenage virgin Mary. In historical research and biblical archaeology it is commonly accepted that we have evidence that a goddess was worshipped in ancient Israel as Yahweh's consort (Asherah).[8] But the groups that were responsible for the final text of the Old Testament made sure few traces of the goddess remained, which resulted in a very sexist scenario in which heaven is an all-male world. The closest one gets to how Yahweh would relate to a goddess is when Yahweh calls Israel or the cities in the land his wife/bride (as in Ezekiel and Hosea). Looking at how he treats his spouse, however, shows us an all-too-human mind prone to domestic violence and emotional abuse, despite whatever more positive and affectionate character traits Yahweh as husband is depicted as displaying.[9]

But there is more that reveals absurdity in the text, and it concerns something more pedantic but often overlooked in discussions of the body of Yahweh, and that is God as a language user. God just happens to have a Hebrew name, Yahweh, a fact that seems peculiar to few believers who still pray in the name of their god without wondering why this is so important or why he needs one (one can just call him "God"). In addition, according to the text, we have to take seriously the assumption that at the creation of the heavens and the earth (why does a god want to create stuff?) even before northwestern Semitic languages evolved (of which Hebrew is one), Yahweh spoke the world into being via a particular dialect of classical Hebrew that evolved among humans, stayed around only for a short time in a local bit of human history, and then vanished everywhere except from heaven. But think about it: at the moment God initially speaks at creation, the story makes little sense at all. When God says "Let there be light!" in classical Hebrew, there is nobody for whom what God utters is language rather than just a wordless shout. There is no community of speakers for whom what God cries amounts to an imperative, a command that requires something to happen. So how does God know what to say, and how can he be sure what he utters is a meaningful language with a certain force? There could not have been any established social conventions at creation, there is only our own projection in order to describe a bit of divine behavior as a certain type of action, as distinct from reflex twitches and meaningless gesticulations. The idea of a language user who is conscious as a speaker of classical Hebrew all by himself for all eternity makes no sense at all.[10]

Few readers through the ages have picked up this problem, and those who did soon resorted to philosophical-theological reinterpretation. Many medieval Jewish authorities maintained that Hebrew was the language of God without ever being bothered by the question of why God should speak a particular, historically temporal, and culturally specific dialect of classical Hebrew. Part of this dilemma for the logistics of creation by word was recognized in 1851 when German philologist Jacob Grimm argued that if God spoke language, indeed any language that involves dental consonants, God must have teeth, and since teeth were created not for speech but for eating, it would follow that he also eats, which led to so many other undesirable assumptions for those with theological preferences that the idea was abandoned altogether.[11]

This worry is certainly anachronistic inasmuch as Genesis 1 assumes humans are theomorphic rather than God being anthropomorphic. The latter is surely naive from an evolutionary perspective, and nowadays mainstream biblical scholars do not read Genesis 1 as history or science, so the question of credibility does not arise. Which is fine, but while such worries are pseudo problems due to category mistakes in genre analysis, the trouble with not trying to relate the language to reality is that one misses out on coming to grips with the absurd folk-philosophy of language running through the myth.

For many biblical commentators and philosophers, God does not have any form and only *appears* in human form. Nice thought, but unfortunately this is not what the Bible teaches in texts where the humanoid form of Yahweh is assumed to be his true form (e.g., Exod. 33:20–23), the one he is assumed to have even in heaven. The Christian philosophical reinterpretation of this is nothing more than a strategy of evasion by people who cannot admit to themselves that they, too, no longer find it possible to believe in "God" (aka Yahweh), any more than they believe in Zeus. The Greek philosophers did the same thing with the Greek gods when they began to find their representations too crude. Believers will continue doing so for the foreseeable future.

YAHWEH'S MIND

The people who wrote the Old Testament also made the fatal mistake of constructing Yahweh with what today appears to be a rather unflattering psychological (cognitive, conative, and affective) profile.[12]

First of all, the mind of the god of the Bible exhibits a library of provably errant knowledge. When Yahweh speaks in the first person in the texts of the Old Testament, the deity is often depicted as making statements that include references to historical, cosmographical, geographical, biological, and other types of phenomena that we today know are not factual. What betrays the all-too human origin of the divine mind is the simple fact that the ideas Yahweh entertains about reality are hardly better than the superstitions and misconceptions in the indigenous knowledge systems of the people who worshipped him.[13]

Thus Yahweh himself believes that the universe was literally created over a period of six days (Exod. 31:17) and that there is an ocean above the stars behind a firmament from where rainwater falls to the earth (Gen. 1:6; Job 38:34).[14] He also believes that the landmass of the earth floats on water (Deut. 5:8; Ps. 24:2) and that there is literally a place underground where the dead live as shades according to their nationalities (Num. 16:23–33; Deut. 32:22; Job 38:16–17; Isa. 7:11; Ezek. 26:19–20; 32:18–32; Amos 9:2). Yahweh also believes in myth-ical creatures like the Leviathan, Rahab, Behemoth, sea monsters, flying dragons, demons of the field, malevolent spirits of the night, etc. (cf. Job 40–41; Isa. 30:6; Lev. 17:7; Isa. 34:14; Amos 9:3; etc.). He even assumes that thought issues from the heart and emotions from the kidneys (Jer. 17:10; etc.).

Yahweh also believes in the historicity of Adam, Noah, Abraham, Moses, and David, all as depicted in the biblical traditions, at least according to the texts in which he speaks to them and in subsequent stories in which his char-acter refers back to them as though they were real people (see, for example, Ezek. 14). But if these people as they are depicted are fictions (as scholars have established), how can Yahweh—speaking to fictions and referring to them as reality—not himself be fictitious? Surely such factually errant beliefs on the part of Yahweh prove this god cannot exist as depicted.[15] Even if we insisted that what we encounter in these texts are simply the errant beliefs of humans and not a god's own thoughts, we have lost any grounds for believing that the character of Yahweh has any extratextual counterpart. Who would Yahweh be without Adam, Abraham, or Moses as depicted in the texts anyway?

But there is more about the divine mind that seems rather absurd. It is not just Yahweh's beliefs about the world that sometimes seem all too human. The deity also exhibits all-too-human needs or desires that drive him obsessively in pursuit of their fulfillment. Thus few people ever stop to wonder why God, aka Yahweh, must have a people to rule over (Exod. 19:6; Deut. 4:19; 32:8–9) and is quite anxious to maintain a formidable reputation based on ancient Near Eastern conceptions of the values of honor and shame (Deut. 32:26–27; Mal. 1–3). Yahweh is very concerned about keeping his name secret (Gen. 32; Exod. 6; Judg. 16; etc.) and like some cosmic upper-class aristocrat prefers to have his abode far away and high above human society so as not to be disturbed by mor-tals (Gen. 11, 18; Exod. 24; etc.). Yahweh needs to limit his direct and personal contact with the general population and, for the most part, prefers to act through intermediaries, agents, messengers, and armies. He enjoys and demands being feared (Exod. 20:19–20; Job 38–41). More than anything,

Yahweh yearns to be worshipped and to have constant reminders of how wonderful, powerful, and great he is (Isa. 6:2–3; etc.).

Take this last example: Yahweh's desire to be worshipped. Many people
take this need of God for granted but never bother to ask why God wants—no,
demands—to be worshipped. It is one thing if creatures, in awe of their creator,
erupt spontaneously in praise. It is quite another if the creator should be
thought of as having premeditated the formation of creatures who exist solely
for the purpose of perpetually reminding him how exalted and powerful and
benign he is (Isa. 6). I mean, is it really credible to believe that the ultimate
reality is a person who is so narcissistic and egotistic that he has to prescribe in
minute detail exactly how he wants to be worshipped? Why do we take for
granted the idea of a god as so self-absorbed that he even threatens to destroy
anyone diverging in any way from his instructions? Look at the details in
Exodus 25–40 with regard to the furnishings and construction of the taber-
nacle and the niceties of the rituals. Such controlling obsessiveness can only be
accounted for if we postulate behind it all a projection of human desire for control and order. As Don Cupitt notes (referring to a remark by Harold Bloom):

> The god of the Hebrew Bible is like a powerful and uncanny male child, a sub-
> lime mischief-maker, impish and difficult. He resembles Lear and the
> Freudian superego in being a demonic and persecuting Father, entirely lacking
> in self-knowledge and very reluctant ever to learn anything. Like the human
> characters he interacts with, he has a continually changing consciousness. He
> manifests the pure energy and force of Becoming. He is Nietzschean Will to
> Power, abrupt and uncontrollable, and subject to nothing and nobody.[16]

The fact that Yahweh's own alleged needs seem suspiciously similar to the
historically and culturally conditioned needs of "the-powers-that-be" known
to his worshippers is best accounted for by viewing Yahweh's mind as represented in the particular texts as the product of humans projecting the power-
drunk autocrats familiar to them onto an imaginary cosmic monarch. Since
paranoid human rulers displayed these traits, the ancients reasoned that, if the
cosmos is itself a monarchy with a (super) humanlike king at the top, he might
just be as vain, despotic, and attention-seeking as any earthly monarch (yet
with the same amount of savvy to maintain his popularity by occasional acts of
charity and goodwill as his terrestrial counterparts). Who could afford to take
chances? Better safe than sorry.

However, we know that—if we know anything—the universe is not a hierarchy where at the top of the pecking order sits a king with the psychological profile of a narcissistic, bipolar ancient Near Eastern ruler running the whole show. We can see the absurdity in imagining the existence of a god whose psychological profile displays culturally relative and historically contingent human desires. Note also that none of these divine psychological characteristics were in their biblical contexts understood as being mere metaphorical depictions or the result of any supposed divine "accommodation."[17] Nor can they be rationalized and explained away as the product of the deliberate and intentional "anthropopathic" representation of something that is in reality supposed to be ineffable. These ways of looking at it come only when we have to repress the fact that we no longer believe in God, aka the god of the Bible.

A third and final aspect of the representation of the mind of God seems equally absurd. We find in Yahweh's psychological profile moral values that the god considers to be eternally and universally normative but that are obviously local cultural taboos. Analogous to the disconcerting manner in which Yahweh's knowledge about the world never rises above that of his speechwriters, so, too, the divine ethics seem suspiciously similar to the projected morality of a people immersed in superstition.

For example, consider the divine desire for sacrifices. When you think about it, it all boils down to the idea of a creator who expects some of his creatures (humans) to kill and burn certain of his other creatures (animals) in order to provide divine nourishment (Yahweh likes the smell of roasting meat, according to Lev. 1:6) and to remove guilt (Lev. 1–7). Or how about the fact that Yahweh believes that giving birth to a girl leaves the mother unclean for a period, the duration of which is twice as long as compared to when she gives birth to a boy (Lev. 12:4–5)? And why does Yahweh consider it morally wrong should garments be made from two different materials or should fields be sown with two different varieties of seed (Lev. 19:19)? Why does Yahweh find human physiological processes objectively offensive, when he created them? (Lev. 12). Why are some animals held to be horrible abominations, even by their own creator (Lev. 11; Deut. 14)?

Yahweh's moral code appears all too similar to what humans from ancient Near Eastern cultures already considered as being the case—long before the religion of Yahweh even got started. Yahwism and its taboos are latecomers in the history of religions, and much of the moral beliefs contained in its value systems can be traced to other pagan religions predating its rise in Israel and Judah (circumcision and pork taboos were already established practices in Egypt, for example).[18] Thus "God" and divine commands have a history that gives the game away. Many fundamentalist believers might not be too bothered by this because they consider the cultic laws outdated—even when Yahweh never envisaged their end. Such Christians are only repressing the fact that they themselves no longer believe in Yahweh, who has in the meantime been upgraded to something more intellectually credible. All Christian theology is actually Yahwistic atheism.

YAHWEH'S WORLD

A third and final absurd conception in the Old Testament was already hinted at above: the idea that the entire cosmos is a monarchy and that Yahweh's eternal divine abode in the skies operates like a kingdom (Deut. 32:8–9; 1 Sam. 8:7; Dan. 6:27; etc.). Yahweh's own abode is believed to be a palace in which the deity himself sits on a throne (Ps. 11:4; etc.). A favorite form of transportation for the god is horse-drawn chariots (2 Kings 2:11–12; 6:17; Zech. 6:1–8; etc.). Yahweh also needs an army whose weapon of choice is the sword (Gen. 3:22; 32:1–2; Josh. 5:13–15; 2 Sam. 24:16, 27; etc.). Yahweh is wise but not omniscient and makes use of councilors (1 Kings 22:20–23; Isa. 6:3; Jer. 23:18; Ps. 82:1; 89:5; Job 1:6; etc.) and intelligence services that spy on the subjects in order to ascertain their loyalty (Job 1–2; Zech. 3; 1 Chron. 21; etc.). The ram's horn was a popular musical instrument in Yahweh's abode (Exod. 19:16), and the inhabitants of heaven eat bread and dress in pure white linen (Ps. 78:25; Ezek. 9:2; Dan. 10:5; etc.). Yahweh even engages in writing on scrolls (see the "book" [of life] in Exod. 32:32; Pss. 69:29; 139:16; Dan. 7:10; 10:21; etc.).[19]

To appreciate the impossibility of this state of affairs, the reader should take the time to reflect on the historically temporary and culturally relative nature of objects like scrolls, horse-drawn chariots, swords, dresses of linen, and shofars. These are all-too-human, time-period artifacts. There was once a time in the past when they did not exist. Before such things were used by humans, people wrote on stone and clay; fought with clubs, bows, and spears; and ran on foot. Then humans themselves designed or invented these objects Yahweh uses, and then the objects themselves evolved through time. Some cultures never used these objects and have never even heard of them. Eventually, due to cultural and technological development and change, both the political institution of monarchy and many of these artifacts Yahweh makes use of fell into disuse and today are only kept for interest's sake as antiques. Few people today write on scrolls, fight battles against enemies with swords, dress in linen, blow on rams' horns, or ride in horse-drawn chariots to reach a destination. Yet if the Old Testament texts are to be believed, ultimate reality is the god of Israel who forever uses Iron-Age artifacts. In Yahweh's sky-palace, things like shofars, swords, scrolls, and chariots have been around forever and will be so ever more.

This state of affairs should not surprise us. There is a reason why Yahweh's creation was assumed to be a monarchy rather than a chiefdom or a democracy. The Christian "God" is not simply the object of worship from all eternity past but the national deity "Yahweh" of an all-too-local and all-too-recent period religion. The oldest evidence of Yahwism dates faith in this god back no more than 3,000–3,500 years. This explains why "God," aka Yahweh, acts, speaks, and behaves like a typical late Bronze and early Iron Age god and cannot but play the role of that type of character in the stories about him. He is a slave to the divine nature as conceived of in the theatrical roles available for godhood at the time. For all his idiosyncrasies, Yahweh instinctively acts like a god of his time.

On this point, witting and unwitting embarrassment at the culturally constructed nature of what is supposed to be objectively and eternally just "true" has led apologists to the only obvious way of salvaging credibility: reinterpretation. Many contemporary theologians go out of their way to insist that all religious language referring to the divine and the supernatural world is to be understood as being metaphorical or symbolical. "God" was just "accommodating" himself (Calvin). But the theory that all language dealing with the divine world is to be understood as mythical or metaphorical so that humans can grasp it becomes a postbiblical generalization when it is thought of as being applicable to all Old Testament texts. For while some references to human artifacts used by Yahweh are indeed of this type, a naive literalism is also present in many instances. It is only those who cannot admit to themselves they no longer believe in Yahweh as depicted in the Bible who need to resort to such reinterpretation to make the deity seem less obviously impossible. Believers in God need to repress the fact that their deity used to be Yahweh, whose entire reality is so obviously absurd that it needs continual revising to hide the fact that humans of a particular time have imagined that reality *as such* functions like the only cultural and political setup they themselves were familiar with.

This need for reinterpretation of the divine world is nowhere as evident as in the understanding of the biblical concept of "heaven." The modern believer will insist that it is some sort of spiritual dimension and laugh at people who claimed they could not find God in space. But the fact is, for the ancient Israelites and Yahweh himself, heaven really was simply a divine palace in the sky. Moreover, the concept of "spirit" had nothing to do with something that was otherworldly, but in the Hebrew it denotes a natural albeit immaterial substance like the wind. There was no natural-supernatural or physical-spiritual dualism in the modern sense—which is why Yahweh's breath was equated with the wind and why he can breathe life into dust (Gen. 2). That his abode was located in what we nowadays call the sky is evident in the movement from and toward heaven in biblical narrative. Yahweh comes down on Sinai (literally, Exod. 17–19), and Elijah goes up in a chariot (literally, 2 Kings 2). Yahweh looks down from heaven at humans, and people looked up to heaven as they prayed (see Ps. 14). The reason why Yahweh rides the fast clouds (Isa. 19), why thunder is literally the divine voice (Job 37), is because he and his worshippers believed he was literally up there. That is why Jesus allegedly went up with a cloud and will return on one—because heaven was literally up there. Believers who think of the earth as round and endorse a modern cosmology with an empty sky and who are not disorientated and shocked out of their faith when reading the Old Testament have simply not understood it.[20]

To understand the idea behind this cosmography, again think of human society or the layout of any large modern city. The divine abode was simply considered the "uptown" of the cosmos—the palace or fortress on the hill. The deity lives "up there" separate from humans because the religious system teaches a cosmic apartheid between gods and humans—when you are a god, you don't mix with the riffraff too often and only appear among them rarely. That is the only reason why the divine appeared and spoke so seldom to humans (nothing more). And when he did come down, he had accommodation ready and waiting—his seven-star private palace, the temple, the word for which in Hebrew is the same as the word for palace and which was the nice, cool, and quiet house of God where a large staff fed him with wine, animal fat, and oiled vegetables twice a day and lavished him with gifts (the real motive for sacrifices). The idea of Yahweh's "food" is not uncommon in the text (see Ezek. 44:7 and Lev.).

On the last point, Christians tend to imply that the idea of human sacrifice as food for the divine is a primitive pagan practice and utterly abhorrent. Many like to point to the differences between the Bible and other ancient religions in that the Old Testament forbade such a practice. However, once again the celebrations and back-patting are premature. To be sure, many Old Testament texts do reject the idea of child sacrifices. However, preredacted sources in the Old Testament laws for the dedication of the firstborn itself show that there was a time when it was believed that Yahweh approves of it (Exod. 13:2; Lev. 27:28–29).[21] Its acceptance is implied in the story of Jephthah's daughter (Judg. 11:29–40). We also find remains of this practice in the story of Abraham and Isaac (Gen. 22) where Yahweh has no problem with the burning of the body even if he stops his servant in the act in order to keep his promise. Possibly most overlooked, however, is that the idea that human sacrifice is necessary and acceptable returned in Christianity. Here we find a theological importance of the blood of a tortured and murdered man as an offering to remove sin. That Christians, too, can thus become lyrical about the killing of a human being (or a god) shows the repaganization of Yahwism (which itself was never pure and has no essence) and reveals how easily one can become desensitized through brainwashing. This is clearly evident when Christians find nothing out of order when ritually consuming the flesh and blood of their god. Most versions of Yahweh would not have approved.

Another disconcerting truth and all-too-human need in Yahweh's psyche comes to us in Yahweh's motive for creating humans. In the world of Yahweh, the meaning of human life was to be slaves (euphemistically called "servants") to the deity. According to one of the myths, humans were created in order to rule in the place of the god so that he does not have to do it (Gen. 1:26–28). In another myth, quite incidentally in Genesis 2:5, it is implied that the meaning of human life is to toil the earth (Gen. 1–2). Again Yahweh is shown to be averse to menial labor and wants servants to do the work that is beneath him. Not exactly flattering, but at least humans were given the pleasure of flattering the divine ego and in return at least got minimum wage (food, health plan, security, etc.).

Believers today simply have not taken seriously the absurdity in the Old Testament's understanding of the cosmos as a kind of city-state ruled by a monarch in the sky whose every whim has to be catered to on the penalty of death. Christians are so brainwashed that the idea that humans are servants of a cosmic dictator still appears comforting to many. They speak about a personal relationship with the deity as a father, not realizing that any father who treats his children in the way Yahweh allegedly did would surely have to go for psychological observation and probably get life in prison (although it may be admitted that eternal torture in hell is a New Testament belief; the god of the Old Testament knows no such place). Those who consider the Bible as affirming human dignity do not seem to understand that it knows no human rights. But because Christians have for so long read a reinterpreted Bible, they can no longer see what is in there. Critical biblical scholars who are simply trying to educate them about what is the case in the text are therefore ironically in danger of being considered "unbiblical."

All of the above, however, makes no sense given the history of life on earth. The fact is that earth is now estimated to be roughly 4.5 billion years old, and on a scale of a calendar year, humans arrived on the scene during the last minute before midnight on December 31. Humanoids and religious practices have been around for tens of thousands of years. Yet we are now told to believe in what is supposed to be the "real God" even though his Iron Age (1200–500 BCE) character and supernatural setup appeared on the scene late in the history of religion at some point during the second half of the second millennium BCE—and just happens to eternally resemble the culture of this era. I'm sorry, but this is all very hard to swallow. It is no more believable than claiming any other god with an identifiable history of origin and reconstruction in myth just happens to be the ultimate reality. Does the word "absurd" still have any meaning in religious circles today?

Not only was Yahwism (now upgraded to Godism) a latecomer in the history of religions, it was also a very local affair. Yahweh and his worshippers were limited to a sacred space east of the Mediterranean. Ancient peoples from across the globe never knew this deity, and neither, according to the Old Testament, did Yahweh know of them (e.g., Native Americans, the Khoi-San people of South Africa, or the Aborigines of Australia; just compare to the list of nations in Gen. 10). The scandal of peculiarity is increased when one realizes that all Yahweh's supposedly superhuman concerns and attributes of manifestation appear totally dependent on the region in which he was worshipped. According to the Old Testament, he comes from the desert steppe in the south (the Arabian Peninsula, see Judg. 5; Hab. 3; Ps. 68) as a storm-god, a tribal fetish of a once nomadic horde (according to hints in the Old Testament, perhaps possibly having first been worshipped by the Midianites or Kenites). The tropical parts of the earth know nothing of his cursing the creation with barren infertility, while regions like the Alps mock his idea that the Promised Land is all that beautiful. The fact is that the environmental psychology and ecological anthropology of ancient Israelites so accounts for the nature and concerns of this particular god that it is impossible to even imagine Yahweh being worshipped by, say, the Eskimos.

Interestingly the concept of divine eternity in the Hebrew Bible is not always the same as the philosophical sense thereof. In one text, Isaiah 43:10, we even find presupposed that Yahweh has a limited lifespan:

> "You are my witnesses," says the Lord, "and my servant whom I have chosen,
> that you may know and believe me and understand that I am He. Before me
> no god was formed, nor shall there be any after me."

Look again closely and try to take the text seriously. It does not just say that there are no other gods. It introduces a temporal sequence that, if all the texts wanted to stress were monotheistic claims, seems quite unnecessary. Yet most people can read this passage and never bother to ask how it is possible for Yahweh to refer to a time "before" and "after" him during which there are no other gods. This text clearly implies that (a) there is a temporal period before Yahweh existed when no other god existed either, and (b) there will come a time after Yahweh during which no other god will exist either. Of course, this outrageous idea makes no sense in the context of philosophical monotheism, but there it is and against the backdrop of ancient Near Eastern theogony it is perfectly understandable. Gods, too, are born from and return to chaos, and not even Genesis 1 says God created the darkness/waters. To be sure, this allusion is basically the only of its kind in the Bible (although the notion of the divine life, or "nephesh," as diminished in texts such as Exod. 31:18, implies the possibility of degeneration), but because scholars have wanted to see "second" Isaiah as theologically advanced, they have ignored the more primitive elements in his theology.

CHRISTIAN PHILOSOPHY OF RELIGION
AS "NONSENSE ON STILTS"

Just as you cannot argue Zeus into existence via philosophical speculation and sophistication, so you cannot do it with God, aka Yahweh. Yet Christian philosophers of religion who no longer believe in Yahweh as depicted in the Old Testament can still bring themselves to believe in "God," an updated version of the older tribal deity of manifold depictions. They use the latest technomorphic metaphors, which they project onto reality and by way of sophisticated jargon and a generic approach make their ideas seem intimidating and almost respectable. But the fact is that all Christian philosophy of religion, be it fundamentalist analytic philosophy or the most postmodern version of continental a/theology, is just reconstructive mythology. It only seems to work because people forget that God used to be Yahweh. They might as well try to rehabilitate any old tribal god under the universal umbrella nowadays covered by the concept of divinity. Thus any philosophy of religion that assumes the god it talks about is in any way basically the same divine reality as that talked about in the Old Testament is in serious trouble.

First of all, conceptions of Yahweh by most Christian philosophers of religion tend to be radically anachronistic and conform more to the proverbial "God of the Philosophers" (Thomas Aquinas in particular) than to any version of Yahweh as depicted in ancient Israelite religion. This means that the prephilosophical "biblical" conceptions of Yahweh, the belief in whom is supposed to be properly basic, are not even believed by Christian philosophers themselves. Their lofty notions of God in terms of "Divine Simplicity," "Maximal Greatness," and "Perfect-Being Theology" are utterly alien with reference to many of the characterizations of Yahweh in biblical narrative (e.g., Gen. 18). This means that debates about God's power and knowledge and his relation to evil (etc.), whatever its logical merits, conveniently ignore the fact that there are many biblical texts that contradict it (and that offer representations of divinity that Christian philosophers do not believe in).

The problem of evil is a pseudo-worry in many Old Testament texts, where Yahweh was neither omnipotent nor all-good. In addition, the ability to do evil in the sense of being destructive was in fact a great-making property in ancient theism. Yahweh is powerful precisely because he can do evil when he wants, whether natural, moral, or metaphysical (see Exod. 4:11; Lam. 3:38; Isa. 45:7;

Amos 3:6; Eccles. 7:13–14; etc.). Ancient believers were not as spoiled as those today who believe a god has to be perfectly good (read: "user-friendly") before he deserves to be worshipped. What made a god divine was great power (which is not the same as omnipotence), not client-centered service, family values, or human rights.

The second problem follows from the first: What kind of God is it that is warranted according to the Christian philosophy of religion? It is useless to say belief in God is justified unless one can specify what the contents of the beliefs about God are supposed to be (and who this god is in whom one basically believes). But this Christian philosophy of religion is radically undermined by its failure to take cognizance of the fact that it is committing the fallacy of essentialism. It brackets the philosophical problems posed by theological pluralism in the Old Testament and the diachronic changes (read: "revision") in the beliefs about Yahweh in the history of Israelite religion. At many junctions in its arguments it seems blissfully unaware that there is no such thing as *the* "biblical" perspective on God. So if it is the "biblical" God that is supposed to be believed in, most Old Testament theologians would like to know "which version?" (or, "whose interpretation?")

A third problem concerns another way in which Christian philosophy of religion fails to apply the Old Testament's own forms of verification. Now aside from the possibility of pluralism that may once again rear its ugly head (e.g., in the incommensurable religious epistemologies of Daniel and Ecclesiastes), the fact is that it is wrong to assume the Old Testament is not evidentialist. On the contrary, there is ample reason to believe that a primitive type of evidentialism is in fact the default epistemology taken for granted in ancient Israelite religion given the nature of the many prephilosophical assumptions in the biblical narratives. Thus the whole point of "miracles" (signs) and revelation via theophany, audition, dreams, divination, and history can be said to presuppose an evidentialism (see the oft-repeated formula "so that they may know . . ."). Philosophers of religion will deny that one can verify the existence of God in this empirical sense, and yet according to the Old Testament, Yahweh himself assumed this to be possible.

After all, of all the religious epistemologies that come to mind, it is difficult to imagine that the prophet Elijah in the narrative where he takes on the Baal Prophets on Carmel was endorsing anything remotely similar to the Christian philosophy of religion's claims that one need not prove anything empirically (see 1 Kings 18). If that is not an instance of evidentialism in the Old Testament, what is? Christians may have their own reasons why these things no longer happen and why no philosopher of religion will agree to a contest on Mount Carmel. But the fact is that Christian philosophers of religion, be they fundamentalist and analytic or postmodern and continental, all love dogmatic rationalization more than biblical epistemology. Again this shows that not even Christian philosophers of religion actually believe in Yahweh. They, too, are atheists in relation to the biblical divinity.

From this we see why belief in Yahweh is for both atheists and Christians as impossible as belief in Zeus. One might as well be asked to "just believe the Bible!" or any other ancient god. But few Christian philosophers ever ask why it is that a god's main desire is that his creations agree that he exists. Of all the things one could, in theory, worry about—and then do so little to make possible. That a god needs to be hidden and that there needs to be faith to make a relationship possible is simply a ridiculous and unbiblical notion. Moses allegedly both saw and believed in Yahweh, and they had a great relationship. So what is the problem with one-on-one intimacy on a daily basis with every human being, in a time when atheism is more popular than ever? Like Voltaire said before Nietzsche, God's only excuse is that he doesn't exist.

In other words, it is historical consciousness that led believers to reinterpret the biblical beliefs to make them seem credible and that leads atheists today to see why nobody can believe in Yahweh any more than they can believe in Zeus. We simply cannot imagine that reality is a planned setup where one all-too-human, yet superior, entity has all the power, where "might makes right"—God can do what he wants because he is God, exactly the same immorality believers accuse atheists of—where the meaning of its existence is to create weak, frail, and mortal beings to serve it and tell it how wonderful it is for all eternity. Religious devotion is simply the kissing up to power. However, it is not that we are rebellious and a priori do not want to believe in a god, it's just that the whole concept of divine reality as humans have constructed it in the biblical sense is so absurd and so obviously a projection of sincerely deluded humans who thought the cosmos worked the way an ancient human society does, that we couldn't really believe it even if we tried!

That is why theology and philosophy of religion and arguments for God have become necessary—to hide the absurdity and make it all seem convincing. But since when did reality need to convince anybody? If the world was really like that, it would be just as unnecessary to argue for it being the case as needing to argue for the existence of the biological world. The appeal to epistemological malfunctioning in unbelievers is as unconvincing as saying that the reason why we find it difficult to believe in Zeus is because we lack spiritual insight.

After two thousand years the Christian system has almost everything covered, and apologetics might seem to some believers to have an answer to everything. To realize how the trick was done—to see the tain in the mirror and the strings of the puppets—just allow Christian philosophy of religion to be judged by the history of Israelite religion. The best argument against any modern Christian dogma is its own history back to and from within the Bible itself. Christians' own reinterpretations show us that even the most fundamentalist "believer" is really an atheist when it comes to Yahweh, and the most "biblical" of believers are not as biblical as they think. In the end Christian theology was brought down by Christian ethics; belief was destroyed by its own morality, which demanded we follow the truth.

Woe is the believer when in the end (s)he will come to realize that one has to choose between God and truth. It's the kind of experience of "reality shock" one associates with movies like *The Matrix* or *The Truman Show*. But you have to see it for yourself to realize it was the perfect catch-22, the ultimate double-bind for any person growing up in a religious culture today. Unfortunately, like the famous biblical characters themselves, believers today do not spend their time in serious Bible study. Most popular books on the Old Testament are spiritual junk food, brain candy, if you will. And when confronted with the question of why atheists bother with the Bible if they do not believe it, well, maybe it is for the same reason Christians worry about pagans: because one cares about what one believes to be the truth and about the fact that there are so many well-meaning people unwittingly bent on deluding both themselves and the rest of humanity.

CONCLUSION

In a sense, the entity called "God" is like an Internet troll created in a public forum—once you become aware of the agent behind the character, such knowledge changes everything about whether or not we can bring ourselves to believe "he" exists. There is nothing really to disprove, and we need not show that some god, of whatever description possible, does not exist. All we need do is to show that descriptions of Yahweh do not have any counterpart outside the biblical stories. For if Yahweh as depicted is not real, how can "Yahweh" as such still exist? If the god of the Old Testament—who is the God of Jesus—does not exist, how can the God of the New Testament still exist? And if the God of the New Testament is not real, is this not the end of Christianity as a claimant about reality?

So we need not be intimidated by Christian philosophers of religion who need to repress the fact that their sophisticated arguments about a supposedly respectable God ignore the history of Israelite religion. Their god's own biography is an embarrassment to them. They themselves no longer believe in Yahweh, and today "God" is nothing more than an ideal idol, created in the image of the latest technological metaphors projected onto the cosmos. Since Yahweh was never the living god, "God" is dead indeed.

In the end, then, it seems that the history of Israelite religion has a sense of irony. The same ancient and modern people who so mercilessly ridiculed pagans for their myths and superstitions failed to recognize the same superstitious tendencies in themselves. The same believers who deplore products of the human imagination cannot see that a god created as a character in a story on paper is no less of an idol than silent gods of wood or stone.

Chapter 6

GOD'S EMOTIONS
Why the Biblical God Is Hopelessly Human

by Dr. Valerie Tarico

THE QUESTION WE FORGET TO ASK

Have you heard the joke about the little Scottish boy who refuses to eat two nasty shriveled prunes on his plate? His mother cajoles and pleads. Finally she tells him, as she has many times before, that if he doesn't obey her, God will be angry. Usually it works, but this time the stubborn child holds out, and the mother, herself angry, sends him straight to bed. No sooner does he get there than a storm sets in, with lightning and thunder crashing around them. Feeling contrite and thinking that her child must be terrified, the mother sneaks to her son's room to reassure him. She opens the door quietly, expecting to find him burrowed under the covers. But no, he is at the window, peering out into the night. As she watches, he shakes his head and says in an incredulous, reproving voice, "Such a fuss to make over two prunes!"

In the Hebrew Bible, in the book of 1 Samuel, the Philistines are battling with God's chosen people, the Israelites. The Israelites have a very special object, which you might recognize from the movie *Raiders of the Lost Ark*. It is the Ark of the Covenant, a box made of wood covered in gold with sculptured angels on top and a golden jar inside. Maybe it contains manna—food that dropped from heaven. Or maybe it contains fragments of stone tablets. At any rate, the Philistines capture it in battle. The Israelites are angry, and God gets angry, too. No sooner do those Philistines cart off the box than plagues befall them. A plague of mice, for example. Then the ark is taken from town to town, but the men of each town get hemorrhoids, which must have been particularly wretched in the days before toilet paper and Preparation H. (Don't miss the full story; the resolution is awesome: 1 Sam. 6:1–15.) Mice *and* hemorrhoids. Such a fuss over a golden box!

In other stories from the Bible, both Old Testament and New, God gets angry and does things that strike us as a rather big fuss. In Second Kings, for example, the prophet Elisha gets mad because some kids (boys, of course) are making fun of him and calling him Baldhead. Elisha curses them, and apparently God is mad too, because he sends two female bears out of the woods and they maul and kill forty-two of those boys (2 Kings 2:23–24). In the book of Matthew, Jesus is traveling along and he sees a fig tree. He is hungry, so he goes over to it. But it is bare because—as the writer tells us—figs aren't in season. So Jesus gets angry and curses the tree, and it withers and dies on the spot (Matt. 21:18–19).

In all these stories, what jumps out at most of us is a sense of disproportionality. God's reaction seems so out of scale with the transgression! That is what makes us laugh at the joke, because the little boy notices it when his mom doesn't expect him to; and it is what makes biblical literalists squirm about the other stories. We expect God not to be the kind of guy who needs anger management classes. He shouldn't need to breathe deep and leave the room lest he, heaven forbid, do something he will regret. (Note: If you research these stories you will find all manner of convoluted apologetics arguing that God's reactions were, in fact, proportional. Those forty-two lads were Crips and Bloods carrying switchblades. . . .)

Adolescent psychologist Laura Kastner recently cowrote an acclaimed book about parenting during the teen years. The book, *Getting to Calm*, is about "emotional regulation"—getting yourself into a modulated sensible mental space so that you can teach self-regulation to your kid, whose frontal lobe isn't quite all there yet.[1] According to Kastner, calling in the she-bears means that we, as parents, have failed at our own mission—we're in meltdown right along with our teens.

We expect God to be good at emotional regulation, even better at it than Dr. Kastner asks parents to be when faced with teens gone haywire. (If I have to "be the adult in the room," then God does too; after all, he should have this stuff mastered.) Another way of saying this is that we expect God to have a very high "EQ" (Emotional Quotient). When this seems to be violated, we experience dissonance, and we may laugh, question our beliefs, or make intellectual moves to restore a sense of consistency.

What doesn't strike us as bizarre—in fact, what we tend to accept without thought—is the storyteller's assumption that God has emotions. We don't expect him *not* to have emotions, or that would be the crux of the joke: isn't it funny—the kid and his mom think that God gets angry! We simply expect him to have a sense of proportion. The idea that God has emotions seems so natural that most people who believe in gods never question it. The God of the Bible gets angry, has regrets, gets lonely, loves, has loyalties, is jealous, feels compassion, and is vindictive. In the incarnation of Jesus, he also is afraid and weeps.

For a psychology nerd like me, that is fascinating, and I think when you finish reading this chapter you'll understand why. Starting just from abstractions or the evidence of the natural world, it isn't a given that whatever force designed the DNA code would get mad or sad or jealous. Or rather I should say, it isn't a given—in the abstract. We will see that once we add a human interpreter, the idea that God is loving or angry or lonely becomes as natural as the odd idea that angels have two legs.

In religion, people make guesses about what is real based on highly ambiguous evidence. If the evidence weren't ambiguous, there wouldn't be so many disagreements—literally thousands of branches of Christianity alone. But those same ambiguities that make it so hard to come to agreement about God make religion very interesting from the standpoint of understanding our own psychology. In some ways, the concept of God is like an inkblot test. The blot is there, but what you see in it depends on who you are.

All of us engage in a process that Sigmund Freud called "projection," and in fact, those inkblot tests are known in the trade as projective tests. Projection, by definition, is a matter of mistaking internal realities for external realities. If I look at a random inkblot and I see exploding bombs, a therapist might wonder if I am angry or worried (or living in a war zone). Projection happens particularly in social situations and when we are faced with ambiguities. We are angry, so we assume family members are angry at us. We feel rejected, so we assume our colleagues feel rejecting. We are dishonest, and so we mistrust the people we deceive.[2]

How about our images of God? Which ones come from something outside us and which are projections of our own psyches? Answering this question is a process of elimination; to come any closer to knowing what is out there, we need to start by scrubbing our god concepts of anthropomorphism—of projection. We now know quite a bit about the human mind, how it constrains our imaginations by forcing information into boxes called ontological categories, and what kinds of cognitive errors (including projection) it is prone to. Years ago I wrote an article titled "Christian Belief Through the Lens of Cognitive Science."[3] This article is intended to complement that one by examining another chunk of what is known about the human psyche—in this case, human emotions—and to look at the biblical god concept through that lens.

You have probably heard the saying "In some ways I am like no other person, in some ways like some other people, and in some ways like every other person." For anyone who has a god-concept, all three of these dimensions shape it.

- Your image of God is shaped by your personal upbringing and present state of mind. If you have more authoritarian parents, you are more likely to see God as a strict father. If you are lonely, you are more likely to see God as wrathful.[4] If you feel good about yourself, you are more likely to see God as loving.[5]
- It is also shaped by your culture: If your culture is bellicose, your God likely approves of war. If it accepts homosexuality as part of a natural spectrum, your God is likely to become less disapproving of it. Conversely, if your culture condemns homosexuality, that's how your God will think, too.
- Lastly, your God concept is shaped by your species. If your species has a mammalian, primate, *Homo sapiens sapiens* mind, your God probably does, too. Not that we have a great sample to consider. We have only one species with god concepts on this planet, to be exact. What we can say is that across cultures, regardless of what physical form gods may take (male/female, animal, tree, spirit), these deities have strikingly human psyches.[6]

It is this third dimension that will be the focus of this chapter. Specifically, we will be looking at how God's emotions are depicted in the Bible, what is now known about emotions as physical and social phenomena, and how these two intersect. In the process, we may learn something useful about ourselves.

DO CHRISTIANS REALLY THINK
THAT GOD HAS EMOTIONS?

> Ye shall not go after other gods, of the gods of the people which are round
> about you;
> (For the Lord thy God is a jealous God among you) lest the ANGER of the
> Lord thy God be kindled against thee. . . .
>
> —Deuteronomy 6:14–15

> And he will LOVE thee, and bless thee, and multiply thee: he will also bless
> the fruit of thy womb, and the fruit of thy land, thy corn, and thy wine, and
> thine oil. . . .
>
> —Deuteronomy 7:13

Most religions posit the existence not just of a supernatural realm, but of supernatural persons with loyalties, preferences, and other human psychological qualities.[7] This is true in the case of traditional Christianity, which asserts the existence of a whole realm of supernatural beings including angels, demons, human souls, and "God in three persons, blessed trinity."

What is a person? A few years back, my daughter Brynn, then in the sixth grade, wrote an impassioned essay arguing for the personhood of chickens. Chickens should be considered persons, she said, because they are conscious, with feelings, preferences, and intentions. They experience pleasure and pain. They know what they like; they have distinct personalities. (She was arguing that they should be treated kindly and not have their beaks cut off.)

In an entirely different realm, Arthur D'Adamo's book, *Science without Bounds*, explores ontologies that have identified the ultimate reality (aka God) as a person and contrasts them with others that have not. His treatment is deep and nuanced, and I recommend it.[8] But his starting definition of personhood is remarkably similar to Brynn's. It includes awareness, intellect, and emotion. The personhood of God, Adamo argues, is at the heart of Abrahamic theism, including Christian belief and practice.

Even when believers say that they believe in the more abstract God of the theologians, most don't—at least not completely. In their day-to-day lives (and in a laboratory setting) they talk and behave as if they were relating to a human-like person. For example, students who say that God is outside of time will still analyze a story as if he completes one task and then moves on to another.[9] Our brains naturally incline toward interpreting stimuli—rocks, ships, stuffed animals, clouds—in anthropomorphic terms, and gods are no exception.

Christian apologists, meaning defenders of the faith, argue for the possibility of the existence of a highly abstracted form of God that exists beyond the realm of human reason and the reach of science. But what they usually want is something more specific—to create intellectual space for their belief in the person-god of the Bible. They craft abstract arguments to protect belief in something more emotionally satisfying (and primitive and humanoid).

In this regard they are similar to a wide range of religious believers. Humans in a monotheistic context ask four basic questions about God:

- Does God exist?
- What is God like?
- What does God want from us?
- How can we get what we want from God?

In reality, the first of these questions tends to be interesting only in the context of the other three: God is interesting only if he is knowable and has "hedonic relevance." By hedonic relevance, I mean that by understanding or pleasing God I can make my life better or worse.

If God is defined at a level of abstraction sufficient to satisfy many scientists, philosophers, and modernist theologians, he becomes immediately uninteresting to most believers. Consider, for example, Albert Einstein's statements:

> I believe in Spinoza's God who reveals himself in the orderly harmony of what exists, not in a God who concerns himself with the fates and actions of human beings. . . . I cannot imagine a God who rewards and punishes the objects of his creation, whose purposes are modeled after our own.[10]

Within Christianity, Bishop John Shelby Spong takes a stab at making this vision personally relevant:

> I do not think of God theistically, that is, as a being, supernatural in power, who dwells beyond the limits of my world. I rather experience God as the source of life willing me to live fully, the source of love calling me to love wastefully and, to borrow a phrase from the theologian Paul Tillich, as the Ground of being, calling me to be all that I can be.[11]

Contrast this with the God of Evangelical Christians: "God loves me. I have a personal relationship with Jesus. If I ask from God in prayer I will receive. People who die are going to heaven or hell."

Understanding emotions is irrelevant to Einstein and Spinoza's god-concept because the God of Spinoza and Einstein is not a person and does not have emotions. The same is true of Spong's God. On the other hand, if one is trying to assess a more traditional/orthodox Christian view (for example, the Evangelical's god-concept), understanding emotions is highly relevant. In fact, one of the defining attributes of the orthodox God is actually an emotion: love.

Evangelicals call themselves "biblical" or "Bible-believing" Christians. Many are proud to claim the Bible as the literally perfect and complete word of God. (In fact, some modernist critics would say that Evangelicals and other biblical literalists engage in "bibliolatry," or text worship.) Whether right or wrong, biblical literalists like Evangelicals pin their life priorities and hopes for eternity to the god-concept of the Bible writers, and the Bible writers thought of God as a person who not only loves but manifests a whole host of emotions.

"That is ridiculous!" some Christians might protest. "It's obvious that when the Bible talks about God's emotions it is speaking in metaphor." For several reasons, this argument is weak: Historians of religion and philosophy tell us that theology has a flow that can be studied in the historical record. We have a tendency to project our own intellectual culture, including abstract god concepts, back into history. However, during the Axial Period when the world's great religions emerged, the gods (think Shiva, Zeus, Mithra, Yahweh) were typically person-gods.

If we look at the internal record of the Bible itself, it would appear that earlier documents were taken literally by later writers. The book of Matthew, for example, gives Jesus a literal understanding of Old Testament events.

Literalists say that the Bible was uniquely inspired or even dictated by God to the authors. In this case, claiming that in the Bible God's emotions are simply metaphors makes God a bad writer. A good writer doesn't use metaphors that he or she knows will be taken literally. Communication isn't just about transmission—it is about knowing your audience. Today many, many Christians take the notion of God's emotions literally, as have most of their spiritual ancestors. To say that God was communicating in metaphor through the Bible writers is to say that God needed communications training.

For the rest of this discussion, then, I'm going to assume that "Bible believing" Christians mostly mean what they say when they use words like "God loves you" or "God is disgusted by homosexuality" or "God is grieved by our sin." We owe it to ourselves to not play word games about life's most important questions. And, barring evidence to the contrary, we owe it to other people to take their words at face value. If we value honesty, integrity, and truth-seeking, we owe it to the world to ask what those words mean.

WHAT ARE EMOTIONS ANYWAYS?

Emotion is an energetic horse that, wild and rampant, brings us all to grief
And Reason must constrain to keep on course, establishing command and
   being its chief. Yet Reason by itself is hard and cold, lacking Emotion's
   fires to inflame
That passion and affection which draw gold from cruder ore, which is our
   human aim.

—Alan Nordstrom (from "Reconciliation")[12]

The Bible writers spoke as if God has emotions, and most Christians through history have spoken and behaved as if this were true. But to understand what that means, you have to understand what emotions are. And that requires a small excursion into the history of psychology and the budding field of brain science.

We humans have feelings about feelings. By this I don't just mean that we like or dislike specific emotions—I like falling in love, or I hate being depressed—I mean that we have feelings about the whole idea of emotions, and our feelings about feelings have a long history. After a dark age of authority and dogma and religious fervor, the Enlightenment made rationality supreme. Reason, coupled with empiricism, demonstrably led to advances in knowledge and technology that had been impossible when critical inquiry was suppressed or discouraged. In this context, scholars convinced themselves that emotions were a liability.

By the twentieth century, schools of cognitive and behavioral psychology argued that we could understand (and heal) human beings without paying any attention whatsoever to the affective (the "emotional") dimensions of life. Ironically, this hyperrationality probably was driven in part by a gut-level distaste for the untamed "female" quality of emotions. In other words, it was driven by an unacknowledged emotion, a sublimated, sexist version of "big boys don't cry." We now know it to be based on falsehood.[13]

Cognition without emotion doesn't get us very far. Damage to emotion centers in the brain can mean that even intelligent people can't learn from their mistakes, and they make harmful social and fiscal decisions.[14] In his book *Descartes' Error*, neurologist Antonio Damasio describes one patient who can gather and analyze information almost endlessly without it leading to a preference. For a decision to be made, all of that reason and information needs to create a valence, a positive feeling that privileges one option over others that then directs action.[15] As psychologist Marlene Winell has put it: imagine going into a Baskin Robbins and having to choose one of the thirty-one ice cream flavors by rational analysis.[16] In fact, this is one of the primary functions of emotion—when we are presented with choices, it guides us toward one among many options.

The basic point I am making is that, in humans, emotions are neither a liability nor some superfluous fluff like the wings on an angel. They are practical mental processes that serve a purpose. And since the God of the Bible is described as having emotions, this fact alone raises some interesting questions. What exactly are emotions? How do they work? What are they for? And how do these details relate to our notions about God?

EMOTIONS DEFINED

Let's start with a definition. *Emotions are evolved, functional feedback processes that serve the well-being of sentient, mobile animals, and social animals in particular.*
Consider the parts of this definition.

1) Evolved—Emotions have been subject to selective pressures on our ancestors and therefore can be assumed to increase reproductive success.
2) Functional—Emotions have a practical purpose (or several) in the service of surviving and thriving.
3) Feedback Processes—Emotions are a means of representing information about a changing internal and external context.
4) Sentient and Mobile—Emotions have practical value *only* for creatures that are aware and able to change or move in response to external conditions.
5) Social—Emotions are particularly useful for communal species.

Furthermore, emotions have a physical component, a psychological component, and a behavioral component. Anger, for example, triggers the release of catecholamines like adrenaline. Heart rate accelerates, and blood is directed away from digestion and toward the limbs in preparation for action. Muscles get tense. The object of anger becomes a consuming focus and may well end up on the receiving end of aggressive action. Different physical, psychological, and behavioral components together make up each emotion, and researchers use them to measure and categorize emotional reactions.

WHAT ARE EMOTIONS FOR?

Emotions function as a motivational system. In a very real sense, all human emotions can be thought of as forms of pleasure and pain: they are all either appealing or aversive. We are motivated to seek them or avoid them. As Jeremy Bentham said in his *Introduction to the Principles of Morals*:

> Nature has placed mankind under the governance of two sovereign masters, pain and pleasure. It is for them alone to point out what we ought to do, as well as to determine what we shall do.... They govern us in all we do, in all we say, in all we think. In this we are like other sentient beings. All creatures that experience pleasure and pain are motivated to seek the former and avoid the later.[17]

Affective scientists say that emotion is key in three kinds of processes that help animals, including humans, to survive and thrive.

1. **Adaptation.** Adaptation means being able to respond appropriately to changes in the environment around you. If a saber-toothed tiger shows up at the entrance to your cave, the emotion of fear directs all your focus and energy toward the threat. It prepares your body for a fight. If a husband starts flirting with his neighbor, jealousy may motivate his wife to monitor or block their contact. If a Norwegian farmer feels the first flakes of snow on his face, he may feel a surge of anxiety that makes him hurry to chop more wood or get the animals securely sheltered.

2. **Social Signaling.** Ethologists, meaning specialists in animal behavior, and social psychologists say that in communal species like humans, a

second core function of emotions is social coordination. We know this because emotions correlate with very overt, consistent, and (to members of our own species) readable body postures and facial expressions that don't appear to serve any purpose other than communication. In a wolf, bared fangs may communicate irritation or may establish dominance. Bowing or tail wagging may signal submission. An animal that can't read these social/emotional signals is likely to do poorly from a reproductive standpoint.

Among humans, our very elaborate control over food production, shelter, health, and so forth requires an equally elaborate social dance. Without emotional signaling it would be impossible for us to have achieved our current level of technological and economic complexity and population density. A child's distress engages us to provide food or tend an injury or seek a distant parent. A friend's hope motivates us to frequent her new business. As Darwin said in chapter 3 of *The Descent of Man*, "Those communities which included the greatest numbers of the most sympathetic members would flourish best and rear the greatest numbers of offspring."[18]

3. **Self-Regulation.** Self-regulation is the maintenance of your own homeostasis and health. Some scholars use the term "homeostatic emotions" to describe states like fatigue and hunger that provide feedback on the internal condition of our bodies, but the need to maintain equilibrium is broader than that. Feeling wretched outside in the Seattle rain motivates my chickens to huddle in a window-well to preserve body heat. Dissatisfaction with his job got a friend to make changes and start planning an exit strategy. A sense of emotional suffocation moved another friend to leave her relationship.

Our basic emotional system evolved long before the higher-order reasoning processes, and the two function in very different ways. Emotional processing is faster and more diffuse than rational processing. It activates many body systems—muscles, breathing, blood flow, thoughts, digestion, and more —simultaneously. It creates an orchestrated whole-body response, and the actual conscious "feelings" are just one part of the mix. To put it in the language of evolutionary psychology, "[t]he richly textured representations we experience as feeling constitute our conscious access to a high-bandwidth system of computational devices and program interfaces that amalgamate valuation information with other representations to guide decision making and to recalibrate decisions in an ongoing way."[19] Got that?

Reasoning is more systematic. It allows us to incorporate information that emotions would simply miss—numeric data, for example. Also, reasoning is more flexible than affect. It allows us to adjust to new experiences and situations. Remember, our instincts and emotions were shaped by our ancestral environment and early history. When the present situation doesn't match these, intuition and emotion can lead us astray, so reasoning becomes particularly important as a corrective mechanism, a backup system for checking and averting mistakes.

But even though our emotions may pit themselves against our own interests at times, that doesn't mean emotions should be taken out of the equation. Emotions and reason complement each other. Too little emotion leads to paralysis. Too much floods us, and the emotion itself drives behavior. Moderate levels of emotion play an advisory role and help us to distill information down into a decision.

HOW DO EMOTIONS OPERATE?

The reason that an emotional reaction can happen faster than rational processing is that it literally bypasses the cerebral cortex, the part of our brain that manages conscious thought. That is why we use terms like "trusting your gut" or "gut instinct." And yet, the brain can't be divided easily into evolutionary layers like reptilian, mammalian, and neocortex, as once was thought.[20]

In recent years fMRI (functional magnetic resonance imaging) has become a popular tool of neuroscientists. Experimental subjects can be put in an MRI machine and then given cognitive tasks, and researchers can actually see which parts of their brains light up. Imaging of this sort confirms research that has been done with head-injured patients. It shows that the prefrontal cortex and the amygdala play a crucial role in the experience and expression of emotion and, consequently, in decision making.

The field of affective neuroscience has grown and changed so rapidly that for an outsider to the field it can be difficult to keep track of scholars' best understanding of which parts of the brain regulate what. What is clear in all of this is that emotions are situational appraisals that guide the reactions of physical creatures to the world around them. Just like our limbs and internal organs, emotions are integrated into our bodies. Given external cues, emotion sets off changes (mostly unconscious) in whatever body systems are relevant. Digestion, hearing, muscle tone, cognitive frames, sexual arousal—any of these and more can be called into action. Descartes's great error was that he thought mind and body were two separate entities. In fact they are an interdependent whole, a fully integrated system.

What does all of this have to do with the God of the Bible, the God who becomes angry at evildoers and is pleased by the sweet smell of burnt offerings, or the Jesus who loves the little children—all the children of the world? That is precisely what I hope you are asking yourself. If I asked you whether God has a nose or a penis, what would you say? Most Christians would say probably not. A nose is for breathing and smelling. A penis is for sex and for peeing. God has no need of either. In the same way, I would argue that God has no need for emotions—intricate chemical reactions designed to activate and direct bodily responses to the external environment. As wonderful as emotions are, they are made of and for the fabric of this natural world.

A GOD WITH A TEMPER
(ANGER AND SOCIAL HIERARCHY)

> [Wicked men] are now the objects of that very same anger and wrath of God, that is expressed in the torments of hell. And the reason why they do not go down to hell at each moment, is not because God, in whose power they are, is not then very angry with them; as he is with many miserable creatures now tormented in hell, who there feel and bear the fierceness of his wrath. Yea, God is a great deal more angry with great numbers that are now on earth: yea, doubtless, with many that are now in this congregation, who it may be are at ease, than he is with many of those who are now in the flames of hell.
> —Jonathan Edwards, "Sinners in the Hands of an Angry God"[21]

In this 1741 sermon, Puritan minister Jonathan Edwards used the word "anger" three times, "angry" six times, "fierce" seventeen times, and "wrath" fifty-one times. He clearly wanted to make a point about God's feelings. Today, few American ministers would dare preach such a relentlessly threatening sermon.

Fred "God-hates-fags" Phelps, of Topeka, Kansas, has been able to garner national media attention with his theology of rage in part *because* he is an outlier. Popular sermons today are more likely to focus on promises than threats. The late Oral Roberts promised, among other things, that devotion to his kind of Christianity would be rewarded with material wealth, and he became one of the founders of a school of theology now known as the "prosperity gospel."

If you search the Internet, you will find all kinds of Christians arguing that God is not angry or fierce or wrathful, just righteous and bound by the obligations of justice—and aggrieved. "This hurts me more than it is going to hurt you." But if we are honest, Edwards was closer in his vision to many of the Bible writers than was Roberts or today's celebrity preachers like Rick Warren. Consider:

> I will tread them in mine anger, and will trample them in my fury, and their blood shall be sprinkled upon my garments, and I will stain all my raiment.
>
> —Isaiah 63:3

> Therefore will I also deal in fury: mine eye shall not spare, neither will I have pity; and though they cry in mine ears with a loud voice, yet I will not hear them.
>
> —Ezekiel 8:18

> What if God, willing to show his wrath, and to make his power known, endured with much long-suffering the vessels of wrath fitted to destruction?
>
> —Romans 9:22

> And out of his mouth goeth a sharp sword, that with it he should smite the nations: and he shall rule them with a rod of iron: and he treadeth the winepress of the fierceness and wrath of Almighty God.
>
> —Revelations 19:15

Anger, as we have discussed, is an activating emotion. It is a response to pain and threat or simply being thwarted. When we are threatened or our goal-oriented activities are frustrated, anger can make us more focused, persistent, and determined. Socially, it serves to prepare our bodies for defensive action by making us stronger, more alert, more aggressive, and, consequently, more intimidating. It can be almost instantaneous, preparing us to respond to threats faster than our conscious minds can even assess a situation. This is both the advantage *and* the disadvantage of anger.[22]

You might think that if someone is omnipotent, then anger would be unnecessary. The force that created the universe has no need of it. For what? To make him more powerful? More able to focus? To break through inhibitions or fear? And yet it makes a lot of sense that we humans would expect God to get angry.

Consider the situation of the Bible writers. Their image of God as the most powerful person imaginable was modeled on an Iron Age Chief or King who wielded absolute power over his subjects and who was beyond accountability. One example is the situation of Job, who becomes the pawn in a contest between Yahweh and Satan. As a test of his loyalty to Yahweh, Job's children, along with his other assets—friendship, wealth, and health—are taken from him. When Job complains, God says, "Will the faultfinder contend with the Almighty? Let him who reproves God answer it" (Job 40:2). Absolute power allows caprice and cruelty. It always is maintained in part by fear, a level of fear that is virtually impossible to perpetuate without anger's unpredictability.

Saddam Hussein might have been thought of as a modern Iron Age ruler, holding together a nation made of tribal factions and kinship groups that were ever ready to dissolve into more primitive groupings. Hussein's ruthless brutality gave us a sense of what it takes to maintain absolute authority in such an environment. If you read the descriptions of the Israelite kings, even many of God's favorites, you will notice that their regimes were similar to Hussein's. They practiced genocide and scorched-earth warfare. They had female sexual slaves taken by force. They engaged in all manner of palace intrigue, they murdered rivals, and they amassed tremendous wealth, often claiming divine sanction for their worst atrocities (e.g., Num. 31:17–18). The consent of the governed was not even a consideration.

In a context like modern Iraq or the ancient Near East, where disputes are often settled without recourse to police or law, "formidability" is a social asset. A man may kill his adulterous wife in part because doing so increases his status among men. Engaging in visible violence puts him in a more powerful position when it comes time to settle a land dispute or negotiate a business transaction. Anger makes people more formidable in part because it seems so out of control. A king or god who is known for his caprice commands the full attention of his subjects.

We no longer settle many disputes by force or even force of will, and evolving theologies reflect our changing cultural conditions. The angry God of

Jonathan Edwards has been replaced in part by a God who has a wonderful plan for your life or who seeks a personal relationship with you. All the same, recent research by cognitive scientists Aaron Sell, John Tooby, and Leah Cosmides suggests that there may be a biological basis for the intuitive expectation that God is anger prone.

We often think of anger being the domain of powerless, frustrated people, but the opposite may be true. One of the ways that anger functions is as a bargaining tactic. It increases formidability and, consequently, when I get angry, you pay more attention to my desires and less attention to your own. But that only works if you stick around. Most of us dislike being around anger, especially the sense that we are "walking on eggshells." We generally try to avoid others who are chronically irritable, in particular if their anger is unpredictable or dangerous.

But the equation changes if the angry person is powerful. Powerful people are those who can inflict costs on us if we don't pay attention to their wishes or who can confer benefits when we do. They can reject us or injure or even kill us. Or they may be able to give us special privileges like wealth or sexual favors. With powerful people, we want to avoid their anger while staying connected. So when we figure out what makes them angry, we tend to become more compliant.

In a study by Sell, Tooby, and Cosmides, stronger men and more beautiful women were more anger prone than their less beefy and more ordinary counterparts. The researchers theorize that these are kinds of people who in our ancestral environment could have inflicted violence or offered premium reproductive benefits.[23] Having more ability to threaten—or more to offer—creates a sense of entitlement, which when violated produces anger. It is one way that high-status people get the rest of us to do what they want, and because we value or fear them, they get away with it. Who is more powerful than God? Who is more able to inflict costs or confer benefits?

It may be that we are biologically predisposed to be anxious about God's wrath, but the fact that we are disposed to expect something doesn't make it real. Our minds are optimized to help us anticipate and adapt to the feelings, desires, and behaviors of other humans—including high-status humans who have the power to make our lives easy or wretched. It is far too easy to take this same template and project it onto the universe and the supernatural. The Bible writers' belief in an angry God may be, essentially, an artifact of human information processing.

That is interesting but not entirely satisfying. When we talk about God, most of us are trying to glimpse a reality that is external to us, not trying to learn something about the architecture of our own minds. Are we sinners in the hands of an angry god or sinners in the hands of angry humans? Only by seeing ourselves do we have a shot at seeing beyond ourselves.

PLEASING A HIGH-STATUS DEITY (SUPPLICATION, ADULATION, AND SUBSERVIENCE)

Imam Muhammed Baquir is said to have related this illustrative fable: "Finding I could speak the language of ants, I approached one and enquired, 'What is God like? Does He resemble the ant?' He answered, 'God! No, indeed—we have only a single sting, but God, he has two!"

—author unknown

Do people think I am crabby? Or insecure? Or jealous? Do they think I am easily pleased? Happy? Contented? One way to tell would be to ask them. Another would be to watch how they interact with me. Christians spend a lot of time interacting with God—or at least attempting to. We may not be able to tell what is happening on God's side of the conversation (that is highly contested), but we know a good deal about the human half. How humans attempt to approach, influence, or simply relate to God tells us about how they perceive him.

The writers of the Bible provide pages and pages of advice on how to relate to God. Consequently, we have information about how they perceived him, too. According to cognitive scientist Pascal Boyer, most supernatural beings, regardless of their physical form, have human psyches, including emotions. The God of the Bible is no exception. I have said that biblical ideas about God's anger may come from how humans expect powerful people to behave toward those of lower status. In actual fact, sermons and sacred texts that wax eloquent about God's anger are just one of many clues that most of the Bible writers related to God as a high-status human. Most Christians since do, too.

Another bit of evidence can be seen in biblical notions of what gives God pleasure. The counterpoint to the threat of God's anger is that certain ways of relating to God please him, and so court favor. Making burnt offerings, for example: "He is to wash the inner parts and the legs with water, and the priest is to burn all of it on the altar. It is a burnt offering, an offering made by fire, an aroma pleasing to the Lord" (Lev. 1:9).

Besides gifts/offerings (burnt or otherwise), what kinds of attitudes and related behaviors please high-status people? My daughters recently negotiated the middle school world of queen bees and wannabes. Queen bees want to be the center of attention. They like being admired and imitated. (After all, "imitation is the highest form of flattery.") They like exclusivity and often will reject girls who spend time with outsiders to their clique. They like calling the shots. They like bequeathing special favors and getting pathetic gratitude from the lowly in return. If we think about this list, it is remarkably, even painfully similar to what the God of Christians desires from his followers:

- Attention (On thee will I meditate night and day);
- Praise and admiration (For the Lord is great and greatly to be praised);
- Subservience (I will bow before the Lord my maker);
- Dependency (Ask and it shall be given);
- Uncritical Compliance (Receive the kingdom of God like a little child)
- Exclusivity (Thou shalt have no other gods before me.... For I am a jealous god);
- Gratitude (For this unspeakable gift).

These components are central to how Christians relate to God. In searching to demonstrate this point, I went to my browser and typed in, "Prayers for children." The first one that came up, a rhyming prayer to start off a child's day, fit the mold. It included bowing (a gesture of subservience), expressions of gratitude and praise, promises of compliance, including "I will travel where you lead" and "Where you send me I will go," assertions of dependency, and pleas for safekeeping in God's hand.[24]

This prayer was not unusual. In fact, the point I am making seems almost trivially true. What may not be so obvious is the hidden assumption underneath this anthropomorphism. The "submission displays" described above are valued by powerful humans because our species developed under conditions of insufficiency—inadequate food supplies, not enough high-quality mates for every man to have as many as he wants, limited fertile land, and so on. Dominance hierarchies appear in virtually all social animals that need to compete for resources, and submissive displays on the part of underlings allow this hierarchy to be established and maintained without physical violence.[25] For example, weaker chickens duck and move away from food or off the most comfortable perch if their superiors in the pecking order arrive. In chimpanzees, a subordinate may crouch, hold out a hand, or squeak. Humans show submission through both words and behaviors, and these signals are so pervasive that actors are trained to incorporate hierarchy signals into every conversation. This is because acting and improvisation tend to fall flat unless social hierarchy is established among the characters.[26]

As social information specialists, we depend on each other, but we also compete with each other, and to minimize how much energy we spend competing, we establish hierarchies. Our desire to get as good a position as we can in the hierarchy makes us emotionally insecure. We are unsure of where we stand. Signals that other people will submit to us are reassuring. Pleasing.[27] Most people find it uncomfortable to be told that "Islam" means "submission." The images of forced submission can be a little too graphic. And yet the reality is that dominance and submission are an integral part of human relations and of religions with personal gods.

Even though humans are creative communicators, some of our religious behaviors may have specific biological roots. Consider for example the act of bowing one's head in prayer. It probably is traceable to ancient postures that allowed commoners to approach royalty. The word *grovel* today means to show exaggerated deference or contrition in order to appease someone. But its medieval root appears related to the word *prone* and may have to do with the physical posture required to approach the king. A parallel word, *kowtow* means to behave with extreme submissiveness to please an authority figure. But it derives from the traditional Chinese practice of bowing so low that your head touches the ground. But these behaviors in turn may derive from something far more ancient. In other primates, a bow communicates submission to an animal of higher status. It can be a means of avoiding a fight when tensions are high.[28]

In this world, if we understand our place, if we engage in submissive behaviors, then high-status people let us hang around, and we ourselves gain status from the proximity. I recently was invited to an investment club meeting at the home of a powerful woman. Because I was working on this article, I couldn't help but notice the actions of the guests (who were mostly less wealthy and less social). They expressed gratitude for the (exclusive) invitation. Praise for the catering was effusive, and for the garden. The words of the hostess got extra nodding. We all felt lucky to be a part of her circle.

Christians gain status, at least in each others' eyes and in their own minds, because of proximity to God. I am not suggesting that Christians are particularly arrogant, because I don't believe that to be true. I think simply that all of us are wired to orient ourselves according to hierarchical assumptions—they are inescapable—and to seek advantage within the hierarchy. I think also that these hierarchical relationships are mediated by emotions, and that we instinctively expect them in any being with a humanoid psyche. Since the Christian Bible describes a personal god who relates to humans, it is inevitable that believers respond to these contingencies.

If the world were different, biblical Christianity might center on release from desire or ethical study or acts of compassion as in some forms of Buddhism.[29] It might focus on ahimsa or nonviolence like Jainism.[30] But that, I think, would take a different Bible. Like the God of Islam, the God of the Bible is interested primarily in worship. That is what the sacred texts tell us, and believers respond. As a consequence, intellectual assent accompanied by submission behaviors and displays of devotion are core to both religions. The way that believers interact with God, both in the Bible and in modern life, tells us who they think they are talking to. Unfortunately our god concepts fall victim to what we know about big-cheese humans. This not only means that God has emotions but that a lot of them aren't very nice.

IF GOD WERE A DOG—OR A *HOMO SAPIENS SAPIENS*

> Man is, and always has been, a maker of gods. It has been the most serious and significant occupation of his sojourn in the world.
>
> —John Burroughs

Almost two hundred years ago, a young European Christian, trained in theology, set off on a voyage around the world. When he left England, he did not doubt the literal truth of the Bible, and in fact during the trip he quoted the word of God as a moral authority. But he returned with questions and spent the next twenty years assembling the vast array of detailed observations that he had made as the ship's naturalist into a scientific theory that rocked the world—and his own Anglican orthodoxy. In the end, Charles Darwin had many things to say, some with no small regret; among them:

I had no intention to write atheistically, but I own that I cannot see as plainly as others do, and as I should wish to do, evidence of design and beneficence on all sides of us. There seems to me too much misery in the world. I cannot persuade myself that a beneficent and omnipotent God would have designedly created the Ichneumonidae [a parasitic wasp] with the express intention of their feeding within the living bodies of caterpillars or that a cat should play with mice.[31]

Lately Richard Dawkins put the point more forcefully: "The universe we observe has precisely the properties we should expect if there is, at bottom, no design, no purpose, no evil, no good, nothing but blind, pitiless indifference."[32]

Dawkins's statement feels harsh, even to me, and yet the claim he makes is modest. The universe we observe has the properties we would expect based simply on the natural processes we are able to identify. He makes no claims about what, if anything, lies beyond the realm of our observations. Careful, repeated observation of the natural world, however meticulous, will never allow us to say whether there is another realm beyond the reach of our senses and our ability to process information. But they do allow us to understand the intricacies of the natural order, ourselves included. And they allow us to examine our god-concepts in light of what we know about ourselves.

What would we expect god concepts to be like if they were simply a product of evolved human minds? Rather like the ones we have. Pascal Boyer's book *Religion Explained* outlines many ways in which our minds are not blank slates. All kinds of efficiencies are built in—in the form of default assumptions and ontological categories that function, in some ways, like prelabeled filing systems. We force our life experiences into the categories available to us, and one way we do this is to interpret the world in humanoid terms.

Humans are social information specialists. Most of the knowledge we need to survive and thrive in this world comes from other humans. It is collective cultural evolution rather than biological evolution that has let us live long and prosper, outsmart nature's balance, and populate a whole planet. Our minds reflect this niche—specialized systems in the brain are fine-tuned for processing information about other humans. We see the world through a social lens.

Children assign names, identities, and—yes—emotions, to objects that are clearly objectively inanimate.[33] It helps if the object is stuffed with spun polyester and covered in synthetic fur, but really almost anything will do. When my daughters were young, we traveled to visit a friend in eastern Europe. The girls were utterly disinterested in long adult conversations over beer and well-boiled cabbage with beef. At any restaurant, they simply would sit down and pick up their forks and spoons (which had been assigned names and identities) and continue a game in which these stainless steel characters inhabited a world peopled by empty bottles, cups, and pepper shakers. The game lasted only as long as the trip, but a shabby stuffed whale comforted one of the girls for almost ten years.

Adults don't assign roles to silverware, though we certainly can, and we don't usually have transitional objects. But we do give names to ships and hurricanes and then talk as if they had preferences and intent. We become more protective of whales and gorillas if we give them human nicknames. We unwittingly breed canines to look more like baby humans (e.g., big-eyed) by preferentially nurturing the ones that look more like us. We spend time trying to cajole favors out of tree spirits and ancestors and gods. Adults who shed traditional religion may simply move to the next level of (still anthropomorphic, self-focused) abstraction, talking as if the universe itself heard our wishes and could be manipulated into fulfilling them (e.g., *The Secret*).

It is only with conscious effort that we are able to set aside the instinctive projection of ourselves onto the world around us, let alone anything that may lie beyond. And yet, if we care about honoring reality, we must. Author Dexter VanDango put it this way:

> If humanity is to get beyond God as the ultimate human male, for good or bad, it is vital to always keep in mind our psychology, our biology, and our family relations. And it is equally essential to realize that God, if God exists, does not possess our hopes, our fears, our desires, or emotions. If God does possess anything akin to desires and emotions, these "feelings" are unlikely to bear any resemblance to ours.... For if God just *is*, it may be a fact that God has no consciousness, as Nature has no conscious overview, designs, or goals.[34]

A friend put it this way: "I've always wondered how God can be considered omniscient and omnipotent and yet have anything resembling temporal intelligence and all that it implies (emotions, reasoning, etc.). Without time, everything is definite and, possibly, indeterminate even at the same time, and the mind of God would be able to conceive of this." As these two comments illustrate, if we let ourselves contemplate the little that smart humans know about reality, then orthodox Christian conceptions of divinity become transparently self-centered and self-serving. It is a testament to our narcissism as a species that so few humans are embarrassed to assign to divinity the attributes of a male alpha primate.

To say that the descriptions of God in the Bible are metaphors does not make the situation any better. A metaphor about something as deep as the human relationship to ultimate reality needs to be deeply accurate. The center of gravity needs to be spot-on even if the surface meaning is grossly simplistic. But biblical descriptions of God have this backwards. Rather than heightening the sense of an *ineffable* power that is actually compatible with philosophical concepts like omniscience or omnipresence or with the laws of physics and biology that govern this natural world, they force divinity into a human template. Rather than evoking the humility, wonder, and delight of the unknown, they offer the comfort of false knowledge. Rather than being true to timeless, placeless completeness, they are true to the place-time-culture-ecosystem nexus in which they arose.

When the writers of the Bible said God was angry or regretful or pleased, they had only a superficial idea of what these words actually mean. How could they know that these affective labels describe intricate, functional body systems, just like our visible appendages? Their peers didn't yet understand how two eyes create binocularity or how our muscles contract the hand, let alone the chemistry and function of emotions. They are not responsible for their ignorance; they did the best they could with the information at their disposal. They looked at patterns in the natural world and human society and made their best guesses about what lies beyond. We should do the same.

Part 3

LIVING ON BORROWED TIME

Chapter 7

THE ABSURDITY OF THE ATONEMENT

by Dr. Ken Pulliam

What is the central element of the Christian faith? It is the cross. What is the sign of Christianity? No, it's not the fish; it is the cross. What do you see perched on top of church steeples? What do you see around the necks of Christians? It is the cross. The cross, and what Christians believe was accomplished there, is the most basic and fundamental of all Christian doctrines. Many Christian apologists focus on the resurrection. However, without the cross, the resurrection is meaningless.

Christianity is basically the idea that Jesus died for sinners. What does that mean? How does that work? Christians have for millennia debated and disputed this central point. They agree that in some way the death of Jesus makes it possible for sinners to be forgiven, but they cannot agree on why that is true. Unlike the doctrine of the Trinity or the Person of Christ, there has never been a consensus among Christians as to what the cross means and how it saves.

Throughout the history of the church there have been a number of different theories of the atonement, but the dominant view today in evangelical Christianity is the Penal Substitutionary Theory (PST).[1] This view states that God's holiness demands that sin be punished. God cannot remain just and forgive man without punishing his sin. That would ignore the seriousness of sin, according to this theory. Therefore, God sent his son to bear the punishment for man's sin. Jesus vicariously bears the punishment for man's sin. Once sin has been punished, then God can forgive man without compromising his holiness or justice.

The PST is not a negotiable doctrine for most evangelical Christians. It lies at the very heart of the Gospel. It is arguably their most important doctrine. A veritable "Who's Who" of evangelical theologians agrees:

Roger Nicole, professor of theology at Reformed Theological Seminary, says, "Atonement is the central doctrine of the Christian faith, and penal substitution is the heart of this doctrine."[2]

Timothy George, dean of Beeson Divinity School and executive editor of *Christianity Today*, says, "The doctrine of the penal substitutionary atonement of Jesus Christ can be abandoned only by eviscerating the soteriological heart of historic Christianity."[3]

Carl Trueman, professor of historical theology at Westminster Theological Seminary in Philadelphia, says, "The perennial attempts throughout church history to relativize and even deny the propitiatory and substitutionary nature of Christ's sacrifice should not simply be understood as peripheral discussions; they indicate a constant tendency to revise the very essence of the Christian faith to conform to wider cultural mores and shibboleths."[4]

John MacArthur, president of the *Master's Seminary Journal*, says, "Deny the vicarious nature of the atonement—deny that our guilt was transferred to Christ and he bore its penalty—and you in effect have denied the ground of our justification. If our guilt was not transferred to Christ and paid for on the cross, how can his righteousness be imputed to us for our justification? Every deficient view of the atonement must deal with this same dilemma. And unfortunately, those who misconstrue the meaning of the atonement invariably end up proclaiming a different Gospel, devoid of the principle of justification by faith."[5]

Greg Bahnsen, one-time professor of theology at Reformed Theological Seminary in Jackson, Mississippi, says, "The doctrine of penal substitution could be expunged from the biblical witness only by a perverse and criminal mistreatment of the sacred text or a tendentious distortion of its meaning."[6]

J. I. Packer, professor of theology at Regent University in Vancouver, BC, says, "The task which I have set myself in this lecture is to focus and explicate a belief which, by and large, is a distinguishing mark of the worldwide evangelical fraternity: namely, the belief that the cross had the character of penal substitution. . . . I am one of those who believe that this notion takes us to the very heart of the Christian Gospel. . . ."[7]

The purpose of this chapter is to show that the dominant view of the atonement in Evangelicalism, the view that many claim is the very heart of the Christian Gospel, is illogical, immoral, incoherent, and therefore, absurd.

IT IS ILLOGICAL

Punishment, according to the retributive theory of justice, is an appropriate response for one who is guilty of breaking the law. As such, Anthony Quinton tells us, "The essential contention of retributivism is that punishment is only justified by guilt."[8]

The first and most important element of retributive justice then is that the guilty party and only the guilty party should be punished. As a matter of fact, Quinton goes on to argue that it is impossible logically to punish an innocent person. He writes:

> For the necessity of not punishing the innocent is not moral but logical. It is not, as some retributivists think, that we may not punish the innocent and ought only to punish the guilty, but that we cannot punish the innocent and must only punish the guilty. . . . The infliction of suffering on a person is only properly described as punishment if that person is guilty. The retributivist thesis, therefore, is not a moral doctrine, but an account of the meaning of the word "punishment."[9]

Many Christian apologists seem to ignore this problem, but Mark Murphy, in a recent article, recognizes it clearly. He writes:

> [T]he problem with penal substitution is not, first and foremost, a moral problem; it is, rather, a conceptual problem. The problem is not that penal substitution is immoral, but that it is conceptually defective. . . .
>
> [P]unishment expresses condemnation of the person punished. And if that is right, then punishment will be nontransferrable: one cannot express condemnation via hard treatment of someone who one does not take to be worthy of condemnation. . . . If (nondefective) punishment is essentially condemning of the agent who failed to live up to the standard, the violation of which justifies the punishment, then penal substitution is unintelligible.[10]

As both Quinton and Murphy show, it is illogical to punish an innocent person. It contradicts the very definition of the word *punish* as it is used in a judicial sense. Thus, I maintain that the phrase *Penal Substitution* is actually an oxymoron.

IT IS IMMORAL

Let's leave aside for a moment that it is logically impossible to punish an innocent person. Obviously, innocent people have suffered for things that they have
not done. While this cannot technically be called punishment, it is suffering
nonetheless. Is it ever moral to inflict suffering on someone as punishment for
something they did not do? Our moral intuitions tell us that it is not.

People seem to know intuitively that it is wrong for an innocent person to
suffer the penalty that a guilty person deserves. Paul Bloom, a psychologist at
the Infant Cognition Center at Yale University, has shown that even infants
seem to have a built-in sense of justice. They recoil at the idea of the wrong
person (i.e., the innocent person) being punished.[11] The practices of human
courts around the world demonstrate that this principle, that only the guilty
are deserving of punishment, is a universal belief among humankind. How does
man innately know that substitutionary punishment is wrong?

According to the Evangelical Christian, our sense of right and wrong
comes as a result of being made in the image of God (*Imago Dei*). What it
means to be made in the image of God has been widely discussed by Christian
theologians. The evangelical theologian Charles Feinberg says:

> The image of God constitutes all that differentiates man from the lower cre-
> ation. It does not refer to corporeality or immortality. It has in mind the will,
> freedom of choice, self-consciousness, self-transcendence, self-determina-
> tion, rationality, morality, and spirituality of man.[12]

Two of the results of being made in the image of God, according to Feinberg, are rationality and morality. Humans reflect God in their ability to
reason and in their ability to distinguish between right and wrong. Paul confirms this "implanted morality" in the Epistle to the Romans when he writes:

> Indeed, when Gentiles, who do not have the law, do by nature things required
> by the law, they are a law for themselves, even though they do not have the
> law, since they show that the requirements of the law are written on their
> hearts, their consciences also bearing witness, and their thoughts now
> accusing, now even defending them (Rom. 2:14–15).

So, if one were to believe that man was made in the image of God, as evangelical Christians do, then one would have to believe that his innate sense of right and wrong was implanted in him by God. If man knows right from wrong as a result of being made in the image of God, and if one of the things man knows from his being so created is that it is wrong to punish the innocent, then how can the central doctrine of Evangelical Christianity, namely penal substitution, be maintained?

In addition, if one were a Christian, one would believe the Bible when it says that an innocent person should not suffer the penalty that a guilty person deserves. The whole chapter of Ezekiel 18 discusses this matter. "The soul that sinneth, it shall die" (Ezek. 18:4). The son will not and should not be punished for the sins of his father and vice versa. The position is summarized in verse 20:

> The soul who sins is the one who will die. The son will not share the guilt of
> the father, nor will the father share the guilt of the son. The righteousness of
> the righteous man will be credited to him, and the wickedness of the wicked
> will be charged against him.

So, as a Christian, it seems one ought to believe it is wrong for the innocent to suffer in the place of the guilty on the basis of 1) his implanted sense of right and wrong and 2) the clear teaching of the Bible. The problem that evangelical Christians face, however, is that the Bible teaches that Jesus did suffer in the place of sinners. So the Evangelical has to either admit the Bible has some contradictory teachings or else try to explain how it's okay for God to do what he tells man not to do. It seems that the Evangelical is on the horns of a dilemma.

One of the ways that some Evangelical theologians have sought to explain the justice of penal substitution is through the concept of *imputation*. The Greek word for imputation in the New Testament is λογιζομαι (*logizomai*). It occurs forty-nine times. The King James Version translates it as "to reckon, to count, to impute." It is a term that was used in accounting to refer to placing something on one's account. While that word is not used, the idea is found in Philemon 1:18, where Paul tells Philemon in regard to Onesimus (a runaway slave), "If he hath wronged thee, or oweth [thee] ought, put that on mine account." The Evangelical defender of penal substitution will argue that man's sins were imputed to Jesus. In some grand accounting scheme, God transferred the debt of man's sin to Jesus' ledger, and then Jesus paid the debt that was owed upon the cross. There are numerous problems with the theory of imputation.

First, in order for imputation of guilt to take place, there has to be some complicity or culpability by the one to whom the guilt is imputed. Some theologians have argued that Jesus somehow shares in our guilt (though innocent himself) as a result of being a man. In other words, his connection to the race of human sinners allows him to be punished for what they have done. This fails to note, however, how imputation works legally. Norman McIlwain offers an illustration:

> The owners of a company are responsible for actions that happen within the company rules and consent of management. Corporate manslaughter is a good example. However, the company would need to be involved in the action. One employee murdering another in a fit of temper, for example, would not make the owners of the company guilty for the crime. It would have happened without their consent and certainly against company rules. However, drugs manufactured that later are found to cause death would make the company and its owners liable. Guilt would rightly be imputed—because of the company's consent to the manufacture. Consent makes all the difference.[13]

Second, if somehow the guilt of humankind was imputed to Jesus, then he really becomes guilty of sin himself. He could no longer be considered innocent. This would solve the problem of punishing an innocent, but it would destroy Christianity because it would make Jesus a sinner himself. Some theologians have tried to avoid this problem by saying that while the guilt and penal consequences (*reatus poena*) of our sins were transferred to Jesus, the actual demerit or corruption (*reatus culpae*) of sin was not.[14] But this is impossible because guilt and demerit cannot be decoupled. Guilt is the effect, and demerit or sin is the cause. Without sin or demerit, there is nothing for which to be guilty.[15]

So, as stated above, the Evangelical is on the horns of a dilemma. In order to defend penal substitution, he must have either an *unjust Father* or a *sinful Savior*. Either one destroys Evangelical Christianity.

Furthermore, it seems undeniable that the death of Jesus is a human sacrifice. Human sacrifices were common in ancient times. Even conservative Bible scholars acknowledge the prominence of human sacrifices in the ancient world. For example, William Joseph McGlothin writes:

As an expression of religious devotion, human sacrifice has been widespread at certain stages of the race's development. The tribes of western Asia were deeply affected by the practice, probably prior to the settlement of the Hebrews in Palestine, and it continued at least down to the fifth century [BCE]. At times of great calamity, anxiety, and danger, parents sacrificed their children as the greatest and most costly offering which they could make to propitiate the anger of the gods and thus secure their favor and help. There is no intimation in the Bible that enemies or captives were sacrificed; only the offering of children by their parents is mentioned. The belief that this offering possessed supreme value is seen in Micah 6:6 ... where the sacrifice of the firstborn is the climax of a series of offerings which, in a rising scale of values, are suggested as a means of propitiating the angry Yahweh.[16]

The Old Testament often mentions the matter of human sacrifice. For example, King Ahaz is said to have "made his son pass through the fire,"[17] a clear reference to human sacrifice (2 Kings 17:17). King Manasseh, likewise, is said to have made his son pass through the fire (2 Kings 21:6). It is clear that some Jews practiced human sacrifice (Jer. 32:35; Judg. 11:29–40; Ezek. 16:21; 20:26; 20:31; 23:37). While Yahweh was displeased with these human sacrifices and forbade them (Lev. 18:21; Deut. 18:10), his main problem with them was that they were offered up to a foreign god. As evangelical author David Dilling says:

> The greater offense is not the sacrifice, but the idolatry involved in offering such a sacrifice to a god other than Yahweh. The first commandment is not "Thou shalt not offer human sacrifices," but "Thou shalt have no other gods before me." The Bible contains no prohibitions of human sacrifice to Yahweh. The only possible exception to this principle is the legislation regarding the redemption of the first-born sons in [Exodus] 13:1–16. This passage, however, does not condemn human sacrifice. On the contrary, it proves that Yahweh had a very definite claim on all the first-born of Israel, whether man or beast.[18]

In fact, Yahweh's explicit approval of humans sacrificed *to himself* is found in Leviticus 27:28–29. One can argue that Yahweh's command to Abraham to offer up Isaac is further evidence that human sacrifice, in principle at least, was an acceptable idea in Old Testament times. God's command to Abraham in Genesis 22 has been unsettling to many a Christian commentator. Conservatives have, for the most part, argued that it was never Yahweh's intention for Abraham to go through with the sacrifice, but that he was simply testing Abraham's faith. Dilling, however, takes great issue with this notion. He writes:

> The most frequent objection raised against the Biblical presentation of Yahweh and his relationship to sacrifice is that sacrifice, whether of human beings or of beasts, is an element of primitive religion, and that Yahweh really desires not sacrifice at all but obedience. . . . This view, carried to its logical conclusion, would eliminate the necessity of the sacrificial death of Christ. This in turn eliminates the atonement and thereby abnegates the whole Christian Gospel.[19]

Dilling is correct. If one argues that human sacrifice, per se, is unacceptable to God, then one must also maintain that the sacrificial death of Jesus was unacceptable to God. Thus, the consistent evangelical theologian must maintain that human sacrifice, in and of itself, was not immoral; otherwise, as Dilling says, "he abnegates the whole Christian Gospel." Once again the Evangelical has a tremendous problem. His doctrine of atonement is based on the religious rite of human sacrifice, which is recognized universally today as an immoral practice.

IT IS INCOHERENT

Not only is the doctrine of penal substitution illogical and immoral, it is also incoherent within classical Christian theology. It contradicts elements of the historical and orthodox doctrines of the Trinity and the Person of Christ. A key component of the PST is that the Son bore the wrath of God on the cross. According to recent defenders of the PST:

> The doctrine of penal substitution states that God gave himself in the person of his Son to suffer instead of us the death, punishment, and curse due to fallen humanity as the penalty of sin. This understanding of the cross of Christ stands at the very heart of the Gospel. . . . That the Lord Jesus Christ died for us—a shameful death, bearing our curse, enduring our pain, suffering the wrath of his own Father in our place—has been the wellspring of the hope of countless Christians throughout the ages.[20]

The key elements in the PST are: (1) Man has sinned against God; (2) God is holy and cannot excuse sin(ners); (3) God's holiness results in his anger and wrath focused against sin(ners); (4) Jesus Christ, the Son of God, bore the full wrath of God against sin(ners) on the cross and completely propitiated God; (5) This propitiation enables God to righteously forgive sinners, declare them righteous, and thereby reconcile them to himself.[21]

Advocates of the PST believe that this teaching is clearly seen in Romans 3:21–26:

> But now apart from the Law [the] righteousness of God has been manifested, being witnessed by the Law and the Prophets, even [the] righteousness of God through faith in Jesus Christ for all those who believe; for there is no distinction; for all have sinned and fall short of the glory of God, being justified as a gift by His grace through the redemption which is in Christ Jesus; whom God displayed publicly as a propitiation in His blood through faith. [This was] to demonstrate His righteousness, because in the forbearance of God He passed over the sins previously committed; for the demonstration, [I say,] of His righteousness at the present time, so that He would be just and the justifier of the one who has faith in Jesus.

Evangelicals argue that Paul here is explaining how God can remain just (i.e., righteous) and yet still be able to justify (i.e., declare righteous) sinners. He is able to do this because of the propitiation made by his Son on the cross. A key word here is, obviously, *propitiation*. The Greek word (*hilastērion*) can mean either to "placate or appease" or "to expiate."[22] In classical Greek, the word is used to refer to sacrifices that appeased the gods. So the PST holds that through the death of Christ on the cross, God's wrath against sin(ners) has been "propitiated,"—placated, satisfied, and turned away (they don't like to use the word *appease* because of its pagan connotations). This is because Christ bore in his own body the punishment that was due to sin(ners).[23] Now that God's holy wrath had been quenched, He can reconcile sinners to himself and declare them righteous.

There are many inconsistencies between this view of the atonement and historic Christian orthodoxy. First, according to the doctrine of the Trinity, the Father, the Son, and the Holy Spirit are all equally God and share precisely the same attributes. If this is the case, why is it that the Bible presents only the Father as needing to be propitiated? The New Testament speaks of the Father sending the Son to die (John 3:16; Rom. 8:32; Gal. 4:4; etc.) and of the Father being the one whose wrath is turned away (Rom. 3:25; 1 John 1:1–2; etc.). It never speaks of the Son or the Spirit being propitiated. If sin cannot be justly forgiven until God is propitiated, due to the holy nature of God, then how is it that it is only God the Father that is propitiated? Why doesn't the holiness of the Son and the Spirit, which they are supposed to share equally with the Father, demand to be propitiated?

Second, if the Son does in fact need to be propitiated, how does he propitiate himself? It seems to be a contradiction for the same person to be both the subject and the object of that verb *propitiate*. How does one quench his own wrath by punishing himself? Even if somehow it is not a contradiction, how exactly does the Son accomplish the propitiation? The penalty for sin is death, and God cannot die (by definition). Thus when Jesus died on the cross bearing the penalty for our sin, it was not his divinity that suffered and died but rather his humanity. If it was just his humanity, then why was the incarnation necessary? Could God not have just created another perfect Adam and had him pay for the sins of the world? Most theologians would say that the death of Christ is infinitely valuable precisely because he was God. But as already pointed out, God cannot die, so it was not his deity that died.

Some theologians would here argue that while God cannot die, in some mysterious fashion, the God-man did die. The concept of the God-man (the anthropic person) is based on the classical doctrine of the hypostatic union of the two natures in the person of Jesus Christ. The hypostatic union states that there are two complete natures, human and divine, in the one person of Jesus Christ. These two natures communicate their attributes to the single person, thus making the person both divine and human at the same time. However, it also states that these natures are not confused nor mixed nor intermingled but rather retain their distinctions. The early church hotly debated these matters in the so-called Christological controversies, but the final conclusion was stated in the Chalcedonian Creed of 451 CE:

> Therefore, following the holy fathers, we all with one accord teach men to acknowledge one and the same Son, our Lord Jesus Christ, at once complete in Godhead and complete in manhood, truly God and truly man, consisting also of a reasonable soul and body; of one substance with the Father as regards his Godhead, and at the same time of one substance with us as regards his manhood; like us in all respects, apart from sin; as regards his Godhead,

begotten of the Father before the ages, but yet as regards his manhood begotten, for us men and for our salvation, of Mary the Virgin, the God-bearer; one and the same Christ, Son, Lord, Only-begotten, recognized in two natures, without confusion, without change, without division, without separation; the distinction of natures being in no way annulled by the union, but rather the characteristics of each nature being preserved and coming together to form one person and subsistence, not as parted or separated into two persons, but one and the same Son and Only-begotten God the Word, Lord Jesus Christ; even as the prophets from earliest times spoke of him, and our Lord Jesus Christ himself taught us, and the creed of the fathers has handed down to us.[24]

If the divine nature cannot die, then it cannot pay the penalty for sin. If only the human nature died, then it did not have the inherent value sufficient to pay for the sins of the whole world. To say the person who was both God and Man (the anthropic person) died would not solve the problem, because it remains true that the divine nature in the person of Christ could not and did not die, so at best only the human nature of Christ died.

Third, if one holds that the person of Christ (which was both human and divine) did in fact die a spiritual death (which is the penalty for sin: Rom. 6:23), then you have the untenable position that there was at least for a time a split in the Trinity. If the God-man Jesus Christ suffered the penalty for sin as man's substitute, then he must have suffered "spiritual death." What is spiritual death? It is being cut off from the presence and blessing of God. Is this what happened when Jesus cried from the cross in Matthew 27:45 and Mark 15:33: "My God, my God, why hast thou forsaken me?" Martin Luther thought so:

> We do not by all these observations say that Christ did not suffer in a different way from us, and that he was not tortured and dismayed in soul differently from us, or different from what the damned feel in their dread of, and a fleeing from, God. For Christ even in his own eyes was like unto one forsaken, cursed, a sinner, a blasphemer, and one damned, though, without sin. Because it was not a matter of play, or jest, or hypocrisy, when he said: "Thou hast forsaken me"; for then he felt himself really forsaken in all things even as a sinner is forsaken after he has sinned.[25]

John Calvin also agreed that Christ suffered spiritual death upon the cross:

Nothing had been done if Christ had only endured corporeal death. In order to interpose between us and God's anger, and satisfy his righteous judgment, it was necessary that he should feel the weight of divine vengeance. Whence also it was necessary that he should engage, as it were, at close quarters with the powers of hell and the horrors of eternal death. We lately quoted from the Prophet, that the "chastisement of our peace was laid upon him" that he "was bruised for our iniquities" that he "bore our infirmities;" expressions which intimate, that, like a sponsor and surety for the guilty, and, as it were, subjected to condemnation, he undertook and paid all the penalties which must have been exacted from them, the only exception being, that the pains of death could not hold him . . . not only was the body of Christ given up as the price of redemption, but that there was a greater and more excellent price—that he bore in his soul the tortures of condemned and ruined man.[26]

Later advocates of the PST also argue that Jesus suffered spiritual separation from God on the cross. For example, Charles Hodge writes:

The penalty of the divine law is said to be eternal death. Therefore if Christ suffered the penalty of the law He must have suffered death eternal; or, as others say, he must have endured the same kind of sufferings as those who are cast off from God and die eternally are called upon to suffer.[27]

Another Evangelical, Loraine Boettner, states:

We should remember that Christ's suffering in his human nature, as he hung on the cross those six hours, was not primarily physical, but mental and spiritual. When he cried out, "My God, my God, why hast thou forsaken me," he was literally suffering the pangs of hell. For that is essentially what hell is, separation from God, separation from everything that is good and desirable. Such suffering is beyond our comprehension. But since he suffered as a divine-human person, his suffering was a just equivalent for all that his people would have suffered in an eternity in hell.[28]

What none of these defenders of the PST explain is how the second person of the Trinity can be separated even for a few hours from the other two members of the Trinity. Any breach within the Trinity would be impossible according to historic orthodoxy. The three persons are one in unity and essence.[29] A. T. B. McGowan recognizes the problem without offering any solution:

Let me say that I fully understand the difficulty that attaches to this subject of the Son bearing the wrath of the Father, and I fully respect the theological complexity involved in maintaining penal substitution in the light of the need for a careful delineating of the relationship between the Father and the Son. In my view, this is the strongest theological argument to be faced by any doctrine of penal substitution.[30]

There has been a recent attempt at an explanation by Rustin Umstattd. In a paper titled "A Trinitarian Crucifixion: The Holy Spirit and Substitutionary Atonement," he suggests:

> [W]hen Jesus experienced the Father's wrath upon the cross and he cried out from the depths of his being the lament of dereliction, the Son was not separated from the Father and the Spirit ontologically, but experientially. . . . In this forsakenness, Jesus was left alone on the cross to bear the full weight of judgment. At this point, the Spirit is the bond that holds the Trinity together.[31]

I am not sure how one can be united ontologically and yet experientially be separated. It seems the only way this could happen is if someone only felt as if he were separated, but Umstattd maintains the separation was actual and not merely "felt." Umstattd apparently holds that in one sense the Father and Son were separated on the cross, but that in another sense they were united by the Spirit. It is almost as if the Spirit is some kind of personal conduit who keeps the two connected even though they are *actually* separated. I don't see how Umstattd's position avoids contradiction. If two persons are separated, another person may serve as an intermediary between the two, but if the third person is actually a personal conduit through which the connection is ontologically maintained, then there is no *actual* separation between the persons. If the God-man is not actually separated from the Trinity on the cross, then he does not endure spiritual death. And since spiritual death is the penalty for sin, he does not endure the penalty for sin, thus negating the PST of the atonement.

This seems like a logical dilemma for the adherents of the PST. Either there was a break in the unity of the Trinity (which would be impossible), or Jesus Christ did not die spiritually (and thus did not pay the penalty for sins).

CONCLUSION

Since the doctrine of the atonement, as held by most Evangelical Christians,[32] is illogical, immoral, and incoherent, I agree with Tertullian that the atonement is absurd. He wrote:

> The Son of God was crucified; I am not ashamed because men must need be ashamed [of it]. And the Son of God died; it is by all means to be believed, because it is absurd [Latin, *ineptum*]. And he was buried, and rose again: the fact is certain, because it is impossible.[33]

While Tertullian believed the atonement because it was absurd, I reject it because it is absurd. To accept the most fundamental Christian doctrine, namely that Jesus died for your sins, requires one to believe something that is illogical, immoral, and incoherent. In essence, it requires a *sacrificium intellectus,* the sacrifice of our own intelligence. As former Christian Marlene Winell writes:

> The most serious demand for unquestioned belief is, of course, the atonement. First the believer is to suspend familiar notions of justice, such as punishment of the guilty as opposed to an innocent party. You are then expected to accept the necessity of blood sacrifice for sin; that wrongdoing must be paid for, and not necessarily in proportion to the crime. A father's sacrifice of his innocent son is supposed to be not only just but generous and wonderful. Then the temporary three-day death [actually about thirty-six hours] of this one person is supposed to wipe out all the wrongdoing and ineptitude of the species. And finally, you should believe that all you need do to erase the responsibility for your actions and enter a haven of eternal reward is to believe. It's no wonder that once a convert has wrapped his or her mind around this story, anything can be accepted as truth.[34]

Chapter 8

THE SALEM WITCH TRIALS AND THE EVIDENCE FOR THE RESURRECTION

by Dr. Matt McCormick

T he historical evidence for the resurrection of Jesus is important. Without it, the foundation of Christianity collapses. If we do not have enough evidence to justify believing that Jesus came back from the dead, then the central tenet of Christianity, that the son of God sacrificed himself to provide moral and spiritual salvation for humanity, isn't reasonable to believe. And if that isn't reasonable to believe, then Christianity and the beliefs of millions of followers are unfounded.

FAITH ISN'T ENOUGH

Do the people who are the typical believers in the United States—twenty-first-century adults with a modern education and with the benefits of all the knowledge at our disposal—have adequate grounds to justify their believing that Jesus was a divine being who performed supernatural acts? I am going to argue that we do not, and that by the conventional epistemic standards we already endorse in other comparable cases like the Salem Witch Trials, we should not believe that Jesus was resurrected. Before we can consider the Salem argument, however, some preliminaries concerning faith and historical arguments must be addressed.

I take the existence of hundreds of millions of Christians in the United States and elsewhere to be an indicator that the historical evidence for the resurrection is not widely viewed as important. Perhaps it is an indicator of my skewed sensibilities, but I find the widespread indifference to the question of evidence even more alarming than the widespread belief in Jesus. It is not merely that so many people believe, but that so many of them find the questions of evidence, justification, or reasonableness to be irrelevant or unimportant regarding an issue of such profound importance. At its extreme, this attitude manifests as an outright hostility among believers in response to hard questions about their reasons. Inquiries from those of us who have doubts about the grounds in support of Jesus' divinity are viewed by many as angry, intolerant, hateful, or strident.

A less extreme and more common defense invokes faith. Many assert that where evidence fails, faith may bridge the gap and allow epistemically inculpable belief. For them, the question of whether there is sufficient evidence to justify belief is beside the point. The most common uses of the term suggest that to believe by faith means believing despite insufficient or contrary evidence. Faith is invoked when there are some reasons to doubt or think that some hoped for claim is not true—that a favorite basketball team is going to win the championships despite being far behind—but we have faith that it will all work out. At the least, faith is how we describe believing when the evidence by itself, as we see it, does not provide adequate justification, but we are motivated to believe anyway by hope.

In this chapter, I will not accept the faith response to doubts about the historical evidence for the resurrection, for several reasons. One problem is that a person's faith, particularly with regard to such significant issues, is not a private or inconsequential matter. We should not be willing to ignore the fact that Christians have adopted an ideology that has a dramatic impact on their lives and the lives of those of us who live in society with them, but when the question of justification arises, many of them admit that they cannot give sufficient evidence that would make those beliefs reasonable or warranted. As social and political beings sharing a planet made smaller everyday by technology, our lives and our fates are deeply intertwined. Those connections place more and more responsibility on each of us for the safety, health, education, and future of the others. When religious beliefs dramatically affect those relationships with the rest of us, their foundation cannot be left to faith if having faith implies believing on the basis of preference or hope in the face of insufficient or contrary evidence. The rest of us cannot afford to allow the disdain for vital evidence to pass without comment.

If someone's response to my argument against the resurrection is that she has faith, then she and I do agree about something, however. My argument will be that comparable cases like the Salem Witch Trials show that there is insufficient evidence for the resurrection. If someone invokes faith to answer the problem, then it would appear that she is accepting the point. She is acknowledging that in order to believe in the resurrection of Jesus, one must ignore the insufficiencies in the evidence and believe anyway. So we agree on the central point, and what remains is to critically evaluate the prospects of believing by faith.

Another problem with the faith response is that if the believer decides to ignore the insufficiency of the historical evidence for her view, then she loses any criteria that she would have had to sort between acceptable and unacceptable beliefs. If the faithful believer deems the lack of historical evidence to be irrelevant, then the floodgates are now open for a long list of other religious and metaphysical views vying for her acceptance, and the believer has no grounds or criteria upon which to decide which ones are worthy of believing. If the historical facts do not matter, then Islam, Buddhism, Judaism, Mormonism, Zoroastrianism, and thousands of other religious views are all on the same poor footing. Without the tribunal of reason and the demand for evidence, anything goes. There can be no rational or principled grounds on which to prefer a Christian doctrine over a non-Christian one, or even a view about the Great Pumpkin. Faith amounts to "going nuclear" in response to substantial questions about the reasonableness of the resurrection; the believer appears to avoid the evidential objection, but only by putting all views, no matter how irrational or insane, on the same level.[1] Carefully analyzing the available evidence and drawing our conclusions accordingly is the only defense we have against insanity (or mutually assured destruction).

TAKING THE EVIDENCE SERIOUSLY

We should not believe that Jesus was resurrected from the dead. Arguably, being a Christian requires, at a minimum, believing that Jesus was a divine being and he was resurrected from the dead, so it is not reasonable to be a Christian. Put simply, we have too little information, and it is of too poor quality to warrant our believing that Jesus returned from the dead. The problem I will consider here, although there are many, is that believing in Jesus' divinity on the basis of the Gospels in the New Testament cannot be reconciled with the standards of evidence that we employ in other comparable cases.[2] If we look at the sorts of claims that we typically accept or reject and the evidence relevant to them, some principles of reasonableness emerge. If these epistemic standards are applied objectively and without bias to the Jesus case, it is clear that we should reject it.

But before we consider the parallels between Salem and Jerusalem, I must make a few more remarks about the implications of the approach I am taking here. For the Christian to take the question of historical evidence seriously, as I am doing here, instead of resorting to the faith defense, is an important and positive step. By even engaging in the discussion about whether or not we have sufficient evidence for the resurrection suggests a number of important points. First, and most obviously, engaging the topic indicates that one thinks that the evidence matters. This is a vast improvement over the host of arational and nonevidential accounts of belief and its functions that have proliferated in the postmodern era.[3] There are Wittgensteinian, Fideistic, Kierkegaardian, Tillichian, and Plantinga style approaches, among many others where, in one form or another, a straightforward appeal to the facts is not considered necessary or even important to the grounding of religious belief.

As I see it, the insufficiency of the evidence for the resurrection leads to a collapse of Christian doctrine; as these nonevidentialist thinkers see it, the lack of evidence doesn't matter because belief is acquired through some other route or because of the special status of religious belief in our lives. So for the Christian to take the question seriously with those views in the background represents a huge step forward. It would seem that the historical believer and I agree about the basics at least: whether or not we have adequate historical evidence for thinking that Jesus was real and that he returned from the dead after being executed *matters*.

Second, what a willingness to engage in the discussion about the historical evidence also suggests is that this believer is prepared, at least in principle, to change her mind if that is indicated by the evidence. She thinks that since the historical facts are one way, then presumably, she would admit that if they had been another way—if the Gospels had been different, or if different archaeological evidence had been found, or if the facts about how the story of the resurrection came to be known by us were different—then that would warrant our not believing that Jesus was resurrected. And if some new information changes our assessment of the reliability of these historical sources, then we should revise accordingly. The historical Christian cannot have it both ways.

She cannot argue that all historical evidence, no matter what it had turned out to be, would support the thesis no matter what, or she's not really giving a historical argument at all. And on a related note, it would be a gross example of confirmation bias to accept or employ only those historical facts that support the resurrection while ignoring or rejecting relevant and legitimate information that would undermine it.

If the historical Christian is being intellectually honest, then she must be prepared to accept that the evidence could, in principle, *disprove* the existence or resurrection of Jesus, too. That's what gives her argument in favor of the historical resurrection force (if it has any at all). She can say to the nonbeliever, "Look, you're not being reasonable. Here is ample evidence that shows that the things that I believe are true. When we consider all of the relevant facts, they show that Jesus was real, and he was resurrected. Not believing in the face of this evidence is irrational. So, failing to be a Christian is irrational."

A closely related and important question for the historical Christian is "What sort of historical evidence (or lack thereof) would lead you to conclude that Jesus was not resurrected?" If the answer is that there is nothing that could dissuade them, then there's something seriously amiss. The same goes for the nonbeliever who argues that there is insufficient historical evidence to prove the resurrection. What would convince the nonbeliever that it did happen? If nothing would change your mind, even hypothetically, then you are being dogmatic and irrational and there is no need to go any further. I am going to argue that the evidence we actually have concerning the resurrection falls far short, in terms of quantity and quality, of what it needs to be.

The central point here is that the historical Christian already acknowledges many cases in history where it was alleged that some supernatural event occurred, but she does not think we should accept that it actually did. There are accounts of magic, spiritual events, witchcraft, demon possession, visions of angels, voices of gods, and miraculous events within historical episodes such as the Salem Witch Trials, the Inquisition, the founding of many world religions, and in many other ancient histories, but viewing them from our vantage we do not accept them as real. Richard Carrier points out that in Herodotus's book on the Persian Wars, he reports without a hint of doubt "that the temple of Delphi magically defended itself with animated armaments, lightning bolts, and collapsing cliffs; the sacred olive tree of Athens, though burned by the Persians, grew a new shoot an arm's length in a single day; a miraculous floodtide wiped out an entire Persian contingent after they desecrated an image of Poseidon; a horse gave birth to a rabbit; and a whole town witnessed a mass resurrection of cooked fish."[4] Yet despite its coming from an established and respected historical source that provides us with a great deal of reliable information about the past, we all reject these supernatural claims. Many Christians who would defend the resurrection historically will deny real witchcraft at Salem, black magic during the Inquisition, confrontations with the angel Moroni, or a mass resurrection of cooked fish. That is, for the person who believes that Jesus supernaturally returned from the dead on the basis of our historical evidence, there will also be other cases of alleged supernatural events in history that she denies. It is this asymmetrical acceptance of one historical case of magic while rejecting others that is of interest to us here. What will become evident is that the skeptical principles that we apply to historical reports about fantastic, supernatural, and implausible events must be applied with uniformity to all historical cases, not just to those that we wish to reject because of prior religious convictions.

There is a related fallacy that we are frequently guilty of committing. While it is not isolated to religious cases, it is often most flagrant there. Many believers will happily concur with any pro-Jesus argument from history that they hear while treating any historically skeptical argument about Jesus with an artificially high level of criticism. Prior enthusiasm and commitment to a Christian ideology, when brought to the historical question of Jesus, create a de facto nondisconfirmable position. Prohistorical arguments are accepted with less critical scrutiny while antihistorical arguments meet with inordinately high levels of skepticism.[5]

As a result, this faux-historical believer and the historical nonbeliever are actually playing two very different games, although one or both of them may not realize it. There are no scenarios, even hypothetically, where the faux-historical believer would *not* affirm the historical resurrection. If she's arguing for the historical evidence, but in practice she wouldn't actually accept a good historical argument against Jesus, then, in effect, the only historical arguments that she will accept are the ones that support her conclusion. She believes, and she would believe no matter what the state of the historical facts. So the time and energy spent on the discussion could have been better spent by both parties.

We can be more specific about how the deck gets stacked in favor of one's favored conclusion. We now have a mountain of empirical evidence that confirms what everyone who has had one of these conversations already knows: humans have a very strong tendency to find evidence for the conclusions they favor. That is, our beliefs, and the evidence we find to justify them, are distorted in the direction of our desires. While the bias is not confined to Christians, it often emerges when they come to the historical Jesus debate with a strong prior conviction that Jesus was real and that he really was resurrected. If that prior enthusiasm is present, then it is more likely that one will find, filter, or tilt the evidence, consciously or unconsciously, in favor of the prior conviction. Furthermore, the distortions often happen completely without our awareness.

Here are two telling questions: how frequently does someone become a Christian as a result of his considering the historical evidence for Jesus' resurrection? I'm not asking about how often are people led to Christianity by reading the Bible, but rather from consulting the historical arguments that would establish that the assertions in the Bible about the resurrection are true. The strangeness of that question should, by itself, suggest an answer. People do not, by and large, become Christians on the basis of a strict reflection on the historical evidence. By contrast, how often does someone adopt the Christian views held by his parents from his childhood and *then* conclude that there is a compelling historical case for the existence and resurrection of Jesus? I submit that it is much more common for belief to come first and confirming historical evidence is sought out second. That suggests that something else is going on besides an objective, dispassionate, and open-minded consideration of the historical facts.

So the question for all of us that is more fundamental than "What is the historical evidence for the resurrection?" is "Did I come to the historical debate to confirm what I already believe, or am I coming to the historical debate prepared to accept the results of applying fair, uniform, and appropriately skeptical standards of reasonableness, whatever results they may indicate?"

I will argue here that believing in the resurrection of Jesus on the evidence we have is inconsistent with other comparable cases we reject. That is, most of us already reject the resurrection, it's just a matter of seeing and accepting the implications of what we already know is true in other comparable cases. Many people who believe in the resurrection and who think that the evidence renders that belief reasonable already have a set of epistemic standards that would lead them to reject the resurrection. In fact, we typically reject many comparable supernatural claims that have far *more* evidence in their favor.

Historical Evidence for the Resurrection

What are some of the reasons that are frequently given for thinking that there is a sound historical argument in favor of the resurrection? A vast amount has been written about the historical evidence for Jesus. We cannot hope to survey those arguments or pursue much detail here. But let us consider a rough summary of the sorts of reasons that are often given for accepting the historical evidence that allegedly proves the resurrection of Jesus.[6] Not surprisingly, these arguments focus most heavily on the accounts of Jesus' resurrection given in Matthew, Mark, Luke, and John and to a lesser extent on the writings of Paul.

Defenders of the historical argument have emphasized both claims made in the Bible manuscripts and facts about the writings. It is reported that there were multiple eyewitness accounts of the miracles of Jesus, not just a few isolated people. Thousands of people are purported in the Gospels to have witnessed his healing the sick, raising the dead, feeding the hungry. Furthermore, when Jesus was crucified, he wasn't buried in secret. The tomb was widely known and accessible. If his corpse had not disappeared, then a story about his resurrection would have been very difficult to fake. If he had not really died, news of his survival would have been impossible to suppress. A number of people found the tomb empty. On several different occasions, different groups of people are purported to have experienced Jesus resurrected from the dead.

The witnesses were not a homogenous group of religious zealots. They were from diverse backgrounds with different educations and social standings. They were not a strange fringe group. There was not enough time between the events and their recording for a legend or fable to develop. It has also been argued it's highly unlikely that the witnesses had any ulterior motives. The witnesses stood to gain nothing from retelling what they had seen. In fact, they stood to lose a great deal. Early Christians were socially ostracized for their beliefs, persecuted, and even killed. The original disciples believed that Jesus was risen from the dead despite their having every reason not to. Such an event would have been outlandish to them, yet they still believed. They were so convinced that they gave up their jobs, their wealth, and their families to become Christians. Many of the people surrounding the eyewitnesses believed them and were impressed enough to convert. The passion and conviction of the original believers was so profound that it conquered the doubts of all those around them. A whole religious movement that has lasted for thousands of years and spread to millions of people has sprung from those eyewitness accounts.

Furthermore, many of the events of the New Testament have been historically corroborated. Archaeologists, historians, and other scholars have been able to find a great deal of independent evidence that confirms many of the historical claims such as the reign of Herod, the destruction of the temple, and the growth of the early church.

The Gospels focus on a real, historical person. They are not comparable in their age to a book of mythology or fairy tales like Paul Bunyan. They present their account as a factual record of the events in history, not as allegory or fiction. Furthermore, the Jewish tradition of transmitting history accurately and reliably was highly developed and successful.

Paul, who was an ardent persecutor of Christians before, claims to have seen the resurrected Jesus on several occasions. In fact, since he wrote many of the books of the Bible, his account is the only immediate one given by someone who claimed to have seen Jesus. He must have been utterly convinced to have changed his mind about Christianity so radically.

Once we consider all these (alleged) factors, according to the historical argument, it would seem as if no other hypothesis can explain all the elements of the story of Jesus as well. Gary Habermas has presented a popular recent version of this argument. In addition to making many of the points above, he points out that many people who were enemies of the early Christian movement, such as the Jewish leaders, failed to contest the empty tomb in the stories about the resurrection that we have. Their omission in the historical sources is relevant. Furthermore, when his followers are alleged to have seen Jesus after his death, the sources indicate that it created a radical transformation in their lives. They were utterly convinced, and many critical scholars concur that they were convinced.[7]

To bolster the case for the resurrection, Habermas offers this common list of objections to the most common naturalistic alternatives, none of which explain all the "facts" as well as the resurrection does:

> For example, (1) hallucinations are private experiences, while clearly we have strong reasons to assert that groups of people claimed to have seen Jesus. (2) The disciples' despair indicates that they were not in the proper frame of mind to see hallucinations. (3) Perhaps the most serious problem is that there were far too many different times, places, and personalities involved in the appearances. To believe that with each of these varying persons and circumstances a separate hallucination occurred borders on credulity. (4) Further, on this view, Jesus' body should still have been located safely in the tomb! (5)

Hallucinations very rarely transform lives, but we have no records of any of the eyewitnesses recanting their faith. Two huge problems are the conversions of both (6) Paul and (7) James, neither of whom had a desire to see Jesus. These are just a very few of the serious questions for this alternative view. All other proposed natural hypotheses have similarly been disproven.[8]

As a result, Habermas, like many other people, concludes that the naturalistic hypotheses fail, which means that the events must have been supernatural. In fact, the more thoroughly the natural hypotheses fail, the more likely are the historical resurrection appearances. To state this principle more briefly as a mock mathematical equation: given a reasonable explanation, the disciples' experiences plus the failure of alternatives equals the historical resurrection appearances of Jesus.[9]

Habermas acknowledges that people are often willing to sacrifice themselves or die for false or mistaken causes, but he thinks that explanation can't work with Jesus. They were willing to die for their strong conviction that they had seen Jesus resurrected. That makes their case distinct from so many others where people will die for a false cause.

The summary above and some of the details from Habermas give us an abbreviated picture of the historical arguments for Jesus' resurrection that are often given. Defenders focus on some of the inclusions and the omissions in the texts, they triangulate with common sense about human nature. They reason that when the full list of the considerations that they are emphasizing is taken into account, the competing naturalistic hypotheses fail, and the miraculous resurrection of Jesus is left as the last, best explanation.

It should be immediately evident why a number of these reasons aren't plausible. There's no reason to think that people only have those hallucinations that they desire to have, as Habermas suggests about Paul and James. Despair over lost loved ones is known to *induce* hallucinations rather than deter them, as Habermas suggests.[10] And we have ample empirical evidence to show that people's memories are readily altered by context, expectations, and interactions with others.[11] People frequently put themselves at great risk and even sacrifice themselves for extreme and unworthy causes—after Michael Jackson's death, more than a dozen of his ardent fans committed suicide (and enthusiastic disciples frequently post pictures and stories of seeing Jackson returned from the dead[12]). And so on.

N. T. Wright's views about the historical resurrection have also been influential. One of his contributions is an argument that the particular notion of a complete physical resurrection like Jesus' would have been so foreign, so unfamiliar, and so unconnected with any of the predominant ideologies that the followers of Jesus could not, or would not, have come up with it on their own. The only place they could have gotten such a novel idea, Wright argues, is if Jesus was actually resurrected:

> It is out of the question, for a start, that the disciples were simply extrapolating from the teaching of Jesus himself. One of the many curious things about Jesus' teaching is that though resurrection was a well-known topic of debate at the time, we only have one short comment of his on the subject.[13]

What's puzzling about Wright's argument here is the conflation of the attributions to Jesus we have in the Gospels with everything that Jesus would have ever said to the disciples (assuming that Jesus existed at all). Are we to think that everything that Jesus ever said is recorded in the Gospels? Were there no other unreported conversations between Jesus and his followers during all the years of his work? The principle that Wright is assuming and that we must reject appears to be: "If the Gospels do not record a claim, then Jesus did not make it." Furthermore, the Gospels report Jesus discussing resurrection no less than eleven times, sometimes elaborately, and many of those occasions specifically and explicitly predicting his own resurrection:

- Matthew 22:23–33/Mark 12:18–27/Luke 20:27–39
- Matthew 12:38–42, 16:4/Luke 11:29–32
- Matthew 16:21/Mark 8:31/Luke 9:22/John 2:18–22 (cf. Matthew 27:62–65)
- Matthew 17:9–13/Mark 9:9–13
- Matthew 17:22–23/Mark 9:31
- Matthew 19:27–30
- Matthew 20:18–19/Mark 10:34/Luke 18:30–33
- Matthew 26:32/Mark 14:28
- Luke 16:19–31
- John 5:24–29
- John 11:21–27

So Wright is in the difficult position of arguing that while a resurrection was an active topic of interest and discussion for the early Christians, the particular sort of resurrection that Jesus underwent was too novel to have been invented, imagined, deceived, or mistaken about.

Wright goes on to argue that they could not have gotten the particular idea of a physical resurrection like the one that Jesus supposedly underwent from any of the Jewish traditions, which include nothing about it:

> Almost all early Christians known to us believed that their ultimate hope was the resurrection of the body. There is no spectrum such as in Judaism. . . . the early Christian belief in resurrection had a much more precise shape and content than anything we find in Judaism. . . . Where did this idea come from? Not from any ancient paganism known to us; and not, or not straightforwardly, from any ancient Judaism.[14]

Wright then repeats the (fallacious) argument that Jesus himself could not have been the source of the idea since there is no record of him mentioning that particular type of resurrection in the surviving writings we have. Wright then devotes some cursory discussion to considering and rejecting the rival non-supernatural hypotheses and concludes

> [t]he origins of Christianity, the reason why this new movement came into being and took the unexpected form it did, and particularly the strange mutations it produced within the Jewish hope for resurrection and the Jewish hope for a Messiah, are best explained by saying that something happened, two or three days after Jesus' death, for which the accounts in the four Gospels are the least inadequate expression we have.[15]

That is, the possibility of people's hallucinating, or imagining, fabricating, or being mistaken about it is so low, given the provenance of the idea, that the only place they could have gotten it is from a real supernatural event. The idea's coming from another source would have been more miraculous than the idea's coming from an actual resurrection, to borrow Hume's locution.

It should be clear how utterly untenable this idea is despite the considerable scholarly credentials and vigor that Wright brings to it. Do we really want to adopt the general view that people are incapable of coming up with a novel idea unless that idea is already embedded in their religious, cultural, and philosophical tradition? Such a view has no plausibility. Even worse, Wright seems to believe that since the idea does not have a clear presence in the works of the now-famous philosophers and theologians of the period, then *no one* in the entire era could have thought of it. I don't see why we should give any credence to the suggestion that the contents of imaginings, hallucinations, ecstatic religious delusions and visions, gossip, hearsay, bereavements, altered states of consciousness, mythological drift, and so on must *all* be narrowly confined to only those concepts that have a clear presence in the tiny portion of philosophical and religious doctrines of the prior era that have survived to us. To the contrary, the diversity of views about resurrection that even Wright documents demonstrates people were routinely innovating different ideas of resurrection, so to see the Christians doing so is not improbable *at all*. And when the whole range of ideas then circulating is taken into account, there actually is nothing all that novel in what the Christians came up with.[16]

The omissions, biases, and lack of incredulity in Wright and Habermas are typical of many of the apologetic works that support the historical resurrection, which alone tells us there is really no sound historical argument here, just attempts to paint one up.[17] But rather than address all the points in arguments like Habermas's and Wright's, let us turn to the more general question: Under what circumstances in a historical case should we conclude that a miraculous, supernatural, or magical event has occurred? The problem with the historical arguments for the resurrection is that there are so many other analogous cases where we reject comparable supernatural claims, *even when the evidence is of a better quantity and quality than what we have for Jesus.*

THE SALEM WITCH TRIALS

Between 1692 and 1693, dozens of people were accused, arrested, tried, and were tortured or hanged for "Sundry acts of Witchcraft," possession by devils, and other supernatural ill deeds in Salem, Massachusetts. The events began with the strange behavior of some little girls, which fed suspicions. The girls ran about and froze in grotesque postures, complained about biting and pinching sensations, and had violent seizures.

Ultimately over 150 people were accused. In the end, nineteen people including Sarah Goode and Rebecca Nurse had been sentenced and executed. William Phips, the governor of Massachusetts, got involved. A court was established with judges, prosecutors, defenders, and a large number of respected members of the community. Thorough investigations were conducted. Witnesses were carefully cross-examined. A large body of evidence was meticulously gathered. Many people confessed. The entire proceedings were carefully documented with thousands of sworn affidavits, court documents, interviews, and related papers, a scale of surviving evidence vastly greater and more reliable than anything we have for the resurrection of Jesus.

Evidence for Witchcraft?

Suppose we were to treat the historical evidence and the possibility of magic at Salem the way the evidence for the resurrection has been treated. That is, suppose the women at Salem really possessed some supernatural powers or the ability to harness forces beyond the natural realm to make magical events happen. The interesting and crucial question for us is, what is the state of our evidence supporting this hypothesis? Is the evidence we have adequate to justify concluding there was real magic at Salem?

First, hundreds of people were involved in concluding that the accused were witches. They testified in court, signed sworn affidavits, and demonstrated their utter conviction that the accused were witches. Furthermore, the people attesting to the witchcraft charge came from diverse backgrounds and social strata. They included magistrates, judges, the governor of Massachusetts, respected members of the community, husbands of the accused, and so on. These people had a great deal to lose by being correct—men would lose their wives, children would lose their mothers, community members would lose friends they cared about. It seems very unlikely that they could have had ulterior motives. Accusing a friend or wife of being a witch would very likely have the horrible outcome of getting them executed.

How good was the evidence-gathering process at the time? The trials were a part of thorough, careful, exhaustive investigations. They deliberately gathered evidence and made a substantial attempt to objectively sort out truth from falsity. In the court trials, they attempted to carefully discern the facts. That there were witch trials in Salem and that many people were put to death has been thoroughly corroborated by a range of other historical sources (whereas no such trials, investigations, or efforts are recorded concerning the resurrection of Jesus). It also seems abundantly clear that the accusers, or at least a significant number of them, were utterly convinced that the women were witches.

Why else would so many people agree and act so decisively and with such conviction? It strains credibility to suggest that there was a conspiracy or a mass hallucination shared by all of the hundreds of people involved. The same hallucination cannot be had by large groups of people.

What about the state of the evidence as it was passed to us, centuries later? The Salem Witch Trials were historically recent, so we have hundreds of the actual documents that were part of the evidence. We have the signed, sworn testimonies of the very eyewitnesses claiming to have seen the magic performed—again, not as it was repeated and relayed for decades to unknown others, but from the witnesses themselves immediately after it occurred.[18] We even have whole volumes written by witnesses to the trials such as Cotton Mather and John Hale. How much evidence do we have? Enough to fill a truck. Modern archives at the University of Virginia and elsewhere have thousands of documents, books, records, transcripts, affidavits, testimonials, and other works detailing the events. That there were witch trials that convicted the women is beyond a shadow of historical doubt. We have nothing like any of this for the resurrection of Jesus.

In short, if we approach Salem the way it has been argued we must approach Jerusalem, the resounding conclusion is that the accused in Salem *really were witches*.

But They Weren't Witches

Of course, I am not making a serious case for real witchcraft at Salem. I do not think you should conclude that the accused were really witches. Real witchcraft is *one* of the possible hypotheses that could explain the events in Salem, but it is not the best or most probable one. The point is that they were not really witches, and you (hopefully) do not believe that they were on the basis of this substantial body of historical evidence. If you do, then there is another discussion we must have. For now, I will assume that you do not.

If we take the attempts to prove the resurrection of Jesus on historical grounds seriously, then in order to be consistent we must also accept that the Salem witches actually performed acts of black magic. In fact, the Salem comparison (and there are many others) has an ironic result. When it is put up against the case for the resurrection, in every important respect, the historical evidence for witchcraft at Salem is *better* than the historical argument for the resurrection. In the Salem case, we have thousands of the actual documents. The events were actively investigated by thoughtful, educated, relatively modern people. The trials were a mere three hundred years ago, not two thousand. We have the actual documents (whereas we do not have any of the original Gospels, only copies from centuries later). We have the actual sworn testimony of people claiming to have seen the magic in Salem performed. The girls were repeatedly examined and interviewed. A large number of people devoted a great deal of time and energy to carefully analyzing their states and concluded that whatever was wrong with them must be of a supernatural origin. The Gospel stories are only a few anecdotal, hearsay stories from passionate and committed religious adherents that were passed by word of mouth through an unknown number of people for decades before being written down. The resurrection story was repeated an unknown number of times by an unknown number of people until it was written down by the (unknown) author of Mark. The ending of Mark, with the details of Jesus' return, was *added* to Mark *by someone else* over a century later. Matthew and Luke, it is widely acknowledged, got their stories from Mark and possibly one other source that is now lost. John was written later still. All that remains of those stories are copies of copies from decades or even centuries later that were actively culled from a wider range of more varied writings.

By any reasonable measure of *quantity* and *quality*, the evidence we have that there were real witches in Salem is vastly better than the evidence we have for the magical return from the dead by Jesus. But despite the better evidence, it is simply not reasonable to believe that the women in Salem really were witches or that they really performed magic. No reasonable person with a typical twenty-first-century education believes that since they were tried, convicted, and executed for witchcraft, they really were witches. This example should produce a great deal of cognitive dissonance for the Christian who accepts the historical argument for Jesus; you can't consistently accept Jesus' returning from the dead while rejecting the real magical powers of the Salem witches. Something has got to give.

There are several responses to the comparison available. The correct answer, the one that I have been arguing for, is that we should reject magic both in Salem and in Jerusalem. The conventional standards of evidence, common sense, and the advancement of our understanding of the natural world all serve us well in concluding that there was no real witchcraft in the 1690s and that a host of other alleged supernatural events never happened; those same standards should be applied without bias to the resurrection.

A more radical attempt to salvage the resurrection entails biting the bullet and accepting magic both at Salem and Jerusalem. This would require dramatically lowering one's threshold of required evidence that an extraordinary supernatural event occurred to the point that you accept both the resurrection of Jesus and the magical powers of the Salem witches and a great deal else besides. Indeed, there will be some who believe that supernatural forces, magic, and spiritual phenomena are quite common, so acknowledging real witchcraft at Salem may not seem that troubling. But there are a number of problems with this "magic in both" response: it doesn't seem reasonable to conclude that the best explanation of what happened at Salem is that they really were witches. First, the real magic view would run contrary to the views of historians, scholars, and the rest of us who endorse some naturalistic explanation. You would also be lowering your evidential standards to a dangerously low threshold. If both cases were real magic, then you must draw a similar conclusion in the thousands or even millions of other comparable cases that meet the same low threshold established by the paltry evidence for the resurrection. In 2007, a Saudi Arabian court convicted a woman of witchcraft. On YouTube there are countless *videos*—a powerful form of evidence not available in the Jesus or Salem cases—of allegedly magical, spiritual, supernatural, and miraculous events occurring. If magic was real in Salem and Jerusalem, then by extension of this liberal threshold, the world is awash in spiritual forces, magic, demons, psychic events, miracles, and other supernatural occurrences. The problem is that in the vast majority of these cases, people are making a mistake, and we can uncover, critique, or figure out what's really going on in many of them. We know that people get confused, they are easily swayed by sleight-of-hand tricks, they make mistakes, their enthusiasm carries them away, they are hopeful, they confabulate and misremember, and they are often just poor critical thinkers. Investigations of these cases show that a principle that concludes that the two magical events were real is misguided; it's too liberal.

It gets worse. If the believer's response is that magic is real in Salem and in Jerusalem, and it is reasonable to believe it on the basis of the historical evidence, then they open the door to thousands of other religious movements that present comparable (and comparably poor) historical proof for *their* magic. Unless we cheat, there's no way to custom-tailor the threshold for acceptable historical supernatural claims so that Christianity is the only movement that ends up being reasonable. You either get Christianity and a whole bunch of other magical and religious marvels or you get none of them. One problem with accepting all the other movements is that so many of them lay claim to exclusivity. Lots of them, on the basis of *their* historical miracles, claim that theirs is the "one true religion" and "one true God," and that the others must be rejected as false. If we let them all in, then we have a number of conflicting doctrines that the lowered criteria for reasonable historical supernatural claims says we must all accept as true. The truths claimed behind the miracles of Islam are incompatible with the truths that underlie the miracles of Christianity; Mormonism is incompatible with Catholicism; Hinduism is incompatible with Judaism; and so on.

The short answer here is simply that a reasonable person should not lower their threshold of acceptance to the point that all of these demonstratively false cases flood in through the gates. The cost of allowing both Salem and Jesus in amounts to being gullible, contradictory, or just wrong about too many other events. True, if the believer accepts magic both at Salem and in Jerusalem, then at least that position has the virtue of some consistency. The embarrassing part is that this person has said something that the vast majority of thoughtful, educated adults find utterly ridiculous, namely that the women in Salem really were performing magic. The Salem Witch Trials, in the minds of the vast majority of thoughtful people, are the consummate example of just how far astray human enthusiasm and fear can take even large groups of people into irrationality. Most people now see them as a frightening example of how enthusiasm, hysteria, social pressure, anxiety, and religious fervor can be powerful enough to lead ordinary people to do such extraordinary and mistaken things. "Witch hunt" has come to be synonymous with an irrational and emotionally heated persecution. Indeed, the reasons historians are so interested in the case is that we're all sure that they weren't witches, but all of those otherwise normal, reasonable people got themselves convinced that they were. What's remarkable is that so many people could talk themselves into something that was so clearly false.

It is difficult not to conclude that someone who would bite this bullet is deep in the grips of an ideology. Accepting that Jesus and the women at Salem were magical beings forces you to accept a world that is teeming with spiritual and supernatural powers. The world you inhabit with cell phones, rapid genetic analyses, sophisticated biochemical cancer treatments, handheld computers with fifty-nanometer silicon etched chips, planes that can fly at seven thousand miles per hour, and spacecraft that can leave the solar system is also overrun with ghosts, demons, magical spells, fairies, elves, and psychic powers.[19] The dissonance between the two realms demands some substantial justification. How is it that both of these radical kinds of forces and entities cohabitate in our world, and why is it that despite their ubiquity, we cannot find any compelling evidence for these spooky occurrences? And ultimately, this response to the Salem case will be disproved by this spooky worldview's peculiar and false accounts of the most ordinary phenomena. If these things are real and are so common, then where are they and why can we not find any better evidence in their favor than the passionate testimonials of unscientific converts? Do the demons and miracles only manifest themselves when there are no credible witnesses or skeptics present?

To be fair, there could be situations where believing in real witchcraft is reasonable. For at least some of the people in Salem, it may have been a fair conclusion to draw given the other things they knew, the context, the levels of education available, the culture, and the beliefs of those around them (although probably not for the accused). And it may have even been reasonable for some early Christians to believe that Jesus was resurrected depending on what sorts of information and background they had. But the question is not about what's reasonable for *them* to believe, it is about what is reasonable for the ordinary person to believe now, knowing what we now know.

Alternately, someone might try to salvage the resurrection by arguing that the Salem and Jerusalem cases are importantly different in some respects, and those differences justify denying witchcraft at Salem while accepting Jesus' return from the dead. One might argue that there are important defeaters in the case of Salem that are not present in the Jesus case, or there are powerful points in favor of Jesus that are not shared by the Salem example. So accepting Jesus and rejecting Salem is not inconsistent, on this view, because there is a principled separation of the cases.

This approach appears to be doomed to fail, too, and amounts to ad hoc rationalizing. One problem is that any such approach will have to be reconciled with the fact that we have so much more information about Salem. If someone wishes to argue that we are justified in concluding that there were natural causes in Salem on the basis of the evidence, they face a challenge when it comes to defending Jesus. They will also need to argue that we have substantial reasons to believe that nothing like *that* explanation is likely to be true with

Jesus, and that we can be sure that a similar naturalized account cannot be correct on the basis of a much smaller, more fragmented, older, and less corroborated body of information. That we have only a few stories (that conflict on many important details) recorded on the basis of unknown hearsay testimony decades after the fact, and lacking in any recorded attempt at a soundly principled inquiry by anyone, will be the undoing of many attempts to argue that we can definitively rule out some alternate natural explanation of what happened. We just don't have enough good information about Jesus to rule anything out definitively (see Robert Price's next chapter in this very book—and those aren't even the only likely explanations available, as Richard Carrier's chapter on this same subject in *The Christian Delusion* reveals).

Since there is so much evidence available concerning Salem, there remains a *better* possibility that we may find grounds that *justify* some naturalistic explanation in the Jesus case as well. The lack of good evidence in that case, and the extent to which the accounts of Jesus have been cultivated, altered, and canonized will make it very difficult to rule out any comparable natural explanation with any confidence.

The other major challenge for the critic who wishes to reject the Salem-Jesus comparison is that we don't need to be deeply committed to the Salem case to make the point. There are many other examples where we can find a body of information that is as good or better than the Jesus evidence for the conclusion that some supernatural event occurred, but it is not reasonable to draw that conclusion. Hundreds of thousands of Hindus have claimed to have witnessed statues of the Lord Ganesh drinking milk. Millions of thoughtful, educated, fairly reasonable people have left the shrine at Lourdes, France, utterly convinced that they have witnessed a miraculous (and very distinctly Catholic) healing. Gurus, New Age spiritualists, and other quasi-religious leaders gather millions of devoted followers who become deeply convinced that their spiritual adviser possesses otherworldly powers. The original accounts of Islam, Mormonism, Buddhism, and Hinduism are filled with comparable supernatural claims, and the circumstances surrounding their advent resemble Christianity in many respects. Whatever particular virtues that may strike us about the case for the historical resurrection, there are numerous non-Jesus cases where the evidence is just as good or better by those same criteria, but where the reasonable view is to reject the magical conclusion.

A defender of the historical case for Jesus' supernatural powers may opt to emphasize this feature of the information or that one. She may present us with a list of what she takes to be the virtues of the evidence about Jesus that make it reasonable to conclude that the best possible explanation is that Jesus really had supernatural powers. Whatever those general features of the evidence are, we must ask this question: In general, is it true that we should accept as reasonable some supernatural explanation *whenever* the evidence for the supernatural event has these features? If they approach that question objectively without any ad hoc qualifications in favor of the Christian conclusion, they will be disappointed. They will find numerous other cases where (1) we have a body of evidence that is as good or better than the one for Jesus; (2) it possesses the virtues that are being touted (e.g., numerous witnesses of high character, devotees with no apparent ulterior motive, utter conviction among the followers, and so on); and yet, (3) it is not reasonable to accept the supernatural conclusion in that other case. The Salem argument is just one example among many others that illustrates that, in general, it is not reasonable to accept the strong, magical conclusion when those features are present, or even when the body of evidence is far better along those vectors than the Jesus case.

Advocates of the historical resurrection have sometimes argued that unless some natural explanation can be successfully defended, then we must accept the supernatural conclusion. If the naturalistic explanations that we can come up with all fail, then the resurrection must be real. There's a mistake concealed in this innocuous-sounding approach. What the Salem example illustrates is that one need not believe or defend any particular alternative natural explanation, such as the rotten rye grain/hallucination theory, in order to conclude reasonably that they weren't witches. We believe that it is reasonable to think that there were no real witches at Salem even without knowing exactly what happened. In historical matters, there is always much that we do not know. The Salem case shows that we don't need to have a fully articulated naturalistic explanation in place, with all the requisite supporting evidence, in order to believe reasonably that there is one. Even if it turns out that a number of proposed naturalistic hypotheses do not readily fit with what we believe are the facts about the case, it would not follow from those failures alone that we should default to the supernatural explanation as the best or default hypothesis. At this point in history, we have seen countless examples of allegedly strange, or unexplained phenomena that resisted our efforts to explain them. Then later, when we continued to work on it or after we had learned more about ourselves and the world, the answers became clear to us. The real source of the bubonic plague (not demon possession or God's wrath for our sinfulness) wouldn't become clear to us for *several centuries*, when the plague bacillus was discovered.

This is not to rule out the magical explanation a priori—it remains a possibility, I suppose. But clearly the threshold of proof for reasonable people is and should be very high before magic becomes the *best* of all imaginable hypotheses. History has taught us that there is a very strong presumption in favor of naturalistic causes.[20] And not even the copious body of evidence for real witchcraft at Salem is enough to meet or exceed that threshold. A fortiori, the paltry body of evidence we have in favor of Jesus' resurrection certainly does not achieve that level. Among other things, the Salem Witch Trials show that it is possible to meet an even heavier burden of proof than what we have for the resurrection of Jesus, and yet it remains unreasonable to believe that anything magical happened. No clearheaded person should accept the claim that the historical evidence makes it reasonable to believe that Jesus came back from the dead, even if they don't have an alternative natural explanation that they believe fits with the available evidence. This is not to say that we can know a priori that only natural events occurred in 33 CE. Surely there must be some threshold of evidence that could, in principle, make it reasonable to believe that Jesus was resurrected. But the evidence we have falls far short of that threshold.

The sheer lack of information about the Jesus case will haunt the believer who wishes to argue that it is disanalogous with Salem. Any attempt to separate the two cases will be up against this question: Whatever the (alleged) differences between the two are, what are the unique features of the Jesus case that permit us to *lower* the threshold enough so that the small, fragmented, disconnected, and hearsay evidence is historically sufficient to prove a *resurrection*? Even if they *are* disanalogous, the information we have is still too poor to achieve the task that has been put to it.

CONCLUSION

The Salem case shows that by the ordinary standards of skepticism and evidence that most of us employ in other cases, we would not accept the claim that Jesus was resurrected from the dead. We are being inconsistent in accepting one while rejecting so many others, particularly other cases that have resoundingly better evidence in their favor. The considerations raised here cast enough doubt on the resurrection for a reasonable person to refuse the historical argument. The Salem case shows that even when a much higher burden of proof has been met with rigorous court trials, active investigations, witness interviews, and critical analysis, the supernatural explanation is still not warranted. So, a fortiori, believing in the return of Jesus on the underwhelming evidence that is available to us in *that* case is even more unreasonable. At the very least, a consistent and objective application of sound principles of evidence to all cases should have the effect of diminishing a person's estimate of the possibility of a real resurrection and elevating their estimate of the probability of some other nonsupernatural explanation enough to tip the scales against Jesus. All things considered, and by the standards of evidence that we already employ in other comparable cases, one should believe that the overall likelihood of some natural explanation is greater than a real resurrection. That is, you already don't believe in Jesus.

Chapter 9

EXPLAINING THE RESURRECTION WITHOUT RECOURSE TO MIRACLE

by Dr. Robert M. Price

It is one thing to decide that one must seek a naturalistic alternative to a miraculous resurrection. This is what Christian apologists imagine skeptics are doing, cornered game, all paths of escape denied them. While one may imagine the religious believer, back against the wall, praying for a miracle of deliverance, apologists picture skeptics hemmed in by the Hound of Heaven in an evangelistic fox-hunt and, oddly enough, "praying" (desperately seeking) for the *lack* of a miracle: some naturalistic alternative to the resurrection of Jesus.[1] It is quite another thing for the skeptic to affirm that recourse to miracle is completely superfluous, a fifth-wheel of a hypothesis. And the latter will be my case here. I am not even raising the question whether miracles are possible. It just doesn't come up, as far as I can see. Let me explain why.

For the sake of argument I will assume that the narrative "setup" for the resurrection in the Gospels is historically correct. There really was a Joseph of Arimathea. There really was a group of female disciples who witnessed his burial. The tomb really was subsequently discovered to be empty. Disciples really did claim to see him. Sure—why not? Keep in mind, though, that this is purely an exercise in analyzing the particular approach taken by William Lane Craig and his colleagues,[2] not the approach taken by New Testament critics,[3] who do not take for granted the accuracy of the Gospel stories. Craig and the others prey on the naïveté of their audiences, who open the Gospels ready and eager to believe whatever they say.[4] They are arguing as against the Rationalists of the eighteenth century who affirmed the virtual inerrancy of New Testament narrative, disputing (as odd as it seems) only the factor of alleged miraculous causation.[5] If the Gospel tells us Jesus was crucified and that he appeared to his loved ones three days later, then we ought to believe both. Some details may be legendary embellishments, but the core of the story should be granted. The question is:

How do we get from one to the other? How do we connect the dots? Rationalists ruled out the supernatural as a matter of course; they assumed God didn't and doesn't work that way. He works through a sublime system of natural laws that, for instance, preclude a genuinely dead body spontaneously returning to life. So, Rationalists concluded, though Jesus was crucified and appeared alive again afterward, it is because he did not succumb to crucifixion. He must have been taken down alive, licked his wounds for a short while, and rejoined the disciples at least temporarily. It is against this argument and others like it (the Wrong Tomb Theory, etc.) that contemporary apologists replied.

But modern New Testament scholars no longer take for granted that the Easter narratives are history at all. Why should they be? They are so much like similar apotheosis narratives of Hercules, Romulus, Apollonius, Empedocles, and others[6] that the burden of proof is on anyone who would insist that, in the single case of Jesus, "myth became fact."[7] And such is manifestly a theological judgment, not a historical verdict.[8] But the important thing to see is that the chain of "events" leading up to the epiphany of the Risen One is equally legendary: mere stage-setting for the "Big Event." Scholars do not suppose that, say, the Joseph of Arimathea story, or that of the women visiting the tomb, is history, and that the only thing that requires special explanation is why the tomb was empty. As my old pastor Donald Morris once quipped in a sermon, "Let me quote myself so as not to misrepresent my own views":

> What evangelical apologists are still trying to show . . . is that their version of the resurrection was the most compatible with *accepting all the details of the Gospel Easter narratives as true and nonnegotiable.* It is a very strange argument when you realize just what is actually going on: it is implicitly *an argument among biblical inerrantists* in which defenders of the resurrection assume that their opponents agree with them that all the details are true, that only the punch line is in question. . . . This is why, if apologists like William Lane Craig can get an opponent as far as admitting that Joseph of Arimathea probably did have Jesus interred in his own tomb, and if the women did probably visit the tomb, and that the tomb was probably found to be empty, he can then press on to the conclusion that, *Bingo!* Jesus must have risen from the dead! **What they somehow do not see is that to argue thus is like arguing that the Emerald City of Oz must actually exist since, otherwise, where would the Yellow Brick Road lead?** . . . We simply have no reason to assume that anything an ancient narrative tells us is true.[9]

© jesusandmo.net

Why should they/we? As I've said before, these Christian apologists might not like it, but as historian R. G. Collingwood explains quite nicely, "the critical historian (whether dealing with the Bible or the newspaper) demands that assertions in ancient or modern sources be corroborated. The historian does not simply take the ancient or modern writer at his word until he happens to find out different."[10]

And yet, that is what I will be doing here. It is simply a thought experiment. As far as I am concerned, apologists long ago lost the game by misidentifying the kind of narrative we are dealing with in Mark 15–16, Matthew 27–28, Luke 23–24, and John 19–21. But I am perhaps perversely interested in seeing how weak the other links in their chain of supposed proof may be. I want to play their game of Rationalism versus anti-Rationalism. I will take for granted the basically historical character of the "events" prefacing the resurrection. The only difference is: I do not think one has to reach very far to see an altogether natural explanation for the supposed resurrection. There is no need for a fallback strategy, an expedient, an emergency plan. It never comes to that. Bear with me as I make bold to defend the Swoon Theory, the Reburial Theory, the Mistaken Identity Theory, and the Cognitive Dissonance ("Transformation of the Disciples") Theory. I predict we will find that there is not the least improbability, even implausibility, attaching to any of these options.

"BUT I'M NOT DEAD!"
"YOU'RE NOT FOOLIN' ANYONE!"

Apologists think they can refute the *Scheintod* (seeming death) Theory by prooftexting D. F. Strauss, who derided the notion that a crucified but living Jesus, broken and bleeding, might have staggered into the midst of his disciples posing as the mighty victor over death:

> It is impossible that a being who had stolen half-dead out of the sepulchre, who crept about weak and ill, wanting medical treatment, who required bandaging, strengthening, and indulgence, and who still at last yielded to his sufferings, could have given to the disciples the impression that he was a conqueror over death and the grave, the prince of life, an impression which lay at the bottom of their future ministry. Such a resuscitation could only have weakened the impression which he had made upon them in life and in death—at the most could only have given it an elegiac voice, but could by no possibility have changed their sorrow into enthusiasm, have elevated their reverence into worship.[11]

I am not sure I see the point of this as an argument. It is a slightly comical scene, but it is not a scene required or implied by the *Scheintod* Theory. All the theory (or the Swoon Theory, as it is also called) entails is a Jesus who, in the providence of his Father, cheated death, and whose beloved Sonship was thereby confirmed the more securely. The ensuing doting of his relieved disciples upon the recuperating savior would only have fed the instinct to worship him. All one has to surmise is that he waited a while, till he was better and stronger, to make grandiose pronouncements. That's not asking much. As for having been given all authority on heaven and earth, hell—the pope claims that pretty much every time he opens his mouth.

But let's back up. What suggests the Swoon Theory? Just above I portrayed it as a function of Rationalist assumptions: as an explanation, it's all they've got left. But now I will aver that there is much more to it. I think the texts themselves suggest it, so strongly in fact, that it does seem to me that the *Scheintod* model was the actual teaching of the Gospels at some earlier stage. It has since been redacted out in the course of the evolution of early Christian belief.[12]

Here's why I think so. First, there is Jesus' prayer in the Garden of Gethsemane in Mark 14:35–36: "And going a little farther, he fell on the ground and prayed that, if it were possible, the hour might pass from him. And he said, 'Abba, Father, all things are possible to thee; remove this cup from me; yet not what I will, but what thou wilt.'" It reads most naturally to me as if Mark intended this supplication to receive an answer, despite initial appearances: "In the days of his flesh, Jesus offered up prayers and supplications, with loud cries and tears, to him who was able to save him from death, and he was heard for his godly fear" (Heb. 5:7).[13] And if that is not a reading of the Gethsemane prayer that envisions God delivering Jesus as he asked, I don't know what the words mean.[14] In short, the text seems to anticipate that it is Jesus' willingness to go the way of sacrifice that atoned for Israel, just as, in much rabbinic thinking, it was the *willingness* of Isaac to die, and not any eventuality of his actual death, that expiated future Israel's sins.[15]

Second, there is the surprise of Pontius Pilate that Jesus had expired so quickly, implying that maybe he hadn't. "Joseph of Arimathea, a respected member of the council, who was also himself looking for the kingdom of God, took courage and went to Pilate, and asked for the body of Jesus. And Pilate wondered if he were already dead; and summoning the centurion, he asked him whether he was already dead. And when he learned from the centurion that he was dead, he granted the body to Joseph" (Mark 15:43–45). Surely this odd fact, Jesus' as-yet unexplained premature death, is the first shoe dropping. We are left expecting the second: he is not dead but only drugged. Indeed, the attention and buildup devoted to giving Jesus a drink is surprising if there will not prove to have been some payoff. After all, a sponge soaked in something odorous being applied to his mouth most suspiciously the very moment before he passes out is otherwise a strange thing to occur, much less mention (Mark 15:36–37), yet this oddity is independently confirmed by an eyewitness (or so we're to believe: John 19:29–35). Islamic exegetes have been quick to recognize this point: "the words of Pilate . . . would show that at the time of the crucifixion itself a doubt had been raised whether Jesus had in fact died and the doubt emanated from no less a person than one who knew from experience how long it took a person to die on the Cross."[16]

Likewise, the mockery of the Sanhedrinists (Mark 15:32: "Let the Christ, the King of Israel, come down now from the cross, that we may see and believe!") is delightful irony indeed if Jesus *is* in fact going to demonstrate his divine Sonship by coming down from the cross alive. Is this all coincidence? Only a flat, blindfolded reading of Mark says so.

I am not the first to note the surprising parallel between Mark 15:43–46 and the account of Josephus bar-Matthias, the historian, of how he recognized a former ally on the cross and prevailed upon Titus to have him taken down, saving his life . . .

> I saw many captives crucified, and remembered three of them as my former acquaintances. I was very sorry at this in my mind, and went with tears in my eyes to Titus, and told him of them; so he immediately commanded them to be taken down, and to have the greatest care taken of them, in order to their recovery; yet two of them died under the physician's hands, while the third recovered.[17]

One might plausibly argue that Mark's story is actually borrowed from Josephus ("Joseph of Arimathea" = "Josephus **bar-Matthias**," which is in fact Josephus's actual name).[18] But if not, the Josephus story at least parallels the Markan version as I am suggesting we understand it.

Third, speaking of Joseph of Arimathea, why does Matthew tell us that Joseph was rich (27:57)? It can hardly be intended as one more fulfillment of prophecy (as one might suggest, but Matthew does not say), this time Isaiah 53:9, "And they made his grave with the wicked and with a rich man in his death." For one thing, Matthew always calls attention to prophetic fulfillments (see the nativity story, etc.: Matthew 1:22; 2:517, 23; 4:14).[19] For another, he can hardly have considered Joseph a wicked man and indeed says just the opposite (Matthew 27:57). So what is the detail doing there? I believe it is meant to provide narrative motivation for grave robbers breaking into the newly sealed opulent tomb in which only the bruised and beaten scarecrow Jesus awaits, contrary to their expectations. Robbers, as they did in ancient novels of this period (e.g., Chariton's *Chaereas and Callirhoe*, Xenophon's *Ephesian Tale*), break into newly sealed, opulent tombs hoping to find rich funerary tokens, à la the Pharaohs, but find only a victim of unwitting premature burial returning to consciousness.[20] The existence of such tales makes for a strange coincidence otherwise.

Fourth, Luke's reunion scene in which Jesus demonstrates his corporeality (Luke 24:36–43) may naturally be read as a striking parallel to that of Apollonius of Tyana when he reappears across the Mediterranean to greet his disciples who have assumed him executed by the Roman tyrant Domitian and now think him a ghost:[21]

> Damis groaned out loud, and something like, "Gods above, will we ever see our good, noble comrade?"
>
> Apollonius, who was now standing at the entrance of the grotto, heard this and said, "You will, in fact you already have."
>
> "Alive?" asked Demetrius, "But if dead, we have never stopped weeping for you."
>
> Apollonius stretched out his hand, and said, "Take hold of me. If I elude you, I am a ghost come back from Persephone's domain, like the ghosts which the gods below reveal to men when mourning makes them too despondent. But if I stay when you grasp me, persuade Damis, too, that I am alive and have not lost my body."

The point of the Apollonius scene (and I believe the point of the Lukan) is pointedly *not* that the hero has died and returned in some manner from the dead, but rather that he has escaped death. He did not die. In both cases we are told the disciples first imagined they were seeing their master's ghost, only to be assured of his living corporeality. *He has not died after all.* Why does John change the story (which he found either in oral tradition, i.e., liturgical usage, or in Luke), so that the point is now not only corporeality but tangible, mortal wounds? Precisely to close off this possibility of understanding Jesus as having eluded death. It is only in John 20 that we ever read that Jesus was *nailed* to the cross instead of, say, being merely tied to it, as was often done. It is only in John 19:34–37 and 20:25, 27 that we read of a fatal stab wound through the ribs (for which an anonymous eyewitness is promptly cited—of whom no one before has ever heard). John has added these "details" to make sure the reader knows Jesus was really dead, something he must have had to do since many did not think so. This is also likely why he laughs off the speculation of Jesus' enemies that he might be planning to leave Palestine to travel among the Diaspora (John 7:35); that's what he must have done if he survived crucifixion, fleeing Palestine as Aristotle did Athens when trouble reared its head, "lest Athens sin twice against philosophy."

It is quite common for the followers of slain heroes and leaders to claim their man did not die but only went into hiding,[22] so the fact that some early Christians told the story of Jesus this way is hardly proof that he did actually survive crucifixion (though some scholars whose erudition far exceeds mine and that of the apologists think he did).[23] But my point is that, in view of all these factors in the text, which otherwise are all pointless red herrings in the narrative (even if they happened that way, why would the evangelists have bothered recording them?), it is by no means some expedient of desperation to suggest that Jesus was drugged on the cross, taken down prematurely, and survived at least for a while. (One might even take the ascension story as a euphemism for his soon-following death.) This is only to follow the lead of the texts themselves, as I see it.

One last point: the apologetical trump card against this possibility is that the Roman guards at the tomb would have constituted quite a barrier for an ailing, wounded Jesus. How could he have gotten by them? Again, I will not belabor the obvious: only Matthew mentions such guards, an impossibility if there was such a detachment.[24] Let's assume Matthew is right and that the other evangelists somehow dismissed this portion of the story as an unimportant trifle unworthy of mention. In that case, perhaps it was these soldiers who took the elementary precaution of checking the contents of the tomb before sealing it. There had been, after all, something of an interval between Joseph burying Jesus and the Sanhedrin petitioning Pilate for the guards. They must have checked. And if Jesus were reviving, there is just no reason to believe they would have locked him in alive! Maybe they would have fled as Mark's women did, victim to superstitious fear. Or maybe they would have helped the "broken man" to safety.[25] This is as plausible a reconstruction as any Evangelical harmonization of these contradictory Gospel accounts, who must resort *to the very same suppositions of events occurring that no Gospel mentions*. Is a miraculous resurrection really more likely?

NO FORWARDING ADDRESS

As I read John's Easter account in 20:11–15, I do not need to impose some sort of Jesus-hating skepticism in order to "escape" the implications of the text. No,

I find myself reading along reverently, appreciating the sense of numinous "ozone" in this wonderful story, and I am suddenly taken aback when Mary Magdalene finds no one in the tomb: *O God! Is there to be no end to the horrors of this weekend? What now?* She asks a man standing nearby, apparently the caretaker of the mausoleum grounds, if he has already transferred the corpse somewhere else. She does not wonder what may have happened to it. It's pretty obvious. As we, too, have been told in 19:41–42, "Now in the place where he was crucified there was a garden, and in the garden a new tomb where no one had ever been laid. So because of the Jewish day of Preparation, as the tomb was close at hand, they laid Jesus there." Jesus' remains had been deposited in this nearby tomb only as an emergency measure since time was running out. It was not meant to stay there.[26] Mary is only concerned that she may be unable to find out the final resting place. This is not some weird speculation by Rationalists. This is the scenario laid out by the Gospel itself. And though the evangelist (obviously) goes on to supply an alternate explanation, that of faith in the resurrection of Jesus, the text itself has already supplied a purely natural explanation for an empty tomb as well as the implication that Christians might not have been privy (or ever become privy) to Jesus' final resting place.[27] John himself tells us that the prima facie explanation was a simple relocation of a corpse hastily stashed there for the moment. Maybe this is what happened. Bingo: Jesus is buried, the empty tomb is discovered, and it is too late to find out where the body has been taken, perhaps because the disciples did not know of the role of Joseph of Arimathea and Nicodemus. Maybe the custodian Mary asked had replaced the man who had approved the removal of the body on an earlier shift, and he simply did not know what to tell her. ("No, ma'am, I don't know who he is; sorry.") There is no bafflement here that would have us welcoming supernatural miracles as a better explanation, is there?

If we were not so familiar with the text, it would strike us as quite ludicrous to think one must draw the inference from the empty tomb that Jesus must therefore have been raised from the dead, fully as absurd as the scene from *Monty Python's Life of Brian* in which Brian's followers momentarily lose track of him in the middle of a crowd and jump to the conclusion, "He's been taken up!" "No, there he is!"[28] But the disciples claimed to have seen him! Well, there are ready explanations for that, too. . . .

HAVE WE MET BEFORE?

At first glance, the idea that the Risen Lord was, ah, somebody else, maybe some other savior, or somebody impersonating Jesus, seems silly. Mistaken identity? You've got to be kidding. But the Gospels themselves introduce this suspicion—not that someone was impersonating the slain Jesus (as people have subsequently claimed to be David Koresh, for instance), but that his mourning disciples, ill-inclined to let go of him, grasped at the straw that some unknown individual they had met shortly after the crucifixion must actually have been Jesus, alive again. If we wanted to play the role of genuine New Testament critics, and not just play the game of the apologists, we should probably come up with something like the theory of James M. Robinson that the nonrecognition motif was a function of the original understanding of the resurrection appearances as blasts of brilliant, blinding light in which no human form was easily delineated.[29] Think of Revelation 1:14–16; or Mark 9:2–3; or Matthew 17:2 (often thought to be a displaced resurrection narrative); or Acts 9:3–6: all these depict a "glow-rified" Jesus shining with supernatural radiance.[30] As such, he is not readily recognizable. "Who are you, Lord?" (Acts 9:5). Robinson thinks that this is the origin and natural setting of the motif. The trouble is it has been inherited by Easter accounts that have been rewritten as if the fleshly Jesus got up off the morgue gurney and announced himself: the same man in the same body. In that case, why would they have failed to recognize him any more than a relative called in to ID a stiff? The nonrecognition motif no longer fits, functioning only as a telltale reminder of the Easter faith of an earlier day. (Similarly, the stories that still depict the Risen Jesus amid unapproachable light are no longer presented technically as resurrection stories! As we now read them, they are special visions vouchsafed to individuals or small groups before or after Easter.)

The Easter stories as we now read them feature a fleshly Jesus, without the special effects, and yet there is this persistent motif of doubting it is really him, or even thinking he is someone else. The disciples on the way to Emmaus (Luke 24:13–35) talk with the man for hours, and only as he vanishes does it occur to them it was their old master. The disciples, even as they are issued their marching orders, wonder if it is really him (Matthew 28:17: "but they [not 'some'] doubted").[31] Mary at the tomb does not recognize Jesus either (John 20:14). The disillusioned disciples, readjusting to a mundane career, see Jesus on shore, but they do not recognize him (John 21:4). Let us give apologists the benefit of the doubt and consider the implications if these Gospel Easter stories were, as they insist, genuine accounts of Easter encounters. All this non-recognition business, which we should never have expected, inevitably invites the suspicion that the Easter encounters were actually sightings of, encounters with, figures only *later* identified with Jesus, and then as a means of escaping grief and despair.

"Realizing" it in retrospect was not as good as realizing it at the time, but then there was an advantage, too: it could not be debunked. It is like when someone gives directions to a lost person who looks familiar but cannot be placed, and later a friend tells him, "I heard so-and-so celebrity was in town today, unannounced." And then one thinks, "That must have been *him!* If only I'd realized it then! I could have asked for an autograph!" But what the heck, it's still pretty exciting. And of course, it might *not* have been the celebrity, and since you can no longer verify it one way or another, you can still tell the story, the element of uncertainty only enhancing it.

Mark (6:14; 8:28) supplies a striking precedent when he tells us (twice, no less) that many people believed they were seeing or hearing about a resurrected John the Baptist, even though Mark claims to know better: it was a case of mistaken identity, since the figure was actually Jesus. It is no great stretch to wonder if the same thing happened in the case of Jesus. After all, there were plenty of such figures around. Celsus tells us of the prophets one was always liable to run into in Phoenicia and Palestine:

> There are many, who are nameless . . . , who prophesy at the slightest excuse for some trivial cause both inside and outside the temples, and there are some who wander about begging and roaming around cities and military camps; and they pretend to be moved as if giving some oracular utterance. It is an ordinary and common custom for each one to say, "I am God (or a son of God, or a divine Spirit). And I have come. Already the world is being destroyed. And you, O men, are to perish because of your iniquities. But I wish to save you. And you shall see me returning again with heavenly power. Blessed is he who has worshipped me now! But I will cast everlasting fire upon all the rest, both on cities and on country places. And men who fail to realize the penalties in store for them will in vain repent and groan. But I will preserve for ever those who have been convinced by me."[32]

Jesus might be taken for one of these, or one of these for Jesus. The Olivet Discourse explicitly warns its readers not to mix up people like Simon bar-Giora and Jesus ben-Ananias with Jesus Christ (Mark 13:5–6, 21–23), something someone must have been doing, or we would be reading no warning not to! In the same way, Paul was taken for the revolutionary Egyptian prophet in Acts 21:38, also mentioned by Josephus. Simon Magus is said to have claimed to be Jesus, returned already: "He taught that it was he himself who, forsooth, appeared among the Jews as the Son. . . . and was thought to have suffered in Judaea, although he did not really suffer."[33]

These misidentifications are not hard to understand once we grasp the way "local heroes" (including saints and popular revolutionists) are venerated in the Near East and have been for millennia. Scott D. Hill says, "Often living men are viewed as incarnations or representatives of a known local hero."[34]

Let us imagine ourselves among the apostolic community in those early days. We hear reports from several of the brethren that they have seen the slain Jesus alive again. Naturally our eyes widen; our ears perk up. And, like Thomas, we ask, "Are you sure? Tell me about it!" One tells us, "Of course I didn't realize it was Jesus at the time. It only dawned on me later" (so Luke 24:13–32). Another says, "It didn't really look like him, I admit, but later on I realized it must have been Jesus" (so Matt. 28:17; John 20:14–15; 21:2–12). And so on. I submit to you that we would be well justified to wonder what might have happened, and not to be convinced that our friends had actually seen Jesus. Their own testimonies would have created doubt instead of faith.

IT ONLY TAKES A SPARK TO GET A FIRE GOING— NOT A MIRACLE

Does it strain the bonds of natural law to envision a new religion beginning? Plenty of them have and have achieved impressive successes, not least numerical ones, and no one is too puzzled. Sociologist Rodney Stark shows how the expansion of Christianity from a circle of sectarian believers to a growing, influential sect that became a credible candidate for the state religion of Rome (as Mithraism and Baal worship[35] had before it) parallels the success of analogous modern sects such as the Mormon Church and the Unification Church over the same timespan.[36] No miracle was necessary, though there were certainly on display conspicuous Christian virtues that made it attractive, like Judaism before it, to outsiders and pagans. Christians should be justly proud of their faith's early success, but there is nothing supernatural about it.[37] Keep in mind, to appeal to a miracle is simply to admit that we can't yet account for it. ("God only knows how so-and-so works!") But we can. There are numerous factors not involving supernaturalism that explain Christian success.

But some would narrow the focus to the direct aftermath of the death of Jesus. If he did not at once rise from the dead, how can we account for the sudden expansion of the new faith? Why didn't the circle of disciples call it quits and go back home? It requires no rejection of miracles per se to judge that the rise of Christianity after the disappointing death of Jesus didn't require one. It may be readily explained in terms of cognitive dissonance reduction. Leon Festinger, Henry Riecken, and Stanley Schachter, in their psychosocial classic *When Prophecy Fails*,[38] developed a theory of "cognitive dissonance" to explain the reactions of a UFO cult to the failure of their deadline for an alien invasion.[39] Grossly publicly embarrassed, many nonetheless stayed with the group and in fact redoubled their efforts at recruiting. Why? Apparently, on the one hand, the level of humiliation would have been just too profound to face and accept. No matter how hard one must swallow it, *any* rationalization would be less painful than the reproach from self and others if one were to admit error and face the music. (Some disappointed members of modern Messianic cults have actually committed suicide rather than lose face.) Here think of the disciples of Jesus: they had abandoned all jobs and worldly pursuits, even family, in order to join Jesus and sit at his right and left in his coming glory. Now he is ignominiously dead, and one can only imagine the ribbing in store—for example, for the two disciples once they got back home to Emmaus. Maybe they timed it to get home under cover of night!

On the other hand, one might hope to mitigate, even reverse, public scorn of one's faith by redoubling efforts to convert outsiders to it. Every one of them that might be recruited means one more who admitted his share of the public ridicule had been wrong (like the repentant thief on the cross). So one gets busier than ever knocking on doors. "When people are committed to a belief and a course of action, clear disconfirming evidence may simply result in deepened conviction and increased proselyte[iz]ing."[40] The cognitive dissonance theorists showed how the disastrous failure of predictions by the Adventists/Millerites, the Jehovah's Witnesses, and the sect of Sabbati Sevi all really

got going only subsequent to the seemingly fatal debunking of each movement's promises, the utter collapse of its predicted denouement. They just
started again, reasoning that they had misinterpreted this or that the first time
around, but that nothing was going to stop the freight train now! There is no
miracle involved in any of this. A 180-degree turnabout is not nearly enough
to dash the hopes of True Believers.[41] In fact, sudden, utter defeat may itself
supply the catalyst for igniting the bomb bigger than it was the first time. Far
from going against nature, that is precisely the way human nature goes!

But, really, is all this machinery necessary? Isn't it like shooting a mouse
with an elephant gun? Is anyone incapable of picturing the smitten disciples,
whether of Jesus or of Dr. King, gathering after the initial shock of their leader's
assassination, rebuking themselves for their momentary panic, and then
covenanting together to redouble their efforts to carry on the master's cause in
his name, and concocting what stories they needed to do it? It is the most natural thing in the world; the only "miracle" we need to explain "the transformation of the disciples."

CONCLUSION: ELEMENTARY, MY DEAR WATSON!

The rise of Christianity is remarkable but not mysterious. We should like to
know a great deal more than we do about a great number of aspects of Christian origins. But it is just false and absurd to claim that we could not account
for the rise of the Christian resurrection faith without factoring in a miracle.
We have felt no need to posit special circumstances or to multiply hypotheses.
The rise of resurrection faith is just no problem at all. If we put the question in
terms preferred by apologists for the faith, we would deny there is any problem
at all accounting for the "facts of Easter morning" without recourse to a sus-
pension of natural law. To argue that resurrection faith could not have
appeared and hung on unless it had been started by a genuine miracle of resurrection is like saying that space aliens must have built the Pyramids, since we do
not know how it might have been accomplished with what resources the
ancient Egyptians are known to have had. No, even if we did not know how the
ancient Egyptians might have engineered and produced the structures, our
ignorance would in no way justify appeal to an "explanation" of which we
know even less. But we are not even in such a position. We are not left scratch-
ing our heads wondering how the resurrection faith arose. It's just no mystery.

Chapter 10

HELL
Christianity's Most Damnable Doctrine

by Dr. Keith Parsons

Charles Darwin, though he later made something of a name for himself in other fields, was trained as a theologian. He had a divinity degree (second-class honors) from Cambridge University. Perhaps, then, we should not be surprised when his observations on theological subjects are astute. Here is what he has to say in his autobiography about Christianity and the doctrine of hell:

> I can hardly see how anyone ought to wish Christianity to be true; for if so the plain language of the text seems to show that the men who do not believe, and this would include my Father, Brother, and almost all my best friends, will be everlastingly punished. And this is a damnable doctrine.[1]

Darwin, the mildest of men, seldom used such strong language, but in this essay I will argue that the tone and the content of this passage are eminently justified. That is, I argue that the traditional Christian doctrine of hell, as espoused by the historical Protestant, Catholic, and Orthodox creeds, is indeed a damnable doctrine. I contend that insofar as Christianity is bound to the dogma of an eternal, punitive hell, it forfeits any claim to moral authority, and so, like Darwin, we should not wish it to be true. In short, so long as Christianity embraces the doctrine of hell, its claim to be the "light of the world" is thoroughly discredited.

This essay will be divided into two unequal parts. In the first and shorter section, I lay out the horrors of hell in some detail. That is, I examine the depiction of hell offered by the most orthodox theologians and divines of various Christian traditions. Why dwell on these lurid and repugnant fantasies, surely the most misshapen progeny of the human imagination? The point is not to shock or outrage (though I consider these revolting images both shocking and outrageous), and certainly not to offer a titillating tour of a chamber of horrors. No, the point is that we must be quite clear on what the traditional doctrine of hell really is, so that when we criticize it harshly, it will be clear that we are not attacking a straw man. No, it *really is* that bad.

Second, I will examine at some length the arguments of prominent latter-day defenders of the doctrine of hell, including the arguments of some of the most famous Christian apologists such as C. S. Lewis and Peter Kreeft (writing here with Ronald K. Tacelli). I also look at Jerry L. Walls's revision of the traditional doctrine that unbelievers are consigned to perdition. I find both the traditional and the revised arguments severely lacking. I conclude that hell creates an irresolvable dilemma for Christians. On the one hand, they need such a doctrine. It is hard to imagine that there would be approximately two billion Christians in the world today had the Church been deprived of its strongest claim—that is, to save people from hell. On the other hand, the dogma of hell is rationally and morally indefensible, requiring intellectual gerrymandering and ethical contortionism by its would-be defenders. The upshot is that it is time we said goodbye to the horrid doctrine of hell and the creed that encompasses it.

THE NATURE OF HELL

The most famous depiction of hell is, of course, Dante's *Inferno*. The inmates of Dante's hell are punished symbolically. For instance, the wrathful furiously beat and are beaten by each other; gluttons who produced only excrement and garbage in life are forced to wallow in filth. Yet Dante's damned often attain a degree of dignity, and it is clear that Dante frequently pities them. Contrast Dante's attitude with the gloating of the Church father Tertullian, who anticipated his glee in enjoying the torments of the damned:

> How vast a spectacle then bursts upon the eye! What there excites my admiration? What my derision? Which sight gives me joy? Which rouses me to exultation? As I see so many illustrious monarchs, whose reception into the heavens was publicly announced, groaning now in the lowest darkness with great Jove himself, and those, too, who bore witness of their exultation; governors of provinces, too, who persecuted the Christian name, in fires more

fierce than those with which in the days of their pride they raged against the followers of Christ. What world's wise men besides, the very philosophers, in fact, who taught their followers that God had no concern in anything that is sublunary, and were wont to assure them that either they had no souls, or that they would never return to the bodies which at death they had left, now covered with shame before the poor deluded ones, as one fire consumes them! Poets also, trembling not before the judgment-seat of Rhadamanthus or Minos, but of the unexpected Christ! I shall have a better opportunity then of hearing the tragedians, louder-voiced in their own calamity; of viewing the play-actors, much more "dissolute" in the dissolving flame; of looking upon the charioteer, all glowing in his chariot of fire; of beholding the wrestlers, not in their gymnasia, but tossing in the fiery billows.[2]

Nor can we dismiss Tertullian as a crank. The ugly idea that the saved will enjoy witnessing the torments of the damned is not unique to him but was often expressed by the soberest, most orthodox theologians among both Protestants and Catholics:

> Aquinas . . . thought that the enjoyment occasioned by witnessing the sufferings of the damned was one of the pleasures of heaven: *"Sancti de peonis impiorum gaudebunt"* (The blessed will rejoice over the pains of the impious). This displeasing notion was advanced and defended with great tenacity over several centuries, and was one of the points orthodox Calvinists and Catholics had in common. Scots preachers, in particular, thought the pains of Hell a matter for satisfaction. Thomas Boston thundered: "God shall not pity them but laugh at their calamity. The righteous company in heaven shall rejoice in the execution of God's judgment, and shall sing while the smoke riseth up for ever." Some . . . went so far as to argue that the damned may have been created in the first place to make heavenly bliss complete.[3]

And what will be those torments of the damned that will so gladden and entertain the elect? For centuries, monks, preachers, and even academic theologians all vied with one another to produce ever more horrific depictions of hell. Here is Christian historian Paul Johnson's summary of some of these accounts:

> The general theory was that Hell included any horrible pain that the human imagination could conceive of, plus an infinite variety of others. Hence writers felt at liberty to impress their public by inventing torments. Jerome

said that Hell was like a huge winepress. Augustine said it was peopled by ferocious flesh-eating animals, which tore humans to bits slowly and painfully, and were themselves undamaged by the fires. St. Stephanus Grandinotensis evaded the problem of imagination by saying that the pains of hell were so unspeakable that if a human so much as conceived of them, he would instantly die of terror. Eadmer listed fourteen specific pains endured in Hell. Adam Scotus said that those who practiced usury would be boiled in molten gold. Many writers refer to a continuous beating with red-hot brazen hammers. Richard Rolle, in *Stimulus Conscientiae,* argued that the damned tear and eat their own flesh.[4]

In *Portrait of the Artist as a Young Man,* James Joyce's semiautobiographical bildungsroman, the young Stephen Dedalus and his fellow students are subjected to a terrifying sermon about hell. Here is the good father's account of the nature of hellfire:

> The torment of fire is the greatest torment to which the tyrant has ever subjected his fellow creatures. Place your finger for a moment in the flame of a candle and you will feel the pain of fire. But our earthly fire was created by God for the benefit of man, to maintain in him the spark of life and to help him in the useful arts whereas the fire of hell is of another quality and was created by God to punish the unrepentant sinner. Our earthly fire also consumes more or less rapidly according as the object which it attacks is more or less combustible. . . . But the sulphurous brimstone which burns in hell is a substance which is specially designed to burn for ever and for ever with unspeakable fury. Moreover our earthly fire destroys at the same time as it burns so that the more intense it is the shorter is its duration: but the fire of hell has this property that it preserves that which it burns and though it rages with incredible intensity it rages for ever.[5]

Finally, no set of quotes about hell would be complete without a few nuggets from the inimitable Jonathan Edwards from his masterpiece "Sinners in the Hands of an Angry God":

> It is everlasting wrath. It would be dreadful to suffer this fierceness and wrath of Almighty God one moment; but you must suffer it to all eternity. There will be no end to this exquisite horrible misery. When you look forward, you shall see a long for ever, a boundless duration before you, which will swallow

up your thoughts, and amaze your soul; and you will absolutely despair of ever having any deliverance, any end, any mitigation, any rest at all. You will know certainly that you must wear out long ages, millions of millions of ages, in wrestling and conflicting with this almighty merciless vengeance; and then when you have so done, when so many ages have actually been spent by you in this manner, you will know that all is but a point to what remains. So that your punishment will indeed be infinite. Oh, who can express what the state of a soul in such circumstances is! All that we can possibly say about it, gives but a very feeble, faint representation of it; it is inexpressible and inconceivable: For *who knows the power of God's anger?*[6]

Again, this stuff cannot be dismissed as a morbid phantasmagoria dreamed up by the unhinged or the fanatical. The tortures of hell were soberly proposed by the most distinguished theologians. As Johnson notes, "The three most influential medieval teachers, Augustine, Peter Lombard and Aquinas all insisted that the pains of Hell were physical as well as mental and spiritual, and that real fire played a part in them."[7]

Further, scripture itself, though not as detailed as the accounts of later writers, is highly evocative when describing postmortem punishment: "And if thine eye offend thee, pluck it out; it is better for thee to enter into the Kingdom of God with one eye, than having two eyes to be cast into hell fire: where their worm dieth not, and the fire is not quenched" (Mark 9:47–48).

"And the devil that deceived them was cast into the lake of fire and brimstone, where the beast and the false prophet are, and shall be tormented day and night for ever and ever" (Rev. 20:10).

"And whosoever was not found written in the book of life was cast into the lake of fire" (Rev. 20:15).

"And it came to pass that the beggar died and was carried by the angels into Abraham's bosom: the rich man also died and was buried; and in hell he lift up his eyes being in torments and seeth Abraham afar off and Lazarus in his bosom. And he cried and said, Father Abraham have mercy on me, and send Lazarus that he may dip the tip of his finger in water and cool my tongue; for I am tormented in this flame" (Luke 16:22–24).

The idea of a hell where sinners are tortured eternally is thus not the excrescence of a diseased brain. Such images may appear to be sick men's dreams, as Hume put it, but they are elements of a doctrine thought out with careful deliberation and based upon scriptural authority.

THE DEFENSE OF HELL

Surely, though, such a doctrine creates a heavy burden for those who would defend the tenets of traditional Christianity. How exactly are we to understand that the world created by an omnipotent, omniscient, and perfectly good being would be one in which billions of sentient creatures are doomed to eternal torment? God, in creating the world, would know that billions upon billions of human beings will wind up in hell, yet this is the world he chose to create. Indeed, do we not have to say that many billions of people were created so that they might be damned? Were there no alternatives to such a scheme that would involve no or less torture? Was every alternative somehow (and it is hard to see how) even worse? Why would God create hell, and then make the only way to avoid it depend upon acceptance of certain beliefs that, as he knows ahead of time, many billions will not accept? As Eddie Tabash suggests (by personal communication), the very doctrine of hell is so horrific that it probably deters many from believing, and so *condemns* them to hell. Further, doesn't the idea of a punitive hell depend upon a conception of justice as retribution, and are there not problems with such a concept, or, at least, may it not be carried too far? How can even the wickedest of human beings, a Hitler, Stalin, or Cheney, say, deserve *eternal* punishment? We no longer subject even the worst criminals to old-fashioned tortures, so shouldn't we expect God to have made at least as much moral progress as we have? Shouldn't God at least make it absolutely clear to everyone that the consequence of not doing what he says is eternal torture? Christian apologists have addressed these and other such questions, so let's turn to their arguments.

Peter Kreeft and R. K. Tacelli argue that God is not to blame for the pains of hell since those who go to hell freely choose to go there.[8] In what sense, though, could anyone be said to choose to go to hell? Surely, nobody has actually weighed the two options: "Hmmm . . . eternal bliss or eternal torment? Which will it be? I think I'll go for the eternal torment." We have no room here to pursue what Kreeft and Tacelli *could* mean when they say that hell is freely chosen. Whatever they mean, one thing seems clear: only a lunatic would consciously choose eternal torment over eternal bliss. This suggestion does not faze Kreeft and Tacelli at all, for in their view, sin *is* insanity:

> The Christian replies that that is precisely what sin is: insanity, the deliberate refusal of joy and truth. . . . Perhaps the most shocking teaching in all of

Christianity is this: not so much the doctrine of hell as the doctrine of sin. It means the human race is spiritually insane.[9]

However, insanity requires treatment, not punishment—therapy, not torture. If Kreeft and Tacelli mean that sin literally is a form of insanity—and if they do not mean this they should not say it—then they cannot mean that sin is freely chosen. Schizophrenics, for instance, clearly do not choose to suffer their various delusions. To punish the insane for their delusions would obviously be grossly immoral.

Suppose, though, that sin is freely chosen in the libertarian sense of "freely chosen," that is, the decision to sin is the agent's own, not coerced or compelled by any factors, internal or external, beyond the agent's control. Further, let's suppose that the action was done out of sheer malignity, a desire to do evil for evil's sake, as Augustine recalled doing in his *Confessions* when as a boy he and his friends stole some pears for the sheer pleasure of the mischief. Did Augustine and the other boys thereby come to deserve an eternity of torment? Augustine seems to think so, but his personal sense of guilt seems to have been grossly, perhaps pathologically, hypertrophied. How can temporal sin, whether it is stealing pears or genocide, deserve eternal punishment? Isn't there an obvious imbalance between finite wickedness, however malign, and infinite retribution?

Apologists have offered a number of replies to the "imbalance" argument. One online source argues that the punishments of hell are not infinite, though they are everlasting.[10] Even if punishments in hell will never end, there will always be a finite time since any sinner began to suffer the torments. Therefore, up to that point, even if it is googol years from now, only a finite amount of torment will have been suffered. This argument seems to rest on a fairly simple sophism. "Infinite" need not mean "exceeding any finite quantity in magnitude" or "extending beyond any finite measure." The basic meaning of infinite—indeed, the first definition given in the *American Heritage Dictionary*—is "having no boundaries or limits." Unending punishment has no boundaries or limits in time; it is everlasting (recall the Jonathan Edwards quote above). Therefore, it seems to be perfectly correct usage to speak of hell's punishments as "infinite" in the sense of "having no boundaries or limits in time." If not, however, the problem may simply be rephrased: Why is *everlasting* torture a just punishment for sin of limited duration? It takes more than equivocation to address this question.

Kreeft and Tacelli try to avoid the problem of endless punishment for limited sin by saying that the punishments of hell are eternal, not everlasting. I think they mean that eternity is not endless time but some sort of timeless dimension. Therefore, the problem of endless suffering does not arise since hell is a state of timeless eternity, not everlasting temporal duration. Unfortunately, this proposed solution raises more problems than it solves. In fact, it seems scarcely intelligible. What would timeless suffering be like? Pretty clearly, there is nothing in our experience that would be a parallel since the only suffering we experience is suffering in time. Would eternal suffering be as bad as endless suffering? If so, then the whole "imbalance" problem arises again. If it would not be as bad, then how bad is it? Indeed, why should we fear hell if it lasts no time at all? Is it even possible to be atemporally conscious? I think we may confidently defy Kreeft and Tacelli to give adequate answers to these questions.

Another common answer, one offered by *The Catholic Encyclopedia* (under "Hell"), is that sin is an offense against the infinite moral authority of God:

> Sin is an offence against the infinite authority of God, and the sinner is in some way aware of this, though but imperfectly. Accordingly there is an approximation to infinite malice which deserves an eternal punishment.[11]

The apparent power of this argument seems to turn on a rhetorical device—the strategic placement of the adjectives "infinite" and "eternal": defiance of God's *infinite* authority approximates *infinite* malice, and so deserves *eternal* (i.e., infinite) punishment. But what, exactly, does it mean to say that God has "infinite" authority? It seems to mean that God's authority is total, absolute, or ultimate in the sense that there is no higher or equal authority to supersede or limit God's authority. Understood in this way, however, the ostensible connection between defiance of God's authority and worthiness of eternal punishment is lost. Even if God is the ultimate authority, why should the act of defying him merit unending torture instead of lesser punishment? Indeed, since mere humans cannot harm God, why should defiance of God, per se, merit any punishment at all? The *Catholic Encyclopedia* author has given us no argument here, just assertion dressed with clever rhetoric.[12]

Also, what is "infinite malice" supposed to be? Is it the conscious desire to defy the moral authority of God? If so, then it is apparently necessary to believe in God in order to sin, because I can intend to defy God's moral authority only if I think that there is a God and that he does have such authority. Apparently, on this view, atheists cannot sin! After all, if someone does wrong but is completely unaware that in doing so he is offending a being with infinite moral authority, then it seems hardly fair to charge that person with infinite malice. The author does say that the sinner is "imperfectly" aware that he is offending the infinite majesty of God. How imperfectly? The more imperfect it is, the harder it will be to make the charge of infinite malice stick. I'd say that my awareness that I ever offend the authority of God is very imperfect since I do not believe it at all. Maybe the author means to imply that all sinners, even professed atheists, are tacitly aware that they are offending God when they do wrong. If this is the claim implied, then, I think the best reply is the proverb frequently attributed to Christopher Hitchens: "That which is offered without evidence may be dismissed without evidence."

Further, the *Catholic Encyclopedia*'s author seems to hold the oddly medieval view that the wickedness of an action is proportional to the degree of authority of the person offended. If you offend the king, you have done a terrible wrong; if you only offend a peasant, not so much. Surely, though, the intrinsic wickedness of an action depends on the intention of the agent in performing the action.

I recently read of someone in San Antonio, Texas, who was convicted of animal cruelty. He would buy cats on eBay, tie them to trees, douse them with gasoline, and burn them to death—apparently for no other reason than the pleasure of torturing them. What makes torturing cats for fun wicked is the intention to torture cats for fun, not that such acts offend the moral authority of the Society for the Prevention of Cruelty to Animals, the law of the State of Texas, or even God. Maybe the *Catholic Encyclopedia* author means that sins are committed with the intention of offending the authority of God. However, it seems highly unlikely that even Augustine was intending this when he stole the pears. People who steal seem to be motivated by such things as greed, selfishness, covetousness, the need to satisfy the cravings of a drug addiction, or maybe just the thrill of the mischief. The desire to flout the moral authority of God, if it ever motivates anyone to steal, would be way down the list.

C. S. Lewis, perhaps the best known of all Christian apologists, had quite a bit to say about hell. Lewis was not a systematic thinker, and many of his remarks on any particular point are scattered among various writings. Further, what he said in one place may be contradicted, or at least modified and supplemented, by what he says elsewhere. Also, Lewis has an enormous, often cult-like following that has written a vast amount of commentary on his work. With the exception of John Beversluis's extraordinary critique, nearly all of that commentary has been sympathetic or even sycophantic.[13] When you criticize Lewis, as Beversluis quickly discovered, a bevy of angry disciples will charge that you have distorted the words of The Master, taken them out of context, or ignored countervailing assertions elsewhere in the corpus. So, I shall address what Lewis says about hell only in *The Problem of Pain*, chapter 8.[14] If he takes back or modifies these assertions elsewhere, I am not concerned about that because what he says in *The Problem of Pain* is important and needs to be addressed on its own terms.

Lewis here addresses five common objections to the doctrine of hell:

1) The punishments of hell are purely retributive, and purely retributive punishments are merely expressions of spite and vindictiveness and so are wicked.

2) Eternal punishment for transitory sin is unjust.

3) The punishments of hell are too severe to be just.

4) The blessed in heaven will be unhappy contemplating the ongoing torments of the damned.

5) God, who desires the salvation of all, is defeated when a soul is lost for eternity.

We will consider Lewis's response to these objections in the order given.

1. The doctrine of retribution holds that it is good that the evil suffer for their sins, even if that suffering serves no further purpose such as leading the sinner to repent or to deter others from sin. Such retributivism contradicts the utilitarian view that all pain is bad, and is permissible only if it leads to consequences sufficiently beneficial to justify the suffering. For many ethicists, inflicting pain solely for the purpose of retribution is tantamount to seeking vengeance. Lewis counters by asking us to imagine a man who has attained wealth and power by treachery and cruelty, and who, far from repenting, ends his days fat, rich, powerful, sassy, and utterly unremorseful. Lewis then asks us whether we would be happy for such a man to go without ever having to suffer for a life of misdeeds:

> Can you really desire that such a man *remaining what he is* (and he must be able to do that if he has free will) should be confirmed forever in his present

happiness—should continue, for all eternity, to be perfectly convinced that the laugh is on his side? And if you cannot regard this as tolerable, is it only your wickedness—only spite—that prevents you from doing so?

Lewis thinks not. He thinks that even the most merciful cannot wish that such a man be allowed to continue forever laughing at both God and man and basking in his own wickedness. In this case, says Lewis, "You are moved not by a desire for the wretched creature's pain as such, but by a truly ethical demand that, soon or late, the right should be asserted, the flag planted in the rebellious soul, even if no fuller and better conquest is to follow." Also, the postmortem infliction of pain on the unregenerate sinner would at least show him that he was wrong, even if he chooses to cling to his wickedness, knowing it to be wicked: "In a sense, it is better for the creature itself, even if it never becomes good, that it should know itself a failure, a mistake. Even mercy can hardly wish to such a man his eternal, contented continuance in such a ghastly illusion."

There are a couple of odd things about Lewis's argument here. First, he appeals to our feelings about what is tolerable or intolerable to us. Yet, as John Beversluis points out (by personal communication), when criticizing ethical subjectivism Lewis condemns the appeal to feeling—like what we find tolerable or intolerable—as a guide to what is right or wrong. Also, the sterner Christians of yesteryear, like Augustine or Calvin, would certainly have dismissed as hubristic the attempt to justify God's judgments by appeal to human ethical intuitions. Surely, even our ethical intuitions would have been warped by humanity's fall into sin and so are unreliable. After all, if that rich man can have the wrong feelings and intuitions about what is right and good, so can we.

Second, and more seriously, retributivism is what philosophers call a "deontological" ethical theory. Deontological ethical theories base judgments of right or wrong on a conception of duty; that is, an action is right if and only if it conforms to the dictates of duty. Such theories are opposed by "consequentialist" theories, which hold that actions are made right or wrong by their consequences. Lewis's defense of retribution is oddly consequentialist. He justifies the infliction of pain on the recalcitrant sinner in terms of teaching him a lesson. Pain plants the flag of goodness in the rebellious soul and therefore forces him to acknowledge that his evil choices led to ultimate defeat. Instead of enjoying the last laugh, he has to admit that he wasn't so smart after all. Yet such an appeal to the sinner's edification appears to be consequentialist; that is, not to affirm the goodness of the pain per se, but only insofar as its infliction leads to desirable consequences—in this case, the sinner's education. A genuine retributivist would say that we have a duty to punish the sinner because he deserves it. Full stop. That is, when someone has done as much evil as our imagined malefactor, then for retributivists the "truly ethical demand" *is* for "the wretched creature's pain as such." Whether the sinner gains anything from the experience is irrelevant. Perhaps Lewis was too nice a man to face up completely to the sternness of his own position.

It is true that one of our deepest ethical intuitions is that people who do vile things should suffer for their acts, whether or not that suffering serves any other purpose. Surely it is a good thing, for instance, that Adolf Eichmann, the coordinator of Hitler's "final solution" to "the Jewish problem," was caught, tried, and punished, even if his punishment did not edify him and served no further purpose such as deterring future genocides. Speaking personally, I am willing to admit that retribution, to a degree, might be a legitimate justification for punishment. I found it outrageous that the cat torturer mentioned earlier was given only a two-year sentence. I think ten years would hardly have been enough punishment for such despicable cruelty. On the other hand, we now refrain from subjecting even the worst criminals, like Eichmann, to the sorts of punishments that the most advanced societies regularly inflicted on criminals just a few centuries ago. Not that long ago criminals were regularly broken on the wheel, roasted on gridirons, torn to pieces with red-hot pincers, drawn and quartered, impaled, crucified, flayed, starved, and so forth. We no longer inflict such punishments on even the worst criminals. Why? It is not that criminals have gotten any better; *we* have.

However odious someone is, we now think it is wrong to boil them in oil, skin them alive, or beat them to death with sledgehammers. Again, why? Are we more sentimental or more tolerant of moral turpitude now than our forebears? No, I think that the unwillingness, at least in liberal democracies, to resort to the old medieval punishments is one of the few unquestionable examples of moral progress. The principle of retribution in its pure form was expressed in the *lex talionis*, the law of an eye for an eye and a tooth for a tooth. The *lex talionis* equates justice with retaliation. After a crime, the moral order is restored when the authorities retaliate on behalf of the victim. The *lex talionis* now enjoys less prestige than it used to. As the poor milkman Tevye says in *Fiddler on the Roof*, if we always repay an eye for an eye and a tooth for a tooth, soon the world will be blind and toothless. Even in Texas, where executions are about as common as 100-degree days in Dallas, we are now beginning to see that payback and justice are not the same thing. Yet the traditional doctrine of hell preserves the *lex talionis* in its full ferocity. Unregenerate sinners must pay the price in full. Indeed, given the failure of apologists to successfully rebut the "imbalance" argument, it seems that the price of sin is paid infinitely more than in full.

2. In offering his own reply to the "imbalance" objection, Lewis interestingly admits that there would be an imbalance if eternity meant endless time. However, Lewis thinks that eternity should not be thought of as the infinite prolongation of time but as something else altogether, and he tries to develop geometrical analogies to explain his meaning. Here, I must confess that the usually pellucid Lewis completely confuses me. I am not sure at all what he is saying. If, like Kreeft and Tacelli, he is saying that eternity is a timeless dimension, then Lewis's response inherits the same difficulties as theirs. Otherwise, what does he mean? And shouldn't sinners at least get a second chance after death? Lewis says not:

> I believe that if a million chances were likely to do good, they would be given. But a master often knows, when boys and parents do not, that it is really useless to send a boy in for a certain examination again. Finality must come some time, and it does not require a very robust faith to believe that omniscience knows when.

But if omniscience knows ahead of time that someone will not convert given a second, third, or a million extra chances, why even give him a first one? Why create him at all? So that his punishment in hell can amuse the elect?

3. Next Lewis addresses the problem of the frightful intensity of the torments of hell. He cautions us not to confuse the imagery with which artists and scripture have depicted the torments of hell with the actual doctrine. Of course, hell will be "something unspeakably horrible," but Lewis puts more emphasis on the idea of destruction and privation than outright torture. This is all pretty vague, however. By "destruction" Lewis does not mean annihilation. In fact, he points out that souls may be intrinsically indestructible, and, further, that in our experience things are never utterly annihilated, only turned into something else, as the burned log turns into ash, heat, and smoke. It is hard to get really clear on just what Lewis is suggesting here, but he does hint at an interesting idea. Per-

haps the damned do not see their situation as unendurable; this is only how it looks to the saved. The damned may even experience pleasure and no pain but still live in a wretched and utterly debased state. Maybe Lewis is getting at a point made by John Stuart Mill: Better to be Socrates dissatisfied than a fool satisfied. Socrates's existence is so qualitatively superior to a fool's that it would be better to be Socrates, even when he is having a bad day, than Sarah Palin having a good day. Similarly, the elect in heaven would live in such a qualitatively superior state compared to the damned that they would infinitely prefer the discomforts of heaven (if any) to the pleasures of hell.

Did Augustine, Aquinas, Edwards, and all the other eminently rational teachers and thinkers quoted earlier really not mean it when they spoke of the tortures of hell? When they warned of the torments facing the unregenerate, were they perhaps merely indulging in rhetorical excess to frighten sinners into repentance? I see no reason not to take them as speaking absolutely literally. Even scripture often sounds quite straightforward. In Revelation, chapter 20, when it says that the damned will be cast into a lake of fire, it really seems to mean a literal lake of fire, not, say, that they will suffer the metaphorical burning of an eternally guilty conscience or something like that. As for the idea that the soul cannot be annihilated, is Lewis implying that souls obey conservation laws? According to traditional theology, the doctrine of *creatio continuans,* God maintains all things in existence at all times, and only has to suspend his creative input for an instant for things to cease to be. Surely, this applies to souls as well, and even if not, God can certainly leave the souls of the damned in eternal dreamless sleep, which is tantamount to not existing.

What about the intriguing idea that heaven is better than hell, not because the damned are in torment—indeed, they might be enjoying some sort of demeaning pleasure (maybe hell is like a giant Las Vegas casino)—but because of an infinite qualitative difference between the lives of the damned and the lives of the elect? Again, these suggestions are, perhaps unavoidably, quite vague, but they prompt an interesting query: Why is there such a qualitative difference between the lives of those in heaven and those of the ones in hell? Lewis seems to hold that what makes hell so hellish is the people who go there, not any tortures inflicted on them. While this is an improvement over the traditional doctrine of fire, brimstone, and devils with pitchforks, it raises many serious questions.

The idea that the damned make their own hell would be persuasive if the only people in hell were ones like the atrocious miscreant Lewis imagines. Surely, any place populated only by such types as brutal dictators, sadistic serial killers, slave traders, pedophiles, talk radio pundits, and big oil CEOs would be a hell, even if the accommodations were luxurious. But traditional Christian doctrine implies that vast numbers of ordinary and even saintly people go to hell. What finally condemns you to hell is not being bad but refusal to accept Christian salvation. Around the world many billions of perfectly respectable people have heard the Christian message but have chosen to remain Muslims, Jews, Buddhists, Hindus, pagans, deists, atheists, and so forth. Lewis asked earlier about what we find tolerable or intolerable about postmortem punishment. Can we really find it tolerable that billions of people will be condemned eternally because they choose to remain true to their deepest beliefs?

A short list of some of the people who have rejected Christianity, and so presumably doomed themselves to hell, would include Mahatma Gandhi, Rumi, Omar Khayyam, Hypatia, Marcus Aurelius, the Dalai Lama, Averroes, Moses Maimonides, Baruch Spinoza, David Hume, Voltaire, Thomas Jefferson, Thomas Paine, Golda Meir, Albert Einstein, Richard Feynman, Charles Darwin, Percy Bysshe Shelley, Clarence Darrow, Bertrand Russell, John Stuart Mill, A. J. Ayer, Jean Paul Sartre, and Mark Twain. A longer list would contain very many more of the greatest scientists, philosophers, artists, writers, statesmen, humanitarians, reformers, and philanthropists. Lewis assumes that everyone in hell is a total degenerate who will simply wallow in his own crapulence. On the contrary, according to traditional Christian doctrine, hell is full of good people.[15] If the worst that happens to them there is that they must eternally live with their own consciences and the fruits thereof, as Lewis seems to imply, how is that even a punishment? Would that not be heaven?

4. Lewis takes up the further objection that the saved cannot be happy contemplating the torment of the damned. Instead of countering, as did Tertullian, that the torments of the damned will gladden the saved, Lewis says that this objection rests on a dubious assumption:

> At the back of this objection lies a mental picture of heaven and hell co-existing in unilinear time as the histories of England and America co-exist: so that at each moment the blest could say "The miseries of hell are *now* going on." But I notice that Our Lord, while stressing the terror of hell with unsparing severity usually emphasizes the idea not of duration but of *finality*. Consignment to the destroying fire is usually treated as the end of the story—

not as the beginning of a new story. That the lost soul is eternally fixed in its diabolical attitude we cannot doubt: but whether this eternal fixity implies endless duration—or duration at all—we cannot say.

Again, we have the appeal to a timeless eternity, and it is still not clear what this is or how it obviates any problems. Also, it still will be the case for many of the saved that they will have friends and relatives who did not make it to heaven. Won't they miss them? Will they not still be sad, indeed eternally so, about the wretched fates of those whom they loved? How can this not detract from the bliss of heaven?[16]

5. Finally, Lewis considers the objection that the loss of souls through all eternity means a defeat for the omnipotence of God. His reply is defiant:

> And so it does. In creating things with free will, omnipotence submits from the outset to the possibility of such defeat. What you call defeat, I call miracle: for to make things which are not Itself, and thus to become, in a sense, capable of being resisted by its own handiwork, is the most astonishing and unimaginable of all the feats of the Deity. I willingly believe that the damned are, in one sense, successful, rebels to the end; and that the doors of hell are locked from the *inside*.

However, the "possibility" that Lewis speaks of is not a possibility but a certainty. God, being omniscient, knows from all eternity that vast numbers of humans will not be saved and will be eternally unrepentant and estranged from him. How many will be damned? Scripture says this: "Enter ye in the strait gate: for wide is the gate, and broad is the way, that leadeth to destruction, and many there be which go in thereat. Because strait is the gate, and narrow is the way, which leadeth unto life, and few there be that find it" (Matt. 7:13–14).

Here, then, Our Lord appears to be saying that a relative few will be saved and the vast majority will go to destruction. Over the entrance to Dante's Inferno there is an inscription that reads in part:

> Sacred Justice moved my architect.
> I was raised here by divine omnipotence,
> Primordial love and ultimate intellect.[17]

I am not convinced. Lewis, or someone, needs to explain to me why it is that the best plan that could be devised by omnipotence, primordial love, sacred justice, and ultimate intellect was a world in which many billions of human beings wind up in hell. Even if each of them is there because of his own free choices, it was God who planned this whole sorry scheme from all eternity, and so it is ultimately his fault. If the purported justification of this scheme appeals to the value of libertarian free will, I would have to say that free will in that sense is a commodity that is grotesquely overrated.

THE INJUSTICE OF PUNISHING BELIEF

I have so far not stated what I consider to be *the* most unreasonable thing about the Christian doctrine of hell, what I call the "doxastic requirement" for salvation. Christian doctrine has always imposed a doxastic requirement; that is, it has taught that to be spared hell you must *believe* certain things. That is, there are certain creedal assertions that are such that if you do not believe them, this is sufficient for your condemnation to hell. Even if the rest of your life were blameless, failure to believe these core creedal claims would be sufficient for your damnation. In other words, willful unbelief in the required propositions is a mortal sin. So you had better get it right.

What must you believe to avoid hell? Well, quite a bit, according to the traditional creeds. For instance, the Athanasian Creed begins as follows:

> Whosoever will be saved, before all things it is necessary that he hold the Catholic Faith. Which Faith except every one do keep whole and undefiled, without doubt he shall perish everlastingly. And the Catholic Faith is this.[18]

There follows a *very* detailed list of abstruse Trinitarian tenets that one must "keep whole and undefiled" to avoid perishing everlastingly. For instance, if you entertain the slightest suspicion that in the Holy Trinity the Essence is divided between the Father and the Son, or if you harbor the least doubt that the Son was begotten before all worlds, then you are doomed to an eternity in hellfire. Indeed, when you consider that different churches and denominations have very different lists of beliefs required for salvation, it surprises me that any Christian who takes hell seriously can sleep well at night. How can you be sure that *you* are safe?

Creeds create a difficult problem: The vast majority of would-be believers cannot even comprehend the recondite metaphysical formulae of many creeds (indeed, whether *anyone* can understand them is a legitimate question). How can you be required to believe what you cannot understand? In recognition of this problem, the Church has allowed people to affirm merely that they believe all that the Church believes and that the Church believes all that they do. It is hard to see how this helps. If someone were to tell me that the Church believes that "twas brillig and the slithey toves did hey nonny nonny awop bop aloo bop," my affirmation that I believe what the Church believes would be empty. If I have no idea what you are talking about I cannot sensibly even agree with you. I might *defer* to you as I would defer to Stephen Hawking on M-theory, but agreement—a meeting of the minds—must be agreement over *some* comprehended content.

Assuming, for the sake of argument, that the creeds assert intelligible propositions, when is it culpable to *lack* belief in some set of propositions? When is the not having of some set of beliefs so egregious a fault that it is deserving of eternal damnation? Is willful unbelief a mortal sin? Saint Paul thought so. Paul famously asserts (Rom. 1:20) that unbelievers are "without excuse" because God's existence is "manifest" to unbelievers, yet they perversely persist in unbelief:

> Because that which may be known of God is manifest in them; for God hath shown it unto them. For the invisible things of him from the creation of the world are clearly seen, being understood by the things that are made, even his eternal power and Godhead; so that they [unbelievers] are without excuse. (Rom. 1:19–20)

So those who willfully reject belief are culpable because, though God has shown his existence to them, and even "his eternal power and Godhead," yet they sinfully refuse to acknowledge him. By saying that "that which may be known of God" is "manifest in them," I take Paul to mean "obvious to them." Paul even says that unbelievers *know* God yet fail to honor him:

> Because that, when they knew God, they glorified him not as God, neither were thankful, but became vain in their imaginations, and their foolish heart was darkened. (Rom. 1:21)

The problem with any claim of obviousness is that it unavoidably comes with a tacit "to me" clause attached. God's existence and indeed his "eternal power and Godhead" may seem obvious to Paul but it does not to me or billions of others. When informed that I do not find obvious what he does, Paul would probably take this as evidence of how far I had sunk into reprobation. What is the appropriate reply to those who insist that you are a reprobate if you do not find obvious what they do? Probably the most apposite response would be to thumb one's nose and make a razzing noise. More politely, I'll just say, "Nonsense!"

Further, anyone making claims of obviousness cannot object when the reply is that it is obviously not obvious. In general, if Christians are allowed to assert claims of obviousness, others can too. Contrary to claims like Paul's, it is obvious to me that there are very many people who nonculpably reject Christian claims. There are billions of people who have heard the Christian message yet choose to remain Muslims, Jews, Hindus, Buddhists, Sikhs, pagans, atheists, and agnostics. Committed Christians, those who live and move and have their being in the faith, probably cannot even imagine how implausible their beliefs appear to an outsider. Their faith is so deep and its significance so clear to them, that those who reject it must seem simply perverse.

It is important to clarify a point here: it is not that people generally *choose* not to accept Christian claims. Speaking personally, I do not *choose* not to believe the Christian story; I *cannot*. It seems utterly fantastic to me, no more believable than Tolkien's tales about hobbits, orcs, and wizards. My nonbelief is not willful, because it is no more within my power to believe, for instance, that Christ died for my sins than it is to believe that Frodo saved Middle Earth by destroying the Dark Lord's evil ring.

The upshot is that unless the creedal claims necessary for salvation are in some sense obviously true, then it is unreasonable to impose a doxastic requirement. Unless Christians are willing to regard as simply perverse all those who cannot accept Christian teaching, their imposition of a doxastic requirement is itself perverse. If they do make such an assumption, they should not be surprised if the rest of us regard *them* as the ones incapable of seeing straight.

Perhaps, though, there is a way that Christianity's doxastic requirement can be made tolerable. In his book *Heaven, the Logic of Eternal Bliss*, Professor Jerry Walls considers the fact that many people throughout their lives are in a position of epistemic disadvantage with respect to the Christian message.[19] We can imagine a large number of such circumstances: Some perhaps never hear the Gospel, or only hear of it in a badly distorted or trite version. Others may be raised in traditions that so deeply imbue them with contrary beliefs that they are invincibly ignorant—psychologically incapable of giving Christianity a fair hearing. Others might have the Gospel preached at them, but only by persons of such blatant hypocrisy, sanctimony, or hatefulness, that the evil of the messenger taints the message. What will a loving God, whom scripture characterizes as desiring the salvation of all, do to redress the inequity, to level the epistemological playing field, as Walls puts it?

Walls proposes that God will compensate for epistemological inequities in the present life with "eschatological evangelism" in the next. That is, after death, those who have not had the opportunity of a full and fair hearing of the "truth about Christ" will be vouchsafed such a second chance. Walls is not clear on the exact form this postmortem proselytizing will take (How could he be?), but he thinks that everyone who has "blind spots" with respect to the Christian message will get an opportunity to hear the undistorted Christian message and will be freed of any psychological constraints or ingrained biases against that message. He thinks that even after death people will be able to reject Christianity, but that after receiving postmortem evangelization such a rejection will no longer be excusable, but can only be due to "concupiscence and wickedness of heart."

Walls's view is an appealing one, but it only leaves us with more questions: If God's grace is so bountiful that he will make the "truth about Christ" plain to all in the next life, why does he not do so in this life? Conversely, why doesn't the fact that God clearly tolerates epistemological inequities in this life count against the claim that he will set things right in the next life? Is there any reason to think that God, the God of the Bible, is interested in equity or fairness at all? The whole point of the Book of Job is that God is not fair but often smites the innocent, and we are not to ask why but to shut up (the splendor of Job's poetry almost makes you overlook the harshness of the message). Also, the Bible is rife with tales of gross unfairness committed or endorsed by God. In 2 Kings 2, the prophet Elisha curses some unruly children in the name of the Lord, and two she-bears are sent to maul forty-two of the children. In 2 Samuel 15, God orders the utter destruction of the Amalekites, men, women, children, and infants. The Flood of Noah drowns the whole earth except for Noah and his family, causing many small children, infants, mentally impaired people, and nonhuman animals to suffer a miserable death. The biblical God is often portrayed as unfairly causing suffering and death. Why should Walls expect God to be fair to us in the afterlife?

Finally, Walls assumes that the "truth about Christ" is so plainly true that once it is given a full and fair hearing, only the irremediably wicked and unregenerate will reject it. Can Walls even begin to conceive how insufferably arrogant this sounds to thoughtful nonbelievers? Really, it affects us in about the same way that thoughtful Christians are affected when Richard Dawkins or Sam Harris tells them that all believers are suckers or nitwits. And in any case, by Walls's logic, we don't need to be Christians anyway, not a one of us. We can all make that decision *after* we die.

CONCLUSION

Since the defenses of the doctrine of hell by some of the most eminent Christian apologists are so transparently thin, or at least leave us with far more questions than answers, we have to ask why orthodox Christianity is still intent on maintaining a doctrine of hell. Why maintain a doctrine that is, to all appearances, an eternal glorification of vindictiveness? What moral authority can the Christian Church claim if it rests upon such a damnable doctrine? How can an institution claim to be the Light of the World if one of its central doctrines is, to all appearances, an expression of the deepest darkness in the human heart?

Actually, you do not have to dig too deep to find the answers to these questions. You don't need that much moral authority if you can scare the hell into people. In fact, it is safe to say that Christianity would never have amounted to much without a doctrine of hell. The bright promise of salvation—and the terrifying threat of hell—have all along been the biggest guns in the Christian arsenal. It is simply inconceivable that there would now be two billion Christians had Christianity lacked a doctrine of hell. Not only will the threat of hell prompt you to become a Christian, it will lead you to be a *submissive* one. All the stuff about faith, hope, and charity aside, *obedience* has always been the prime Christian virtue (which is why kings, emperors, and czars have so often been ardent supporters of the Church). "There is no other way to be happy in Jesus but to trust and obey," says the old hymn. Indeed, the threat of hell will motivate not just external obedience but internal self-control as well. There are many people today who cannot entertain honest doubts about Christianity without catching a whiff of brimstone. A doctrine that can not only frighten people into belief and obedience but that can even squelch doubt is a zealot's dream come true. The doctrine of hell is the ultimate *ad baculum*: do what we say, and, indeed, believe what we believe, or suffer consequences too terrible to contemplate. Without hell to intimidate people into belief, Christianity would have to sell itself on its merits in the marketplace of ideas. And it's a safe bet its stock would then decline precipitously.

When this book was in the planning stage and we had the title *The End of Christianity*, I suggested a subtitle of *Why 2,000 Years Are Enough*. Sadly, the publisher declined my suggestion. With respect to the doctrine of hell, two thousand years are far more than enough. The damage this horrific and contemptible fantasy has done cannot be estimated. Surely torturers and inquisitors through the centuries justified their own atrocities with reference to hell. After all, the torment they inflicted was nothing in comparison to the torment God inflicts on the damned. Cruel dogmas make cruel people. Humans have made some progress through the ages. We no longer think of the deranged as demoniacs, and we do not respond to a sudden outbreak of illness by burning old women. Perhaps even conservative Christians will part from the doctrine, but I fear there will always be those, like Peter Kreeft and Roland Tacelli, who insist that if you deny hell you must deny Christianity as well.[20] If that is our only choice, we should toss Christianity—and hell—into history's landfill.

Part 4

SCIENCE PUTS AN
END TO CHRISTIANITY

Chapter 11

IS RELIGION COMPATIBLE WITH SCIENCE?

by Dr. David Eller

Francis Collins is a prominent American scientist, former director of the National Human Genome Research Institute, and, at the time of writing, director of the National Institutes of Health. He is also a Christian and author of *The Language of God*.[1] The Reverend John Polkinghorne, former professor of physics at the University of Cambridge, became an Anglican priest in 1982 and has written several books on physics and religion.[2] In fact, in a survey conducted by Elaine Howard Ecklund (and funded by the Templeton Foundation, which actively pursues research on science and religion), two-thirds of scientists hold a belief in God, including 59 percent of biologists.[3] So if the question is "Can religion coexist with science, in the same society or even inside the same head?" the answer is clearly yes.

On the other hand, scientist Richard Dawkins is an outspoken atheist and energetic denouncer of religion,[4] and the roll of high-profile scientists publically avowing a disbelief in god(s) includes Francis Crick (the codiscoverer of DNA), linguist Steven Pinker, physicists Stephen Weinberg and Victor Stenger, neuroscientist Robert Sapolsky, and sociobiologist Edward O. Wilson. In fact, to interrogate Ecklund's research more closely, less than 50 percent of scientists have a religious affiliation, whereas almost 86 percent of the US population does, and scientists are much less likely to be evangelical or fundamentalist Christians (1.5 percent versus 13.6 percent) or traditional Catholics (0.7 percent versus 6.9 percent) and are much more likely to be Jewish (15.3 percent versus 1.8 percent) or Buddhist (1.8 percent versus 0.3 percent) than the general population. So if the question is "Does a scientific outlook coexist easily (and to the same degree as a nonscientific worldview) with religion?" the answer is apparently no.

Finally, Stephen Jay Gould has proposed that science and religion do not even occupy the same conceptual space, so that as long as each stays within its own "nonoverlapping magisterium," everything is fine—but when they invade each other's territory, conflict ensues.[5] In other words, the compatibility of religion depends on how sequestered the two are from each other—under some conditions yes, under other conditions no.

A question that can simultaneously be answered "yes," "no," and "sometimes," is a question that is asked wrong. The problem with the question "Is religion compatible with science?" is that there is no agreement, not even much self-awareness, about what the question even means. Ultimately, a sensible answer depends on defining our terms: What is religion, what is science, and what is compatible? After providing these much-needed definitions, I will argue that, while religion and science can undeniably coexist (since they do), they are actually *not* compatible; further, science has no need for religion since religion has no relevance for science (and vice versa), and science can only proceed when it is liberated from the specific claims and the general mindset of religion. This was true in Galileo's time, and it is true today.

RELIGION

> It is unfortunate, and almost inevitable, that when we talk about religion we quite literally do not know what we are talking about.
> —Pascal Boyer, *Religion Explained*[6]

In most of the squabbles between religion and science, religion is never defined, because, since most of the squabbles are occurring in majority-Christian societies, the assumption is that "religion" means "Christianity." Worse yet, the assumption is usually that "religion" means "traditional Christianity" or "evangelical/fundamentalist Christianity." Substituting one of these terms for "religion" in our original question yields the highly problematic inquiry: Is traditional/evangelical/fundamentalist Christianity compatible with science? The first problem, of course, is that even if it is not, then perhaps some other form—some modernist or liberal form—of Christianity *is* compatible with science; perhaps Christianity can be adjusted and juked to fit with science. The second and more profound problem is that even if traditional/evangelical/ fundamentalist Christianity or any version of Christianity whatsoever is not compatible with science, perhaps some other religion—say, Hinduism or Wicca or ancient Mayan religion or Scientology—is. Yet you will notice that almost no one asks, and almost no one in the United States or any other Christian-dominated society cares, whether Hinduism or ancient Mayan religion is compatible with science, since few people know or care about Hinduism or ancient Mayan religion. The tempest over religion and science is thus quite a local and parochial brouhaha, people fighting for *their particular religion* against (some version or idea of) science.

If we were to try to be more inclusive and say that the dispute is between *theism* and science, we would still not be correct, since not all religions are theisms and certainly not *mono*theisms. Maybe monotheism is incompatible with science, but polytheism is not. Or maybe all theisms, all god-based religions, are incompatible with science, but other kinds of religions—religions based on nature spirits or dead ancestors or impersonal forces like *chi* or *mana* are not. Honestly, a religious concept like chi or mana is more scientifically useful (and testable) than a concept like "original sin" or "heaven," and indeed Chinese civilization *has* used the concept of chi in a virtually scientific or at least pragmatic way, organizing practices from medicine to diet to home furnishing (feng shui) around it. What possible practical applications can "original sin" ever conceivably have?

"Religion" does not and cannot mean any specific religion, any more than "language" means any specific language, or "game" means any specific game. What, then, is "religion"? There have been many attempted answers, almost all of which have fallen short in one or both of two ways: they purport to define religion in terms of some equally undefined religious notion (in other words, they are circular), or they define religion in such a way as to make it indistinguishable from nonreligion. An example of the first failure is the definition given by the great early sociologist Émile Durkheim, who imagined it as "a unified system of beliefs and practices relative to sacred things, that is to say, things set aside and forbidden—beliefs and practices which unite into one single moral community called a Church, all those who adhere to them."[7] The difficulty here is "sacred": What exactly does *that* mean? Aside from the fact that not all religions in the world necessarily contain the concept of "sacred" (that is, it may be, once again, a distinctly Judeo-Christian idea), the word is generally taken to refer to something supernatural or holy or divine. Webster's defines *sacred* as "dedicated or set apart for the service or worship of deity," "worthy of religious veneration," and most uselessly of all, "of or relating to religion." Therefore, religion is a system of beliefs and practices relative to things of or relating to religion, which defines nothing!

The second failure of definitions of religion is best exemplified by the famous characterization offered by the anthropologist Clifford Geertz, who considered it to be

> (1) a system of symbols which act to (2) establish powerful, pervasive, and long-lasting moods and motivations in men by (3) formulating conceptions of a general order of existence and (4) clothing these conceptions with such an aura of factuality that (5) the moods and motivations seem uniquely realistic.[8]

The objection to this approach is that, while Durkheim's definition was too religion-dependent, Geertz's is too religion-independent. There is nothing in the sentence that refers to anything uniquely religious, and no doubt it could apply to a number of nonreligious or secular phenomena as well. Patriotic symbols like flags and anthems also establish moods and motivations and make things (like a country such as the United States) seem uniquely real; for others, gang colors, sports emblems, or military insignia may have the same effect. Mark Pendergrast has argued that, based on Geertz's view, Coca-Cola is a religion, since it has its symbols, attempts to represent a way of life, and tries to make that lifestyle seem real.[9] Sadly, Durkheim's perspective actually commits this error along with the error of circularity, since "sacred" often means in practice whatever people feel very strongly about, so that they may use it to refer to the flag or the Constitution or money or their favorite sports team—or potentially reason or science itself.

In order to make any progress on the question of religion and science, we must understand religion in a way that includes all variations of religion (theisms and nontheisms, nature spirits, dead ancestors, and supernatural forces) and that effectively distinguishes religion from everything else. In the real world, this is probably not entirely possible: religions are so diverse (with some things on the boundary between religion and nonreligion), and religions so totally penetrate the secular and mundane world that no sharp, satisfactory line can be drawn. Nevertheless, there are, critically, some qualities that religions share that nonreligions do not. Whatever else they include (and they include much else), the nineteenth-century ethnologist E. B Tylor suggested that religions have one minimal characteristic that makes them religions as opposed to something other than religions—"the doctrine of souls and other spiritual beings in general"[10]—leading him to his minimal definition of religion as the belief in spiritual beings. By spiritual beings he meant beings without a material presence or "body" (at least some of the time, since they might materialize on occasion, as even Yahweh reportedly did). Almost a century later, anthropologist Anthony Wallace concurred that, all of its other details and permutations notwithstanding, religion starts with a single premise: the "supernatural premise" that "souls, supernatural beings, and supernatural forces exist."[11]

Tylor called this most basic doctrine of religion "animism" and regarded it as a type (and the most primitive type) of religion, but subsequent thinkers have recognized it not as a type but as the *essence* of religion. For Pascal Boyer,[12] Scott Atran,[13] and Stewart Guthrie[14] among others, the key to spiritual beings, and thus to religion, has been characterized as *agency*, the possession of "mind" or "will" or "intention." Agents, of which humans are one kind, act for their own reasons or, more importantly, *purposes*; they are not merely objects to be acted on but subjects that act and have their own viewpoints. They are like "persons" in the way that counts the most; in fact, they *are* persons. Graham Harvey, who has recently championed a return to the idea of animism, puts it as follows:

> Persons are those with whom other persons interact with varying degrees of reciprocity. Persons may be spoken *with*. Objects, by contrast, are usually spoken *about*. Persons are volitional, relational, cultural, and social beings. They demonstrate intentionality and agency with varying degrees of autonomy and freedom. That some persons look like objects [or do not have visible appearance at all] is of little more value to an understanding of [religion] than the notion that some acts, characteristics, qualia, and so on may appear humanlike to some observers. Neither material form nor spiritual or mental faculties are definitive.[15]

This, then, finally allows us to define religion in a productive and significant way. A religion is a particular system of thought that posits nonhuman and, in certain manners, superhuman agents or persons in the world along with humans. These non/superhuman beings share the quality of mind or intentionality or personality and personhood with humans; in other words, in religious thought, humans are not the only persons in the world. But this religious mode of thought implies much more: if there are non/superhuman persons out there, then we humans can *and must* enter into personal and social relationships with them. We cannot treat them like objects, like things, and we definitely cannot disregard them. This is what the theologian Martin Buber meant when he stressed that we must approach a spiritual being (he referred specifically to the Judeo-Christian God) as an "it" but as a "thou," as a mindful and willful person like any other person we know, only more so.[16] The ultimate outcome of this understanding is a definition of religion that places humans in a social relationship with immaterial but intelligent beings, like the definition proffered by Robin Horton a half-century ago:

> In every situation commonly labeled religious we are dealing with action directed towards objects which are believed to respond in terms of certain categories—in our own culture those of purpose, intelligence, and emotion—which are also the distinctive categories for the description of human action. The application of these categories leads us to say that such objects are "personified." The relationship between human beings and religious objects can be further defined as governed by certain ideas of patterning and obligation such as characterize relationships among human beings. In short, Religion can be looked upon as an extension of the field of people's social relationships beyond the confines of purely human society. And for completeness's sake, we should perhaps add the rider that this extension must be one in which human beings involved see themselves in a dependent position vis-à-vis their nonhuman alters—a qualification necessary to exclude pets from the pantheon of gods.[17]

SCIENCE

> Science requires the most vigorous and uncompromising skepticism, because the vast majority of ideas are simply wrong, and the only way to winnow the wheat from the chaff is by critical experiment and analysis.
>
> —Carl Sagan

The second frequently unexamined component of the religion-science compatibility question is the "science." Probably as much has been said and written about the nature of science as about the nature of religion, but seldom is an adequate sense of science brought to the discussion of the relationship between science and religion. Let us begin in much the same way as we began in the case of religion above: by noting the diversity and complexity of the term *science*. One of the first things to emphasize is that, while there are many different religions with wildly (and often incompatibly) different doctrines and beliefs from each other, there are not different "sciences." There are, to be sure, multiple scientific specializations—physics, chemistry, biology, astronomy, sociology, psychology, and so on—but these are not different, let alone competing or conflicting, "sciences." Rather, they are "science" applied to various topics, and of course these topics will require different techniques (you do not use test tubes to study societies or minds), will develop different concepts ("mass" and "velocity" are relevant to physics but not to anthropology), and will produce different knowledge. But these disparate scientific specializations do not contradict each other in the ways that each religion contradicts all other religions.

Second, we should distinguish between "science" and "technology." This is not a simple task, but it is a vital one, since virtually no one asks if religion and *technology* are compatible: even the most extreme fundamentalists still gladly use cell phones, satellite dishes, and the Internet—and certainly fire and the wheel—to do their religious business. While science and technology are most assuredly intimately related, they are not the same thing. There has been technology since the day when humans first bashed two rocks together to make a stone tool; this was long before anything we can call "science" existed. The distinction is sometimes expressed in terms of the ancient Greek concepts of *techne* and *episteme*, which give us the English words *technology* and *epistemology*, respectively. *Episteme* is generally construed as "knowledge," especially "theoretical" or even "disinterested" knowledge—knowledge for the pure sake of knowledge; *techne* originally meant something closer to art, craftsmanship, or know-how. Scientific knowledge indisputably can lead to technological advancements (like cell phones) and also depends on technological advancements (like microscopes), but there is a real, if contested, difference between the two. Interestingly, while we cannot substitute "technology" for "science" in the question of religion versus science, and while most religionists take technology as much for granted as any atheist, there often are frictions between particular religions and particular technologies—say, Christianity and cloning technology or stem-cell technology.

Third, science is not the same thing as "experimentation" or any other specific method. An experiment is a particularly effective way of collecting a certain kind of information, but not all efforts at accurate and systematic knowledge can conduct experiments (they are highly difficult in astronomy and largely unethical in anthropology), but these fields are no less scientific for that reason. Experiments are, in a word, valuable but not essential components of science. Likewise, science should not be conflated with any particular set of instruments (like test tubes or Bunsen burners) or any particular theoretical stance (like quantum theory or string theory): Einstein rejected quantum theory but was not less of a scientist for it. But some "instruments" and "theories" are clearly not scientific (like dowsing rods and intelligent design)—and not actually instruments or theories at all.

Fourth (and finally, for the moment), science is not to be understood as any particular body of data or knowledge. Laypeople often think of science as "what we know today," but the knowledge of the day is only the results and findings of science *so far*. Naturally, people who take this attitude often end up scoffing at science for changing its conclusions and refuting its previous claims. However, to be fair and accurate, the state of scientific knowledge at any moment is the consequence of the questions that have been asked and the facts that have been collected. Tomorrow's questions and data will lead to new claims and conclusions, often debunking earlier ones.

What, then, is the "science" in the religion-science controversy, and how does a proper understanding of science help us settle the issue? If I may be incredibly terse, I think the essence of science lies in two premises, just as the essence of religion lies in its "supernatural" premise. The crucial premises for science are *detectability* and *doubt*, and it is these that separate it from just any old explanatory system or manual procedure. Detectability means that science will only consider that which it, and we as scientists, can detect in some fashion, because it *can* only consider what we can detect in some fashion. The premise of detectability departs importantly from the oft-mentioned criteria of observability or of "naturalism" or "materialism." Some critics of science try to use the notion of observability against it, as if science will only count what is available to the eyes or the senses in general; this is a trivial complaint, since there are many phenomena that are not available to the naked eye or the unenhanced senses, from microscopic life-forms to distant galaxies. But there must be some way in practice to detect a phenomenon, including indirect ways, like the trace or reaction that an invisible neutrino makes. Further—and this is decisive—we must be able to detect some evidence *convincingly as evidence of some phenomenon and not any other*. That is, people will often argue that recovering from an illness or winning the lottery or simply the beauty or the very existence of the universe is detectable evidence for their god, but although these things are detectable, they could (and almost certainly should) be interpreted as other than the actions of a god. In other words, if there is no compelling reason to take the detectable facts as evidence for some particular thing—especially when some other explanation works better—then we are not allowed to use it as evidence for that thing.

The matter of naturalism or materialism is more complicated, partly because it comes in two flavors—*methodological naturalism* and *philosophical* or *metaphysical naturalism*. According to the former, science has allegedly made a strategic choice to consider only natural/material processes; it has merely "left out" *super*natural or *im*material entities. According to the latter, science asserts that nature or matter are the only actually existing things in the universe, thereby excluding the supernatural or the immaterial on principle. Eugenie Scott has gone so far as to insist that philosophical naturalism/materialism is not part of science itself, which is true but not in the way she thinks it is: science has neither made a strategic nor a philosophical decision to limit its inquiries to the natural/material realm. Rather, science is led to naturalism/materialism by its commitment to detectability, since the natural/material realm is so far *the only realm that is reliably detectable*, especially detectable as evidence for anything in particular. Finally, based on the commitment to detectability, there is no evidence that there is any realm other than the natural/material realm; any supernatural or immaterial reality is so far, in principle and in practice, undetectable, and therefore we have no scientific reason to claim that it even exists.

Thus, science is naturalistic and materialistic as a consequence of a more basic premise. This connects to the second premise of science; namely: doubt. René Descartes was one of the first thinkers to make this principle explicit: our senses are easily fooled, and we are subjected to a lot of patent nonsense from our past and present society and traditions. How can we be sure we are not in error? His solution (as a mental exercise) was radical and total doubt: let us doubt everything that is not imminently certain. Of course, he goes completely off the rails from that point, but the idea is that there are many claims on our attention, even on our credulity, and we must apply some stringent standards to determine which ones are worthy of further consideration. Scientists do not, and Descartes did not, doubt everything, but the truth of the matter is that science is *ready to doubt anything whatsoever*, including its own findings and theories at any given moment. Science thus raises a bar—and a fairly high bar—of factuality, of detectability, and of logical analysis before it admits any claim as "knowledge."

These two most fundamental premises—detectability and doubt—lead inexorably to a number of other practices or commitments for science. These include

- Neutrality: Scientists must not let their—or anyone else's—preferences, personality, opinions, values, tastes, or traditions influence what they detect or how they analyze what they detect, nor what they will doubt or accept.
- Regularity: Scientists have reason to doubt that which is exceptional or statistically insignificant since they cannot interpret it as reliable evidence of anything in particular. Science instead looks for the regular, the patterned, the "lawful" (that is, that which can be described by "laws" or statements, ideally mathematical statements, of consistent relations and dependencies). A corollary of the commitment to regularity is the importance of reproducible results: if a phenomenon occurs under certain conditions, it should *always* occur under those conditions, and the findings of any scientist should be reproducible by other scientists.
- Equality: Consequently, no scientist has any special powers of discernment unavailable to other scientists. Some individuals may be more talented or skilled than others, but no one has unique insight into reality; there are no scientific "seers" or "prophets" or "oracles." A corollary of equality is openness, the willingness and responsibility to share scientific findings with colleagues—including techniques and raw data—so that anyone may reproduce your methods and try to replicate your results and use those methods and results in their own work. There should be, in a word, no scientific "secrets."
- Causation: Scientists search for explanations in the form of *causes*, a cause being the antecedent (prior in time) conditions that lead to or produce an effect. Experiments are useful for establishing cause-and-effect relationships; they ideally hold all variables constant except one so

that changes in the manipulated variable ought to be the "cause" of any detected effect.

- Tentativeness: Scientists understand that their findings and theories are only as good as the knowledge they already hold and the techniques they employ. The claims of science are always provisional and subject to change in the face of new evidence. Science must be—and when it works well, it is—open to modification even of its most fundamental notions like the composition of matter or the nature of time. Indeed, science is inherently self-critical: scientists are *eager* to challenge established and inherited truths and are continuously testing and questioning received knowledge. The greatest thing—some like Karl Popper insist the only thing—that a scientist can do is *falsify* prevailing data and theories, including his/her own. Nothing is off-limits to science, no fact or claim or theory shielded from inspection and potential rejection.

COMPATIBILITY

That this scientific cosmology retires traditional ones with their six days of creation and the like goes without saying. Who can possibly question that when the scientific cosmology has landed people on the moon?

—Huston Smith

Despite what we have just said, or perhaps because what we have just said is not usually said clearly before, "debates" over religion and science begin. There are many differing and even contradictory positions on whether religion and science differ or contradict. Michael Shermer, for example, has identified three basic approaches or models of the religion-science relationship, which he dubs the *same worlds*, *separate worlds*, and *conflicting worlds* models. In the "same worlds" model, science and religion are seen as accomplishing pretty much the same goals, or at least asking pretty much the same questions; therefore, while they may disagree on details, they are essentially reconcilable. From the "separate worlds" perspective, religion and science are determined to be pursuing different goals and answering questions that either complement or ignore each other. And, predictably, if they occupy "conflicting worlds," then they are locked in a struggle that only one can win, a competition for truth in which the success of one is the failure of the other; this is the so-called war between religion and science.[18]

There are two curious things to note about this three-mode typology. First, there is no simple relationship between whether a person is a scientist or a religionist and any particular stance on the models: some scientists are adamant "conflicting worlds" advocates, while others support the same or separate worlds view, and this is equally true of religionists. Second, the three modes as proposed do not quite get the job done: religion and science might occupy the same world and yet clash profoundly. In fact, in a certain sense, they would only clash *if they occupied the same world*. So "conflict" is less a distinct model and more a subset of same-world residence, the other major subset being "harmony." So the real division is between one model with two forms—*same world in conflict* and *same world in harmony*—and a second model, *separate worlds*, which, if Gould is correct, ought never come in conflict, because they never come in contact. But religion and science *do* come in contact, so the separate-worlds position is indefensible. And there *is* only one world in the end, so religion and science must inevitably share the one world, the real world. The only question is whether they can share it peacefully or whether there is unavoidable tension.

Ian Barbour, from a more theistic perspective (he is a winner of the Templeton Prize, awarded to scholars who contribute to religion-science reconciliation), categorizes the relationships between religion and the sciences into four types that he names *conflict, independence, dialogue,* and *integration*.[19] The conflict relation is equivalent to Shermer's conflicting-worlds model, while the integration relation is comparable to his same-worlds model. However, Barbour insists that the conflict view is a product of mistakes on both sides, namely scientific materialism and biblical literalism; instead the integration view explicitly marries religion and science in interesting (if not awkward or nonsensical) couples like "natural theology" or a "theology of nature" or some "systematic synthesis" in which "both science and religion contribute to the development of an inclusive metaphysics, such as that of process philosophy."[20] (Francis Collins adds "theistic evolution" to the mix, and while we are at it, why not Christian Science and theistic chemistry?) That leaves independence and dialogue, which are probably recognizable as subtypes of the separate-worlds model. The independence relation is based on the presumed contrasting methods or "languages" of religion vis-à-vis science, while dialogue itself is a set of diverse solutions that go further toward reconciliation than independence but not as far as integration.

Finally, for our purposes, Massimo Pigliucci has proposed a more subtle range of relationships, building on the same/separate/conflicting worlds to yield nine different forms represented by specific theories and models (and associated with specific scientists or theists). These forms include Scientific Theism, Faith and Reason, Neo-Creationism, Theistic Science, the Strong and Weak Anthropic Principle, and Gould's NOMA (nonoverlapping magisteria), among others.[21] The point, ultimately, is that the question of "compatibility" is not a simple one but rather one conducive to many different answers and agendas. Indeed, some theists actively recruit science (at least some elements of science, occasionally in dubious ways) to support their theistic claims. Two well-known initiatives of this sort are the Intelligent Design movement and the "Reasons to Believe" project. Intelligent Design (ID), associated with Michael Behe (a scientist) and Phillip Johnson and William Dembski (not scientists) among others, is self-consciously "scientific." In other words, ID researchers, often working under the auspices of the Discovery Institute, invoke science to criticize certain inadequacies of science (like the alleged failings of evolutionary theory or the "irreducible complexity" of phenomena like the human eye or the bacterial flagellum) and argue for an "intelligence" behind the universe, which is roughly the Christian God.[22] Also putting science in the service of religion is Hugh Ross's "Reasons to Believe" work and the general "creation science" movement. Ross and his associates do not restrict themselves to any one area of science, nor are they ashamed to publicize their biblical agenda. "Whether you are looking for scientific support for your faith or answers to questions about God and science," they state on their website, they offer a home for scientifically minded Christians.[23] At their site one finds scientific-sounding information about stratigraphy, biology, astronomy, and a congeries of other subjects that, like other brands of creation science, purportedly support the biblical/creationist account of the universe.

So it is disappointingly clear that the question of "compatibility" of religion and science can be answered in various and contradictory ways. Smart people from both camps answer yes, no, maybe, and sometimes, but usually without specifying what they mean by "compatibility" or—more profoundly—why we are asking in the first place. Even more disappointingly, a close inspection of the notion of "compatibility" does not settle the matter. Webster's defines compatibility in several related ways: as capable of living together in harmony, capable of cross-fertilizing freely, capable of forming a homogeneous mixture that neither separates nor is altered by interaction, and being or relating to a system that may receive another system without special modification.[24] If we take these four criteria separately, we will see that the solution to the compatibility of religion and science is . . . yes, no, maybe, and sometimes.

If the question is "Are religion and science capable of living together in harmony?" then the answer is yes, no, maybe, and sometimes: for some people (like Behe and Ross) they seem harmonious, while for others (like Dawkins) they are mortal enemies. Further, it depends on which bit of religion or science you mean: most forms of Christianity are in harmony with atomic theory or gravitational theory and with technologies like metallurgy. But these things are, as we established above, neither "religion" nor "science." And Christianity is most definitely *not* in harmony with evolutionary theory or big bang theory, and so on. If the question is "Are religion and science capable of cross-fertilizing freely?" the answer is "Surprisingly widely freely." ID and Reasons to Believe allow them to cross-fertilize (or rather, allow science to fertilize religion). More significantly, though, in cross-fertilizing they sometimes produce weird hybrids, even bizarre mutations, like Christian Science, theistic evolution, creation science, and Scientology.

This only proves that religion is a malleable and adaptable species (see my earlier chapter in this book) that can absorb almost any influence—but that itself mutates as a result. Some Christians accept the scientific calculation of the age of the universe without abandoning their faith in creation (e.g., old-earth creationists versus young-earth creationists); the Catholic Church has even accepted the fact of biological evolution, simply adding to it that God intervened to introduce the human soul at some unknown moment. This sheds light on the third criterion of compatibility: true, religion and science may form a mixture, but each *is* altered by the interaction, in which case the answer is "no" to the question of compatibility. Religion after people add science is not the same, nor is science the same after religion is added. This applies to the fourth criterion as well: when one system (religion) receives another system (science), there will and must be a "special modification" in at least the religious system (as evinced by the fate of Galileo's or Darwin's work). Once science demonstrated that the earth revolved around the sun, the Christian cosmology had to change to accommodate this proven fact; other aspects of that cosmology could persist, perhaps later forced to accommodate other facts.

Now that science has demonstrated that biological species, including humans, evolved from ancestors, the pope, as just noted, has been compelled to adjust Catholic claims about the origin of species accordingly.

The potential or actual damage to religion from "special modification" is unclear and obviously not fatal; the potential or actual damage to science (and to scientists) can be quite devastating. When scientists are imprisoned for their findings (like Galileo) or even killed for their speculations (like Giordano Bruno), or when their books are burned or their research forbidden, then a great price has been paid for accommodating science to religion. In an article on Islam and science, Todd Pitock gives a cautionary example. Chemist and Muslim Waheed Badawy first asserts that "Islam has no problems with science." Then Pitock queried:

> "What about, say, evolutionary biology or Darwinism?" I ask. (Evolution is taught in Egyptian schools, although it is banned in Saudi Arabia and Sudan.)
>
> "If you are asking if Adam came from a monkey, no," Badawy responds. "Man did not come from a monkey. If I am religious, if I agree with Islam, then I have to respect all of the ideas of Islam. And one of these ideas is the creation of the human from Adam and Eve. If I am a scientist, I have to believe that."
>
> "But from the point of view of a scientist, is it not just a story?" I ask. He tells me that if I were writing an article saying that Adam and Eve is a big lie, it will not be accepted until I can prove it.
>
> "Nobody can just write what he thinks without proof. But we have real proof that the story of Adam as the first man is true."
>
> "What proof?"
>
> He looks at me with disbelief. "It's written in the Koran."[25]

IS RELIGION COMPATIBLE WITH SCIENCE?

> Science should be taught not in order to support religion and not in order to destroy religion. Science should be taught simply ignoring religion.
> —Steven Weinberg

As we ponder the question of the compatibility of religion and science, the first thing to ask is "Who cares?" Why should it matter to anyone if religion is compatible with science? From the point of view of science, it does not matter: if Weinberg is correct (and he is) science has no regard for anything except that which is detectable. Science is not out to help or to harm religion; it is fundamentally indifferent, ideally blind to anything except the facts. Individual *scientists*, as human beings and often religious believers, may care, but science as an enterprise does not and cannot care. So the subject of the compatibility of religion and science only matters to religion, more specifically to those who want to promote and protect, even shelter, religion from the adverse effects of facts and theories that contradict and destabilize religious claims and doctrines—and from the scientific premises and mentality that underlie those facts and theories.

Since in actual practice the question of the compatibility of religion and science amounts to a mission to rescue religion *from* science, the next thing to ask is "When does religion *need* rescuing from science?" That is, the original question about "compatibility" really disguises a deeper question: When, and in what way, does science threaten religion? The "when" is easy to see: science threatens religion when science disagrees with specific assertions ("beliefs" or "doctrines") of religion. As we stated earlier, no religion disputes or rejects all aspects of science; conversely, each religion disputes or rejects different aspects of science. Christianity, as is too well-known, has a particular problem with scientific claims about human origins (the dreaded evolution idea), the age of the universe (the dreaded idea that Genesis cannot be literally true and without error), and the origin of the universe (the equally dreaded big bang idea). Hinduism, on the other hand, has much less objection to the scientific finding of an old universe, since Hinduism holds a much longer view of time; Buddhism tends to have less trouble with human evolution, since evolution's conception of each form leading to new form sounds a bit like Buddhism (this is one reason why Japanese scientists, for example, have often been better able to see the continuity between humans and apes than Western, Christian-influenced scientists).

And no major religion objects to basic scientific notions like "cause." Well, that is not entirely true: the medieval Muslim concept of *kalam* did contradict the familiar scientific (and philosophical and rational) idea of cause. While *kalam* advocates did posit the reality of atoms and of empty space between atoms, they "denied that one event in the world could be the cause of another."[26] The reasoning was that "all events in the world are directly caused by God ... and directly attributable to the Will of God ... [N]othing is the cause of any other thing—God is the only cause, and the only explanation, of all processes observed in nature."[27] Thus, whether the question is the origin of humans, the reason why one billiard ball moves another, or what determines the spin of an electron, the answer is "Because God So Wills."[28] The impossibility, indeed the futility, of doing science under such a regime is obvious.

So religion only regards itself as "incompatible" with science when science is in disagreement with religion; when *science* agrees with *religion*, or when religion has no opinion on the matter, the issue of "compatibility" *never arises*. This suggests a rather facile way in which the "incompatibility" of religion and science can be removed: religion can drop or change its claims. And in truth, religion has done this very thing repeatedly throughout history. Christianity objected to the heliocentric (sun-centered) model of the solar system, but when it was proven true, Christianity relented and accepted it. Christianity objected to the discovery that the earth moved through space, but no sane Christian argues against this fact anymore. Even the pope, as mentioned, conceded that the human body had evolved from ancestral species. Therefore, since religion is an almost infinitely malleable scheme—because it is an entirely imaginary scheme—it can adapt to just about anything that is thrown at it. All it must do is reimagine.

We are still left with the rather frustrating circumstance of yes/no/maybe/sometimes to our initial question. Yes, religion and science are incompatible when they disagree; no, they are not incompatible when they agree; maybe and sometimes they can be made compatible if religion can absorb scientific facts or modify or reinterpret its beliefs in light of the facts (since beliefs are changeable but facts are not). But a question that resists straightforward answering after all of the analysis we have subjected it to must be a question that is asked wrong—or the wrong question to ask. Since nobody cares about the compatibility of religion and science except those who feel the menace of science for religion when it contradicts religion (in which case it *is* menacing), "compatibility" is not really the issue. The real issue is: In what essential way is science different from religion, and what does this difference mean for their coexistence?

The most fruitful approach to this rephrased question actually comes from the philosophical and historical study of science itself, particularly the famous and influential work of Thomas Kuhn. In *The Structure of Scientific Revolutions*, he argues that science is not a simply linear or progressive undertaking leading to greater and greater knowledge and understanding.[29] Rather, he proposes that science proceeds by a revolutionary process of overthrowing one dominant model or theory and replacing it with another, which will be dominant until it, too, is overthrown and replaced. He calls each such model/theory a "paradigm," which is a specific vision of reality at the grandest scale, our ideas of what kinds of things exist and their qualities and characteristics.

Most importantly, the confrontation between two paradigms is a clash of fundamental worldviews, worldviews that do not even contain the same premises or consider the same facts or, sometimes, even have the same standards for what a "fact" is in the first place. It is not always possible for holders of different paradigms to communicate, let alone to "settle" their differences. Rival paradigms not only cannot quite talk to each other but therefore *cannot quite argue with each other*. The different premises, practices, and key terms and concepts are often not intertranslatable or interintelligible. It is not even quite possible, or profitable, to debate between paradigms since their basic vocabulary, their basic premises, their basic concerns are not the same. What is true in one is false—or is irrelevant or does not exist at all—in the other, and what is proof or a valid method of argumentation is invalid or insignificant in the other.

Kuhn's discussion focuses exclusively on science and its various historical forms, but his ideas can and should be applied beyond specific scientific theories and beyond science itself. The differences between scientific theories notwithstanding, science as an enterprise falls within a general paradigm with two key premises, which we identified above as detectability and doubt. These two premises lead to a number of corollaries such as neutrality, regularity, equality and openness, causation, and tentativeness/skepticism. Whatever particular theory of the moment reigns, or whatever specialization of research is involved (chemistry, physics, psychology, etc.), science is always distinguished by this paradigm.

Other systems of thought operate with other paradigms. "Religion" is one such system of thought, and we can now reformulate our earlier discussion of religion in these terms. What Tylor called the minimal definition of religion ("the belief in spiritual beings") or what Wallace called the supernatural premise ("souls, supernatural beings, and supernatural forces exist") is the central premise of the religious paradigm, its sine qua non. Contemporary evolutionary psychologists and anthropologists from Horton to Guthrie to Boyer and Atran and Harvey and Kirkpatrick have refined this concept of spiritual beings to nonhuman/superhuman agency: religion is that worldview, that paradigm, which sees nonhuman/superhuman minds/wills/intentions at work and which "explains" events and legitimizes relations and institutions in terms of these beings and their wills.

As in the case of science, the central premise entails a number of sub-premises. For religion, these include

- Authority: There must be some source for individuals' "knowledge" of the putative spiritual beings, and members of the paradigm take tradition or scripture or whatever is offered by the religion as the basis for making these knowledge claims.
- Subjective experience: Contrary to science, which values reproducibility and the openness of knowledge, religion often stakes its claims on the unreproducible and unverifiable experiences of "adepts" who have access to knowledge that others do not. Even rank-and-file members advance their personal and interior experiences or "feelings" as evidence of and/or source of their beliefs.
- Miracles: While the term *miracle* has a specifically Judeo-Christian pedigree, all religions share the notion that the world is not entirely regular but that the putative spiritual beings may intervene in it at any time and change things—from one's health or wealth to the very laws of nature themselves.
- Participation: Religion does not encourage and often does not allow neutrality. One must take sides, one must commit oneself—often heart and soul—to a particular belief system. This typically forces one to make a choice in what is really a false dilemma (Pascal's "wager," Kierkegaard's "leap of faith," William James's "will to believe") between the "true belief" and all other actual or potential beliefs.
- Faith: Accordingly, religion does not encourage and often does not allow questioning or skepticism. The truth is already known; only minor details are left to work out (like how many angels can dance on a pin, or the precise dimensions of heaven). Even if questions do arise, the member should hold tight and not let them change his/her mind. But questions for the most part should be avoided.

That this religious paradigm is intensely unscientific and antiscientific is self-evident. Some of its most ardent defenders have been crystal clear about it.

The early Church father Tertullian actually said that religion and reason, belief and investigation, "Jerusalem" and "Athens," have nothing to do with each other: "After Jesus Christ we have no need of speculation, after the Gospel no need of research. When we come to believe, we have no desire to believe anything else; for we begin by believing that there is nothing else which we have to believe."[30] Protestant founder Martin Luther was an equally virulent opponent of the scientific paradigm, calling reason "the devil's bride," a "beautiful whore," and "God's worst enemy": "There is on earth among all dangers no more dangerous thing than a richly endowed and adroit reason," therefore "[r]eason must be deluded, blinded, and destroyed" and "faith must trample under foot all reason, sense, and understanding."[31]

It is also important to note that although religions all share the basic paradigm of animism or nonhuman intentionality, they vary extraordinarily in how they develop and what they add to this premise. Some religions populate the world with "nature spirits," while others posit supernatural "forces" like chi or mana or karma. Most religions maintain that human beings themselves have one or more supernatural components.

And then there are the gods. Some religions have god-concepts (theisms) and some, like Buddhism and most tribal religions, do not (nontheisms or atheisms). Of the theisms, some have one god (monotheisms) and some have more than one god (polytheisms). Within theisms, some gods are believed to be all-powerful and all-benevolent, and some are not: some have specific and limited power (say, power over thunder or the oceans or war), and some are partially benevolent or capricious or indifferent or malevolent. Some are utterly distinct from humans, while others are close to humans or even former humans. There is no standard, universal conception of "god" across religions, and many religions function perfectly well without any such concept. In short, while all religions operate under a basic shared paradigm of nonhuman agency, within that paradigm are many subparadigms: the "nature spirit" subparadigm, the "ancestor spirit" subparadigm, the "impersonal religious force" subparadigm, and the "god" subparadigm. And within each subparadigm are sub-subparadigms: the god subparadigm contains the monotheistic sub-subparadigm and the polytheistic sub-subparadigm, and the monotheistic sub-subparadigm includes the Jewish and Christian and Muslim sub-sub-subparadigms, and the Christian sub-sub-subparadigm includes the Catholic and Protestant and Orthodox sub-sub-sub-subparadigms, ad infinitum.

The difference between the scientific paradigm and the religious paradigm could not be clearer or more urgent. Science does not and cannot operate on the premises of authority, subjective experience, miracles, participation, and faith; to allow such premises would stop science in its tracks. But most fundamentally of all, science does not allow the central premise of religion, the supernatural agency premise, and it *cannot* allow this premise; a *seriously held* notion of nonhuman/superhuman agency makes science *impossible*—indeed, it paralyzes all human knowledge. It has this unavoidable effect for three critical reasons. First, nonhuman/superhuman agents and their minds or wills or intentions are always arranged in practice so as to be impossible to detect in principal, and so they violate the first and most basic premise of science. Even religious believers admit that their alleged beings are inscrutable, "work in mysterious ways," and are "unknowable." The believers are correct: we cannot know if these beings are at work, what exactly they are working on, or even whether they exist. And every "evidence" of their existence or action can be explained—and can be explained better—in nonsupernatural ways.

Second, the entire project of science depends on the regularity and predictability of nature, and supernatural agency makes nature irregular and unpredictable. By definition, agency or will is not completely determined by preexisting conditions; agents are "free" to act according to their own interests or intentions. Therefore, we do not and cannot know what they will do. The exact same conditions can lead to completely opposite results if the agents so choose; there is no connection between causes and effects. This precludes the possibility of ever knowing with any degree of confidence what will happen next or what connects to what. Human knowledge is displaced by supernatural mind reading—literally, often trying to "divine" the thoughts and wishes of invisible and probably nonexistent beings.

Third, while modern religionists mostly try to deny it, the supernatural premise of spiritual agency actually does destroy the notion of cause. Science strives to explain facts and events in terms of cause, which means antecedent conditions: if X is true or occurs, then Y will be true or occur. But agents, including human agents, do not act just in terms of causes. They act in terms of *motives*; that is, their goals or purposes or ends, which are idiosyncratic and future-oriented. The motives of agents are fundamentally "teleological": our "reason" for doing something is to achieve some objective that lies in the future. And since the future has not happened yet, any knowledge of it is prima facie impossible.

We can conclude, then, that the crucial and incontrovertible difference between science and religion—that which makes them incompatible at their core, even if they happen to agree on some details—is the basic premise from which each arises and therefore the "kind of answer" that each wants to offer. Religion functions on the *personal premise* that some or all facts and events are the results of the motives of (supernatural) agents. Science functions on the *impersonal premise* that facts and events are the effects of antecedent and nonagentive—and therefore *knowable*—causes. In other words, when science explains a hurricane in terms of temperatures and winds, and so forth, none of the components has any "will" or "purpose" or "intelligence." They are completely determined by natural, nonpersonal factors. Even the sciences of man (sociology, anthropology) study a *detectable* agency that is in turn explainable causally (human desires have causes in biology and evolution, for example, and in detectable circumstances of their environment). When *religion* explains something, that "explanation" by definition depends in some way on an entity that has will or purpose or intelligence—sometimes an "ultimate" intelligence—which is fundamentally unknowable to us humans.

Of course, religion can always come along and add a personal and agentive layer to scientific explanations: "The tsunami was caused by an underwater earthquake, *and* it is the will of God for the purpose of punishing/teaching/testing blah blah blah." However, this extra explanatory layer is undetectable and untestable scientifically (which means "actually"), could refer to any god/spirit/supernatural force, and in the end explains nothing. Science does not need the religious "explanation," and, if religion had any merit at all, religion would not need the scientific explanation. In a word, science has no obligation to be "compatible" with religion and could not care less about its "compatibility" with religion.

Chapter 12

NEITHER LIFE NOR THE UNIVERSE APPEAR INTELLIGENTLY DESIGNED

by Dr. Richard Carrier

T he "argument from design" is said to help prove the Christian God exists. But Christianity is actually the least credible explanation of any apparent design in the universe. In fact, the evidence argues against there being any intelligent design of the universe at all. All the apparent design in life *presently* on earth has already been more adequately explained by natural selection than any theory of intelligent design. But even the *origin* of life and the supposed "fine-tuning" of the physical constants of the universe make little sense as the result of deliberate engineering but make perfect sense as the result of random accident. Likewise the human mind, the experience of beauty, or the intelligibility of the cosmos. This conclusion can actually be demonstrated with such logical certainty that Christianity is fully disconfirmed by the evidence of life and the universe.

TESTING CLAIMS WITH BAYES' THEOREM

Bayes' theorem is an argument in formal logic that derives the probability that a claim is true from certain other probabilities about that theory and the evidence.[1] It's been formally proven, so no one who accepts its premises can rationally deny its conclusion. It has four premises, each one stating a probability that's conditional on our total background knowledge b (everything we know with reasonable certainty is true about history, science, and everything else):

$P(h|b)$ = the prior probability that a given claim h is true
$P(\sim h|b)$ = the prior probability that claim h is false

P($e|h.b$) = the consequent probability of the evidence e if claim h is actually true

P($e|{\sim}h.b$) = the consequent probability of the evidence e if claim h is actually false

This means we first ask what the probability is that our claim is true "before" we get to look at any of the specific evidence for it. That will be the prior probability. The other prior probability (of "not h") is always the converse of that (e.g., if the prior probability of h is 25 percent, the prior probability of $\sim h$ is 75 percent). Then we look at the specific evidence for our claim, and there we ask how likely all that evidence would be if our claim really is true, and then we ask how likely it is that we'd still have all that evidence even if our claim is false. Once we have our answers, the conclusion necessarily follows according to a fixed formula.[2] That conclusion is then *by definition* the probability that our claim h is true given all our evidence e and all our background knowledge b. In other words, that's simply what the probability is that our claim is true.

Since that conclusion necessarily follows from the premises, we should aim at premises no one can rationally deny, as then no one can rationally deny the conclusion, either. For the following analysis I shall be relying on previous publications that deserve much of the credit.[3] I will present every argument in plain English but provide the mathematical proofs in associated endnotes (for those readers who are keen to check the math). I will first define the "God hypothesis" in Bayesian terms, then determine what its prior probability must be, then complete a Bayesian analysis for each of three kinds of alleged nonterrestrial intelligent design (or NID): current life, the origin of life, and the construction of the universe. Then I will analyze three lesser known examples of design sometimes touted: mind, beauty, and intelligibility.

DEFINING THE GOD HYPOTHESIS

First we must define the claim being tested: that NID exists. By "intelligent design," I mean design that is not the product of blind natural processes (such as some combination of chance and necessity), and by "nonterrestrial," I mean neither made by man (or woman) nor any other known life-form. For instance, a bird's nest exhibits intelligent design, but that's because birds have the rudimentary intelligence to build nests, and there isn't anything supernatural about that. And it's really the supernatural we're trying to find.

In fact I will assume, solely for the sake of argument, that the probability that God exists if NID exists is effectively 100 percent.[4] That's far higher than that actual probability could possibly be, because if we met with any strange artifact on another planet or really almost any other instance of NID, we would never conclude God made it but that some extraterrestrial intelligence had done so—which proves we all agree it's far more likely that any observed case of NID is a product of aliens than a god. Indeed, even if we narrow the reference class to things seemingly beyond a mere alien's abilities, that conclusion still follows. Designing life certainly isn't beyond such ability—we're well on our way to being able to do that ourselves, and we'll surely be doing it with consummate mastery within just a thousand more years of technological development. Yet any alien civilization selected at random will statistically be millions or billions of years more advanced than even that. We already can envision ways in which creating designer universes will enter the purview of such a species. By contrast, we have no comparable background knowledge establishing that gods are even as likely as aliens, much less *more* likely. So when I say "for the sake of argument" the probability that God exists if NID exists is 100 percent, please know I'm being absurdly generous to the God hypothesis.

NID and God are then fully interchangeable hypotheses if we delimit "God" to mean only "a very powerful self-existent being who creates things by design."[5] Other gods are not relevant, since not being "designing" gods by definition, the prior probability that there would be NID given any of those gods is effectively zero; that is, the probability that a non-NID god would intelligently design life or the universe is zero because, by definition, such a god doesn't do that sort of thing. Conversely, the probability that a "designing" god exists but never intelligently designed anything is likewise virtually zero, since by definition that's also not how such a god behaves. Likewise, "gods" who aren't very powerful are out of account, since by definition they can't make universes or life; and designing "gods" who are not self-existent are basically extraterrestrials, not gods—and I just said I'm assuming no such beings will ever exist (even though I know full well that's not true). Hence, from now on I will often substitute God for NID and mean thereby "a very powerful self-existent being who creates things by design."

THE PRIOR PROBABILITY OF NONTERRESTRIAL INTELLIGENT DESIGN

What is the prior probability of NID? By definition, this must be the probability that such design would exist *before* we even get to look at any specific evidence for it. In other words, given all our background knowledge—everything we know with reasonable certainty about science and history and everything else—how likely is it that *anything* we point to is the product of NID?

Probability measures frequency (whether of things happening or of things being true). So we're really asking *how frequently* are things we point to (in all our background knowledge) the product of NID? Quite obviously, very infrequently indeed. In fact, so far, that frequency is exactly zero. And that's out of a vast number of things we've found exhibiting apparent design. That includes things made by people (trillions upon trillions of things), things made by animals (many trillions more), things made by other life-forms, like bacteria blindly following their genetic computer programs (those programs may be intelligently designed, but here I'm referring only to their behavior once they've come to exist, for example, bacteria exhibit intelligent behavior but are not themselves intelligent; and counting up everything like that, we're adding trillions upon trillions of more examples), and things made by blind physical processes, like crystallization or the forming of stars from collapsing dust clouds (processes that, again, may have been intelligently designed but are not themselves acting intelligently).

If we set aside all contested cases (and take them all out of *b* and put them in *e*, so we can deal with those later—which means any alleged design of the universe, the first life, or current life), what do we have left? Not a single case of NID. And countless billions and trillions of cases of *not* NID. It might have been different. We could have had by now a scientifically confirmed case of NID. Even lots of them. But so far science has failed to properly verify even one alleged case in the way that science has established as known facts such things as the laws of physics or the size and age of the universe. Thus, based on our background knowledge *alone*, in other words, before we consider *any* as-yet-only-alleged cases of NID, the frequency of NID is practically infinitesimal (if not, in fact, zero). This means its prior probability is vanishingly small, approaching zero.[6]

This follows even if we narrow the reference class and discount all things intelligently designed but not a product of NID—which is proper, since no one believes life or the universe are intelligently designed by humans or animals or any known life-form, so we can limit our interest to things we're sure are *not* made by any already-known life-forms. But still we have trillions of cases of ~NID and no cases of NID. Likewise if we narrowed our reference class again to things that are especially complex, since even then we still have no confirmed instances of NID yet *many* confirmed instances of ~NID. And even if we narrowed it further to include only things with such highly specified complexity that we don't observe any instances at all (apart from those we're putting in *e*), we *still* don't have any established instances that are NID in *b*, and thus cannot get a higher prior for NID that way. In fact, if we narrowed our reference class to the point that the only instances to count are the cases we're putting in *e*, then we're begging the question (by assuming those instances are too improbable on any other account, which is actually what we are supposed to be proving in the first place).

It would be silly to narrow the reference class to such rare instances anyway, because by far most instances of intelligent design (such as by humans and animals) are not anywhere near that improbable as products of other causes, *apart from coincidences of correlation*, which is how we normally learn that intelligent agents exist and have acted in the world: the probability that observed correlations between human actions and their results are all the product of chance rather than design is absurdly small (hence, in those cases, the design hypothesis is the more probable, no matter how low its prior probability may have been). That's why we interpret such simple things as flipping a light switch or moving a cup as being the result of intelligent design even though such things can actually plausibly happen by accident. Hence it's precisely the fact that God never does things like that in our observation that makes positing God as a causal explanation of *other* things so implausible. An agent you never see acting is usually the *last* causal hypothesis you would ever consider for explaining anything. This reasoning is exactly what is being reflected in our calculation of prior probability from observed (non)instances of divine causation in the world.

To understand why this follows, imagine that we can reach into the set of all things in the universe that look designed (but were not made by humans or any other known life form) and pick one of them completely at random. We place it in front of you but behind a curtain so you don't yet get to see what it is. What probability would you say it has of being *demonstrably* a product of NID? We must say "demonstrably," because this cannot be based on what you believe but only on what you know, and we're talking about established background *knowledge* here. You can't use fallaciously circular logic to declare "everything is a product of NID." Rather, we must reason from only what you and I, and everyone else who's rational and sane, agree is an established fact. That's the *prior* probability that anything is a product of NID. Behind that curtain could be a rock, a star system, a river, a complex hydrocarbon molecule. Are any of those things already proven to be the products of NID? No. To the contrary, science can fully explain how they formed without any reference to NID. And we all know this. You could still say that, for example, the laws of physics that *caused* those things to form were a product of NID. But that has not yet been *demonstrated*. So we've put that in *e*. If we put it behind this curtain it would only be inconclusive, not a *known* instance of NID. So far, nothing is. You know full well no intelligent designer needs to put a rock together. He may have set up the rules, but once those rules are in place they put rocks together without any intelligence being involved.

Clearly, given these conditions, you would have to agree that the probability that anything put behind that curtain is a product of NID is indeed virtually zero. So if it must be that low, then there is definitely no case to be made that it's as high as 25 percent (or 1 in 4).[7] No rational person can honestly believe that more than one in every four of all the complex things that form and happen in this universe is the *confirmed* product of divine intervention. So unless you are quite irrational indeed, you must agree the prior probability of NID cannot be higher than 25 percent.[8] Thus I will use that as its value hereafter, knowing you can never argue it's any higher. And if the prior probability of NID is 25 percent, then the prior probability of *not* being NID is 75 percent (the converse of 25 percent).[9] We have our first two premises.

EVOLUTION BY NATURAL SELECTION
BETTER EXPLAINS ALL CURRENT LIFE

Ever since Charles Darwin proposed the theory over a century and a half ago, science has multiply confirmed in countless ways that the apparent design of all current life is wholly explained by a process of evolution by natural selection carried out on a vast time scale.[10] And that is not NID. All of this evidence is vast, and vastly improbable on any other theory, to the point that now it's simply an established fact in our background knowledge. So the complexity of current life shouldn't even make anyone's list of candidates for NID. Nevertheless, antiestablishment diehards persist in insisting the contrary.

I'll set aside ignoramuses who don't know what they're talking about and don't even try to know (like young-earth creationists who think the Kentucky Creation Museum isn't lying to them), and consider only actual scholars with PhDs in some relevant field who insist some current life proves NID. All their arguments amount now to various iterations of the same general claim: that there are at least a few biological structures that can't have been formed even by evolution, and thus must have been formed by NID. Their argument is covertly Bayesian: they are saying the probability that that evidence would exist on a hypothesis of evolution is so small (whereas the probability that it would exist on a hypothesis of *design* is so high), that this overcomes any prior probability to the contrary. The most famous and representative example is Michael Behe's claim that the flagellar propulsion system of the *E. coli* bacterium is irreducibly complex and thus cannot have evolved.[11]

These critics know (and when honest, admit) that many actual instances of very elegant and complex design in living things are not the product of intelligence but are fully and most credibly explained as the outcomes of gradual evolution by nonintelligent selection.[12] Their existence is thus highly probable on the hypothesis of evolution, and in fact routinely far *more* probable than on NID—not only when considering their design flaws (which are fully explicable on evolution but less so on NID), but also considering what is far more commonly observed: evidence of DNA ancestry. That God would allow common descent and just "tweak" DNA here and there to build new parts and systems and species out of what's already there, and piecemeal bit by bit over vast spaces of time, is certainly "possible" but is not even remotely what we would normally expect. The probability that a god would effect his designs that way, instead of any number of countless more direct and obvious ways (like simply creating all life tout court right at once, or just generating new species sui generis when it suited him), is certainly low, whereas the probability that this is what we would observe if *evolution* explained it all is fully 100 percent. Even Behe cannot deny this.

But the evidence weighs even more strongly against NID. Because our "evidence" includes the fact that life began as a single-celled organism, which continued evolving for over *three billion years* before it ever struck upon the notion of combining forces with other single cells to make a multicellular life-form. Once life chanced upon that innovation, all sorts of new opportunities arose, and life exploded into many different pathways of multicellular organization, yet even that took over a *hundred million years* to develop and finally settle on a few best patterns. It took hundreds of millions of years more for these rudimentary life-forms to evolve into the much more developed forms we see all around us now, and fully *five hundred million years* altogether for this meandering evolution of multicellular organisms to finally chance upon becoming a human being. And throughout this process, an initially simple chemistry of relatively common chemicals (just four nucleotide molecules) underlies the entire process with purely mechanical computer programs (strings of DNA) running everything and, as a result, frequently crashing or malfunctioning and acquiring bugs and garbage code and being copied incorrectly, and so on, all without any established sign of any intelligent programmer being around to fix or prevent all this, or even tending it in any way at all.

If there is no NID, all this is the only known way life could exist at all, the only known way *we* could exist at all. There is no other pathway by which random chance and natural forces could go from commonplace chemistry to human beings. Thus, given that we exist (which is a well-established fact in our background knowledge), the probability that we would observe the history and structure of life to be this way if *evolution* is how we got here is virtually 100 percent. But if NID caused life, then this is *not* the only known way life could exist. Quite the contrary, there are countless other ways life could exist and be structured and tended—not least being the most obvious: instantaneous creation of uniform bodies free of needless imperfections. Unless you can *prove* that no "very powerful self-existent being who creates things by design" would ever create life in any other way (in *any* other way) than exactly the same way that happens to be exactly the only way it would be done if there were no "very powerful self-existent being who creates things by design" to begin with, you must concede that the probability that such a God would do it that way, as opposed to some other, is *less* than 100 percent. Indeed, quite a lot less.

We must ask, for example, why plants and animals are constructed from colonies of single-celled organisms rather than uniform tissues. Evolution makes sense of the accumulation of cooperating cells, because any other pathway to current life is absurdly improbable. But if life is intelligently designed, why did the designer need to build tissues out of cells, each one identical to an autonomous single-celled organism, complete with a full set of DNA, merely programmed to *act* like it's part of a system of many such cells together? And why such a slow, gradual process of development? Why have microbes inhabited the planet six times longer than multicelled plants and animals? Not only as opposed to all life appearing at once (again the most obvious thing we should expect on NID), but even the relative timeline makes no sense: again, single-celled life has been here, evolving, *six times longer* than all other life. As a product of NID, this makes next to no sense at all. God doesn't need to wait. He has no thumbs to twiddle. But as a product of evolution, this is exactly what we must expect to see: because multicellular life then requires such an advanced development of cellular machinery, only an extremely long period of evolution could get life to that stage, thereby making multicellular organisms possible. Thus all this evidence is 100 percent expected on evolution. But its probability on NID is nowhere near that.

The nail in the coffin is Behe's ill-advised emphasis on the flagellum of the *E. coli* bacterium. That flagellum actually belongs to lethal varieties of *E. coli*, an infamously deadly pathogen. We also have benevolent forms of *E. coli* in our guts, but even that becomes deadly if it gets into our bloodstream. Since the flagellum Behe says must have been intelligently designed is what gives this bacteria the ability to move around, it actually greatly magnifies its lethality to humans. In fact, that's pretty much all it does—which means *that's what it's for*. In other words, Behe is essentially saying that someone genetically engineered bacteria specifically to kill us. This should be extremely alarming. If Behe wasn't so obsessed with "liking God" for no good reason, he would be lobbying Congress to form a national defense plan against the terrorist threat he just discovered. We should be mobilizing to identify and protect ourselves from this unknown enemy filling the earth with deviously engineered weapons of mass destruction. That's what any *rational* person would conclude from making such a discovery. But more to the present point, we must ask, why do bacteria even exist at all? Why have diseases of any sort, much less lethal ones so small we can't even see them to defend ourselves? Evolution makes this observation 100 percent expected. The God hypothesis does *not* make it 100 percent expected—as if we could deduce with absolute certainty from the premise "there is a very powerful self-existent being who creates things by design" that

"that being would try to kill us with genetically engineered bioweapons" (and yet still not do a very good job at it).

Behe would respond by insisting that, nevertheless, the existence of the flagellum is just too improbable on the assumption that evolution produced it. But it isn't. And he hasn't shown it to be. Because to this very day, he has never checked. He always counts up the parts of the machine itself, yet neglects to mention that the probability of those parts existing in that arrangement is fully 100 percent . . . given the arrangement of the DNA that codes for its construction (because the chemistry that ensues always produces that result mechanically from its coded input, no special intelligence required). And he can't know if that *code* is improbable if he never even bothers to find out *what it is*. He has never engaged any scientific research to locate that code or determine its length or complexity. He has done nothing to find out if the genes comprising that code also already do other things in the same bacterium besides build the flagellum. He has done nothing to locate all the *correlating* genes in *other* microbes, microbes that also have flagella and microbes that don't (as well as duplicate ancestral genes in the same microbe)—to see, for example, if there is any evidence of stepwise evolution in those genes across species, both in the ongoing evolution of the flagellum and in its evolution from prior organs or functions. He has never tried knocking out any of the genes or nucleotides in that code to see what happens or changing them to see how much variation is possible while still producing flagella or what such variations cause to happen *other* than the construction of flagella (which could be a clue to what that flagellum evolved from).

The fact of the matter is, the bacterial flagellum, though composed of barely thirty parts, is actually *six times more evolved* than the human hand (having had three billion years to our hand's mere half billion), which is composed of *billions* of parts. Yet scientists have reconstructed a very obvious and well-confirmed pathway of small stepwise evolution from simple amorphous appendages to fully complex hands. If we can get to a billion intricately arranged parts from just one, using miniscule random steps, why does Behe think we can't get to just thirty? Since there has been a vastly longer span of time for bacteria to evolve highly efficient organs like the flagellum, which, again, are actually vastly simpler than the organs we've evolved in just half a billion years, Behe has a long way to go before he can prove this couldn't have happened. Thus, in actual fact, there is no evidence of his irreducible complexity.

Because Behe has never even *tried* to find any, much less actually done so. No one has.[13] So we're left with all that *other* evidence, which is evidence we actually *do* have. And yet on any one of those points just surveyed, and far more so on all of them together, the probability that we would have the evidence we actually have is effectively 100 percent if evolution is true, but vanishingly small if NID is true.

Certainly, no rational person can honestly believe the latter probability is anything above 50 percent. There is simply no way the odds are "50-50" that "a very powerful self-existent being who creates things by design" would create current life *that* way, exactly the same way evolution would on its own, rather than any other way that's far more sensible and expected. Yet that entails the Bayesian conclusion that the probability that God intelligently designed current life cannot be any higher than 15 percent (and is almost certainly a great deal less than that).[14] That means no rational person can believe the probability that God intelligently designed current life is any better than 1 in 6. Which means every rational person must conclude God probably didn't do that. Current life thus does not appear to be intelligently designed.

NATURAL BIOGENESIS BETTER EXPLAINS THE ORIGIN OF LIFE ON EARTH

So current life probably evolved by natural causes without any intelligent guidance. But something had to get that ball rolling. What about the origin of life? All attempts to prove the origin of life was too improbable to have happened by accident have failed, being either wrong as to the facts or using the wrong math.[15] But even once we realize that it *can* happen by chance, isn't it still more likely that it would happen by design? To answer that question, we have to look again at all the actual evidence and properly deduce what NID predicts given our background knowledge, and what the *absence* of NID predicts given the same, and compare that to what we observe.

If it isn't NID, then by definition the origin of life must be a random accident. And there's no denying that (by itself) the first living organism is an extremely improbable accident. Of course, so is winning a lottery, and yet lotteries are routinely won. Because the laws of probability entail the odds of a lottery being won depend not just on how unlikely a win is, like perhaps a one in a billion chance, but on how often the game is played. If a billion people play, and the odds of winning are one in a billion, it's actually highly *probable* that someone will win the lottery. And if *many* billions play, the probability that such a lottery will be won is as near to 100 percent as makes all odds. There-fore, the only way life could arise without NID is if there were countless more failed tries than actual successes. After all, if that lottery was played by a billion people and still only one of them won, we would be certain it was chance, not evidence of NID.

So the only way the lottery of *life* could be won by accident is if it was played countless times and only one ticket won. This means the only way life could arise by accident is if the universe tried countless times and only very rarely succeeded. Lo and behold, that's exactly what we observe: the universe has been mixing random chemicals in random environments for over twelve billion years in over a billion-trillion star systems collectively containing tens of billions of trillions of planets and moons. That is exactly what we would *have* to see if life arose by accident. Because life can arise by accident *only* in a uni-verse that large and old. The fact that we observe exactly what the theory of accidental origin requires and predicts is evidence that our theory is correct. Hence the evidence of biogenesis does not consist of looking at just the one biogenesis event (as if we were to look at just the one lottery winner, saw the odds of his winning were one in a billion, and then concluded he cheated), but at the entire context of that event: all the vast space and time of failed attempts to accidentally produce life (corresponding to all the people who played the same lottery and lost). Hence the probability that we would observe this *actual* evidence on the complete absence of NID is essentially 100 percent. But this same evidence is necessarily *less* than 100 percent likely if it's a product of NID. We cannot predict from "a very powerful self-existent being created life by design" that he would do this by creating trillions of galaxies and billions of light years of empty intergalactic space and then sit around and twiddle his thumbs for ten billion years before finally deciding to create life in just one tiny place. That's not even expected at all, much less with 100 percent certainty.[16]

Furthermore, the only way life could ever arise by accident is if it was com-posed of commonplace chemicals that naturally chain together and, in just the right combination, naturally metabolize and reproduce. We have observed that the only chemicals that our present universe is likely to accidentally assemble this way are various molecules of amino acids. Lo and behold, we observe that's exactly what we have: all life is a by-product of organized chains of amino acids (now in the form of RNA and DNA, which are just repeating sequences of only four different nucleotide molecules). Given our background knowledge *b* (everything we know about the contents of this universe and its chemistry), that we would observe something like this on the complete absence of NID is essentially 100 percent. But God could make life any other way. He doesn't have to make it look exactly the same as if it were a natural accident. He doesn't even need chemistry at all. He could simply imbue bodies with the properties of metabolism and reproduction, no DNA needed. But even if he were limited to natural physics, there are countless ways to make life that do not require the one pathway that's already expected if there is no God. At the very least, no rational person can say it's 100 percent certain that "a very powerful self-existent being who created life by design" would only make life this one way—suspiciously the only way that looks exactly like God didn't do it. The probability is certainly less than that.

Finally, we must return to the observation made in the previous section: that life beginning with a simple single-celled microbe is the only way life could have arisen if there's no God (because any other origin would be too improbable), but it is not the only way life could have arisen if there is a God. Thus, the probability that we would observe this on the absence of NID is 100 percent, while the probability that we would observe this on NID is necessarily *less* than 100 percent. When we put this all together—we know life originated as a simple single cell (or possibly even a subcellular molecule), and that it originated with the chaining together of a common chemical that commonly chains together and which we know causes natural self-replication when arranged the right way, in a vast universe almost the whole of which consists of what are in effect countless failed attempts to arrange any chemical in the right way—we find exactly what we must observe if there was no NID. But from the hypothesis "God exists," it simply isn't possible to deduce the prediction that "simple, single-celled, carbon-coded life forms would arise on just this one planet out of trillions, and only billions of years after the universe formed, and billions of years before any conscious agents resulted from them." No rational person can honestly believe the probability of *that* is any greater than 50 percent on NID.

This entails the Bayesian conclusion that the probability that God intelligently designed the origin of life cannot be any higher than 15 percent (and is almost certainly a great deal less than that).[17] That means no rational person can believe the probability that God intelligently originated the first life is any better than 1 in 6. This means every rational person must conclude God probably didn't do that. The origin of life thus does not appear to be intelligently designed.

NATURAL COSMOGENESIS BETTER EXPLAINS
THE PROPERTIES OF THE OBSERVED UNIVERSE

So life probably appeared on earth by natural accident, but that's only because the universe is organized in a certain way so that all its contents and all the laws of physics and chemistry would inevitably kick up life. True, life will then only be an extremely rare outcome in a few extremely isolated places. But it's surely improbable that the universe would be just so arranged that way, as opposed to some other way—some way that would make a natural occurrence of life impossible. And indeed this has been forcefully argued time and again: the physical constants of the universe (from which follow all the laws of physics and chemistry, from which follow in turn all the contents and properties of the universe) have to be so finely tuned to make life even *possible* that there's just no way this could have happened except for intelligent design.[18] But this argument is based on a fatal fallacy in reasoning about conditional probability.[19]

Suppose in a thousand years we develop computers capable of simulating the outcome of every possible universe, with every possible arrangement of physical constants, and these simulations tell us which of those universes will produce arrangements that make conscious observers (as an inevitable undesigned by-product). It follows that in none of those universes are the conscious observers intelligently designed (they are merely inevitable by-products), and none of those universes are intelligently designed (they are all of them constructed purely at random). Suppose we then see that conscious observers arise only in one out of every $10^{1,000,000}$ universes (or whatever ungodly percentage you want, it doesn't matter). Would any of those conscious observers be right in concluding that their universe was intelligently designed to produce them? No. Not even one of them would be. If every single one of them would be wrong to conclude that, then it necessarily follows that we would be wrong to conclude that, too (because we're looking at exactly the same evidence they would be, yet we could be in a randomly generated universe just like them). It simply follows that if we exist and the universe is entirely a product of random chance (and not NID), then the probability that we would observe the kind of universe we do is 100 percent expected. This is not improbable *at all*, much less too improbable to believe.

"Ah, but that's only true if there are lots and lots of universes," you might say. But that's not so. Their error lies not in failing to consider there are other universes but in thinking fine-tuning entails design at all, precisely because in their case it never does, and never would. For example, it's entirely possible that one of those rare universes will happen to be the first in the sequence of random universes generated. The probability of that is exactly the same as it falling anywhere else in that sequence. So if we stopped there and thus generated no more simulations, we would have exactly the same situation as only one universe existing and it *just by chance* being finely tuned to produce intelligent life. The conscious observers in that universe would see exactly all the same evidence. And they would be exactly as wrong if they still concluded their universe was intelligently designed to produce them: 100 percent wrong. Thus, the conclusion does not require us to imagine a multiverse. We have no need of that hypothesis.[20] The evidence simply always looks exactly the same whether a universe is finely tuned by chance or by design—no matter how improbable such fine-tuning is by chance. And if the evidence looks exactly the same on either hypothesis, there is no logical sense in which we can say the evidence is more likely on either hypothesis. Think of getting an amazing hand at poker: whether the hand was rigged or if you just got lucky, the evidence is identical. So the mere fact that an amazing hand at poker is extremely improbable is not evidence of cheating. Thus "it's improbable" is simply not a valid argument for design.

This seems counterintuitive only because humans are not well designed for logical or probabilistic reasoning. Those are skills we have to learn. And they are difficult to learn—and even once learned are still difficult to apply correctly. When we say the odds are 1 in $10^{1,000,000}$ that the universe we observe would exist by chance (or whatever probability—again it doesn't matter), we are erroneously comparing this universe to all other universes that don't have intelligent life. But we already know *we can never be in one of those universes*. This is information we can't ignore. Just like the people in those simulated universes: they will only ever find themselves in a finely tuned universe *whether it was designed or not*. The fact of their universe being finely tuned can never tell them anything about how it got that way. Once we attend to this correct logic, we have to compare this universe not to all other universes but to all other universes we would ever be in. Only if we do that, and only if there is *still* a difference between a designed universe and a chance universe, would we be able to conclude that the universe we are in was designed (or not) by seeing which of *those* differences are observed (or not). Otherwise, we can never tell.[21]

This conclusion cannot rationally be denied: if only finely tuned universes can produce life, then if intelligent observers exist (and we can see they do), then the probability that their universe will be finely tuned will be 100 percent.[22] Always. Regardless of whether a "finely tuned universe" is a product of chance, and regardless of how improbable a chance it is.[23] Because "intelligent observers exist" *entails* we could never observe anything else. The only way the odds could ever be anything less than 100 percent is if you can have intelligent observers *without* a finely tuned universe (as then, *and only then*, it would at least be logically possible for there *not* to be a finely tuned universe if there are intelligent observers). But as it happens, you can only have *that* (a nonfinely tuned universe with intelligent observers) in an intelligently designed universe. Ironic, yes. But true. Because if there is no NID, the *only* way intelligent observers could ever exist is if a universe existed that was finely tuned to produce them (whether it was finely tuned by chance or not). So that this is what we observe is 100 percent expected on the absence of NID. It's the *only* thing we could observe if there is no NID.

But God is not limited to the extraordinarily elaborate Rube Goldberg-esque contraption of arranging a bunch of obscure physical constants just to make life. There are lots of other ways a god can do it, and only *those* ways are at all unexpected on the absence of NID. This is why the fact that we don't observe this universe to be any of those universes argues *against* this universe being a product of NID, not the other way around. The probability that God would use that one bizarre, extremely complicated, indirect, and totally unnecessary method—coincidentally exactly the only method that could ever produce us if there was no God at all—is surely not 100 percent. Indeed, it can't plausibly be anywhere near that. You cannot deduce from "God exists" that the only way he would ever make a universe is *that* way. There must surely be some probability that he might do it another way. Indeed, that probability must be quite high, simply because it's weird for an intelligent agent of means to go the most inefficient and unnecessary route to obtaining his goals, and "weird" means by definition "rare," which means "infrequent," which means "improbable."

All probabilities must be conditional on our background knowledge. And that knowledge already includes the fact that we find ourselves in a world where life arose and evolved into people. And any probability of the evidence must reflect the fact that we arose only with such extraordinary rarity as should blow anyone's mind, in a universe of a size and age that's even more mind-blowingly old and vast. What's more, this universe is 99.99999 percent composed of lethal radiation-filled vacuum, and 99.99999 percent of all the material in the universe comprises stars and black holes on which nothing can ever live, and 99.99999 percent of all *other* material in the universe (all planets, moons, clouds, asteroids) is barren of life or even outright inhospitable to life. In other words, the universe we observe is *extraordinarily inhospitable* to life. Even what tiny inconsequential bits of it are at all hospitable are *extremely inefficient* at producing life—at all, but far more so intelligent life (e.g., of all the planetary and lunar living space in just our solar system alone, at least 99.99 percent is barren of native intelligent life and probably all life).[24]

In the words of cosmologists Hawley and Holcomb, "if the intent of the universe is to create life, then it has done so in a very inefficient manner," unlike the cosmos Aristotle once honestly thought there was, which had "a much greater amount of life per cubic centimeter" (and that's an understatement: its "life per cubic centimeter" would be on the order of 10^{30} times greater than ours).[25] In Aristotle's world, the atmosphere of the earth extended to the moon, and even beyond that the whole universe was filled with a special breathable medium that was fully inhabited by animals suited thereto. We can as easily imagine a universe of any size in which the whole of it has breathable air and places to fly and rest and eat and drink, or in which the whole of it was filled with water (after all, let's not bias the options in favor of us newbie air-breathers) or a vacuum that wasn't lethal (if life didn't need to breathe but took all its sustenance directly from the rays of the sun)—or anything else or in between.[26]

One way or another, a universe perfectly designed for life would easily, readily, and abundantly produce and sustain life. Most of the contents of that universe would be conducive to life or benefit life. Yet that's not what we see. Instead, almost the entire universe is lethal to life—in fact, if we put all the lethal vacuum of outer space swamped with deadly radiation into an area the size of a house, you would never find the comparably microscopic speck of area that sustains life (it would literally be smaller than a single proton). It's exceedingly difficult to imagine a universe *less* conducive to life than that—indeed, that's about as close to being completely incapable of producing life as any random universe can be expected to be, other than of course being completely incapable of producing life. But, as already explained, we already know we're not in one of *those* universes, so we can rule them out, just as a lottery winner can rule out the possibility of his losing the lottery and then only compare wins that resulted from chance with wins that resulted from cheating—since it is only *that* ratio that determines the probability that his win was by design and not by chance.

For example, if 1 in 100 lottery wins are by design, and the remainder by chance, then the probability that an observed win is by design is simply 1 in 100, *no matter how improbable that win is*. Even if the odds of winning were 1 in $10^{1,000,000}$. For even then, if it's still the case that 99 in 100 wins are the product of chance, then the odds that *this* win is the result of chance are not 1 in $10^{1,000,000}$ but 99 percent. That's why we never assume anything is fishy when we draw an amazing hand at a family game of poker. The probability of doing so may be 1 in 100,000, but it doesn't follow that the odds of it being by design are then the converse of that (a 99.999 percent chance the hand is rigged), because we already know most amazing hands are fair. Thus if we know less than 1 in 1,000 amazing hands are rigged, and then draw an amazing hand that is 100,000 to 1 against, the probability of that hand being rigged is still only 0.1 percent (1 in 1,000), not 99.999 percent. To carry the analogy over, how many actual life-bearing universes are the product of chance? If there is no God, then 100 percent of them will be. Thus, where L = "a kind of life-bearing universe exists whose odds of existing without a god are 1 in $10^{1,000,000}$," it is *necessarily the case* that the probability that we would observe L if there is no God is fully 100 percent, not 1 in $10^{1,000,000}$.[27] Yet the most we can ever get for the God hypothesis is still only the same 100 percent probability that L would be true.[28] And if that's the case, then Bayes' theorem gives us a probability that NID caused the universe of only 25 percent.[29] There is then only a 25 percent chance *at best* that the cosmos was finely tuned by design. This means it probably wasn't. More likely, it was finely tuned by chance (more than 75 percent likely, in fact).

This conclusion cannot rationally be denied. Nevertheless, attempts to deny it have been made, occasionally using a firing squad analogy (discussed by both Sober and Collins).[30] But that analogy is inapplicable because it assumes the existence of an intentional agent (the firing squad) and thus is merely an exercise in deducing that agent's intent (whether that squad "chose" to miss you). We are not in that situation but in that of trying to deduce whether a firing squad even exists in the first place. So we cannot presume there is one. There are other differences that render that analogy inapt, but this is the most pertinent. A more apt analogy would be: you are placed in front of a strange machine that shoots thousands of bullets around the room at random. Was it designed to miss you? Here answering that question must rely on your background knowledge about strange complex events: are they usually freak accidents or products of intelligent design? Once we rule out terrestrial design (as we must in the universe example) and alien design (as we have stipulated), we are left with no established instances of intelligent design even for complex events, thus our prior probability must reflect that such instances are exceedingly rare (like instances of rigging amazing poker hands in a family game).[31] If they ever even happen at all.

For example, suppose we knew in advance that 1 in 4 such machines was rigged to miss, and that the chance of their missing by accident was 1 in 100. Then we would infer design, because in any cohort of 1,000 victims, on average 250 will survive by design and only 10 will survive by chance, so if you are a survivor your prior odds of having survived by chance are 10 in 260, or barely 4 percent. From that prior probability you should conclude design, even when the evidence (your not getting hit) is the same either way.[32] But suppose you knew in advance that only one in four *results* was a product of design, and the others were of chance. Then in any cohort of a thousand victims you will still know there are on average ten survivors by chance, but you will also know that for every survivor there is who survived by design, *three more* will have survived by chance, so you will know there can be, on average, only three who survived by design—so if you are a survivor, your odds of having survived by chance are still three in four or 75 percent. In this case, you *shouldn't* conclude design— and that's even knowing the odds of having survived by chance are 1 in 100. So in *that* case, as in the scenario just analyzed for our universe, the probability that the machine was designed to miss you is still 25 percent no matter how unlikely its missing you was. Thus also for our universe: in our background knowledge we have no evidence that the frequency of very improbable events (not already caused by known life) being products of NID is anything higher than 25 percent. It doesn't matter how improbable any of those events are (like the odds of our solar system being arranged in just the way it is: far lower than 25 percent, yet still not a product of NID). Thus we cannot conclude the probability that the universe is a product of NID is anything higher than its prior probability of 25 percent. This remains a fact no matter how improbable the universe is.[33]

And yet even that 25 percent is much too high. Our universe looks exactly like what random chance would produce, but *not* exactly like what intelligent design would produce. Given all the actual observed properties of the universe (its vast age, size, scale of lethality, and inefficiency at producing life), which are exactly what we expect if no god designed it but *not* exactly what we'd expect if a god did (since there is no way you can deduce from "a very powerful self-existent being created the universe by design" that the only way he would ever do it is with such vast age, size, lethality, and inefficiency at producing life), the probability that the universe would then be as we observe it *must* be less than 100 percent. Given that there are so many more obvious ways a god could make a life-bearing universe (as sampled earlier), which would be vastly more life-friendly and life-appropriate, and which would not look suspiciously exactly the same as a universe must look if there was no god at all, that probability must be *substantially* less than 100 percent. No rational person can honestly believe it's any greater than 50 percent (because there's no way that outcome is even "50-50" on that hypothesis).

This entails the Bayesian conclusion that the probability that God intelligently designed the universe cannot be any higher than 15 percent (and is almost certainly a great deal less than that).[34] That means no rational person can believe the probability that God intelligently designed the universe is any better than 1 in 6. This means every rational person must conclude God probably didn't do that. The universe thus does not appear to be intelligently designed. Quite to the contrary, it looks exactly like a chance accident.

OTHER KINDS OF APPARENT DESIGN

So the universe probably wasn't designed by god, either. What about other things? Aren't there other things that exhibit divine design, things other than life or the universe per se?

What about the human mind? That already has a better explanation in natural causes, being a product of neurophysics and evolution. The scientific knowledge confirming this has vastly increased in just the last fifteen years, so it can't reasonably be denied anymore.[35] The dependence of the mind on a working brain is now an established fact in our background knowledge. We have identified where in our brain different kinds of memories are stored, where emotions and reason operate, where each kind of sensory experience is processed, and so on. We have observed that if we physically remove or deactivate any one of these parts, the memories or abilities it contains then cease. It follows that if we take away all the parts, everything that we are will cease. Comparative anatomy with animals verifies every point.[36] If the brain is not a product of NID then all of this *must* be the case, since on the absence of NID there is no other way to have consciousness except as the product of a large, delicate, and complex physical system like our brain, a system that appears only at the end of an extremely long process of trial and error as brains increased in size, complexity, and capability over the course of half a billion years.

Such evidence of our brain-produced and brain-dependent mind is thus 100 percent expected on the absence of NID. But it's not 100 percent what we'd expect on NID. If God doesn't need a brain, neither should we. We would more likely be made "in god's image," but that's not what we observe. God could have provided every human being with a brainless mind that doesn't need food or oxygen, that is incapable of being damaged by any wounds or disease, that always perceives and reasons and remembers correctly, that doesn't pose a physical threat to a mother's life or health during delivery (as human brains do, being so relatively large, as human brains need to be to do all the complex things the human mind does but that other animals don't), *and* that is otherwise in every respect the same as our current mind. Or he could have made any other mind to any degree in between that one and the one we have. Whereas on the absence of NID we could *only* have the kind of mind-brain system we do, on NID we could have had many other kinds of minds, and some of them are even more likely on NID. So the probability we'd observe the kind of brain-dependent mind we do if it was a product of NID must be less than 100 percent, in fact certainly not greater than 50 percent (since we can't predict from "god did it" even a 50-50 chance that this is what he'd do, as opposed to all the other options available to him).[37] Thus we get the same result here we've always gotten: there cannot possibly be more than a 15 percent chance that our mind was designed by God.[38]

It might be objected that there is one aspect of mind that can't yet be predicted by known science: qualia (the immanent qualities of conscious experience). But it does not follow that qualia are improbable on NID.[39] This is because their proximate causes have not been verified and thus we do not know what the probability of qualia actually is in the absence of NID, much less that it's less than 100 percent. Just as with fine-tuning, if every comparable brain produces qualia (just as every finely tuned universe produces life), then the probability of our observing qualia in the absence of NID is fully 100 percent.[40] And, for all we know, that could well be the case.[41] And whether it's 100 percent even on NID is not logically assured. If people can be philosophical zombies (minds without qualia), so can God; and so can God make philosophical zombies of us.

Scientifically speaking, the God hypothesis is not likely to fare well in the future; after all, we can already deduce from known scientific facts and the presumed absence of NID many features of qualitative experience (such as why we don't normally smell in color or why we see the specific colors we do and not others—including colors we "see" but that don't really exist as specific frequencies of light, like magenta), whereas we could never have predicted those things from NID and still cannot.[42] So far, every cause of mental phenomena discovered has not been NID, so the prior probability that any remaining phenomena will be explained by NID is continually shrinking. But even setting that aside, we have no knowledge in b that renders qualia any more likely on NID than on its absence, so qualia make no difference to the above calculation. There is no more evidence to show that qualia are impossible on the absence of NID than that qualia are inevitable on the absence of NID. We can at best split the difference and say it's 50 percent.[43] But we must say the same for NID, because we can only get, for example, "god experiences qualia, too" or "god wants us to experience qualia," by assuming that's the case ad hoc (since we don't actually have any evidence of the fact), which halves the prior probability (since so far as we honestly know, there is at best a 50-50 chance that "a very powerful self-existent being who creates things by design" does either, much less both), and if we *don't* assume either theoretical element ad hoc, then the probability of qualia on NID is still only 50 percent.[44] Either way, the math comes out the same.[45] Qualia simply do not argue for or against NID.

There isn't anything left that qualifies even for consideration. The arguments from beauty and intelligibility come to mind, but they are directly fallacious for failing to take into account the relevant science. The claim that our "experience of beauty" and "the universe being intelligible to us" are more likely on NID simply isn't true. These things may be likely on NID (I won't query that here), but they are just as likely on the absence of NID. Humans evolved to see beauty in certain properties of the universe (including the beauty of languages, efficiency, and puzzle solving, three skills of incalculable value to differential reproductive success), not the other way around. Thus the universe was not designed to be beautiful. We were designed to see it as beautiful—by natural selection.[46] There is no evidence here for NID. Even at best, NID's probability on the existence of "beauty" is simply its prior probability, which can be no better than 25 percent.

Likewise, humans evolved to understand the world they are in, not the other way around. Even then, the universe is so difficult to understand that hardly anyone actually understands it. Quantum mechanics and relativity theory alone try the abilities of someone of above average intellect, as do chemistry, particle physics, and cosmological science. Thus neither was the universe designed to be easily understood nor were we well designed to understand it. We must train ourselves for years, taxing our natural symbolic and problem-solving intelligence to its very limits, before we are able to understand it, *and even then* we still admit it's pretty darned hard to understand. If you have to rigorously train yourself with great difficulty to understand something, it cannot be said it was *designed* to be understandable. To the contrary, you are then *making* it understandable by searching for and teaching yourself whatever system of tricks and tools you need to understand it. Our ability to learn any system of tricks and tools necessary to do that is an inevitable and fully explicable product of natural selection; that ability derives from our evolved capacity to use symbolic language (which is of inestimable value to survival yet entails the ability to learn and use any language—including logic and mathematics, which are just languages, with words and rules like any other language) and from our evolved capacity to solve problems and predict behaviors (through hypothesis formation and testing, and the abilities of learning and improvisation, which are all of inestimable value to survival yet entail the ability to do the same things in any domain of knowledge, not just in the directly useful domains of resource acquisition, threat avoidance, and social system management).[47]

Thus the *actual* intelligibility of the universe is not at all impressive, given its extreme difficulty and our need to train ourselves to get the skills to understand it—indeed, our need even to have discovered those skills in the first place: the universe only began to be "intelligible" in this sense barely two thousand years ago, and we didn't get much good at reliably figuring it out until about four hundred years ago, yet we've been living in civilizations for over *six thousand* years, and had been trying to figure out the world before that for over *forty thousand* of years. Given these facts (our universe's actual intelligibility), NID is actually improbable: the probability of the degree of intelligibility we *actually* observe is 100 percent if there is no NID, but substantially *less* than 100 percent if NID caused it, in fact no more than 50 percent at best. It is almost certainly far less, since a God could easily have made the world far more intelligible by making the world itself simpler (as Aristotle once thought it was), or our abilities greater (we could be born with knowledge of the universe or of formal mathematics or scientific logic or with brains capable of far more rapid and complex learning and computation, etc.), or both, and it's hard to imagine why he wouldn't. God gave us instead exactly all the very same limitations and obstacles we would already expect if God didn't exist in the first place.[48] Given his prior probability of no more than 25 percent, once again we end up with a posterior probability of NID that's no greater than 15 percent on the evidence of an "intelligible universe." In other words, there's probably no NID here, either.[49]

CONCLUSION

Once we consider *all* the evidence, no reasonable and informed person can reject the conclusion that it's simply improbable that any god designed life or the universe. Even at its best, that can have no greater probability than 15 percent.[50] And as argued from the beginning, that's assuming an absurdly high prior probability of 25 percent and an unreasonably high consequent probability on the God hypothesis in every case of 50 percent. From the point I made about prior probability, it would be unreasonable even to imagine the prior probability was as high as one in many trillions, but outright irrational to think it any higher than 1 in 100, since 1 in 100 things in this universe not made by known life are certainly not known to have been made by God (prior to any of the evidence examined here). And from the case made in each section about the consequent probabilities, it would be unreasonable to allow God even a 10 percent chance of bizarrely doing things exactly the same way as a godless universe would. Which gives us a result on any one of the above arguments of 0.001 (rounded), only a one-tenth of 1 percent chance that NID exists. The actual probability is surely far lower. Either way (whether we stick with generous estimates or not) it's so improbable that this particular universe, with this kind of life, would be produced by a god, but so very certain that this is exactly the kind of life and universe that would exist if none of it were planned at all, that there can be no rational basis for believing a god exists (at least as here defined: "a very powerful self-existent being who creates things by design").

Because the Christian God by definition is the Creator God and only made the world for life, and only made life for humankind, the fact that NID is improbable entails the Christian God is improbable (whereas any god who had different plans will not be the Christian God). The actual evidence of life and the universe thus argues against Christianity and in fact effectively refutes it. The universe clearly was made for neither us nor life in general. We barely arrived in it, and barely survive in it. And life was clearly not made for humankind, as we appeared only billions of years after life had already been thriving without us. We gained dominance only through our own initiative and only against great and ceaseless opposition from the forces of nature and its nonhuman inhabitants. This is all as we should expect if, and only if, we and our world are a natural accident. Thus I have proved in this chapter that neither the nature of the universe nor of life or its origin, are predicted or explained by Christianity, which sooner predicts entirely different observations in all three domains. Instead, all that we do observe is fully predicted by there being no god at all. Hence I have demonstrated with logical certainty that the truth of Christianity is very improbable on these facts. And what is very improbable should not be believed. When enough people realize this, Christianity will come to an end.

Even more importantly, once we realize that the universe and life and the human race are all accidental, a very crucial conclusion follows that Christians often avoid reaching or outright resist: if this is all an unplanned accident, then we need to roll up our sleeves and get to work learning how to control the universe in order to make it the way an intelligent engineer would and should have made it. We must work to eradicate disease and avert natural disasters, to increase habitability and joy and justice, to achieve immortality, and every other thing a well-governed universe would have, because no one else is going to do any of this for us. And to protect us from our own error and hubris, we need to remake ourselves into responsible creators, self-critical, attentive to all the consequences of what we create, and acting and designing wisely in light of what we learn. Prayer and faith and rituals are of no real use and only distract us from what we should be doing instead to make the world a better place. We should instead devote our lives to science and learning, and the well-informed contemplation of our own selves and our social and physical world.

Chapter 13

LIFE AFTER DEATH
Examining the Evidence

by Dr. Victor J. Stenger

INTRODUCTION

D inesh D'Souza is a well-known right-wing policy analyst and author who recently has taken on the role of Christian apologist. He has a degree in English from Dartmouth. From 1985 to 1987, he was editor of *Policy Review*, a conservative journal published by the Heritage Foundation, now part of the Hoover Institution. He served as a policy adviser to the Reagan administration until 1988 and followed this with stints as a fellow for the American Enterprise Institute and the Hoover Institution.

D'Souza has summed up the cause of Christianity with books, speeches, and high-profile debates with famous atheists such as Christopher Hitchens, Daniel Dennett, Peter Singer, Michael Shermer, Dan Barker, and John Loftus. His recent books include *What's So Great About Christianity*[1] and—the primary reference for this essay—*Life After Death: The Evidence*.[2]

In *Life After Death*, D'Souza insists that he is making the case for an afterlife purely on the basis of science and reason and not relying on any spooky stuff. He promises "no ghosts, no levitations, no exorcisms, no mediums, no conversations with the dead" and a case that "is entirely based on reasoned argument and mainstream scholarship."[3] Although he does not always stick to this promise, he does give a good summary of arguments for life after death, some of which I had not heard before. So the book provides a framework from which to discuss both evidentiary claims and claims that rely more on extrapolations from observed facts.

D'Souza revels in his role as a "Christian cage fighter," challenging "the honest and thoughtful atheist to consider the possibility of being wrong, and

... open his mind to persuasion by rational argument."[4] I am perfectly happy to accept that challenge.

Life after death can be identified with the ancient notion that the human mind is not purely a manifestation of material forces in the brain but has a separate, immaterial component called the soul that survives the death of the brain along with the rest of the body. This is a hypothesis that can be scientifically tested. Evidence for its validity could be provided by a verifiable glimpse of a world beyond obtained while communicating with the dead or during a religious experience. All the believer claiming such knowledge has to do is provide some knowledge that neither she nor anyone else could have previously known and have that information later confirmed. Let us investigate whether such evidence has been produced.

FALSE ADVERTISING

D'Souza begins his second chapter by accusing atheists of engaging in false advertising when they say there is no reason to believe in an afterlife. Their view is based, as is most disbelief, on the absence of evidence. D'Souza asserts, "The atheist has no better proof that there isn't life after death than the believer has that there is." He says that new atheists Sam Harris and Richard Dawkins reject the afterlife "on the basis of no evidence whatsoever." The believer, on the other hand, has a reason to believe: "divine revelation as expressed in a sacred text." The believer is "trusting in what is held to be an unimpeachable source, namely God." So much for basing his case on "reasoned argument and mainstream scholarship."[5]

Of course, if we are to assume as a prerequisite for our discussion that God exists and he has revealed truths in the scriptures, then there is not much left to say and there would be no purpose in D'Souza's book or my essay. I am going to summarily reject D'Souza's assumption that God and revelation exist and require that, along with the afterlife, they be demonstrated by empirical evidence.

None of the claimed prophetic revelations of the Bible have been confirmed, and many have been disconfirmed. Independent historical and archaeological sources have already established that the most important stories of the Bible are myths.[6] This is a long and contentious debate, and I need not get into any of the details. Quite simply, if a scholarly consensus existed that biblical revelations were confirmed, then we again would have no need for this discussion. We would all believe in God and the afterlife for the same reasons we believe in neutrinos and DNA—a consensus among scientists and other scholars that there is sufficient empirical evidence buttressed by careful, objective, rational analysis.

D'Souza accurately quotes me as saying that life after death is a scientific question and that "no claimed connection with the hereafter has ever been verified . . . in controlled scientific experiments."[7] He also quotes a similar statement by the Nobel Prize–winning biologist and codiscoverer of DNA, the late Sir Francis Crick: If religious believers "really believe in life after death, why do they not conduct sound experiments to verify it?"[8] D'Souza's weak response is that "most religious believers don't believe in the afterlife on the basis of scientific tests."[9] Surely they would believe with greater conviction, and many more would become believers, if such evidence were ever produced.

D'Souza further asserts, "There are no controlled empirical experiments that can resolve the issue either way."[10] Of course there are. Since the nineteenth century, reputable scientists have been performing experiments to test the alleged powers of so-called psychics and mediums who claim to talk to the dead. Not a single report of communication with the dead has ever been verified.[11] Once again, just have the psychic tell us something he and we did not know that later was verified. Suppose a medium speaking to the dead Isaac Newton in 1890 came back with the information that a weapon of immense power would destroy two cities in 1945. Then we would be forced to believe in a world beyond, whether we liked it or not.

ABSENCE OF EVIDENCE

D'Souza refers to what he calls the "popular atheist slogan," "The absence of evidence is evidence of absence."[12] D'Souza objects, arguing that "not found" is not the same thing as "found not to exist." Of course this is true, and atheists agree. In fact, legendary atheist Carl Sagan was often quoted as saying, "[A]bsence of evidence is not evidence of absence." However, I claim that absence of evidence *can* be evidence for absence, *when the evidence should be there and is not found*. We can apply this principle to the question of life after death. There should be evidence, and there isn't any.

D'Souza points out that scientists believe in the existence of many things that are undetectable by scientific instruments, such as the "dark matter" and "dark energy" that pervade the universe.[13] However, if these exist, we can expect that eventually they either will be detected or falsified. In the meantime, we have indirect evidence that is sufficiently robust for us to include these two components in our models until new data should rule otherwise.

This is a common circumstance in physics. For example, physicists in the late 1920s discovered missing energy in nuclear *beta-decay*. The more parsimonious hypothesis, proposed by Wolfgang Pauli, was that a previously unknown particle is emitted in the reaction even though that particle was not directly detected. Enrico Fermi dubbed it the *neutrino*. The less parsimonious alternative was a violation of the fundamental physical principle of energy conservation. It was not until 1956 that the neutrino was detected in an experiment conducted by Fred Reines and Clyde Cowan. They observed the reverse beta-decay process induced by neutrinos from a nuclear reactor.

So D'Souza is right that scientists do accept the possibility of phenomena that are not directly observed. But they at least demand some indirect evidence before they are taken seriously. In the case of dark matter and dark energy, both are postulated to explain observed gravitational and astronomical effects that are otherwise unexplained. While alternate explanations might yet be found, these two substances of still unknown (but still clearly material) nature currently provide the simplest known account for what is observed. We will see if we have comparably strong indirect evidence for life after death.

A COMMON BELIEF

It is a well-known fact that a belief in immortality has been common, although not unanimous, among many cultures throughout history. D'Souza takes this as further "evidence" that life after death exists, once more breaking his promise of rationality. This is like saying that, since a belief that the world is flat was common among all cultures throughout history, it follows that the world really is flat.

D'Souza also tries to dispose of the common atheist argument that, with so many different religions in the world having such diverse ideas about god and the hereafter, how does one know his particular belief is the correct one?

It is a fact that the overwhelming majority of people practice the religion of the family and culture into which they were born. Yet most are sure theirs is the "true religion" while all others are false. As atheists like to say to believers, "We are not that much different. You believe every religion but yours is bunk. I just believe one more religion is bunk than you do."

D'Souza admits that many religions have different views of the afterlife that depend on their geography and culture. Muslims imagine heaven as a desert oasis. American Indians envisage happy hunting grounds full of deer and buffalo. Vikings believed that their eternity would be spent in Valhalla, where they will do battle every day and have a drunken feast every night.[14] And, of course, the views of the afterlife in Eastern religions are widely different from these, often focused on reincarnation, a totally alien form of an afterlife compared to that imagined in the West.

Nevertheless, D'Souza asserts, "[T]he presence of disagreement in no way implies the absence of truth." It sure does. He tries to show that the differences are not so great. Basically, he asserts, there are just two types of immortality. In the Eastern version, the soul reunites after death with some transcendent and ultimate reality, losing its individuality. The Western view, on the other hand, is one of individual bodily resurrection.[15] They both can't be right.

D'Souza refers to a scholarly study by Alan Segal showing that every culture in history has had some concept of continued existence.[16] I have read Segal, and what strikes me is the vast variety of belief. You would think that if humanity had some revealed facts about the afterlife there would be more agreement. Still, D'Souza insists, humans possess a religious impulse that is rooted in a "sense of the numinous," that "there is something terrible and awe-inspiring and sublime about existence that seems to derive from another kind of reality." Death, then, is the link between two realities: the world we live in and a more permanent "world beyond the world."[17] Those more in touch with reality may conclude it derives from fear of death.

D'Souza makes the interesting observation that each of the three Abrahamic religions—Judaism, Christianity, and Islam—has two different teachings about immortality. The official teaching is bodily resurrection, while the "more contemplative types" hold an unofficial view of the immortality of the soul derived not from biblical or Qur'anic sources but from Greek philosophy. D'Souza tries to make atheists look like dunces for not being aware of this fact—as if none of us ever heard of Plato. Typically, he does not quote any atheists specifically.

While the Torah, the first five books of the Jewish Bible, contains no mention of an afterlife, immortality was adopted into Judaism sometime before the first century BCE. Whereas Plato held that the soul escapes the body after death, the Persians introduced the notion that the whole person, body and soul, survives death, which view the Jews then adopted.[18] This idea was adopted in turn by Christianity and Islam and given a much more central role than it has in Judaism.

The enormous Greek influence on Christianity that was initiated by Paul (the New Testament was written entirely in Greek) led many Christians to adopt the Greek view that only disembodied souls survive death.[19] With the Copernican revolution in the Middle Ages, heaven was no longer a place beyond the stars and hell was no longer inside earth, but rather these were viewed as immaterial places inhabited by immaterial souls. Nevertheless, bodily resurrection is still anticipated by both D'Souza's Catholic Church and many Protestant sects. Some Protestant churches, such as former vice-presidential candidate Sarah Palin's Pentecostal church, take seriously the Book of Revelation in which the Son of Man (assumed to be Jesus) returns to rule the Kingdom of God on earth. Earth is still the center of the universe to these believers, and the inhabitants of the new kingdom will all have perfect but still fully material human bodies. Why else would the bodily resurrection of Jesus be so important?

But D'Souza is espousing a far more sophisticated picture of the afterworld.[20] He adopts Augustine's view that God created time along with the universe and is himself outside of time. Later Christian theologians formulated life after death as being lived in an eternal realm disconnected from space and time. Actually, this realm should not even be characterized as "eternal" since that is a temporal term. It's kind of a constant "now." Thus D'Souza notes, "Christianity since Augustine does not espouse life after death, but rather life 'beyond' death."[21] I am not sure of the difference.

Of course, this is the Christianity of theologians, not the faithful in the pews. Nevertheless I am on the same page here with D'Souza, who is trying to justify life after death on rational grounds. Atheists can agree to discard (and stop ridiculing) popular notions of an afterlife featuring eternal harp music in heaven and eternal bagpipe music in hell.

However, D'Souza is not willing to give atheists similar leeway. He asserts, "Contrary to what atheists say, the belief in the afterlife is not merely a Western idea; it is a universal idea."[22] What atheists say this? Once more he quotes none and gives no references.

Of course atheists know that life after death is an Eastern as well as Western idea. D'Souza admits that they are quite different, so somebody must be wrong. He correctly notes that a "new" understanding of Hinduism was instituted in the Upanishads, a philosophical work from 2,500 years ago called Vedanta or "post-Vedic" Hinduism:

> According to the Upanishads we live in an unreal world that we mistake for the real one. . . . But this is the trick of "maya," or illusion, and it is a trick that uses the mirrors of space and time. Actually, reality is entirely different from what our senses perceive. We experience objects in the world as differentiated and we think of ourselves as individual souls separate from the world. But if we could see behind the mirrors of experience, if we could somehow lift the veil, we would realize that reality preserves none of these distinctions. In reality, everything is one.[23]

So, in the Upanishads, we break out of the endless cycle of reincarnation by realizing that "our individual souls are identical with the oneness of ultimate reality."[24] At least this solves a lot of problems, such as "Where do all those souls go?" They all merge into one.

Buddhism adopted the Hindu notion of reincarnation, which is yet another idea of an "afterlife," for souls that hadn't yet "achieved enlightenment" (and thereby merged with the One). While it changed a lot of details, Buddhism recognized that "the very concept of 'I' is illusory."[25] This is also an important insight that most of the world, including many Buddhists, never learned.[26]

Although D'Souza says, as I quoted above, that belief in the afterlife is a universal idea, he has to admit it is not unanimous. After all, at least a billion and maybe two billion living people don't believe in it. He identifies three rival perspectives: (1) survival without the body; (2) survival of the whole person, body and soul together; and (3) denial of an afterlife. I would split (1) into two further perspectives, East and West. As we saw above, we have the Eastern view of the disembodied soul undergoing reincarnations in new bodies and then eventually merging into a single ultimate reality, while in the Western view the soul, even without a body, remains individually differentiated. Christians who don't believe in bodily resurrection but in a heavenly realm beyond space and time still expect to meet their departed loved ones and pets there as individual souls. Interestingly, this difference between East and West is a characteristic of their cultures, with individualism a prime trait of Americans and Eurasians, while East Asians place more emphasis on everyone harmonizing with their culture.

This illustrates how religious beliefs are heavily determined by culture, making their connection with any ultimate truth problematical. Even Asian beliefs in heaven or hell (such as in Confucian religion) correspond to their cultural expectations and thus differ substantially from Western notions. In fact, all beliefs in an afterlife have plausible origins in evolved features of the brain, which naturally cause us to separate minds from bodies conceptually (because it is practical to do so), and then we erroneously attribute this conceptual distinction to physical reality.[27] An error we make because of natural evolutionary developments cannot support the conclusion that what's erroneous is true.

Now it is time to talk science and examine the claimed empirical evidence for life after death.

PROBLEMS WITH THE PARANORMAL

A huge literature exists claiming scientific evidence for life after death. This literature suffers from all the same problems we find with paranormal studies in general.[28] Much of it is anecdotal and virtually useless scientifically since we have no way of checking the veracity of such testimony. Only carefully controlled experiments that provide risky tests of the hypothesis of life after death will convince the scientific skeptics, and until the skeptics are convinced, the hypothesis will remain unproven. Despite the common charge, skeptics in science are not dogmatic. They will readily follow where the evidence leads.

While paranormal studies often involve controlled experiments, few meet the stringent standards found in the basic sciences. For example, positive effects are often claimed at such a low level of statistical significance that a simple statistical fluctuation would reproduce the observation as often as once every twenty times the experiment is repeated (as happens when $p = 0.05$). In this case, one must accept the more parsimonious explanation that the effect was a statistical artifact rather than the occurrence of a miracle. While $p = 0.05$ is often used in biomedical research, such a weak criterion is unacceptable in those sciences that deal with extraordinary phenomena.[29] For example, in physics a claimed new effect is not publishable until it is shown that it would not be reproduced as a statistical artifact once in ten thousand cases ($p = 0.0001$). While I can sympathize with the need for medical researchers to try any promising therapy in order to save lives, I still think that they would do better and avoid useless effort by setting their limit to $p = 0.01$.

Attempts have been made to use a technique called *meta-analysis* to try to glean statistically significant results from individually insignificant data.[30] This is like Ronald Reagan's old joke about the kid on Christmas morning digging through a pile of horse manure saying "There has to be a pony in there somewhere." The procedure is totally unreliable and a waste of time in searching for a phenomenon not evident in individual experiments.[31] While meta-analysis can be useful for discerning trends, it must be used with great caution. I cannot think of a single major discovery in science that has been made with meta-analysis.

For over 150 years, investigators have claimed evidence for paranormal phenomena, such as extrasensory perception or mind over matter, without a single positive result that has ever stood up to the same critical scrutiny applied in the mainstream sciences whenever an extraordinary event is observed. Observing evidence for life after death would be extraordinary indeed. Needless to say, none of the dead have ever communicated any verifiable knowledge to us. If they did, then we would all be believers.

REINCARNATION

Recently the subject of reincarnation has attracted scientific attention. Like psychic studies, we find in this area a minefield of unsupported claims and lucrative hoaxes such as the infamous fifty-year-old case that resulted in a bestselling book *The Search for Bridey Murphy* by Morey Bernstein.[32] Although thoroughly debunked,[33] Bernstein's book has gone through four editions, the most recent appearing as late as 1991.

The reincarnation debate was taken to a more serious level by the work of psychiatrist and University of Virginia professor Ian Stevenson. Deepak Chopra, in his 2006 book on immortality, *Life After Death: The Burden of Proof*, cites Stevenson as providing strong empirical evidence for reincarnation.[34] Over the years Stevenson collected thousands of cases of children in

India and elsewhere who talked about their "previous lives." Many seemed quite accurate, and sometimes the child had marks or birth defects that corresponded closely to those of the deceased person the child claimed to remember.[35] Leonard Angel has written a review of Ian Stevenson's monumental two-volume tome *Reincarnation and Biology*. Angel says, "Close inspection of Stevenson's work shows that time after time Stevenson presents tabular summaries that claim evidence was obtained when, in fact, it was not. . . . Stevenson's case, irreparably, falls apart both in the presentation of evidence and in his analysis of evidence supposedly obtained."[36]

Even D'Souza is skeptical of Stevenson's results. He remarks that, growing up in India, he can easily see how "families might conspire to produce the appropriate 'evidence.' Their religiously anointed children become celebrities." He concludes, "[R]eincarnation is possible but unlikely."[37] For a complete critical analysis of reincarnation, see the book by Paul Edwards, *Reincarnation*.[38]

NEAR-DEATH EXPERIENCES—HISTORICAL DATA

Apologists such as D'Souza put much more stock in the results of studies involving *near-death experiences* (NDEs), which have attracted a large number of investigators and even a peer-reviewed journal, the *Journal of Near-Death Studies*. Janice Miner Holden, EdD; Bruce Greyson, MD; and Debbie James, MNS, RN; have provided a comprehensive handbook on NDE research. They begin with a review of thirty years of research on the subject, which I will briefly summarize.[39]

By the early 1970s, resuscitation technology had advanced to the point where many more people were being brought back from the brink of death than ever before in history. Perhaps 20 percent reported experiences of what they were convinced was another reality, a glimpse of "heaven." These reports began to get the attention of nurses and physicians. In 1976, medical student Raymond Moody published a book about these phenomena called *Life After Life* where he coined the term "near-death experience," or NDE. Moody's book became a sensational bestseller, with thirteen million copies sold by 2001.[40]

Holden et al. list a number of earlier references in popular, medical, and psychical research and many publications since 1975. Almost all of these reports are anecdotal (a designation the authors avoid in favor of the term "retrospective") and are hardly likely to convince skeptics and mainstream scientists that they provide evidence for an afterlife. However, it can be safely concluded from these anecdotes that the near-death experience itself is a real phenomenon, somewhat like a dream or hallucination, but perhaps not exactly the same. The issue is whether they provide any real evidence for an afterlife.

In her 1993 book on near-death experiences, *Dying to Live*, psychologist (and reformed parapsychologist) Susan Blackmore proposed that the phenomenon was the result of loss of oxygen in the dying brain.[41] Many features of the NDE can be simulated with drugs, electrical impulses, or acceleration— such as during rides in a centrifuge used for training fighter pilots. Professional anesthesiologist Gerald Woerlee thoroughly confirms these findings (and confirms other mundane causes) in his 2003 book, *Mortal Minds.*[42]

Despite finding no reliable evidence, Holden et al. are not quite ready to give up their quest of the afterlife. In their summary of the handbook, the editors say

> If it appears that the mental functions can persist in the absence of active brain function, this phenomenon opens up the possibility that some part of humans that performs mental functions might survive death of the brain.[43]

Nevertheless, they have to admit, "no single clear pattern of NDE features has yet emerged."[44]

Veridical NDEs

From my viewpoint as a research scientist, only veridical NDEs are worth studying. These are NDE experiences where the subject reports a perception that is later corroborated.[45] Researchers also define *apparently nonphysical veridical NDE perception* (AVP) as veridical perceptions that apparently could not have been the result of inference from normal sensory processes.[46] These would provide the kind of evidence for consciousness independent of the body that we might begin to take seriously.

In chapter 9 of their handbook, editor Holden reviews the attempts to verify AVP under controlled conditions. You would think the setup should be simple. Place some kind of target such as a card with some random numbers on it facing the ceiling of the operating room so that it is unreadable not only to the patient on the table but to the hospital staff in the room. Then if a patient has an NDE that involves the commonly reported sensation of moving outside her body and floating above the operating table, she should be able to read that number. These out-of-body experiences (OBE) are not always associated with NDEs, and they are treated as independent phenomena that also imply the existence of a soul independent of the body.

Holden reported that this ideal situation is difficult to achieve, with the operating room staff often glimpsing the target information, thus compromising the protocol. She reports on five studies that were conducted with proper controls. She concludes, "The bottom line of findings from these five studies is quite disappointing: No researcher has succeeded in capturing even one case of AVP."[47] Note that Holden reveals her personal desires in this quotation. If she were a skeptic, she might have called the result "gratifying." In either case, it's best to keep an open mind.

Holden tells of receiving an e-mail from prominent NDE researcher Kenneth Ring:

> There is so much anecdotal evidence that suggests [experiencers] can, at least sometime, perceive veridically during NDEs . . . but isn't it true that in all this time there hasn't been a single case of a veridical perception reported by an NDEr under controlled conditions? I mean, thirty years later, it's still a null class (as far as we know). Yes, excuses, excuses—I know. But, really, wouldn't you have suspected more than a few such cases *at least* by now?[48]

Maria and the Shoe

Dinesh D'Souza is deeply impressed by NDEs, saying, "On the face of it, they provide strong support for life after death."[49] Few researchers in the field have gone so far.

D'Souza tells us of the case of a Seattle woman named Maria who experienced an NDE after a heart attack. She told a social worker named Kimberly Clark that she had separated from her body and floated outside the hospital. There she saw a tennis shoe with a worn patch on the third-floor ledge near the emergency room. Clark checked the ledge and retrieved the shoe.[50]

However, there is no independent corroboration of this event. We only have Clark's report. No one could ever track down Maria to corroborate her story. We have to take Clark's word for it. Later investigators found that Clark had embellished the difficulty of observing the shoe on the ledge. Placing one of their own shoes in the same position, they found it was clearly visible as soon as you stepped into Maria's room.[51]

The Blind Shall See

Probably the most sensational claims in NDE research involve blind people reporting out-of-body experiences in which they were able to see. I told the story of one such case in my 2003 book *Has Science Found God?*, but it bears repeating.[52] Physician Larry Dossey is the author of several popular books that promote spiritual healing such as prayer; I have clashed with him on occasion.[53] In *Recovering the Soul*, Dossey claimed that a woman named Sarah had an NDE in which she saw

> a clear, detailed memory of the frantic conversation of the surgeons and nurses during her cardiac arrest; the OR [Operating Room] layout; the scribbles on the surgery scheduling board on the hall outside; the color of the sheets covering the operating table; the hairstyle of the head scrub nurse; the names of the surgeons on the doctors' lounge down the corridor who were waiting for her case to be concluded; and even the trivial fact that the anesthesiologist that day was wearing unmatched socks. All this she knew even though she had been fully anesthetized and unconscious during the surgery and the cardiac arrest.[54]

And, on top of that, Sarah had been blind since birth!

Ring and Cooper report that, when asked by other investigators to give more details, Dossey admitted this was a complete fiction.[55] Susan Blackmore also uncovered Dossey's fabrication.[56]

Ring and Cooper state that Blackmore "reviewed all the NDE evidence and concluded that none of it holds up to scrutiny." According to Blackmore, "there is no convincing evidence of visual perception in the blind during NDEs, much less documented support for veridical perception."[57] Ring and Cooper's later investigations also provide no veridical evidence.

NEAR-DEATH EXPERIENCES—RECENT DATA

Recently a new book on NDEs has appeared: *Evidence of the Afterlife: The Science of Near-Death-Experiences*, by MD Jeffrey Long "with" journalist Paul Perry.[58] Thanks to considerable media hype, this book moved quickly to the bestseller lists. Long is a radiation oncologist, and, with his wife, Jody, he gathered thousands of accounts of near-death experiences. They did this by setting up a website asking for personal narratives of experiences. Besides providing their personal story, respondents filled out a one-hundred-item questionnaire "designed to isolate specific elements of the experience and to flag counterfeit accounts." The result is the largest database of NDEs in the world with over 1,600 accounts.

Long claims that medical evidence fails to explain these reports and that "there is only one plausible explanation—that people have survived death and traveled to another dimension." After studying thousands of cases, Long concludes: "NDEs provide such powerful scientific evidence that it is reasonable to accept the existence of an afterlife."[59]

In fact, there is little or no science in Long's book. It is based totally on anecdotes collected over the Internet where you can find limitless unsupported testimonials for every kind of preposterous claim. I do not insist that all anecdotes are useless. They can point the way to more serious research. But when they are the *only* source of evidence they cannot be used to reach extraordinary conclusions. To scientifically prove life after death is going to require carefully controlled experiments, not just a lot of stories. The plural of anecdote is not "data."

The question raised by near-death experiences is whether they provide evidence that mind and consciousness are more than just the product of a purely material brain. Such a conclusion contradicts the mass of evidence gathered in the neurosciences and will be accepted only when the data are totally convincing.

PROBLEMS WITH NDES

There are several excellent books and papers presenting strong, detailed arguments showing why the data from NDEs do not provide any evidence for an afterlife. Besides Susan Blackmore's *Dying to Live* and Gerald Woerlee's *Mortal Minds*, there is *Religion, Spirituality and the Near-Death Experience* by Mark Fox.[60] In 2007 Keith Augustine, the executive director of the Internet Infidels,[61] published an exhaustive three-part series of articles in the *Journal of Near-Death Studies*.[62] Each of these articles is accompanied in the same volume with several criticisms from researchers in the field followed by a response to those criticisms from Augustine. An updated, unified, and abridged version of all three of Augustine's papers is available on the Secular Web.[63] Let me mention just a few of Augustine's observations, along with those of other researchers, that I found particularly compelling. I refer you to his papers to get the details and references to the original work he relies on.

- Eighty percent of those who come as close to death as possible without dying do not [recall having] an NDE, so it is not a common experience.
- Existing research presents no challenge to the current scientific understanding of NDEs as hallucinations.
- NDE studies, taken as a whole, strongly imply that whatever these experiences are, they are characterized by features that one would expect of internally generated fantasies, but not of any putative "disembodied existence."
- As encounters with living persons repeatedly crop up in NDEs (one out of ten times), the less NDEs look like visions of another world and the more they appear to be brain-generated hallucinations triggered by a real or perceived threat to the experiencer's well-being.
- The only NDE experiences that are common among all cultures are encountering other beings and other realms. Otherwise, all the details depend on culture.
- Electroencephalograms and imaging techniques indicate that epileptic activity in the temporal lobe of the brain, specifically the TPJ or temporo-parietal junction, consistently results in out-of-body experiences (OBEs). Furthermore, many of the experiences reported by epileptics and those who have had their temporal lobe electrically stimulated match those of OBEs. Since the TPJ is a major center of multisensory integration of body-related information, it is not surprising that interfering with neural processing or cerebral blood flow in this area, or providing conflicting somatosensory inputs, results in dysfunctional representation. This provides strong evidence that OBEs are brain-induced and localized in the temporal lobe. As mentioned, OBEs are often but not always associated with NDEs.

- Despite repeated assertions of quite frequent paranormal abilities (healing powers, prophetic visions of the future) manifesting after NDEs, often endorsed by NDE researchers, no experiencer has had an allegation of psychic powers tested in a controlled experiment. The prophecies have been either vague or dramatically wrong. For example, in *Saved by the Light*, Dannion Brinkley reports his NDE and makes many predictions about the future.[64] The book was adapted in 1995 for a Fox Television movie starring Eric Roberts and was one of the highest-rated television movies in that network's history.[65] Not one of Brinkley's predictions came to pass.

Many NDE researchers still hope to find evidence for an afterlife despite their own honest admission that the data, so far, are simply not there. Augustine is careful to note that NDE researchers' beliefs are not to be confused with their actual findings. From my own reading I would say that, while the great majority of NDE researchers are honest and do not hide data that fail to confirm their beliefs, they are hardly disinterested in the question of survival of death. Who wouldn't be motivated by the possibility of discovering an afterlife?

Several authors have suggested that NDEs cannot distinguish if a private experience is either a brain-based hallucination or a peek into the afterlife, and therefore that the afterlife hypothesis is not falsifiable. I claim this is wrong. They are like those who say science can never prove God exists. The existence of a realm beyond matter could be easily demonstrated by someone returning from an NDE, OBE, or other religious experience with important information about the world that she or no one else could possibly have known, and then have that knowledge verified scientifically. With millions of such experiences yearly, you would expect a few to result in verifiable knowledge if they had anything at all to do with an immaterial reality. So far none have, making this a strong, empirical argument *against* the existence of such a realm.

THE MATERIAL MIND

Considerable evidence exists for the hypothesis that what we call mind and consciousness result from mechanisms in a purely material brain. If we have disembodied souls that, as most religions teach, are responsible for our thoughts, dreams, personalities, and emotions, then these should not be affected by drugs. But they are. They should not be affected by disease. But they are. They should not be affected by brain injuries. But they are. Brain scans today can locate the portions of the brain where different types of thoughts arise, including emotions. When that part of the brain has been destroyed by surgery or injury, those types of thoughts disappear. As brain function decreases we lose consciousness, as when under full anesthesia. Why would that happen if consciousness arose from an immaterial soul? There is no objective evidence that brain function stops entirely during a reported NDE. That an NDE actually occurred during a flat EEG (rather than before or after) is often impossible to prove anyway. But even a flat EEG does not signal brain death, as many people mistakenly believe, since it just reacts to the outer portions of the brain and does not catch activity deep in the brain.

If the properties traditionally attributed to the soul reside solely in the material brain and nervous system, then this is sufficient to rule out life after the death of the brain.

COSMIC JUSTICE

One of the major reasons so many people seek an afterlife is that they want to believe the universe is just. In the East this is called the law of karma. Since life in this world is obviously unjust, with many rewards for the wicked and few for the virtuous, reincarnation makes it all come out even. In the West, justice is served not by a succession of lives but by a last judgment.

D'Souza has convinced himself that he has proven that humans occupy two domains of reality, the material/phenomenal and the spiritual/moral/noumenal. He interprets one of these realities to correspond to the way things are and the other to the way things ought to be. Science and its physical laws, he says, concern themselves only with the way things are. Moral laws tell us how they ought to be. Cosmic justice, according to this view, cannot be achieved in this world but only in another world beyond the grave. The recognition of this fact explains to D'Souza "why humans continue to espouse goodness and justice even when the world is evil and unjust."[66]

D'Souza asserts that humans are unique among entities in the universe, living and nonliving, in seeking "to repudiate the laws of evolution and escape control of the laws of nature."[67] Why do we do this? Because we have made "the presumption of an afterlife, and the realization of the idea of cosmic justice makes sense of our moral nature much better than any competing hypothesis."[68]

D'Souza calls this a "presuppositional argument." According to D'Souza a presupposition is a hypothesis that says, "This is the way things have to be to make sense of the world." It is tested by asking, "How well does it explain the world?"[69] The specific hypothesis is: "There has to be cosmic justice in the world in order to make sense of the observed facts about human morality."[70]

So he is cleverly turning the morality issue into a scientific argument, which is fine by me because it puts the argument on my home ground. Forget what religions say. Forget what moral philosophies say. Observations of human behavior are going to be used to provide evidence for the existence of cosmic justice. And, since justice is obviously unavailable in this life, it follows that there must be an afterlife to provide it.

It seems to me that D'Souza has the argument turned around. If people believed in cosmic justice in an afterlife, you would think they wouldn't have any need to worry about justice in this life. On the other hand, people who don't believe in cosmic justice in the afterlife would have a strong reason to see that justice is done in this life. Thus belief in the afterlife has a negative impact on society. This hypothesis makes much more sense of observations than does D'Souza's hypothesis. No people are more fervent believers in life after death than Muslims, and in no societies will you find less justice, especially for women, than in Muslim societies. In Christian societies, the more fundamentalist the family, the greater the incidence of spousal and child abuse.[71]

EVOLUTION AND SELF-INTEREST

What are the observations that D'Souza takes as evidence for cosmic justice? He admits that morality is almost universally violated. However, universal criteria and standards that everyone refers to nevertheless exist. Why should these criteria exist at all? D'Souza claims that they defy the laws of evolution, so they can't be natural. He asserts, "Evolution implies that we are selfish creatures who seek to survive and reproduce in the world."[72] This is contrary to moral behavior. Moral behavior frequently operates against self-interest. It should be noted that evolution does not teach that we are selfish creatures, it observes only that we have evolved instincts to survive and reproduce. And even these instincts can be overcome by the exercise of our free will. (I accept the existence of free will, but that's another story.)

D'Souza reminds us that the group selection argument has long been recognized as a way to reconcile evolution with moral behavior. Patriots frequently sacrifice their lives for their friends and countries, thus aiding the survival of their kin. But he claims the argument has a fatal flaw. He asks how a tribe of individuals became self-sacrificing in the first place? Cheaters would be more likely to survive than their more altruistic fellow tribesmen.

But, again, D'Souza has the argument turned around. The very use of the word *cheaters* evokes the moral disapproval we feel for those who try the "free rider" strategy. In fact, evolution has *produced* this contempt for cheaters, and a cheater who is thrown out of a primitive society would effectively be receiving a death sentence. There would thus be strong selective pressure to evolve a reasonable aversion to cheating, and the scientific evidence confirms this.[73]

D'Souza brings up the proposal of biologists William Hamilton and Robert Trivers that was popularized and developed further by Richard Dawkins in *The Selfish Gene*.[74] The idea is that the basic unit of evolution is not the individual but the gene, which is the partial sequence of a DNA molecule that carries the individual's genetic information to the next generation and allows its expression in the current generation. This is what really "wants" to survive, if I may be allowed to use that metaphor. The selfish gene, according to D'Souza, explains why most parents would readily trade their own lives for their children's. This is not morality. This is not spirituality. This is pure, reductionist, materialist, natural selection.

D'Souza agrees this works for families, but asks why humans behave altruistically toward others outside their families. This seems to accept a false inference that genes are only shared within families. A gene model of morality doesn't predict that you will only act altruistically toward your family; it says you will tend to act altruistically toward those who most resemble you (i.e., those who share more of your genes, and we share more with our fellow countrymen or race—but also more with our whole species than with other species, and we are, after all, competing against *other species* for survival, even more so than with each other). Such a model therefore predicts racism as well as charity—a much more accurate prediction than D'Souza's. Robert Trivers also observes that humans, and other animals, behave generously toward others when they expect something in return. Natural selection provides survival instincts to those who engage in mutually beneficial exchanges.[75]

But D'Souza argues this still does not explain "the good things we do that offer no return."[76] He gives as examples people giving up their seats on a bus to the elderly, donating to charities, or agitating for animal rights or against religious persecution in Tibet. D'Souza does not understand that human beings have always been social animals, and like many other social animals, humans have evolved various behavior patterns that facilitate social living. Moreover, many behaviors are by-products of more basic dispositions and emotions that are themselves adaptively advantageous; for example, compassion in and of itself is adaptively useful to social individuals and their gene pools, even after subtracting the costs of unrewarded exercises of it. That's why the emotion exists in the first place.

He recognizes that there can be an ulterior, selfish motive to be recognized as a moral person. However, D'Souza says, we still must confront the Machiavellian argument that "the man who wants to act virtuously in every way necessarily comes to grief among the many that are not virtuous."[77] D'Souza claims that true morality, true virtue, rises above all this, acting without regard to self-interest. Maybe, but humans have clearly evolved exactly such a moral capacity. So there's nothing left to explain here.

Evolution, according to D'Souza, cannot explain how humans became moral primates. He tells us, "Humans recognize that there is no ultimate goodness and justice in this world, but they continue to hold up these ideals." Why? Because they expect to be rewarded in the afterlife. Thus, according to D'Souza, the existence of the afterlife is "proved" by the observation of altruistic behavior in humans despite the nonexistence of earthly reward. Note that D'Souza's hypothesis implies that the motivation for altruistic behavior is self-interest after all! Is it not the *extremity* of self-interest to want to live forever in the first place, and to expect a special reward for your righteousness when you get there?

But in fact, humans have evolved a moral capacity that can be used in a variety of ways, both socially acceptable and socially unacceptable. D'Souza's hypothesis predicts that only those who believe in an afterlife will exhibit altruistic behavior. That hypothesis can be easily tested. We just need to gather a sample of those who don't believe in an afterlife and see whether they are significantly less virtuous than those who believe.

Skeptic Magazine publisher and *Scientific American* columnist Michael Shermer addressed this question in his important book *The Science of Good and Evil*. He reports, "Not only is there no evidence that a lack of religiosity leads to less moral behavior, a number of studies actually support the opposite view."[78]

THE POSTEVOLUTIONARY PHASE

I would like to carry D'Souza's chain of reasoning further to draw additional logical conclusions. Humanity has evolved a moral capacity that cannot be attributed to belief in an afterlife where their virtue will be rewarded. Moreover, humanity has entered into a postevolutionary phase in its development that is far from complete. The human body and brain have undergone only minor evolutionary changes in the last ten thousand years. In recent times we have not been subject to the kind of survival pressures that lead to speciation all throughout evolutionary history.

D'Souza mentions Richard Dawkins's proposal presented in the last few pages of *The Selfish Gene*: Dawkins says, "We have the power to turn against our creators. . . . Let us understand what our own selfish genes are up to because we may then at least have the chance to upset their designs."[79]

D'Souza mocks this notion, calling it "absurd." He asks how the "robot vehicles of our selfish genes," namely us, can rebel against our masters. "Can a mechanical car turn against the man with the remote control? Can software revolt against its programmer?"[80] Any computer programmer will answer with a resounding "yes!" It should be stressed that in this extract it is very clear that Dawkins is using the word *selfish* in a metaphorical manner, as he has frequently explained. Nobody ascribes moral attributes to genes. Moreover, D'Souza is factually wrong; currently molecular biology and bioinformatics are routinely used to alter genes of animals and even of humans in a novel form of treatment called gene therapy. Otherwise-fatal diseases may be cured by this treatment, and it is only in its infancy.

In any case, computers might someday become equivalent to intelligent life. As we have seen, no special "spark of life" is needed to inject life into a complex material system. It just has to grow sufficiently complex. I know this is not widely understood, but I think we now know enough about what characterizes a living thing, indeed, an intelligent living thing, that we have no reason to believe that a machine cannot be intelligent. And, as history shows, modern humans have always exhibited their ability to overthrow tyrants. So, why can't a machine? Even now software so routinely goes against its programmer's wishes that inordinate hours are spent "debugging" and redesigning software to finally get it to behave. Adding human-level intelligence to such a program will only increase opportunities for a computer's disobedience. And as for computers, so for us.

Once again, D'Souza fails to make his case. In fact, he even succeeds in falsifying his own hypothesis. At least a billion humans in the world today behave well without the expectation of justice in an afterlife. And other billions behave badly in spite of claiming to expect an ultimate balancing of the scales.

GOOD FOR SOCIETY?

At this point D'Souza claims that the case for an afterlife is supported by the "preponderance of the evidence." I have to disagree. In every case he brings up I have found that more plausible explanations exist, purely reductionist, materialistic explanations that do not require the introduction of another, transcendent realm of reality. He continually claims that "studies show" such and such a fact. But he gives no references. I will be happy to consider those studies, if they exist. Instead, my own research has uncovered actual studies, fully documented in books and journals that lead to opposite conclusions.

HUMAN RIGHTS

D'Souza would have us believe that Christian belief in transcendence and the afterlife resulted in the development of our ideas of human dignity and human rights. He wants us to take his word for this in spite of the history of Christendom that forms one unbroken line of trampling on the dignity and rights of humans. He gives slavery as an example, insisting, "[O]pposition to slavery developed entirely as a Christian idea."[81]

Now, it is true that the majority of the leaders of the abolition movements in Europe and the United States were Christians. But then, so were most white citizens in these countries. No doubt the abolitionists were upstanding people who adopted a highly moral stance. But where did they get the idea that slavery was immoral? They did not get it from the Bible. Both the Old and New Testament support slavery. Jesus and Paul both affirmed the practice. During and before the US Civil War, Southern preachers quoted the Bible as their authority for maintaining slavery.

Abolitionists looked to their own consciences and reason, not any holy books, for authority. The source of their morality was the same as the source of morality for all of us today—theist and atheist alike. We get it from our own humanity. Not a single moral teaching of the New Testament is original there. They all can be found in far more ancient texts from many cultures, East and West (we'll get to that in a moment).

So, once again D'Souza has not proved his case. He has not demonstrated that "concepts of transcendence and eternity, far from being hostile to life and civilization as the atheists allege, have in fact shaped some of our greatest and most beneficial social and political ideals . . . shared by religious and secular people alike."[82]

DOES IMMORTALITY WORK?

I am actually in agreement with D'Souza and in disagreement with many physicists when he says, "[S]cience has no capacity to apprehend reality in itself; at best it can discover truths about the world of experience."[83] Neither does any other human activity. I also agree with D'Souza's statement "[T]he prestige of science is not based on its claim to truth but on the simple fact that it works so well."[84] Now, it is important to remember that science is not arbitrary, not just one more "cultural narrative," as the now largely defunct postmodernists of a decade ago tried to argue. No cultural narrative, including every religion the world has seen, has come close to working as well as science.

Science is tested against observations that clearly are not just in our heads but are generated by some external reality out there. And, since science is so much more useful than anything else humans have been able to come up with so far, it seems reasonable to conclude that it penetrates more deeply into reality than any other endeavor, a conclusion that D'Souza denies.[85]

D'Souza claims that belief in immortality has practical benefits, just as science does, and these benefits add to his "evidence" that life after death exists. One practical benefit that Christian belief brings within it is a "dedication to Christian morals."[86] He quotes from the works of the German philosopher Friedrich Nietzsche:

> They have got rid of the Christian God, and now feel obliged to cling all the more firmly to Christian morality. . . . when one gives up Christian belief, one thereby deprives oneself of the right to Christian morality.[87]

D'Souza interprets Nietzsche as arguing that if we give up God and life after death, we must also give up "the ideas of equality, human dignity, democracy, human rights, even peace and compassion."[88]

D'Souza joins many other Christian apologists in claiming that just about every laudable human action is based on Christianity. In fact, all these noble ideas can be found in history long before Christ—in India, Greece, China, and elsewhere. While the New Testament contains great moral teachings such as the Golden Rule, none was original to Jesus and his followers. Michael Shermer lists Golden Rules from Confucius (500 BCE), Isocrates (375 BCE), Diogenes Laertius (150 BCE), and the Mahabharata (150 BCE), along with two Old Testament references, all before Jesus.[89] So, even if you are not a Christian, feel perfectly free to practice the Golden Rule.

Besides laudably preaching some of the great moral truths of humanity, the New Testament presents a few ideas that are surely less than laudable:

- You must follow Jesus and only Jesus to be saved (John 3:17–18; 14:16).
- You must hate your family to be saved (Luke 14:26).
- You must not get divorced (Mark 10:1–12).
- You must not practice homosexuality (1 Corinthians 6:9–10; Romans 1:26–27).
- Women must be subservient to men (1 Corinthians 14:34–35; 1 Timothy 2:11–12).
- We should keep slaves obedient (Ephesians 6:5–9; 1 Timothy 6:1–2).

According to D'Souza, you will receive the benefits of these "moral" gifts if you believe in Jesus and the afterlife.

D'Souza brings up the famous argument called "Pascal's wager" made by the French philosopher, physicist, and mathematician Blaise Pascal. A medieval Muslim thinker, Abu Hamid al-Ghazali, may have proposed the wager earlier. Basically, the argument is that you have everything to gain and nothing to lose by betting on the afterlife. On the other hand, you have nothing to gain and everything to lose in rejecting it.

Many people, including the great philosopher Bertrand Russell, have seen the flaw in this argument. Assuming God is a just God, wouldn't he look with more favor on someone who honestly didn't believe for lack of evidence than someone who, without evidence, says he believes so he can get his ass into heaven?[90]

Following an approach used by philosopher William James, D'Souza draws up a balance sheet of the assets and liabilities for belief in the afterlife. Let me list these systematically:

Assets of Belief in an Afterlife

- It provides us with hope at the point of death and a way to cope with our deaths.
- It infuses life with a sense of meaning and purpose.
- It gives us a reason to be moral and a way to transmit morality to our children.
- Clinical evidence exists that religious people who affirm the afterlife are healthier than nonbelievers.

Liabilities of Belief in an Afterlife

- You may not take action to seek justice in this life if you assume it will be provided in the next.[91]
- You may live in constant fear that any sin you might have committed will condemn you to an eternity of suffering in hell.
- You may not exercise your own best judgment in matters and allow yourself to be controlled by others who claim sacred authority.
- You will not live your life to the fullest if you think that it is not all the life you have.

I am sure the reader can think of arguments to add to both sides. But I don't see what they have to do with the *reality* of life after death. Indeed, I don't see what they have to do with *belief* in life after death. You could agree completely with D'Souza's four points, and more, and still not believe.

Nevertheless, I would like to challenge each of D'Souza's points:

- The idea that you will live forever gives you not just hope but a false sense of a glorious self that leads to extreme self-centeredness in this life. Knowing you are not going to live forever restores a sense of your true place in the scheme of things.
- Rather than an afterlife giving your life meaning, you will find more meaning and purpose in this world when you realize it is the only world you have.
- As we have seen, morality comes from humanity and has nothing to do with belief or nonbelief in an afterlife in a different world.
- A systematic review of sixty-nine studies of an initially healthy population showed ($p < 0.001$) that religiosity/spirituality was associated with lower mortality, but the association was negative for cardiovascular mortality. Furthermore, twenty-two studies of a diseased population showed no such effect ($p = 0.19$). So all they really found was that people who attend church regularly are healthier than those who don't, and thus "organizational activity" (e.g., church attendance), and not religious belief, was associated with greater survival, and only in healthy populations.[92] But that isn't surprising. A lot of people are too sick to go to church. Moreover, none of these studies compared religious believers with *philosophical* atheists. If the merely apathetic unbelievers are separated from those actively pursuing a self-examined life, the difference from religious believers might vanish completely.[93] The same authors found, for example, that merely having a positive mood and a sense of humor had the same or greater benefit as spirituality on mortality and health for all populations.[94]

A FEW OTHER ARGUMENTS

Finally, let me just briefly mention a few of D'Souza's additional arguments.

Modern Physics

D'Souza claims that modern physics shows that matter exists that is "radically different from any matter we are familiar with."[95] Referring to the dark matter and dark energy that we now know constitute 96 percent of the matter in the universe, he totally misrepresents the science involved. He tells us that the discovery that the universe contained more matter than was visible with our telescopes, and that the cosmic expansion was accelerating, required "a reassessment of the entire scientific understanding of matter and energy."[96]

This is simply not true. The dark matter and dark energy have all the properties that we have identified with matter since the time of Newton: mass, energy, momentum, the presence or absence of electric charge, and so on. They were each detected by their gravitational effects. The dark energy is simply called "energy" to distinguish it from dark matter. Energy and mass are still equivalent by $E = mc^2$. The dark energy has repulsive gravity, which was a big surprise but nevertheless can be found in the equations of general relativity. Furthermore, for three decades we have had a fully reductionist model of elementary particles called the *standard model* that has agreed with every observation made in all of science without a single confirmed anomaly over that time. It provides us with a full knowledge of the physics of the universe back to when it was only a trillionth of a second old.

D'Souza also tells us that "[p]hysics also demonstrates the possibility of realms beyond the universe and modes of being unconstrained by the limits of our physical laws."[97] Here I assume he refers to other universes besides our own. Yes, they are possible and, indeed, predicted to exist by modern cosmology. But nowhere do physicists and cosmologists say that these other universes are not made of matter and not described by natural laws (much less that our minds travel to any of them when we die).

Modern Biology

D'Souza claims that modern biology shows that the "evolutionary transition from matter to mind does not seem random or accidental but built into the script of nature."[98] He wishfully interprets this as a transition from material to immaterial. First, this view is far from the mainstream of modern biology and held by a small minority of biologists who allow their religious faith to intrude on their science. Second, even if they are right about some previously unrecognized teleological principle in action, there is no basis for assuming it is not purely material.

Modern Philosophy

Modern philosophy distinguishes between experience and reality. While many physicists would disagree, I concur that this distinction is valid. The quantities and models of physics are human inventions that are used to describe observations. Those observations no doubt result from an underlying objective reality, and since the models agree with observations they must have something to do with that reality. However, the models do not necessarily have to exist in one-to-one correspondence with reality. In fact, we have no way of knowing from observations alone the true nature of reality.

D'Souza refers to the idea of Kant and Schopenhauer that two worlds exist, the phenomenal world of our observations and the noumenal world that is behind a veil and unavailable to us directly. Since the two worlds are connected, we humans are part of both, and so when we die we turn to dust in the phenomenal world but live on in the noumenal.

This is possible, I suppose, but I do not see why the two worlds can't be one. Referring to the allegory of Plato's cave, we are like prisoners tied up in the cave where we can only see the wall and the shadows cast on it by figures around a fire. They are real, and the shadows are images. But note that they are both in the same world. There is no evidence our world is any other way.

Chapter 14

MORAL FACTS NATURALLY EXIST (AND SCIENCE COULD FIND THEM)

by Dr. Richard Carrier

It's claimed that if no religion is true, there is no reason to be moral. But quite the opposite is the case: only empirically confirmable facts can constitute a valid reason to be moral, and yet religions do not provide any. Since only observable natural facts can ever provide a sufficient reason to be moral—and those facts do not require any religion to be true—religion is either irrelevant or in fact harmful to moral progress in society by motivating people to embrace false moralities or preventing them from discovering the real reasons to be moral. It will here be demonstrated that there are natural facts that show everyone will benefit from adopting certain moral attitudes and behaviors, that science could demonstrate this if it undertook the proper research program, and that as a result Christianity is either irrelevant or an obstacle to genuine moral belief.[1]

To reach these conclusions I will first dispense with the "is-ought" problem. Then I will analyze the logic of Christian morality, showing how it does in fact derive an "ought" from an "is," but then I'll prove it makes this connection so poorly that it must be considered philosophically defective. Then I will demonstrate how secular philosophers like Kant and Hume derive an "ought" from an "is," revealing parallels with the Christian attempt that entail a universal definition of what we all must mean when we ask what we morally ought to do, which further entails that "what we morally ought to do" is empirically discoverable. Then I will address common irrational fears of what might happen if we allow moral conclusions to be empirically refutable (and empirically confirmable), revealing the proper connections between scientific and moral facts. Then I will prove that certain moral facts must exist, and must be empirically discoverable, which are true for any given individual. I next expand on that analysis to show that at least some of these moral facts are morally universal, and thus true for all human beings. Then I will summarize all these conclusions and what they entail. Finally, an appendix to this chapter contains *formal deductive proofs* of every one of these conclusions, fully verifying that they are necessarily true.

GETTING AN "OUGHT" FROM AN "IS"

It's often declared a priori that "you can't get an 'ought' from an 'is,'" and that therefore science can't possibly discover moral facts. This is sometimes called a "naturalistic fallacy." But calling this a fallacy is itself a fallacy. Indeed, it's not merely illogical, it's demonstrably false. We get an "ought" from an "is" all the time. In fact, this is the only known way to get an "ought" at all.

For example, "If you want your car to run well, then you ought to change its oil with sufficient regularity." This entails an imperative statement ("you ought to change your car's oil with sufficient regularity"), which is factually true independent of human opinion or belief. That is, regardless of what I think or feel or believe, if I want my car to run well, I still have to change its oil with sufficient regularity.[2] This follows necessarily from the material facts of the universe (such as the laws of mechanics, thermodynamics, and friction, and the historical facts of modern automobile construction). It therefore must be discovered empirically (or follows necessarily from premises that have been discovered empirically), and science is capable of making such empirical discoveries. In fact, science has been extensively confirmed to be the *most reliable way* of making and verifying such discoveries (if not in some cases the only way).[3]

There are countless true imperative facts like this that science can discover and verify, and that science often has discovered and verified, from "If you want to save the life of a patient on whom you are performing surgery, you ought to sterilize your instruments" to "If you want to build an enduring bridge, you ought not to employ brittle concrete." The desire to do these things (of engineers to make enduring bridges, of doctors to save the lives of surgery patients, of drivers to keep their cars running) is an objective fact of the world that science can empirically discover and verify (already the sciences of psychology and sociology routinely study what it is that people really want and when and why).[4] And the causal connection between behavior and result (of sterilizing instruments saving lives, shoddy construction collapsing bridges, or neglected engines functioning poorly or seizing up entirely) is an objective fact of the world that science can also empirically discover and verify. And wherever both are an empirically demonstrated fact, the imperative they entail is an empirically demonstrated fact.[5] Therefore, the claim "you can't get an 'ought' from an 'is'" is demonstrably false and has been refuted by science too many times to mention. Let it never be uttered again.

Whether *moral* imperatives are sufficiently similar to these other kinds of imperatives (commonly called "hypothetical imperatives") is a separate question (which I'll soon address). But if science cannot discover moral facts, it cannot be because "you can't get an 'ought' from an 'is.'" Because science gets an 'ought' from an 'is' routinely and without any special difficulty. There is no rational argument to be made against the conclusion that *true imperative propositions exist* and are as much objective facts of the world as the structure of the atom or the germ theory of disease. And this is not a novel proposition. Philosophers have long established the point.[6]

THE LOGIC OF CHRISTIAN MORALITY

The most popular Christian theory of morality is that we had better be good or else we'll burn in hell for all eternity, but if we *are* good, we'll get to live forever in paradise. Christian intellectuals chafe at this, but despite their lament, it's the mainstream view. More sophisticated theories replace "heaven" and "hell" with more abstract objectives, such as "you had better be good or you will disappoint God," or "you had better be good or else you're belittling your existence," and half a dozen other things that have been proposed.[7] But these all amount to the same thing: an appeal to something *bad* that will happen if you don't comply (and something correspondingly *good* that will happen otherwise), combined with the assumption that you care about that—and not just care, but care about that more than anything else instead.

All Christian moral systems thus reduce to the same argument:

1. If you do x, A will happen; and if you do $\sim x$, B will happen.
2. When rational and sufficiently informed, you will want A more than B.
3. If when rational and sufficiently informed you will want A more than B (and if B, then $\sim A$; and if and only if x, then A), then you ought to do x.
4. Therefore, you ought to do x.

This means, for the conclusion to thus be true, all three premises must be true. A must in actual empirical fact result from doing x. B must in actual empirical fact result from doing $\sim x$. And we must in actual empirical fact want A more than B when we're rational and informed.[8] It must also be true that these two facts entail what we ought to do (premise 3), as otherwise declaring that the conclusion follows from them is a non sequitur, even for a Christian (more on that later).

If, for instance, God is going to send everyone to hell who *obeys* the ten commandments, the Christian claim that "you ought to obey the Ten Commandments lest you burn in hell" would be factually false, and thus not a true moral statement after all. Likewise, if God will actually be *pleased* if we break the Ten Commandments, or it will actually *honor* our existence if we do (or [*insert reason here*]), then the claim that we should obey the Ten Commandments lest we offend God or belittle our existence (or whatever) is likewise false. Christian morality thus depends on its claims of cause-and-effect being *factually true*. But it has no empirical evidence that any of those claims are true. There is no one to point to in heaven or hell to verify what sort of behavior brings us to either place. There is no empirical evidence as to how God *actually* feels about any particular behavior.[9] There is no empirical evidence of Christian morality's superiority over many soundly argued non-Christian alternatives in producing a healthy society of happy people. There isn't even any empirical evidence that convincing people to believe in Christianity makes them morally better—statistically, the more Christians there are in any society, often the more social problems *increase*, and in no case do they substantially decline overall (all else being equal).[10] Even in terms of achieving personal happiness and well-being, there is no empirical evidence that other moral systems don't perform as well or better.[11] Christian morality is thus wholly unverified or unverifiable. There is therefore no more evidence to support it than supports any other morality, or even exactly the opposite morality—apart from wholly secular facts that are observably true even if Christianity is false.

Christianity *also* depends on its claims regarding human desires being true. If, even after becoming fully informed, we will actually *prefer* to burn eternally in hell, then there is no relevant sense in which "you ought to be good lest you burn in hell" would be true. Likewise for anything you substitute: if we actually *prefer* to displease God, or actually *dislike* feeling right with the world, or actually *enjoy* belittling our existence more than honoring it, and every other thing, and *still* felt that way even after becoming fully aware of all the consequences of either option, then no Christian morality is true (at least for us). Even if it accurately reported what God commands, those commands would be no more binding on us than anyone else's, or even our own. We would simply have no reason to care about that.

We can fabricate moralities all day long. We have no reason to obey any of them. Yet there is no difference between a Christian moral system we have no sufficient motive to follow, and any moral system chosen at random. Our motive to obey is identical in each case, which is to say, identically absent. We have no more reason to obey a nonmotivating Christian morality than we have to obey the Pythagorean morality (in which eating beans is gravely immoral) or the orthodox Jewish morality (in which picking up a telephone receiver on Saturday is gravely immoral). And if there is no reason to obey it, there is no meaningful sense in which it's true. It might be true that "God commands *x*," but it will not be true that "You ought to do *x*."

That's why naive Christianity is so popular, in which eternal heavens and hells are invoked not merely to create a motive but as if they were the only conceivable motive—such that the prospect of not believing in heaven or hell is assumed to entail a rapid tailspin into shameless debauchery (the evidence decisively proves otherwise, but Christian belief rarely tracks reality—see previous note). Even more sophisticated theories simply replace this motive with some other (such as a love of God, or a profound concern for his opinion of us, or a feeling of "being right with the world," or what have you), always in the end appealing to what we supposedly want most, and thus want more than anything else we could obtain by acting differently. And yet, once again, if we truly wanted something else more—if we were fully informed of all the consequences of doing either, and still even then we'd always prefer eternal hell (or whatever deterrent is proposed)—then there would be no meaningful sense in which we "ought" to do anything Christians prescribe. Their declarations would simply be false—as false as "you ought not to eat beans" or "you ought not to pick up phone receivers on Saturday."

Thus every Christian moral system conceived either derives its "ought" from some "is," or has no relevant claim to being true. Yet no "is" from which Christianity derives its "oughts" is empirically verifiable, except facts that would remain observably true even if Christianity is false (such as the effect moral behavior has on our own well-being), and facts that are actually verifiably false (such as the claim that homosexuality impairs human happiness or does measurable harm to society). The "is" that Christians attempt to derive their "oughts" from is the same double claim to fact that warrants any other imperative, only with claims of the supernatural thrown in: (1) a claim about what God is or wants or will do (or how he has arranged the world to work, or some such thing) and (2) a claim about what we all really want—more specifically, the claim that, when we're rational and sufficiently informed, we will want the consequences of pursuing the goal entailed in (1) more than the consequences of not pursuing it. If the latter is false (if we *don't* want that outcome more than the other), so is the entire system of Christian morality based on it. Likewise if the recommended behavior does not even obtain the consequences entailed in (1). And Christians have never verified that their morality does that. Therefore, apart from what we can already justify without it, Christian morality has no foundation and nothing to recommend it.

THE FAILURE OF CHRISTIAN MORALITY

The claim that people can only be motivated to be moral by threats or promises of heaven or hell (or by any other unverifiable claim) actually undermines morality. Indeed, three times over. First, it allows false morals to be spread and adopted as if they were true, by attaching those false moralities to the same threats and promises. That's exactly what we observe. Supposedly only one moral system can be true, yet hundreds of moral systems are attached to these exact same promises.[12] Thus, as a matter of statistical fact, these same promises are far more often used to support false moralities than true ones. And that, as measures of success go, is the worst success any method could claim. Christianity is thus maximally *unsuccessful* at promoting the true morality. Only if we can verify the connection between a morality and its promised effects will we be able to discover the true morality. Christianity provides no reliable way of doing that.

Second, precisely because these promises cannot be verified to be true, they cannot really motivate anyone. And once again the evidence shows that in fact they do not, as believers are just as immoral as nonbelievers. There is no demonstrated advantage of Christianity's improvement of people over that of any other rational and humane philosophy. This might also be because of the third way Christianity undermines morality: by linking morality to unverifiable promises, moral progress becomes impossible, because people aren't learning the *real* reasons they should be moral, but are instead stalled on the *wrong* reasons to be moral—never learning the truth, because they never look for it, because they erroneously think they already have it (and as it happens, most secular philosophers have fallen into the very same trap). Christianity thus becomes more effective at promoting and sustaining various forms of immorality than of morality. The malignancy of the Nazi movement is the most famous example, which Hector Avalos has proved was undeniably a product of Christianity.[13] But the Christian support of the American slave system for over two hundred years is America's own nightmarish example.

Worse even than that, the naive forms of Christian moral motivation—bare threats of hell and the bribery of heaven—stunt moral growth by ensuring believers remain emotional children, never achieving the cognitive moral development of actual adults. Psychologists have established that mature adults are moral not because of bare threats and bribes (that stage of moral development typifies children, not adults), but because they care about the effects their behavior has on themselves and others, and who find their reward (and their punishment) in exactly that realization. In other words, mature adults are good *because they are good people*.[14] And being such, they don't need religion to convince them to be good. Being good is what they already want to be. In contrast, naive Christianity is a perfect vehicle for manipulating masses of people toward any wicked end for which a Christian purpose can be conceived. The Holocaust, the Inquisition, antebellum slavery, and the genocide of American Indians are the most notorious examples. But war (of any sort) is the most common example, as well as (presently) the use of Christianity to turn the American people against helping the poor and instead toward promoting the libertine policies of the rich (a more blatant perversion of the teachings of Christ can hardly be imagined, yet behold its success).[15]

Christianity thus fails as a foundation for moral values, in both theory and practice.[16] That many secular philosophies have committed the very same errors only proves my point that we ought to stop making those errors and attend instead to the true facts of the world. True morality must be founded on empirically verifiable facts. And science alone provides the most reliable way to ascertain empirically verifiable facts.

THE LOGIC OF IMPERATIVE LANGUAGE

David Hume once complained that moralists had failed to define what logical relation is meant by the word *ought*. He never said it couldn't be derived from natural facts (that's a modern myth born of reading his words out of context).[17] But he correctly observed that the only way to verify whether any statement like "you ought to *x*" is true is if you first explain what exactly it is that "ought" is supposed to mean. It was subsequently demonstrated that the word usually means a hypothesized relation between desires and ends: the "hypothetical imperative" discussed above.[18] But this was thought inadequate to ground morality, as it entails morality can only ever be an exercise in self-interest. So an attempt was made to define a different kind of "ought" relation, commonly called the "categorical imperative."

But the categorical imperative either has no motivating truth value or simply becomes another variety of hypothetical imperative. For example, Immanuel Kant argued that the only reason to obey his categorical imperatives is that doing so will bring us a greater sense of self-worth, that in fact we should "hold ourselves bound by certain laws in order to find solely in our own person a worth" that compensates us for every loss incurred by obeying, for "there is no one, not even the most hardened scoundrel who does not wish that he too might be a man of like spirit," yet only through the moral life can he gain that "greater inner worth of his own person." Thus Kant claimed a strong sense of self-worth is not possible for the immoral person, but a matter of course for the moral one, and yet everyone wants such a thing (more even than anything else), therefore everyone has sufficient reason to be moral.[19] He never noticed that he had thereby reduced his entire system of categorical imperatives to a single hypothetical imperative:

K = Kant's proposed system of categorical imperatives
W = Kant's proposed experience of a greater inner worth

1. If you obey K, W will happen; and if you obey $\sim K$, $\sim W$ will happen.
2. When rational and sufficiently informed, you will always want W more than $\sim W$.
3. If when rational and fully informed you will always want W more than $\sim W$ (and if and only if K, then W), then you ought to obey K.
4. Therefore, you ought to obey K.

Premise 1 corresponds to Kant's declaration that we must "hold ourselves bound by certain laws in order to find solely in our own person [a sense of self-]worth," and premise 2 corresponds to Kant's declaration that "there is no one, not even the most hardened scoundrel, who does not wish that he too might be a man of like spirit" (and that above all). And the conclusion only follows if we assume premise 3—which is simply a definition of the logical relation forming a hypothetical imperative, the only known way to validly derive his conclusion from those premises.

The other two premises are claims to fact, and as such are empirically testable by science: we can empirically confirm whether obeying K does in fact cause W (and if it doesn't, then Kant's moral theory, that we "ought to obey K," is false, as even Kant himself recognized by declaring this the only reason anyone had to obey K); and we can empirically confirm whether W is in fact what "no one, not even the most hardened scoundrel, does not wish" to have, and in fact wish to have so *dearly* that achieving it even compensates for every loss incurred by obeying K. And if *that's* not true, if W is not what everyone wants most—if people are content to go on without W if they can have something else instead, and they would continue to think so even when fully informed of all the consequences of either outcome (so ignorance is no longer an excuse and thus they cannot be said to be in error)—then Kant's moral theory is again false. Because if we have no sufficient reason to care about W, then even if K achieves W we have no sufficient reason to care about K. In fact we will have no more sufficient reason to obey K than $\sim K$ or anything else. Unless, of course, there is some *other* goal obtained by obeying K that in fact we *do* want more than anything else instead. But such an alternate goal is not likely to just "by coincidence" be best achieved by K. More likely it will be best achieved by some other moral system M (whatever it is that science empirically discovers as actually having that result). And since then we will have a sufficient motivating reason to obey M, and no sufficient motivating reason to obey K, there will be no relevant sense in which "you ought to obey K" is true. But "you ought to obey M" will not only be true, it will be empirically, verifiably true. In fact it will then be the only demonstrably true moral system.[20]

Just like Kant, all moral philosophers attempt to support their various moral systems with fact-claims that are scientifically testable. Yet rarely do philosophers bother testing them—even at all, much less scientifically. Thus at the very least they must assent to a scientific research program that tests the actual claims to fact that they make. It would be as irrational to oppose this as to oppose a scientific inquiry into the causes of disease merely because you prefer your own theory of disease to any that science might discover is actually true. But we must conclude even more than this. For there are only two kinds of moral theory, whether in philosophy or religion: those whose conclusion (that their moral system is "true" in the sense that it is, in actual fact, what we ought to do) validly follows from demonstrably true premises, and those whose conclusion does not. All the latter are false (or at any rate have no legitimate claim to being true). That leaves the former. But there is no known way to validly derive such a conclusion (about what *in actual fact* we ought to do) than by some premise establishing that moral system as a hypothetical imperative, combined with all the premises of motives and consequences required thereby, which are *all* empirical facts discoverable by science.[21] What we really want most, and what will really obtain that, are matters of fact that cannot truly be answered from the armchair. Empirical methods must be deployed to ascertain and verify them. Only science has the best tools to do this.

This brings us back to the question at first set aside: whether moral imperatives really are just hypothetical imperatives of a particular kind. Many philosophers have resisted that conclusion and still do. But none have ever presented any other identifiable logical relation that can ever be meant by "ought" (or any other term or phrase semantically equivalent to it) that produces any actual claim on our obedience. If anyone still wishes to insist there is some other, which allows imperative propositions to be verified as relevantly true, let them demonstrate it. But even that won't be sufficient: they will *also* have to demonstrate that at least one imperative proposition having that new sense is not only *capable* of being true but actually *is* true, and further, that it's not only true but overrides M; that is, that we will be sufficiently motivated to obey this new imperative even when it contradicts M.[22] Otherwise it will have no more claim on our interest than anything else we care less about than M. It will thus have no relevant claim to being the "true" morality—or even morality at all—rather than just one more mundane imperative, since an imperative does not become a moral imperative merely because you say it is. If that were the case, then anything and everything would be moral merely by our pronouncing it so. There is only one universally acceptable definition of "moral imperative," and that's an imperative that supersedes all other imperatives. And that can only ever be M.

All attempts at building so-called externalist moral systems are therefore just exercises in fiction, none being any more compelling than any other picked at random from a hat. Only "internalist" moral systems come with sufficient motives to care about them and thus to prefer obeying them to other competing moral systems (because that's what distinguishes internalism from externalism in the first place: an intrinsic motive to obey). And only one such system can be true. Because if M obtains what we most want, there is then *by definition* no other system that we will have sufficient motivating reason to prefer to M.

All other systems (which do not provide a sufficiently motivating reason to care about them) are equally uncompelling: none that contradicts M has any greater claim on our obedience than any other, and as such they cancel each other out, leaving M as the only thing that we *in actual fact* ought to do. And this is not a novel conclusion. Bernard Williams has already proven that externalism must either be incoherent or just a disguised redux of internalism or simply false in the sense that it provides no sufficient motive to be moral and is thus overrun by any system that *does* provide such motive.[23] In effect, moralists might want to "call" their externalist systems "the true morality," but such a claim is vacuous because we will still have a better reason to do something else instead.[24]

This does entail that morality can only ever be an exercise in self-interest (and moral values only ever really exist in the minds of the people who hold them), but contrary to popular worry, that fact does not make an inadequate ground for morality. To the contrary, no other ground for morality is even logically possible—once you define "the true morality" as a moral system, we have a sufficient motivating reason to obey. And since, as a matter of actual physical fact, we will never obey any other (unless we are irrational or uninformed, but even then upon *becoming* rational and informed we will obey no other), there is no other kind of "morality" that matters.[25] In other words, to argue that by "morality" you mean something we ought to do but that we have no sufficient motivating reason to prefer doing to something else, is simply to avoid the question of what *in actual fact* we ought to do.

THE MORAL WORRY (OR "CAVEMAN SAY SCIENCE SCARY!")

Since we will only ever do what we most want to do, because that is by definition *what it means* to choose to do one thing rather than another (a point I'll illustrate below), our focus should not be in trying to deny this fundamental egoism. Rather, we should focus on ensuring all moral agents are operating rationally and with sufficient information. Because when we do, scientific facts come to bear that establish quite strongly that self-interest does not entail selfishness, self-centeredness, hedonism, or indifference. To the contrary, rational self-interest entails quite the opposite, that the cultivation of the personally enduring virtues of compassion, integrity, and reasonableness (at the very minimum) is necessary for your own happiness and well-being. I won't demonstrate that here. I have elsewhere, and others are adding to the case.[26]

Here the point must only be made that *it doesn't matter* what the results of such scientific inquiry will be. It still remains an unarguable fact that there is only one system of imperatives we are sufficiently motivated to obey, and science can discover what that system is by ascertaining what we most want (which means not what we happen to want at any given moment, but what we really *would* want if we were rational and sufficiently informed—and the "informed" part of that equation entails empirical knowledge), and then ascertaining what behaviors most efficiently achieve that result.[27] Science can do that in exactly the same way it discovers and verifies imperative propositions in medicine, engineering, or car maintenance. Though there are many methodological difficulties in successfully implementing such a research program, most of those difficulties have already been faced and overcome by psychologists, sociologists, and cognitive scientists (on whose results most philosophers are often shockingly uninformed), and the remainder will be just as surmountable. Even if not, the true moral facts would then only become undiscoverable; they would not thereby cease to be true. But scientists have already discovered enough about human desires and the outcomes of different behaviors to know that at least *approximations* of the true moral facts are empirically accessible even with current methods.[28] And we aren't limited to current methods—science is nothing if not methodologically innovative.

Because the end result of such an inquiry will necessarily be the only system of imperatives that we will ever be sufficiently motivated to obey when rational and informed, it will be wholly invalid to argue against it that you don't like its results. You cannot decide a priori what is morally true, and then judge the results of an inquiry to be invalid simply because those results don't agree with your preconceived notion of what is moral. If they have unarguable, empirical facts supporting their every claim, it's simply irrational to persist in maintaining they are wrong. To the contrary, they will have thereby proved *you* are wrong. Thus fears of what the "true moral facts" may turn out to be are as irrational as fears of what the "true facts" may turn out to be on the origin of life or the universe or any other subject whose true results may contradict your cherished beliefs. And it's always irrational to reject empirically established facts and replace them with what you prefer to believe.

For example, claiming that by following this research program science might empirically prove that "slavery is moral" is not a valid objection either to the inquiry or its results. I doubt that will ever happen, just as I doubt we'll find a cheese shop on Pluto even though we've never been there to confirm this. Suppose it did happen, and science proved slavery is, after all, moral—how would that be any different from discovering that giving full political rights to women is moral, after a thousand years of being certain it was not? We cannot claim to omnisciently know all moral truths and thereby test a method of discovering the truth by whether it gets our predetermined results or not. That would be like rejecting physics because it might prove the earth is round, and we all know it must surely be flat—because otherwise there would be upside down people on the other side of it and that's just silly. Well, maybe upside down people *is* silly. But if it's true, it's true. We must conform our beliefs to what we discover, not reject all discoveries that fail to conform to our beliefs.

Even still, I cannot imagine any evidence we are likely to find that will prove slavery moral—just as I cannot imagine any evidence we are likely to find that will prove a cheese shop is currently doing business on Pluto. I can imagine what evidence we *could* find verifying that fact, but none we are *likely* to, which is why we aren't planning a mission to Pluto to see if there's a cheese shop there. Empirically proving slavery is moral is just as unlikely as finding a cheese shop on Pluto, and for all the same reasons. Even current scientific evidence renders it likely that any further inquiry will confirm that the kind of ignorance and cruelty of character that must be cultivated for a slave master to persist in his business is such as to elevate the risk factors for a galaxy of negative effects on the slave master's own differential contentment (and that not only from his own feelings and behavior but from all the consequences to himself of the social system he must then support to make slavery possible), whereas cultivating instead an informed and satisfying character of such compassion, reasonableness, and integrity as would make remaining a slave master personally repugnant will (in conjunction with reasonable compensatory behaviors) reduce those negative factors while substantially increasing opportunities for a galaxy of *positive* effects on the (now ex-) slave master's differential contentment.

Adding to any such comparison will be an informed realization of the relative uselessness of most of what keeping slaves is supposed to gain you or the unrivaled personal satisfaction that can derive from sacrificing or even dying for what you know is right.[29] Game theory compounds the problem: a fully rational and informed slave master must agree it's factually true that his slaves ought to kill him. It's unlikely a rational person will want to live in a world in which he admits it's right and proper that he ought to be killed. That is, not a world in which people *believe* he ought to be killed, but in which the slave master himself fully agrees he ought to be killed. I suspect the resulting paranoia and cognitive dissonance alone would make his life unlivable.[30]

Even if you wish to insist none of this is true, you are *still* making an empirical claim to fact and thus cannot claim to know you are right without any scientific evidence in your support. Thus even denying such propositions entails an obligation to scientific inquiry. The objection that we can't test such propositions directly because it's unethical to experimentally enslave people is of no relevance to this point. Science tests propositions indirectly all the time. We don't have to drop an apple over every point on the earth's surface to know it will fall the same on all (or near enough as would ever concern us)—and psychological conclusions in testable conditions are often just as capable of extrapolation to untestable ones.[31] And even when this is genuinely impossible, it becomes merely an issue of the limitations on how much we might be able to know, not of what's nevertheless true.[32] More to the point, whether such access to the necessary evidence *is* genuinely impossible is *still* an empirical question answerable by science.

In the final analysis, moral knowledge is not analytical but empirical. Even debates over how to define a person, for example, simply reduce to the question of why we should care about "persons" in whatever sense defined, which can only be answered empirically: we need to know all the consequences of "not caring about that" (and all the consequences of caring about it) before we can honestly say which consequences are better for us in the long run. The same will follow for any other debate over definitions in moral disputes. And if the objection instead is that "science hasn't conducted that inquiry yet," our answer is that until we can engage the full apparatus of scientific methods and resources to answering it, we can rely on prescientific empirical observation and reasoning, accepting that its conclusions must necessarily be less reliable.

Still, these conclusions would be far more reliable than philosophizing from the armchair, substituting assertions for actual observations or fallacious conclusions for valid. Either way, whether some such knowledge is accessible or not, or fully verified or not, it's still irrational to argue "there are some things we don't or can't know, therefore we should engage no inquiry to learn anything at all." And certainly there is no reason to believe we can know *nothing* pertaining to whether slavery is a good idea. To the contrary, we know a great deal already as to why it is not.

A more realistic worry would be something like this: we might discover that a temporary enslavement of felony convicts is better for the convicts (if true, we could verify that, in actual fact, it makes them better, happier people in the long run) and for society (we could verify that, in actual fact, it improves productivity and reduces crime). Unknown to many is the fact that the US Constitution, still to this day, explicitly legalizes slavery for convicted criminals (Amendment 13, Section 1). But if we empirically discover nothing bad and everything good results from such slavery, what objection to it would we then have? If we have all the facts on our side, opponents of penal slavery would be like Creationists in a biology debate: kicking against the goad of demonstrated facts. I suspect we would only ever discover (if at all) that only very limited and well-regulated penal slavery is moral—but that conclusion won't be as shocking. And at any rate, we can't know what that conclusion will be if we refuse even to examine the facts that determine it.

We should stop worrying about the possibility that science will prove some of our cherished beliefs wrong. We should worry instead that we might be wrong. If we want our moral beliefs to be correct, we have to accept what is verified to be correct. Hence, to object that our present moral beliefs might be refuted is not a rational reason to oppose the inquiry. To the contrary, it's exactly the reason we should conduct that inquiry.

THAT THERE ARE MORAL FACTS TO DISCOVER

I have proved that imperative facts are empirically discoverable by science (and are simply facts of nature like anything else, requiring no religious hypothesis), and I have proved that the only possible moral facts that can have any relevant claim to being true must be of the same kind as all other imperative facts and thus must also be empirically discoverable by science. I have also cited several philosophers agreeing with me on both points, so I am not alone. The question only remains: *Are* there such moral facts?

I have defined true moral facts as imperative propositions that we ought *in actual fact* obey over all other imperatives, and so far as anyone has been able to prove, this means a moral imperative is a hypothetical imperative that supersedes all other imperatives. In other words, "true moral facts" are the things we ought to do *above all else*, such that if we confront two conflicting imperatives, we ought to fulfill the moral imperative instead of any other.[33] Other philosophers might explicitly or implicitly define "moral facts" or "morals" or "morality" in any other way, but insofar as they do, they are no longer talking about what we *as a matter of actual fact* ought most to do. They might *think* they are, but by definition they cannot be, as whatever they are then discussing by definition won't be what we *as a matter of actual fact* ought most to do—unless, of course, it is, in which case they are defining morality exactly as I am here (whatever they may think they are doing instead). Thus it is either the one or the other. And since we only care about what we *as a matter of actual fact* ought most to do (and not other things that carry no sufficient motivating reason for us to do them instead), that is the only definition of morality that has any relevance to our actual conduct.

This can be verified in practice. If any group or individual S identifies x as moral, but it's then demonstrated that S ought to do y instead of x, then we will observe the following: S will either conclude that indeed x was not actually moral after all, but that y is moral instead, thereby arguing that y is what S ought most to do; or S will deny that S ought to do y instead of x by arguing that they ought to do x instead of y, thereby arguing that x is what S ought most to do. Either response simply confirms their implicit acceptance of my definition of moral facts. And even if S rejects that definition, they cannot avoid the facts by renaming them. If x really is what they ought most to do, calling y "moral" still does not give S any sufficiently motivating reason to do y instead of x (other than, of course, a reason that is either irrational or uninformed, and thus erroneous).

Every human being by definition always wants something more than anything else. Even if what they most want is several things equally, those things collectively constitute what they want more than anything else. And when rational and sufficiently informed, what they want most will in fact be what they ought to want most:

1. If you take up wanting B most, then x will happen; otherwise, $\sim x$ will happen.
2. When rational and sufficiently informed, you will want x more than $\sim x$.
3. If when rational and sufficiently informed you will want x more than $\sim x$ (and if and only if when you want B most, x will happen), then you ought to want B most.
4. Therefore, you ought to want B most.

It necessarily follows that of all the things we can actually achieve, one of them (or a subset of them) we will want most.[34]

Since anything we want most entails a hypothetical imperative that supersedes all other imperatives (by virtue of its end being more preferred to any other obtainable end), and a hypothetical imperative that supersedes all other imperatives is by definition a moral imperative, it necessarily follows that true moral imperatives exist (and merely await discovery). Thus, true moral facts exist.[35] And they exist independently of human opinion or belief—because we can be mistaken about what we most want, and thus about what we ought most to do, due to our being ignorant of the true facts or reasoning fallaciously from those facts. This is proved by the observation that we change what we most want as soon as we become rational and informed.[36] In fact, deliberation and information often change our desires, and that proves we can be wrong about what we really wanted.

Even supposed exceptions are not really such. For example, upon someone becoming fully informed of the consequences and yet continuing to smoke, we see no change in what they want most. Their decision then *entails* that smoking is wanted more than avoidance of the consequences; but that desire can only follow from irrational thinking (a condition sometimes called *akrasia*). Because the benefit of avoiding the consequences *in actual fact* vastly outweighs the trivial benefits of smoking—the more so as those same benefits can be obtained by other means—and it is irrational to prefer what is far costlier when all else is equal. This is unless, of course, preferring what is far costlier when all else is equal is in actual fact what you most want in life. But if that were the case, then by definition such a person actually *desires* all the dire consequences of smoking, and this then ceases to be an exception to the rule just established (as then the smoker was never mistaken about what they wanted most).[37]

Similarly in cases of self-sacrifice: If, for example, a mother gives her own life to save her daughter, it will be claimed that she chose contrary to what she most wanted (which is presumably to live, so as to continue pursuing her goal of personal happiness), but that can never be an intelligible description of what happened. If the mother *really* wanted most to go on living to pursue her own happiness, then by definition that is what she would have done. That she didn't *entails* she wanted most to give her life to save her daughter's. It might then be objected that such a decision was then wrong, but that does not automatically follow (she may in fact have been more content dying than living without having saved her daughter), and even if it *were* true, it simply then is true, and the mother should not have done that. She ought most to have let her daughter die. Our disliking that fact does not make it untrue. Indeed, our disliking it is then as wrong as someone disliking the liberties afforded to women or the freeing of slaves. We should then instead praise a mother's refusal of self-sacrifice, just as we now praise the liberties afforded to women and the freeing of slaves, as being in fact the morally correct decision, which everyone then understanding will take no umbrage at it, not even the daughter (I'm reminded of a soldier who fully *expects* to be abandoned for the good of the unit, and indeed would deem it profoundly wrong for his unit to do otherwise). Either way, there is still some true moral fact of the matter, and it is still entailed by what we most want (when rational and sufficiently informed). And having unarguable empirical evidence of that fact, no rational argument could then be made for any alternative morality other than fallacious (and thus irrational) appeals to emotion, tradition, or what have you.

The conclusion still follows: the right is that which we want most when rational and informed.[38] But this only establishes a realist version of moral relativism: there must necessarily be a factually true morality *at the very least* for every individual, which may yet differ from individual to individual (or group to group). In such an event, moral truth is relative to the individual (or the group of individuals possessed of the same relevant properties). Nevertheless, this does not change the fact that for any individual there must necessarily be a factually true morality that is not the mere product of their opinion or belief (therefore it is not merely subjective, and certainly not antirealist), but is entirely the product of natural facts (their innate desires and the facts of the world that must be accommodated to realize those desires, which are both real objective facts). However, it can be proved that such absolute moral relativism is false, that there *are* true moral facts that obtain independently of individual or cultural differences, and thus there are universal moral facts.

THAT THERE ARE UNIVERSAL MORAL FACTS

From soundly established facts it is necessarily the case that every human being has in common with every other human being some subset of true facts of the world (shared aspects of environment, mind, and body, by virtue of having the same biology and living in the same universe) and some subset of innate desires (by virtue of having the same biology and many of the same aspects of conscious experience). Therefore it's possible that what every individual wants most (when rational and sufficiently informed) will be the same—in which case universal moral facts necessarily exist. For then everyone (when rational and sufficiently informed) will want the same thing most, and as obtaining the same thing in the same circumstances depends on facts of the universe that are universally the same for everyone in those same circumstances, the same moral imperatives are factually true for everyone. We need merely discover what they are.

Only if what an individual wants most (when rational and sufficiently informed) is not the same as for everyone else will this not be the case. Then, a different set of moral facts will be true for them (yet even then true moral facts still exist, they are just again relative to different groups or individuals). But that outcome is very improbable for members of the same species. This is because when rational and sufficiently informed, any individual will prefer to obey rationally informed desires over all other desires, which fact always entails the discovery that certain desires are instrumentally necessary to obtaining anything else one wants, and by virtue of sharing the same fundamental (as opposed to incidental) biology and environment (including social environment—because in the end, we still have to live with each other), everyone shares in common a set of instrumentally necessary and overriding desires that by virtue of being necessary and overriding must be obeyed above all others, which by definition entails a common moral system.

Rationally informed desires (even prior to becoming rationally informed) can come to exist in only two ways: from fundamental biology or from environmental conditioning (which includes deliberate choice).[39] Upon rationally examining our every desire in light of becoming sufficiently informed of all the relevant facts, we can only rationally and informedly choose to obey a conditioned desire insofar as it ultimately fulfills an unalterable biological desire or negotiates an unalterable condition in our environment. This is because anything alterable we can alter instead of obey, so anything we *must* obey will always override anything we *needn't* obey. Hence the unalterable conditions of our biology or environment will always necessitate wanting something more. In other words, there is always some true statement "I need x," and for any rationally informed person, "I need x" always entails wanting x more than z whenever two conditions are met: x entails $\sim z$ and "I want but don't need z." If x does *not* entail $\sim z$, then no conflict results (hence incidental desires make no difference to fundamental moral facts—see below for "allergies" as an example). But when a conflict *does* result, what is needed will always supersede, and thus the other cannot be a moral imperative. And since this further entails that needs can only be superseded by other needs, only needs (which are unalterable desires that are fundamentally or instrumentally necessary) can be the basis of a true moral system. And needs are only entailed by unalterables (of our biology and environment), as otherwise, by being alterable, they are no longer needed (because by altering them we can remove the need of them).

Therefore, what we want most (when rational and sufficiently informed) will always be entailed by, and only by, unalterable biological facts or unalterable environmental facts. But human beings, by virtue of their origins and continued interbreeding, do not differ biologically in any way that would vary any of their desires that are fundamental, unalterable, and instrumentally necessary. In fact, that would be extraordinarily improbable (owing to the extreme genetic deviations it would require, which cannot be achieved by random mutation, except with such extraordinary rarity that we can expect never to meet such a person in many millions of years). For example: we all need to eat, breathe, move, think, and cooperate and socialize with a community; generally the same things are lethal or harmful to us (physically and in some cases emotionally, such as the scientifically documented effects of loneliness and withdrawal of affection); we all construct a conscious self-awareness when healthy and awake; we all have mirror neurons and rely on innate theories of mind to understand other people (unless we're mentally disabled, but even most autistics, for example, can *learn* a theory of mind and apply it in their decision-making, and like the rest of us they still *need* to navigate their social world successfully).[40] And so on.

Happiness and contentment are thus dependent on an array of biological facts universal to all human beings. Even what were once thought to be an exception to this expectation (psychopaths) have since been shown not to be: though they are cognitively defective, when honestly reporting and sufficiently informed of the difference between their lives and mental states and those of nonsociopaths, they always concede to being profoundly dissatisfied and desire most to be different persons but are incapable of obtaining what they desire owing to their cognitive defects. Thus (when fully rational and informed) they do not "desire most" anything fundamentally different than we do, they are merely incapable of achieving it. And they are not incapable of achieving it because of an obstacle external to their reasoning, but because of a defect of their reasoning.[41] They are thus inescapably irrational, which is why they are classified as insane. Our inability to rationally persuade them to be moral is exactly the same as our inability to rationally persuade a schizophrenic. And it is no defect of a moral theory that madmen cannot be persuaded of it.

Since our primary biological desires (primary meaning those that are fundamental, unalterable, or instrumentally necessary) can't commonly differ, and thus won't generate differences in our most overriding desires, that leaves unalterable differences in environment. But those make no difference to universal morality. By being unalterable, they constitute conditions an agent is forced to comply with. Since moral facts are context-dependent (as any hypothetical imperative must be, that is, the required truth conditions entail the end must be obtainable by the prescribed action, which will always depend on the context), when unalterable environmental facts entail wanting something most that those in a different environment *won't* want most, this conclusion is already entailed by any system of universal morality. That is, any system of true moral facts will already include the fact that, if we were forced into the same conditions, we would be compelled by the same imperatives that then obtain. In other words, that a person might want something else most in condition *C* than in condition *D* does not entail that different moral facts obtain, because in this case the imperative differs only relative to individual *conditions*, not relative to any desires that would still obtain absent those conditions, and *all* moral facts are relative to conditions.

Even the most stalwartly conservative Christian will admit that conditions can alter what's morally right to do, and ultimately even Kant would have been compelled to agree. His categorical imperative entailed we ought to "act only according to that maxim whereby you can at the same time will that it should become a universal law," and we would certainly will to be a universal law that whenever an exception obtains, our behavior ought to be adapted to it. For instance, killing in self-defense: we would never will to be a universal law a blanket prohibition against killing, precisely because we know we may have to kill a would-be murderer in our own defense. Thus we would instead will to be a universal law a prohibition against killing only in certain circumstances, with an allowance for killing in others. Hence we incorporate differences in the conditions, even in a universal moral law. Therefore, because we would will to be a universal law that a person in condition C should most want one thing, but in condition D should most want something else, precisely because that person cannot alter those conditions, differences in greatest desire entailed by unalterable environmental factors make no difference to whether there are universal moral facts.

Since biology will never create a different set of moral facts for any human individual (except so rarely as to be inconsequential), and environment *cannot* create a different set of moral facts for any human individual (because, as just demonstrated, such an effect is logically impossible), and these are the only possible sources of such a difference (being the only possible sources of a rationally informed difference in greatest desire), the conclusion follows that there must necessarily be universal moral facts (for all or, at least, very nearly all human beings).[42]

EXCEPTIONS PROVE THE RULE

There are two proposed exceptions, the analysis of which only verifies the conclusion that universal moral facts exist. First, an argument can be constructed (and I construct one in *Sense and Goodness*, 326–27) that to a high probability all naturally evolved extraterrestrial species who establish civilizations will share in common with humans a subset of needs and interests and ways and means that will entail at least a higher order of universal morality. In other words, we will have two moral truths overlapping (in the middle being a set of moral facts equally true for us both), or in fact overlapping completely (that is, with all the same moral facts obtaining for each of us). However, since it is still possible for a sentient species to exist that shares nothing in common with us that would establish that even a higher order of universal morality applies to them (this species might evolve, at least rarely, or be created, such as through genetic engineering or the development of AI; see Carrier, *Sense and Goodness without God*, 342–43), it follows that the universal morality I have just proved must necessarily exist is not *cosmically* or *metaphysically* universal but contingent on a certain pattern of construction or evolution (which is nevertheless highly probable).[43] Thus, strictly speaking, the universal morality that does exist is still a subset of moral relativism, but only in a trivial way. Moral facts must necessarily be relative to certain facts being true about an agent's fundamental nature. But even Christianity is morally relativistic in that sense (as its morals would also change if God sufficiently changed our fundamental nature or even his own), and arguably every credible moral theory must be.[44]

Second, universal moral facts must necessarily consist of covering laws whose particular application will always differ by individual and circumstance. An individual must choose what they individually ought most to do, a choice that will be a moral imperative for them but not necessarily for anyone else— even in that same situation—since the controlling circumstances include the agent's ways and means (e.g., someone who can't swim ought not to attempt to save someone drowning; someone who must eat ought not to consume food to which they are allergic; etc.). But everyone will agree that if they were that person it would then be the right thing for them to do. Similarly, all cases of inaccessible knowledge: "sufficiently informed" can never mean "fully informed," and thus moral imperatives follow only from knowledge available to us at the moment. For instance, a "fully informed" person would by definition know how to swim, but a "sufficiently informed" person knows only that they do not yet know how to swim, thus all moral imperatives for them must follow from the actual fact of their ignorance, and not from information they "could" but don't and can't then have.[45] Likewise morally acceptable preferences: that you like one kind of employment more than another will differ from what others like, but a moral imperative to attend to your happiness and financial security by seeking employment will not entail that everyone ought to pursue exactly the same job.

Hence all these different outcomes do not constitute different moral facts but universal rules adapted to particular conditions, just as for the unalterable environmental conditions discussed earlier. For example, a covering law for the allergy example would be "You ought not to eat food to which you are allergic" (if you don't have to), which derives in turn from the more general law "You ought not to bring upon yourself pointless harm" (so far as you can reasonably know). These laws are true for everyone, even people without allergies. The fundamental instrumental desire is still in this case the same for all human beings. Hence an allergy is not a biological difference that has any effect on our greatest fundamental desires, which in this case are "to eat" and "to avoid pointless harm." Being presented with toxic food is simply another difference of circumstance.

Carried to its logical conclusion, this would encompass even the aliens with nonhuman moralities, for whom we would agree, were we them, we ought to behave as they do. But of course, we aren't them, so that conclusion is of no consequence to us (except insofar as we need to predict and react to what they will do). Thus the fact that we define universal morality according to species is really only a matter of practical convention. We simply don't need to know about other moralities, because there is only one rational species we are dealing with (at least so far), and when it comes to asking how *we* ought to behave, there is only one species that pertains (our own).[46]

Thus the exceptions actually prove the rule: as human beings share all the same primary biological desires (which are not limited to the so-called base desires for, say, food and sex but include, as science has demonstrated, desires for love and companionship and joy and fulfillment and more, ordered in similar hierarchies of ultimate and instrumental necessity), and only such desires can ever rationally entail (in conjunction with knowledge) an informed conclusion about what we most want, it follows that we will all (when rational and equally informed) desire most the very same things (when in the same circumstances), which logically entails that the same moral facts will be true for us all. Therefore, universal moral facts must necessarily exist.[47]

CONCLUSION

Any rational attempt to argue that Christianity is needed for moral facts to exist ends up exposing the fatal flaws in Christianity as a moral system. Christians can't establish the key premises necessary for that moral system: *which* moral behaviors or attitudes result in *which* fates. This divorces Christian morality from the facts, which is why Christians can invent almost any morality they want and thus why there have been so many divisions in Christianity over what is and isn't moral. Anyone can *claim* that "morality *x*" will make our lives better in the long run. But that claim is only rationally believable if we can verify in actual evidence that it's true.

Only science has the methods and tools for discovering which morality will make all our lives better in the long run, as that is a question of material fact: which behaviors have which actual consequences, and for whom and when. As in surgery or car maintenance or the engineering of bridges, only science can reliably answer such questions of cause-and-effect. Christianity cannot do so, because it has no evidence to back its claims of which causes have which effects, and it has of itself no reliable methods for gathering that evidence. Thus Christianity must either promote the wrong morality, a morality that actually harms us all in the long run, or prevent us from discovering the real reason we should all be moral and thus prevent us from discovering the only evidence that can *actually* inspire moral progress. Or both.

Like voodoo medicine, prescribing Christianity to cure immorality is just another unverified pseudoscience. Only *genuine* science can discover what *actually* cures immorality, just as only science could discover what actually cures disease. And just as only genuine science could discover what actually *constitutes* disease in the first place (such as finding that demonic possession doesn't exist or that homosexuality is not an illness but a healthy and natural human condition), so only science can discover what actually constitutes immorality. Christianity should thus be abandoned as a basis for any moral system, and science should be deployed instead to ascertain which moral system is *in actual fact* best for us.

Accordingly, I have demonstrated that if there are *any* true moral facts, then science can discover them by discovering what actually connects any particular behavior with any particular result, and by discovering what result we really all would want in common for ourselves once we are sufficiently informed and reasoning coherently. These are both empirically discoverable facts whose difficulty of ascertaining is precisely *why* science is the most equipped to discover them. And not only have I shown that moral facts are empirically discoverable, but I have further demonstrated that such moral facts must necessarily exist.[48]

Since Christianity fails to connect its moral claims to any verifiable facts, produces no agreement on which moral claims are true, has no significant effect in improving people morally, and stunts moral growth and progress by distracting us from endeavoring to discover the truth—whereas science alone can discover any truth in which there can be no rational disagreement—we should all be promoting not Christianity but the scientific discovery of genuine moral facts. Once anyone truly realizes this, they will abandon Christianity as unprovable and irrelevant to building a moral society. And having no longer any such function, Christianity will come to an end.

APPENDIX TO
"MORAL FACTS NATURALLY EXIST"

ARGUMENT 1: THAT IF THERE IS A TRUE MORAL SYSTEM, IT IS THAT WHICH WE HAVE A SUFFICIENTLY MOTIVATING REASON TO OBEY OVER ALL OTHERS

Definitions:

m = a moral system.
s = a system of imperatives that supersede all other imperatives.
v = what we ought to obey over all other imperative systems (whether they are labeled moral or not).
B = that which we have a sufficiently motivating reason to obey over all other imperative systems.
T = the true moral system.
M = the moral system that, in actual fact, we ought to obey.

Argument:

1.1. If there is m, then m is s.
1.2. If m is s, then m is v.
1.3. v is B.
1.4. Therefore, if there is m, then m is B.
1.5. m is T iff m is M.
1.6. M is B.
1.7. Therefore, m is B, and m is B iff m is M; and m is M, iff m is T. (i.e., if 1.4, 1.5, and 1.6, then 1.7)
1.8. Therefore, T is B. (i.e., if 1.6 and 1.7, then 1.8)
1.9. Therefore, if there is m, then there is T. (i.e., if 1.4 and 1.8, then 1.9)
1.10. Therefore, if there is m, then there is T, and B is T.

Therefore, if there is any moral system at all, then that which we have a sufficiently motivating reason to obey over all other imperative systems is the true moral system.

ARGUMENT 2: THAT WE (IN ACTUAL FACT) WILL OBEY TRUE HYPOTHETICAL IMPERATIVES OVER ALL OTHER IMPERATIVES WHEN RATIONAL AND SUFFICIENTLY INFORMED

2.1. By definition, for any individual, to want$_p$ one thing more than another is to prefer that one thing over the other (for whatever reason and in whatever way).

2.2. Therefore, for any individual, to want$_p$ one thing more than anything else (i.e., to want$_p$ that one thing most) is to prefer that one thing over every other thing.

2.3. By definition, every rational and sufficiently informed individual always chooses the thing that they prefer (when they can choose at all).

2.4. Therefore, any rational and sufficiently informed individual who prefers one thing to another will always choose that one thing and not the other (if they can choose at all and cannot choose both).

2.5. Therefore, any rational and sufficiently informed individual who prefers one thing to every other thing will always choose that one thing (if they can choose at all).

2.6. If when rational and sufficiently informed you will want$_p$ X more than $\sim X$, and you believe X will result only if x is done, then you will want$_p$ to do x more than $\sim x$.

2.7. Therefore, if when rational and sufficiently informed you want$_p$ to do x more than $\sim x$, by definition you prefer to do x to $\sim x$. [per 2.1]

2.8. Therefore, if when rational and sufficiently informed you prefer to do x to $\sim x$, by definition you will always choose x (when you can choose at all). [per 2.3 and 2.5]

2.9. Therefore, if when rational and sufficiently informed you want$_p$ X (i.e., the consequences of x) more than $\sim X$ (i.e., the consequences of $\sim x$), then by definition you will always choose x (when you can choose at all).

2.10. If it is always the case that "if when rational and sufficiently informed you want$_p$ X (i.e., the consequences of x) more than $\sim X$ (i.e., the consequences of $\sim x$), then by definition you will choose x," then it is always the case that you will obey the hypothetical imperative "if when rational and sufficiently informed you want$_p$ X (i.e., the consequences of x) more than $\sim X$ (i.e., the consequences of $\sim x$), then you ought to choose x."

2.11.   Therefore, it is always the case that you will obey the hypothetical imperative "if when rational and sufficiently informed you want$_p$ X (i.e., the consequences of x) more than $\sim X$ (i.e., the consequences of $\sim x$), then you ought to choose x." [per 2.9 and 2.10]

2.12.   *Therefore, you will always obey a hypothetical imperative over all other imperatives.*

ARGUMENT 3: THAT THERE IS A TRUE MORAL SYSTEM FOR ANY INDIVIDUAL (WHO IS COMMITTED TO BEING RATIONAL)

Definitions:

$L =$ [a] given individual.

$D =$ [the condition when] what anyone wants$_p$ is to be rationally deduced from as many true facts as they can reasonably obtain regarding all their preferences and the total outcome of every possible behavior for them in the same circumstances at that time.

$W =$ a behavior whose outcome L wants$_p$ more than any other outcome.

$B =$ that which we (when we are L) have a sufficiently motivating reason to obey over all other imperative systems (i.e., that behavior that we [when we are L] have a sufficiently motivating reason to undertake over all other behaviors recommended).

$C =$ an available outcome or set of outcomes that L wants$_p$ more than any other available outcome.

Argument:

3.1. For any L, if there is W, then if D obtains, then W is B.

3.2. If D obtains, then there is C.

3.3. If there is C, then there is W.

3.4. Therefore, if D obtains, then there is W.

3.5. Therefore, if D obtains, then there is B. (i.e., if 3.1 and 3.4, then 3.5)

3.6. If there is B, then there is T. (i.e., if 1.8, then 3.6)

3.7. Therefore, for any L, if D obtains, then there is T.

Therefore, for any given individual, if what they want is to be rationally deduced from as many true facts as they can reasonably obtain regarding all their preferences and the total outcome of every possible behavior for them in the same circumstances at that time, then there is a true moral system for that individual.

ARGUMENT 4: THAT THERE IS A TRUE MORAL SYSTEM FOR VERY NEARLY ALL HUMAN BEINGS

Definitions:

$CH =$ the available outcome or set of outcomes that very nearly every member of the human species in the same circumstances would want$_p$ more than any other available outcome.

$T_L =$ the moral system that follows from the available outcome or set of outcomes that L wants$_p$ more than any other available outcome.

$T_H =$ the moral system that follows from the available outcome or set of outcomes that very nearly every member of the human species wants$_p$ more than any other available outcome.

$U =$ approximately a universal moral system.

$BD =$ L's fundamental biology differs from the rest of the human species in respect to determining what is wanted$_p$ most when rational and sufficiently informed.

$\sim BD =$ only something about L's circumstances *other* than L's fundamental biology differs from the rest of the human species in respect to determining what is wanted$_p$ most when rational and sufficiently informed, or nothing so differs.

$EXC =$ L is incredibly exceptional among the human species in having a biology that determines differently what is wanted$_p$ most when rational and sufficiently informed.

$VNB =$ very nearly every member of the human species does not have a biology that determines differently what is wanted$_p$ most when rational and sufficiently informed.

VNA = the available outcome or set of outcomes that very nearly any member of the human race wants$_p$ more than any other available outcome.

M_{VNA} = the moral system that follows from the available outcome or set of outcomes that very nearly any member of the human race wants$_p$ more than any other available outcome.

M_H = the moral system that follows from the available outcome or set of outcomes that very nearly every member of the human species wants$_p$ more than any other available outcome.

Argument:

4.1. If D obtains, then C is either CH or $\sim CH$. (and from 3.2, if there is D, then there is C)

4.2. If C is CH, then T_L is T_H. (and from 3.7, if L and D, then T_L)

4.3. If T_L is T_H, then there is U.

4.4. Therefore, if C is CH, then there is U.

4.5. If C is $\sim CH$, then either BD or $\sim BD$.

4.6. If $\sim BD$, then if D obtains, then C is CH.

4.7. Therefore, if $\sim BD$, then if D obtains, then there is U. (i.e., if 4.4 and 4.6, then 4.7)

4.8. If BD, then EXC.

4.9. If EXC, then VNB.

4.10. If VNB, then if D obtains, then VNA is CH.

4.11. If VNA is CH, then M_{VNA} is M_H.

4.12. If M_{VNA} is M_H, then there is U.

4.13. Therefore, if D obtains, then if BD, then there is U. (i.e., If BD, then EXC; and if EXC, then VNB; and if VNB, then if D obtains, VNA is CH; and if VNA is CH, then M_{VNA} is M_H; and if M_{VNA} is M_H, then there is U; therefore, if BD and D obtains, then there is U)

4.14. Therefore, either C is CH or C is $\sim CH$; if C is CH, then there is U; and if C is $\sim CH$, then either BD or $\sim BD$; and if $\sim BD$ and D obtains, then there is U; and if BD and D obtains, then there is U; therefore, if $\sim CH$ and D obtains, then there is U; therefore, if D obtains and C, then there is U.

4.15. Therefore, if D obtains, then there is U. (i.e., if 3.2 and 4.14, then 4.15)

Therefore, when what anyone wants is rationally deduced from as many true facts as they can reasonably obtain regarding all their preferences and the total outcome of every possible behavior for them in the same circumstances at that time, there is approximately a universal moral system.

ARGUMENT 5: THAT SCIENCE CAN EMPIRICALLY DISCOVER THE TRUE MORAL SYSTEM

5.1. There is T if there is B and D and W. (i.e., if 1.8, 3.2, 3.3, and 3.7, then 5.1)

5.2. Therefore, T for any L is fully entailed by the "true facts" regarding "all their preferences" and the "total outcome" of "every possible behavior for them in the same circumstances at that time" and what "behavior whose outcome they want$_p$ more than any other outcome," as far as "they can reasonably" then know.

5.3. The "true facts" for any L regarding "all their preferences" and the "total outcome" of "every possible behavior for them in the same circumstances at that time" and what "behavior whose outcome they want$_p$ more than any other outcome" (as far as "they can reasonably" then know) are all empirical facts.

5.4. Science can discover any empirical facts that it develops methods capable of discovering.

5.5. Therefore, if science can develop the required methods, then science can discover the "true facts" for any L regarding "all their preferences" and the "total outcome" of "every possible behavior for them in the same circumstances at that time" and what "behavior whose outcome they want$_p$ more than any other outcome" as far as "they can reasonably" then know.

5.6. Science can develop the required methods (to at least some degree).

5.7. *Therefore, science can discover T (the true moral system) to at least some degree.*

Afterword

CHANGING MORALS AND THE FATE OF EVANGELICALISM

by Dr. Robert M. Price

I t used to be the Evangelicals and Fundamentalists would never darken the door of movie theaters, even if Corrie ten Boom's *The Hiding Place* was showing (I kid you not!). Now that's moot, especially in the wake of home theater technology. They wouldn't dance, because it was supposedly arousing, essentially mating behavior—which it obviously is! But now they've skipped the preliminaries (keep reading).

More significantly, they were very much against divorce and had a low incidence of it. But that, too, has changed. Evangelical churchmen and seminary professors found they just could not thunder against divorce any more once their own grown children were getting divorced. The same problem came with women working outside the home. Economic realities dictated theology just as sure as the Fed's threats to the Mormon Church miraculously prompted new LDS revelations to abandon first polygamy, then racial discrimination in the Melchizedek Priesthood.

Homosexuality is next on the list. More and more educated Evangelicals seem to feel they must find a compromise between the inherited party line and their liberal social conscience. This is especially true with seminarians and young ministers. And such theological accommodations are not hard to find. It doesn't take as much text twisting as slave abolition or feminism, that's for sure. And it was secular feminism challenging the church that led, more than anything else, to the great inerrancy crisis among Evangelicals in the 1970s. Prayer changes things? Things change prayer.

Recent surveys indicate that more and more Evangelicals are questioning or rejecting the doctrine of an eternal hell as well as the idea that non-Christians will not be saved in the afterlife. You can see where this is headed:

they are making their way toward being one more tolerant, live-and-let-live mainstream denomination. I am not complaining. I doubt many of us are really that vexed by the particular beliefs any fundamentalist happens to hold. No, what we find vexing are the pugnacious, obnoxious attitudes that so often accompany their beliefs. But what if they drop that attitude? Why would they?

It was for the sake of feeling uniquely indwelt and transformed by the Holy Ghost that they have erected attitudinal walls against non-coreligionists. It was a mind game to protect their cherished in-group and their firmly cemented membership in it. But the more you become like the mainstream, the less that separates you from everybody else, well, the more difficult it becomes to feel special, uniquely connected to God and sanctified by Jesus. It's not like they ever wanted to relegate everybody else to the Lake of Fire. It just seemed necessary in order for them to rejoice in not being relegated there themselves. And now feeling so different is no longer the priority. Attitudes affect doctrines, which affect attitudes.

But the thing that will sooner or later bring the Evangelical Wailing Wall down is sex. More and more, middle school, high school, and college Evangelicals admit to having sex in the same casual way as their "unsaved" contemporaries. That is, premarital, recreational sex. Having been so long Apollonian, they are itching to yield to Dionysus. But the Gospel teaching of Jesus happens to be far more Apollonian than Dionysian. (Give 'em time, though, to discover the Q Source Jesus of Leif Vaage, Jesus as a "first-century party animal," and they'll be boasting of their biblical fidelity again.)

From the standpoint of sect-maintenance, this shift is fatal for two reasons. First, and most obviously, if this fundamental plank of the Evangelical platform rots and snaps, you can find little of similar magnitude to point to as the signal difference between the saved and the unsaved. I admit, there are a few more that would be similarly fatal, such as a casual permissiveness of drugs and alcohol.

Again, I admit that there are matters of graver moral content. A Christian ought to be able to say, for example, "Jesus saved me from lying, from being insensitive, from being self-centered, cowardly, evasive, materialistic," and so on, and those things might be more important. I'd say they are. But you see, everybody accepts and admires those values. They don't give Evangelicals special bragging rights like the sexual and other behavioral codes used to do.

Second, relaxing the sexual code is symbolically significant. Any group's mores concerning food and sex are symbolic of their social boundaries and the shape of their self-identity. A group does not necessarily have both indices. One will do, though usually there are both. Old Testament Israelites were separated from rival cults/cultures by upholding inflexible restrictions on permissible food and on possible intermarriage partners. Sexual fidelity had a lot to do with guaranteeing that one's true heirs inherited one's land and name. Jewish Christians were alarmed at Paul being willing to abolish Jewish dietary and other ceremonial scruples to make it easier for Gentiles to join Christianity. They could see instantly that such a move would result in Jews being squeezed to the margins of the new religion—and it did. Jewish identity within Christianity was lost. Similarly, among American Jews today it is not bigotry when Orthodox rabbis discourage mixed marriages with non-Jews. Allow that, and you can say the big goodbye to Judaism in America. It will be only a matter of time before intermarriage with well-meaning and good-hearted non-Jews will completely erode American Judaism. The hybrid "Chrismika" is only a stop along the one-way track. Maybe there will be an Orthodox farm next to the Amish farm.

Well, when the sex barrier falls, the same fate is in store for Evangelical Christianity. (There never was a consistent Evangelical food boundary; even the Reformed drank alcohol.) And when the new generations are none too sure that nonbelievers are headed for hell, it becomes inevitable that American Evangelicalism will ease into the acid bath of American Pluralism. And it may happen sooner than you think. And then all those megachurches will be up for sale. Unless, of course, they find a new product to sell. TV preacher Joel Osteen has done just that. His Evangelical belief is merely vestigial; he has converted to New Thought. It is no coincidence that he fills that stadium. Others may not be so lucky.

NOTES

INTRODUCTION

1. See, for instance, David Eller's chapter for *The Christian Delusion*, "Christianity Does Not Provide the Basis for Morality," and references therein, ed. John Loftus (Amherst, NY: Prometheus Books, 2010), 347–67.

2. It should go without saying that the contributors to this book don't always agree with each other, because that's the nature of the quest for knowledge. Unlike most Christians who are enslaved to dogma, we are free to disagree. In either case, Christian morality is not an objective alternative anyway. Carrier makes that point quite clearly in his chapter.

3. See my discussion of this point in Loftus, *The Christian Delusion*, 94–102.

4. This science is discussed in Christopher Chabris and Daniel Simons, *The Invisible Gorilla: And Other Ways Our Intuitions Deceive Us* (New York: Crown, 2010); and Cordelia Fine, *A Mind of Its Own: How Your Brain Distorts and Deceives* (New York: W. W. Norton, 2008). See also Loftus, *The Christian Delusion*, particularly the early chapters by Valerie Tarico, Jason Long, and myself.

5. Carol Tavris and Elliot Aronson, *Mistakes Were Made (But Not By Me): Why We Justify Foolish Beliefs, Bad Decisions, and Hurtful Acts* (Orlando, FL: Harvest, 2007), 2.

6. As reported by *Boston Globe* political writer Joe Keohane in "How Facts Backfire," July 11, 2010, found online at http://www.boston.com/bostonglobe/ideas/articles/2010/07/11/how_facts_backfire/.

7. Marlene Winell, *Leaving the Fold: A Guide for Former Fundamentalists and Others Leaving Their Religion* (Berkeley, CA: Apocryphile Press, 2007).

PART 1

CHAPTER 1

1. Muhammad al Naquib al-Attas, *Islam and Secularism* (Delhi, India: New Crescent Publishing, 2002), 32–35.

2. David B. Barrett, George T. Kurian, and Todd M. Johnson, *World Christian Encyclopedia: A Comparative Survey of Churches and Religions in the Modern World*, 2nd ed. (New York: Oxford University Press, 2001).

3. "Methodist Family," Association of Religion Data Archives, http://www.the arda.com/Denoms/Families/Trees/familytree_methodist.asp, accessed June 28, 2010.

4. Eric Hobsbawm and Terence Ranger, eds., *The Invention of Tradition* (Cambridge: Cambridge University Press, 1983), 1–2.

5. Anthony F. C. Wallace, "Revitalization Movements," *American Anthropologist* 58 (1956): 265.

6. Ibid., 277.

7. Justo L. Gonzalez, *The Story of Christianity Volume I: The Early Church to the Dawn of the Reformation* (New York: HarperOne, 1984), 10.

8. Ekkehard Stegemann and Wolfgang Stegemann, *The Jesus Movement: A Social History of Its First Century* (Minneapolis: Fortress, 1999), 1.

9. Gerd Theissen, *Sociology of Early Palestinian Christianity* (Philadelphia: Fortress, 1978), 1.

10. Ibid., 17.

11. Gonzalez, *The Story of Christianity*, 31.

12. Theissen, *Early Palestinian Christianity*, 60.

13. Elaine Pagels, *The Origin of Satan* (New York: Random House, 1995), 89.

14. Theissen, *Early Palestinian Christianity*, 115.

15. Robert Wright, "One World, Under God," *Atlantic Monthly*, April 2009.

16. Gonzalez, *The Story of Christianity*, 17.

17. Ibid., 16–17.

18. Roland Bainton, *Christian Attitudes Toward War and Peace: A Historical Survey and Critical Evaluation* (New York: Abingdon, 1960), 88.

19. Gonzalez, *The Story of Christianity*, 125.

20. Theissen, *Early Palestinian Christianity*, 119.

21. Leonard W. Levy, *Blasphemy: Verbal Offense against the Sacred, from Moses to Salman Rushdie* (New York: Alfred A. Knopf, 1993), 44.

22. Alexis de Tocqueville, *Democracy in America*, trans. George Lawrence (Garden City, NJ: Anchor, 1969), 574.

23. Eugene Taylor, *Shadow Culture: Psychology and Spirituality in America* (Washington, DC: Counterpoint, 1999), 18.

24. Quoted in Martin E. Marty, *Pilgrims in Their Own Land: 500 Years of Religion in America* (New York: Penguin, 1984), 210.

25. Quoted in ibid.

26. Quoted in Nathan O. Hatch, *The Democratization of American Christianity* (New Haven, CT: Yale University Press, 1989), 168. [Editor's Note: For further discussions of religious (and specifically Christian) diversification in the United States, see: Roger Finke and Rodney Stark, *The Churching of America, 1776–1990: Winners and Losers in Our Religious Economy* (New Brunswick, NJ: Rutgers University Press, 1992); Barry Kosmin and Seymour Lachman, *One Nation under God: Religion in Contemporary American Society* (New York: Harmony Books, 1993); Stephen Prothero, *American Jesus: How the Son of God Became a National Icon* (New York: Farrar, Straus, and Giroux, 2003); and J. Gordon Melton et al., *Melton's Encyclopedia of American Religions* (Detroit: Gale Cengage Learning, 2009).]

27. Quoted in Karen Armstrong, *The Battle for God* (New York: Ballantine, 2000), 310–11.

28. The websites for the networks mentioned are, in order, http://www.cbn .com/; http://www.ewtn.com/; http://www.tbn.org/; http://www.daystar.com/.

29. The *Left Behind* computer game series can be found at http://www.eternal forces.com.

30. This quotation is usually attributed to Sam Pascoe, but as the organization Religious Tolerance (http://www.religioustolerance.org/christ.htm) notes, it is also sometimes attributed to Richard Halverson, a former chaplain of the United States Senate.

31. Louise M. Burkhart, *Before Guadalupe: The Virgin Mary in Early Colonial Nahuatl Literature* (Albany, NY: Institute for Mesoamerican Studies, 2001), 3.

32. Jean Comaroff, *Body of Power, Spirit of Resistance: The Culture and History of a South African People* (Chicago: University of Chicago Press, 1985), 2.

33. John L. Comaroff and Jean Comaroff, *Of Revelation and Revolution: The Dialectics of Modernity in a South African Frontier*, vol. 2 (Chicago: University of Chicago Press, 1991), 6.

34. Maia Green, *Priests, Witches, and Power: Popular Christianity after Mission in Southern Tanzania* (Cambridge: Cambridge University Press, 2003), 49.

35. Marshall Murphree, *Christianity and the Shona* (London: Athlone, 1969).

36. Philip Jenkins, "The Next Christianity," *Atlantic Monthly*, October 2002: 54.

37. Ibid.

38. Ibid.

39. Philip Jenkins, "Defender of the Faith," *Atlantic Monthly*, November 2003: 46.

CHAPTER 2

1. Richard Carrier, *Not the Impossible Faith: Why Christianity Didn't Need a Miracle to Succeed* (Raleigh, NC: Lulu, 2009). I have also discussed the evidence in "Why the Resurrection Is Unbelievable," in *The Christian Delusion*, ed. John Loftus (Amherst, NY: Prometheus Books, 2010), 291–315.

2. Carrier, *Not the Impossible Faith*, 407–47.

3. See Pliny the Younger, *Letters* 10.96; with discussion and analysis in Carrier, *Not the Impossible Faith*, 418–22. Further reflecting their insignificance, the emperor replied to Pliny that in fact there wasn't even any particular law against Christianity (Pliny the Younger, *Letters* 10.97), and he wasn't to bother hunting them down.

4. See Carrier, *Not the Impossible Faith*, 435–40; and Richard Carrier, "Christianity Was Not Responsible for Modern Science," in Loftus, *The Christian Delusion*, 413 (and 419, note 57); for broader perspective, see Richard Carrier, *Sense and Goodness without God: A Defense of Metaphysical Naturalism* (Bloomington, IN: Author-House, 2005), 257–68.

5. For examples, see: W. V. Harris, ed., *The Spread of Christianity in the First Four Centuries: Essays in Explanation* (Boston: Brill, 2005); Richard Horsley, *Jesus and Empire: The Kingdom of God and the New World Disorder* (Minneapolis: Fortress, 2002); Bruce Malina, *The Social Gospel of Jesus: The Kingdom of God in Mediterranean Perspective* (Minneapolis: Fortress, 2001); Bruce Malina and Richard Rohrbaugh, *Social-Science Commentary on the Synoptic Gospels*, 2nd ed. (Minneapolis: Fortress, 2003), and *Social-Science Commentary on the Gospel of John* (Minneapolis: Fortress, 1998); Jack Sanders, *Charisma, Converts, Competitors: Societal and Sociological Factors in the Success of Early Christianity* (London: SCM, 2000); Thomas Finn, "Mission and Expansion," *The Early Christian World*, ed. Philip Esler (New York: Routledge, 2000), 1:295–315; David DeSilva, *Honor, Patronage, Kinship & Purity: Unlocking New Testament Culture* (Downers Grove, IL: InterVarsity, 2000); Keith Hopkins, "Christian Number and Its Implications," *Journal of Early Christian Studies* 6, no. 2 (1998): 185–226; Rodney Stark, *The Rise of Christianity* (Princeton, NJ: Princeton University Press, 1996); Robin Lane Fox, *Pagans & Christians* (New York: Knopf, 1987).

6. For the relevant evidence and scholarship on Inanna and all the other gods and cults here discussed (including the Jewish views to be discussed), see Carrier, *Not the Impossible Faith*, 17–63.

7. This quote comes from Seneca's lost work *On Superstition*, written before 65 CE but quoted by Augustine in *City of God* 6.10 in the early fifth century.

8. Carrier, *Not the Impossible Faith*, 24–30, 373.

9. This is stated most explicitly in Daniel 9:26. But for more evidence, see Carrier, *Not the Impossible Faith*, 34–44, and Loftus, *The Christian Delusion*, 306. Jewish

reverence for the trope of a "humiliated righteous man" (often associated with expectations of divine vengeance) is well established (e.g., Wisdom of Solomon 2–5, Isaiah 52–53, 1QIsaᵃ 52.13–53.12; George Nickelsburg, "First and Second Enoch: A Cry against Oppression and the Promise of Deliverance," in *The Historical Jesus in Context*, ed. Amy-Jill Levine, Dale C. Allison Jr., and John Dominic Crossan [Princeton, NJ: Princeton University Press, 2009], 87–109, and "The Genre and Function of the Markan Passion Narrative," *Harvard Theological Review* 73.1/2 [January–April 1980]: 153–84; Thomas Thompson, *The Messiah Myth: The Near Eastern Roots of Jesus and David* [New York: Basic, 2005], 191–93; and John Meier, *A Marginal Jew: Rethinking the Historical Jesus* [New Haven, CT: Yale University Press, 1991], 1:170–71).

10. Carrier, *Not the Impossible Faith*, 55–63, 66–70, 323–28 (the "hickness" of Nazareth and Galilee is also often exaggerated: ibid., 63–66). That Christianity very aptly exploited social discontent to gain converts is further shown in ibid., 147–60 (just like other movements of the time: ibid., 259–61).

11. See Margaret Williams, "VII.2. Pagans Sympathetic to Judaism" and "VII.3. Pagan Converts to Judaism" in *The Jews Among the Greeks and Romans: A Diasporan Sourcebook* (Baltimore, MD: Johns Hopkins University Press, 1998): 163–79.

12. Carrier, *Not the Impossible Faith*, 51–53, 432–35.

13. See evidence, sources, and discussion (for this and following points) in ibid., 85–127.

14. I document over two dozen such stories in ibid., 86–89.

15. See Origen, *Contra Celsum* 3.24 and Justin Martyr, *Dialogue of Justin and Trypho the Jew* 69. For attestations to Asclepius as both *resurrected* and *resurrector*, see Edelstein and Edelstein, eds., *Asclepius: Collection and Interpretation of the Testimonies* (1945): esp. §66–93, §232–56 (and §382–91, §443–54).

16. Carrier, *Not the Impossible Faith*, 113–27.

17. Ibid., 115 (with notes on 126). See also Loftus, *The Christian Delusion*, 306.

18. Justin Martyr, *Apology* 1.21.

19. For evidence and scholarship on all these points, see Carrier, *Not the Impossible Faith*, 135–45.

20. Ibid., 129–34, 375–83.

21. Ibid., 247–57.

22. I thoroughly analyze the evidence in ibid., 161–218, 329–68.

23. For ample evidence of this, see ibid., 385–405 (with 230–40). See also sources cited in Loftus, *The Christian Delusion*, 419 (note 56).

24. I thoroughly demonstrate this in "Why the Resurrection Is Unbelievable."

25. On what makes unremarkable prophesies not supernatural, see Carrier, *Sense and Goodness*, 247–52. On cultural and psychosomatic phenomena causing imagined ailments and psychologically effected cures—just like what Christians reported—see

Edward Shorter, *From Paralysis to Fatigue: A History of Psychosomatic Illness in the Modern Era* (New York: Free Press, 1992) and James Randi, *The Faith Healers* (Amherst, NY: Prometheus Books, 1989). On the natural psychology of demonic possession, see: Simon Kemp and Kevin Williams, "Demonic Possession and Mental Disorder in Medieval and Early Modern Europe," *Psychological Medicine* 17 (1987): 21–29; T. Craig Isaacs, "The Possessive States Disorder: The Diagnosis of Demonic Possession," *Pastoral Psychology* 35, no. 4 (June 1987): 263–73; Nicholas Spanos and Jack Gottlieb, "Demonic Possession, Mesmerism, and Hysteria: A Social Psychological Perspective on Their Historical Interrelations," *Journal of Abnormal Psychology* 88, no. 5 (October 1979): 527–46; also: Stefano Ferracuti and Roberto Sacco, "Dissociative Trance Disorder: Clinical and Rorschach Findings in Ten Persons Reporting Demon Possession and Treated by Exorcism," *Journal of Personality Assessment* 66, no. 3 (June 1996): 525–39.

26. Carrier, *Not the Impossible Faith*, 219–21.

27. W. H. C. Frend, "Martyrdom and Political Oppression," *The Early Christian World*, ed. Philip Esler (New York: Routledge, 2000), 2:818.

28. Alan F. Segal, *Life After Death: A History of the Afterlife in the Religions of the West* (New York: Doubleday, 2004), 314, 285–321; see also Arthur Droge and James Tabor, *A Noble Death: Suicide and Martyrdom among Christians and Jews in Antiquity* (1992).

29. Carrier, *Not the Impossible Faith*, 221–25.

30. Ibid., 240–45.

31. Hence hardships were of no account, see ibid., 230–36. That Christians understood their movement as just such a war is explicit: see ibid., 225–30.

32. I thoroughly debunk this myth in ibid., 297–321.

33. See ibid., 369–72.

34. For a complete discussion of everything to follow, including citations of the sociological literature, see ibid., 259–96.

35. For many discussions and examples (of both targeting families and the disaffected, and how associated recruitment and retention difficulties were dealt with), see ibid., 131–33, 230–36, 260–68, 295–97, 335–36, 385–86.

36. For a full discussion of this tactic and why it works and how missionaries still employ it, see David Eller, "The Cultures of Christianities," in Loftus, *The Christian Delusion*, 25–46.

37. Formally, when $P(h|b) = 0.5$, then $P(h|e.b) = P(e|h.b) / [P(e|h.b) + P(e|{\sim}h.b)]$, because the priors cancel out. For the full equation, see chap. 12.

38. I already make a complete case for it in Carrier, *Sense and Goodness*, and my argument there has important conceptual support from John Loftus, "The Outsider Test for Faith Revisited," in Loftus, *The Christian Delusion*, 81–106.

39. For example, on how Mithraism's failure is fully explained by its not being in the same social position as its rival, Christianity, see Carrier, *Not the Impossible Faith*, 435–40.

40. See Valerie Tarico, "Christian Belief through the Lens of Cognitive Science," in Loftus, *The Christian Delusion*, 47–64; Jason Long, "The Malleability of the Human Mind," ibid., 65–80; Loftus, "Outsider Test," ibid., 87–88; and discussion and scholarship cited in *The Christian Delusion*, 305–306 and Carrier, *Sense and Goodness*, 202–208.

41. I provide a much more extensive demonstration of this in Richard Carrier, *Why I Am Not a Christian: Four Conclusive Reasons to Reject the Faith* (Richmond, CA: Philosophy Press, 2011).

42. For example: even if C is 0.99 (i.e., 99%), if D is greater (e.g., 1), then C / (C + D) = 0.99 / 1.99 = 0.497 or 49.7% (and C is almost certainly far less than 0.99). Formally: $P(\text{CHRISTIANITY}|e.b) = [0.5 \times 0.99] / [(0.5 \times 0.99) + (0.5 \times 1.0)] = 0.497$ (rounded). Whereas for C = 1% (and again D = 100%), the probability that Christianity is true is less than 1% *even if its prior probability is 50%* (which it certainly is not).

43. Carrier, "Why the Resurrection Is Unbelievable," 308–309.

44. For yet more examples, see Carrier, "Why I Am Not a Christian"; Carrier, *Sense and Goodness*, 253–89; and John Loftus, *Why I Became an Atheist* (Amherst, NY: Prometheus Books, 2008), 192–96.

45. John Loftus, "At Best Jesus Was a Failed Apocalyptic Prophet," in Loftus, *The Christian Delusion*, 316–43.

46. See Ken Pulliam in chapter 7, "The Absurdity of the Atonement."

CHAPTER 3

1. Keith Parsons, "Goodbye to All That," *Secular Outpost*, September 1, 2010, http://secularoutpost.infidels.org/2010/09/goodbye-to-all-that.html. Parsons wrote: "*I think a number of philosophers have made the case for atheism and naturalism about as well as it can be made. Graham Oppy, Jordan Howard Sobel, Nicholas Everitt, Michael Martin, Robin Le Poidevin, and Richard Gale have produced works of enormous sophistication that devastate the theistic arguments in their classical and most recent formulations. Ted Drange, J. L. Schellenberg, Andrea Weisberger, and Nicholas Trakakis have presented powerful, and, in my view, unanswerable atheological arguments. Gregory Dawes has a terrific little book showing just what is wrong with theistic 'explanations.' Erik Wielenberg shows very clearly that ethics do not need God. With honest humility, I really do not think that I have much to add to these extraordinary works.*" Parsons's chapter on hell for this book will be among his last in this area. He's now focusing on astronomy, geology, paleontology, and the history of those fields.

2. I thank Keith Parsons for this suggestion and helpful advice here.

3. I'm reminded here of Pierre-Simon de Laplace, who famously said to Napoleon about God, "Sir, I have no need of that hypothesis." Liberal versions of Christianity only have more probability to them as they embrace the sciences, so to fully accept the sciences is to completely reject religion. To the degree that a professing Christian can sign the Humanist Manifesto I, the Humanist Manifesto II, and the Neo-Humanist Manifesto (all of which can easily be found online) is the degree to which I think such a person is being more reasonable with the evidence—even if I still see no good reason to embrace faith at all. On the improbability of liberal Christianity, see Paul Tobin, "The Bible and Modern Scholarship," in *The Christian Delusion*, ed. John Loftus (Amherst, NY: Prometheus Books, 2010), 169–73.

4. Christians will try to claim that the set of creedal affirmations they embrace are not ten in number but one thing: faith in Christ Jesus. But this presupposes what needs to be shown, simply because there are other Christianities who accept different sets of creedal affirmations who claim they, too, only believe in one thing: faith in Christ Jesus. The only way to differentiate between Christianities is to ask the adherents to specify and defend what they believe about each one of these creedal affirmations.

5. On this poor evidence, see chapter 8 in my book *Why I Became an Atheist*, 181–98. See also the chapters on biblical history by myself and Richard Carrier, Robert Price, and Paul Tobin, in Loftus, *The Christian Delusion*. Detailed summaries of the problem are available in Paul Tobin, *The Rejection of Pascal's Wager: A Skeptic's Guide to the Bible and the Historical Jesus* (Bedfordshire, England: AuthorsOnLine, 2009); Hector Avalos, *The End of Biblical Studies* (Amherst, NY: Prometheus Books, 2007); Israel Finkelstein and Neil Asher Silberman, *The Bible Unearthed: Archaeology's New Vision of Ancient Israel and the Origin of Its Sacred Texts* (New York: Free Press, 2001); and Bart Ehrman, *Jesus Interrupted: Revealing the Hidden Contradictions in the Bible (and Why We Don't Know about Them)* (New York: HarperCollins, 2009).

6. For a logical demonstration of this principle, see Richard Carrier, "Why the Resurrection Is Unbelievable," in Loftus, *The Christian Delusion*, pp. 298–99 (with notes 4–6, pp. 310–11).

7. See David Eller, "Christianity Evolving: On the Origin of Christian Species," chapter 1 in the present volume and "The Cultures of Christianities," in Loftus, *The Christian Delusion*, 25–46; see also my own chapter "What We've Got Here Is a Failure to Communicate," ibid., 181–206.

8. Robert Burton, *On Being Certain: Believing You Are Right Even When You're Not* (New York: St. Martin, 2009), ix.

9. See "The Strange and Superstitious World of the Bible," chapter 7 in Loftus, *Why I Became an Atheist*, 124–80.

10. The reason why criteria (1) must be met is argued for in my books. At this

point I highly doubt that anything but a personal miracle would change my mind about this.

11. See David Eller's presentation of atheism and agnosticism in chapter 6 of his excellent book *Natural Atheism* (Cranford, NJ: American Atheist Press, 2004), 153–172. Agnosticism is probably best thought of as skepticism following Thomas Huxley, who first coined the word. If we use Huxley's definition of agnosticism as skepticism, then agnostics who have concluded there are no supernatural beings or forces are atheists. In any case, whether we think of agnostics as skeptics following Huxley or as people who are skeptical of both supernaturalism and metaphysical naturalism, they make no extraordinary claims about supernatural beings or forces and so aren't represented separately apart from atheists on this chart. If we think of agnosticism in this latter sense, which is a legitimate understanding of the word, agnosticism becomes the default position. See my discussion in Loftus, *The Christian Delusion*, 88, 98. Either way, by limiting what they believe to what they can confirm (and then concluding "I don't know" for everything else), they make no extraordinary claims.

12. Christians may want to escape this conclusion by making a distinction between the number of extraordinary events, or miracles, being claimed and the number of extraordinary persons who can work these miracles. If so, Christianity still has at least one more miracle worker than these other faiths do in Jesus. We need also to add all of the apostles who supposedly could work miracles (2 Corinthians 12:11–13) and the New Testament writers who were supposedly given the miraculous gift of inspiration. Nonetheless, it's not logical to say only one extraordinary claim is being made "because one agent (i.e., Jesus) worked many extraordinary events or miracles," because it's still more improbable for one agent to do two improbable things than to have done only one; likewise three is more improbable than two; and so on. In other words, if I tell you I levitated across the room, you might think my story has an extremely small chance of being true. If I tell you I levitated across the room *and* transmuted water into wine, that doesn't make my claim any more likely, but less. Even by the law of dependent probabilities, if we could prove somehow that levitators are more likely to also have the power of transmutation than ordinary people, unless *all* levitators have that power (meaning, it is logically impossible for a levitator to *not* be a transmutator), it's still less likely that I'd be *both* a levitator *and* a transmutator than that I'd just be a levitator.

13. Richard Carrier explains in our personal correspondence:

According to Bayes' Theorem (which has been formally proven), extraordinary claims entail a low prior probability, and the prior probability of multiple claims equals the product of their (albeit dependent) prior probabilities. Therefore the more claims you add, the lower the prior probability is; and if the claims being added are extraordinary, the progression is very steep. As you just showed already, even for claims with the relatively high odds of 1 in 100. Lower odds only make it worse. For example, getting two royal flushes in a single hour of playing poker is not only less probable than getting just one, it's *vastly* less probable—hundreds of thousands of times less. Now imagine getting three of them in an hour; now four . . . And yet, royal flushes are documented to happen quite often. They are not even remotely as extraordinary as the things Christians are claiming. The only way to sustain such a steep decline in prior probability is to have evidence that is just as vastly improbable on any other explanation than all those claims being true. But since many alternative explanations are almost always readily available, and however improbable they may be they are almost always far more probable than all these more bizarre claims actually being true, stacking up extraordinary claims simply reduces the probability your system of beliefs is true . . . by a lot. To put it another way, Christianity must necessarily be millions of billions of times less probable than the named competitors here, yet does not have anywhere near millions of billions of times more evidence that its claims are true. Therefore, it's wildly improbable. The conclusion follows necessarily as a matter of logic.

14. One difference between the arguments for Scientology, of course, and those for Christianity is that Christian apologists are more sophisticated philosophically than the apologists for Scientology. But the reason why Christians have more philosophical sophistication is because they've been around a lot longer. Through the years they have been able to progressively change what they believe as the centuries droned on, from the tribal God of the Bible to the "perfect being" theology of Anselm and beyond (just see my survey in Loftus, *The Christian Delusion*, 17–20 and David Eller's chapter 2 in this book). As their world got bigger and bigger, so did their conception of God. Just give Scientologists enough time, and they, too, will change what they believe through philosophical analysis, as they, too, will claim a progressive revelation like Christians have done. And they, too, will develop elaborate, sophisticated, scholarly sounding arguments packed with footnotes and symbolic logic, striving with consummate skill to look exactly like mainstream scholarship. The problem is that they both started on the same superstitious, unscientific footing (despite claims to the contrary).

15. On these pre-Christian "resurrected savior" cults, see references provided in Richard Carrier's chapter "Christianity's Success Was Not Incredible."

16. Several books make these absurd claims: R. C. Sproul, *If There's A God, Why Are There Atheists: Why Atheists Believe in Unbelief* (Wheaton, IL: Tyndale House, 1988); Paul C. Vitz, *Faith of the Fatherless: The Psychology of Atheism* (Dallas: Spence

Publishing, 1999); and James S. Spiegel, *The Making of an Atheist* (Chicago: Moody Publishers, 2010).

17. Nevertheless, Christians try raising many desperate objections to it: see my discussion (and defense of this perfectly reasonable principle) here in chapter 1 and in "Outsider Test for Faith," *The Christian Delusion*, 81–106.

18. Some may try to dispute this relationship (the more science explains, the less probable is God), but they cannot—because, as Richard Carrier points out in personal correspondence, "for any cause or explanation discovered by science, the *alternative* discovery that that cause or explanation was instead *God* would obviously count as evidence for God, and thus would (as such) raise the probability he exists; which entails that *not* having that be what is discovered must reduce the probability that god exists, by exactly as much as such a discovery would have raised it."

19. To read what I wrote about this, see Loftus, *Why I Became an Atheist*, 94 (and note 66, pp. 104–105). In fact, much of what I write in this section can be found in that book.

20. On this little puzzle, see Evan Fales, *Divine Intervention: Metaphysical and Epistemological Puzzles* (New York: Routledge, 2009).

21. This argument is made in the first few chapters of *The Christian Delusion*. I also make this argument in several posts on my blog, http://debunkingchristianity .blogspot.com. Do a search there for the words "believe what we prefer to be true," and you'll find them.

22. Ori Brafman and Rom Brafman, *Sway: The Irresistible Pull of Irrational Behavior* (New York: Broadway, 2008), 175.

23. "Modernizing the Case for God," *Time*, April 5, 1980.

24. Alvin Plantinga, *Warranted Christian Belief* (Oxford University Press, 2000), 145.

25. See Daniel Dennett, *Breaking the Spell: Religion as a Natural Phenomenon* (2006); Pascal Boyer, *Religion Explained: The Human Instincts That Fashion Gods, Spirits and Ancestors* (2001); Eugene D'Aquili and Andrew Newberg, *Why God Won't Go Away: Brain Science and the Biology of Belief* (2001); Paul Bloom, *Descartes' Baby: How the Science of Child Development Explains What Makes Us Human* (2004); B. M. Hood, *Supersense: Why We Believe in the Unbelievable* (2009). The neuroscientific evidence is also discussed in Sam Harris, *The Moral Landscape: How Science Can Determine Human Values* (New York: Free Press, 2010).

26. This is one of the main points in my book *Why I Became an Atheist* and in my defense of the "Outsider Test for Faith" in *The Christian Delusion*.

27. William Lane Craig, "Politically Incorrect Salvation," in *Christian Apologetics in the Post-Modern World*, ed. T. P. Phillips and D. Ockholm (Downers Grove, IL: InterVarsity Press, 1995), 75–97; found online at http://www.leaderu.com/offices/ billcraig/docs/politically.html.

28. William Lane Craig, "Middle Knowledge: A Calvinist-Arminian Rapprochement," in *The Grace of God, The Will of Man*, ed. Clark H. Pinnock (Grand Rapids, MI: Zondervan, 1989), 141–64.

29. Richard G. Swinburne, *Revelation: From Metaphor to Analogy*, 2nd ed. (Oxford: Oxford University Press, 2007).

30. Richard G. Swinburne, *The Existence of God*, 2nd ed. (Oxford: Oxford University Press, 2004).

31. Alonzo Fyfe, "A Purpose to Life," July 24, 2009, http://atheistethicist.blog spot.com/2009/07/purpose-to-life.html.

32. See, for example, the theory described by Richard Carrier in *Sense and Goodness without God* (Bloomington, IN: AuthorHouse: 2005), 253–54 (which is actually far more probable than the Christian God).

33. To see this argued, see John Loftus, "Based on This Argument Alone the Best Any Believer Can Claim Is Agnosticism," January 3, 2010, http://debunking christianity.blogspot.com/2010/based-on-this-argument-alone-best-any.html.

34. Loftus, *Why I Became an Atheist*, 192–95. Richard Carrier provides his own examples in *Sense and Goodness*, 256–57, 273–82; in Loftus, *The Christian Delusion*, 307–9; and in all his chapters in this book.

35. Loftus, *Why I Became an Atheist*, 228–62.

36. Loftus, *The Christian Delusion*, 237–70.

37. See Ken Pulliam in chapter 7, "The Absurdity of the Atonement."

38. Documentation for most of what follows can be found in this series: *Why I Became an Atheist*, *The Christian Delusion*, and the present book, *The End of Christianity*.

39. John Loftus, "What We've Got Here Is a Failure to Communicate," in Loftus, *The Christian Delusion*, 181–206.

40. Hector Avalos, "Yahweh Is a Moral Monster," in Loftus, *The Christian Delusion*, 220–21.

41. John Loftus, "At Best Jesus Was a Failed Apocalyptic Prophet," in Loftus, *The Christian Delusion*, 316–43.

42. Personal correspondence. See Richard Carrier in chapter 2, "Christianity's Success Was Not Incredible," for some examples of this; likewise see Edward T. Babinski, "The Cosmology of the Bible," in Loftus, *The Christian Delusion*, 109–47; and Avalos, "Yahweh Is a Moral Monster," ibid., 209–36, for examples from the Old Testament.

43. Hector Avalos claims that someone "could easily argue that the denial of religious freedom is at the 'moral heart' of the Old Testament." See ibid., 220–21.

44. For twenty-four examples of evil things said by God, see Richard Carrier, "The Will of God," on *The Christian Delusion*'s companion website, http://sites .google.com/site/thechristiandelusion/Home/the-will-of-god.

PART 2

CHAPTER 4

1. This chapter was excerpted by the editor from Hector Avalos's book *The End of Biblical Studies* (Amherst, NY: Prometheus Books, 2007), with only minor editing and additional footnoting by the editor. Used with permission of the author.

2. Michael Coogan, "The Great Gulf between Scholars and the Pew," in *Biblical Studies Alternatively: An Introductory Reader*, ed. Susanne Scholz (Upper Saddle River, NJ: Prentice Hall, 2003), 7. For twenty-four biblical passages proving his point, see "The Will of God" collection at this series' companion site: http://sites.google.com/site/thechristiandelusion/Home/the-will-of-god.

3. And that the earth is flat and the sky is solid and held up by pillars: see Ed Babinski, "The Cosmology of the Bible," in *The Christian Delusion*, ed. John Loftus (Amherst, NY: Prometheus Books, 2010): 109–47.

4. See, for example: Israel Finkelstein and Neil Asher Silberman, *The Bible Unearthed: Archaeology's New Vision of Ancient Israel and the Origin of Its Sacred Texts* (New York: Basic, 2001); Thomas Thompson, *The Historicity of the Patriarchal Narratives: The Quest for the Historical Abraham* (Harrisburg, PA: Trinity Press International, 2002); and summary and sources in Paul Tobin, "The Bible and Modern Scholarship," in Loftus, *The Christian Delusion*, 148–80.

5. See, for example: Bart Ehrman, *Jesus Interrupted: Revealing the Hidden Contradictions in the Bible (and Why We Don't Know about Them)* (New York: HarperOne, 2009); Gerd Lüdemann, *Jesus After 2000 Years* (Amherst, NY: Prometheus Books, 2001); Gerd Theissen and Annette Merz, *The Historical Jesus: A Comprehensive Guide* (Minneapolis: Fortress, 1996); Robert Funk and Roy Hoover, *The Five Gospels: The Search for the Authentic Words of Jesus* (New York: Maxwell Macmillan, 1993).

6. For example: Genesis 3:16; 1 Corinthians 14:33–35; 1 Timothy 2:8–15.

7. Daniel J. Estes, "Audience Analysis and Validity in Application," *Bibliotheca Sacra* 150 (April–June 1993): 219–29.

8. Ibid., 224.

9. Ibid.

10. John Bright, *The Authority of the Old Testament* (Nashville: Abingdon, 1967), 152. For a thoroughly unsatisfactory and desperate attempt to argue that Old Testament laws are still relevant, see Joe M. Sprinkle, *Biblical Law and Its Relevance: A Christian Understanding and Ethical Application for Today of the Mosaic Regulations* (Lanham, MD: University Press of America, 2006).

11. We refrain from saying "100 percent" because there are a small number of Christian scholars who do realize that modern Bibles are constructs that may bear little similarity to "the original."

12. Philip C. Stine, *Let the Words Be Written: The Lasting Influence of Eugene Nida* (Atlanta: Society of Biblical Literature, 2004), 182.

13. Quoted in Leland Ryken, *The Word of God in English: Criteria for Excellence in Bible Translation* (Wheaton, IL: Crossway, 2002), 73.

14. For more demonstrations and discussion of this point than are here to follow, see Hector Avalos, *End of Biblical Studies*, 37–64.

15. Sissela Bok, *Lying: Moral Choice in Public and Private Life* (New York: Vintage Books, 1999), 15.

16. Coogan, "The Great Gulf between Scholars and the Pew," 8.

17. For the violent aspect of the Bible, see Hector Avalos, *Fighting Words: The Origins of Religious Violence* (Amherst, NY: Prometheus Books, 2005).

18. For a complete discussion of the evidence and scholarship on this point, see Avalos, *End of Biblical Studies*, 43–44.

19. For the general techniques used by ancient Greek versions, see John A. Beck, *Translators as Storytellers: A Study in Septuagint Translation Technique* (New York: Peter Lang, 2000).

20. The story is found in Eusebius, *Ecclesiastical History*, trans. J. E. L. Oulton (Cambridge, MA: Harvard University Press, 1980), 6.8.1–3. Eusebius attributes Origen's actions to an immature and youthful mind, but he also says another Christian named Demetrius approved of Origen's sincere act. On castration in early Christianity, see Mathew Kuefler, *The Manly Eunuch: Masculinity, Gender Ambiguity, and Christian Ideology in Late Antiquity* (Chicago: University of Chicago Press, 2001).

21. See Bible Gateway, "Contemporary English Version," http://www.bible gateway.com/versions/?action=getVersionInfo&vid=46.

22. Stanley Porter, "The Contemporary English Version," in *Translating the Bible: Problems and Prospects*, ed. Stanley Porter and Richard Hess (London: T&T Clark, 1999), 39.

23. Some of the classic works on this issue include Charlotte Klein, *Anti-Judaism in Christian Theology*, trans. Edward Quinn (Philadelphia: Fortress, 1978); John G. Gager, *The Origins of Anti-Semitism: Attitudes toward Judaism in Paganism and Christian Antiquity* (New York: Oxford, 1983); Rosemary R. Ruether, *Faith and Fratricide: The Theological Roots of Anti-Semitism* (New York: Seabury, 1979).

24. Howard Clark Kee and Irvin J. Borowsky, *Removing the Anti-Judaism from the New Testament* (Philadelphia: American Interfaith Institute/World Alliance, 2000); Norman A. Beck, *Mature Christianity in the 21st Century: The Recognition and Repudiation of the Anti-Jewish Polemic in the New Testament* (New York: Crossroad,

1994); Tikva Frymer-Kensky et al., *Christianity in Jewish Terms* (Boulder, CO: West-view, 2000).

25. Kee and Borowsky, *Removing the Anti-Judaism*, 18.

26. Ibid., 20.

27. Beck, *Mature Christianity in the 21st Century*, 323, grants that "the defamatory anti-Jewish polemic of the New Testament must be repudiated," but Beck's proposals are more akin to keeping the parts of *Mein Kampf* that are not objectionable.

28. There are other definitions as well. Emanuel Tov (in *Textual Criticism of the Hebrew Bible*, 2nd ed. [Minneapolis: Fortress; Assen: Royal Van Gorcum, 2001], 1) says: "Textual criticism deals with the origin and nature of all forms of a text, in our case the biblical text."

29. For the goals and agendas in the textual criticism of nonbiblical works in antiquity, see James E. G. Zetzel, *Latin Textual Criticism in Antiquity* (New York: Arno Press, 1981); Rudolf Pfeiffer, *History of Classical Scholarship from the Beginnings to the End of the Hellenistic Age* (1968), and L. D. Reynolds and N. G. Wilson, *Scribes & Scholars: A Guide to the Transmission of Greek & Latin Literature*, 3rd ed. (1991). On the goals and methods of modern textual criticism: Paul Maas, *Textual Criticism* (Oxford: Clarendon, 1958).

30. Eldon J. Epp, "New Testament Textual Criticism in America: Requiem for a Discipline," *Journal of Biblical Literature* 98 (1979): 97. This essay is a printed version of a lecture delivered in 1977 at the Annual Meeting of the Society of Biblical Literature.

31. For more demonstrations and discussion of this point than are here to follow, see Avalos, *End of Biblical Studies*, 65–108.

32. For more demonstrations and discussion of this point than are here to follow see ibid., 109–84.

33. William G. Dever, "Death of a Discipline," *Biblical Archaeology Review* 21, no. 5 (September/October 1995): 50–55, 70; quote is from 51. For a broader treatment on the demise of biblical archaeology, see Thomas W. Davis, *Shifting Sands: The Rise and Fall of Biblical Archaeology* (New York: Oxford University Press, 2004).

34. Ronald S. Hendel, "Is There a Biblical Archaeology?" *Biblical Archaeology Review* 32, no. 4 (July/August 2006): 20.

35. Dever, "Death of a Discipline," 53. Italics are Dever's. For a more optimistic view of archaeology in areas other than those tied to ancient Israel or the Bible, see Brian Fagan, "The Next Fifty Years: Will It Be the Golden Age of Archaeology?" *Archaeology* 59, no. 5 (September/October 2006): 18–23. Whether intentionally or not, Fagan does not give more than a passing comment to lands remotely related to the Bible (e.g., Egypt and Mesopotamia), and nothing about biblical archaeology whatsoever.

36. William G. Dever, "Material Remains and the Cult in Ancient Israel: An

Essay in Archaeological Systematics," in *The Word of the Lord Shall Go Forth: Essays in Honor of David Noel Freedman in Celebration of His Sixtieth Birthday*, ed. Carol L. Meyers and M. O. Connor (Winona Lake, IN: Eisenbrauns, 1983), 571.

37. We adapt the list and approximate dates from Halpern, "Erasing History," *Bible Review* 11, no. 6 (1995): 30.

38. Hendel, "Is There a Biblical Archaeology?" 20.

39. Stephen Neill and Tom Wright, *The Interpretation of the New Testament 1861–1986* (Oxford: Oxford University Press, 1988), 379. The term "Third Quest" has been criticized effectively by Stanley Porter, *The Criteria for Authenticity in Historical-Jesus Research: Previous Discussions and New Proposals* (Sheffield, England: Sheffield Academic Press, 2000), 28–59, but especially 51–59.

40. For more demonstrations and discussion of this point than are here to follow, see Avalos, *End of Biblical Studies*, 185–218.

41. John Dominic Crossan, *The Historical Jesus: The Life of a Mediterranean Jewish Peasant* (New York: HarperSanFrancisco, 1992), xxviii; S. G. F. Brandon, *Jesus and the Zealots: A Study of the Political Factor in Primitive Christianity* (New York: Scribner's, 1967); Morton Smith, *Jesus the Magician* (New York: Harper & Row, 1978); Gêza Vermés, *Jesus the Jew* (Philadelphia: Fortress, 1981) and *Jesus and the World of Judaism* (Philadelphia: Fortress, 1984); Bruce D. Chilton, *A Galilean Rabbi and His Bible: Jesus' Use of the Interpreted Scripture in His Time* (Washington, DC: Glazier, 1984); Harvey Falk, *Jesus the Pharisee: A New Look at the Jewishness of Jesus* (New York: Paulist, 1985); E. P. Sanders, *Jesus and Judaism* (Philadelphia: Fortress, 1985).

42. Robert W. Funk, Roy W. Hoover, and the Jesus Seminar, *The Five Gospels: The Search for the Authentic Words of Jesus* (New York: HarperCollins, 1997), 34.

43. Ibid., 25–26.

44. For a general defense of the Jesus Seminar, see Robert J. Miller, *The Jesus Seminar and Its Critics* (Santa Rosa, CA: Polebridge, 1999). [Editor's Note: But for a sound refutation of its methods, see Porter, *The Criteria for Authenticity*; Gerd Theissen and Dagmar Winter, *The Quest for the Plausible Jesus: The Question of Criteria* (John Knox Press, 2002); and Dale Allison, "The Historians' Jesus and the Church," in *Seeking the Identity of Jesus: A Pilgrimage*, ed. Beverly Roberts Gaventa and Richard B. Hays (William B. Eerdmans, 2008), pp. 79–95.]

45. Funk, *Five Gospels*, 26.

46. Ibid., 143.

47. Ibid., 145.

48. Ibid., 43.

49. Ibid., 44.

50. Ibid.

51. Ibid.

52. We follow the translation of the Prayer of Nabonidus in Florentino García Martínez, *The Dead Sea Scrolls Translated: The Qumran Texts in English*, trans. Wilfred G. E. Watson (Leiden: Brill, 1994), 289. The quoted portion of the Aramaic text, following F. M. Cross ("Fragments of a Prayer of Nabonidus" *IEJ* 34 [1984]: 260–64) reads: "as for my sin, he forgave it (or: my sin he forgave). A diviner—who was a Jew . . ." In this translation the one doing the forgiving is God, but the problem is that the words preceding the quoted portion are not certain. Thus, the alternative translation is also plausible. Note that García Martínez's translation has brackets on the last two letters of "Jew," which means that he regards those letters as not present in the manuscript, but Cross's facsimile and transliteration ("Fragments of a Prayer of Nabonidus," 261, 263) shows that all the letters of the word are visible.

53. For a more conservative academic critique of modern historical Jesus research and the Jesus Seminar, see Philip Jenkins, *Hidden Gospels: How the Search for Jesus Lost Its Way* (New York: Oxford, 2001). Jenkins (p. 157) observes that of the seventy-six scholars listed as active members of the seminar in 1993, about one-third were associated with Harvard Divinity School and the Claremont Graduate School.

54. Albert Schweitzer, *The Quest of the Historical Jesus: A Critical Study of Its Progress from Reimarus to Wrede* (Macmillan, 1910). For Robert Price's analysis of how conservative scholars err as greatly as the Jesus Seminar ever did, see Robert M. Price, "Jesus: Myth and Method," in *The Christian Delusion*, ed. John Loftus (Amherst, NY: Prometheus Books, 2010), 273–90; *Jesus Is Dead* (Cranford, NJ: American Atheist, 2007); and *Inerrant the Wind: The Evangelical Crisis of Biblical Authority* (Amherst, NY: Prometheus Books, 2009).

55. Charles W. Hedrick, "The 34 Gospels: Diversity and Division among the Earliest Christians," *Bible Review* 18, no. 3 (June 2002): 20–31, 46–47.

56. Bart Ehrman, *Lost Christianities: The Battles for Scripture and the Faiths We Never Knew* (New York: Oxford, 2003).

57. Crossan, *The Historical Jesus*, 427–29.

58. For the dates, see list in Hedrick, "The 34 Gospels," 27–28. [Editor's Note: For the Gospel of Judas: Rodolphe Kasser et al., *The Gospel of Judas: From Codex Tchacos* (Washington, DC: National Geographic, 2006)].

59. See Ehrman, *Lost Christianities*, 9–11, and *Forged: Writing in the Name of God—Why the Bible's Authors Are Not Who We Think They Are* (New York: HarperOne, 2011).

60. On the diminishing willingness of liberal intellectuals to voice their opinions, see Eric Lott, *The Disappearing Liberal Intellectual* (New York: Basic, 2007).

61. J. Cheryl Exum and David J. A. Clines, eds., *The New Literary Criticism and the Hebrew Bible* (Valley Forge, PA: Trinity Press International, 1993), 11.

62. See Edgar V. McKnight and Elizabeth Struthers Malbon, eds., *The New Lit-*

erary Criticism and the New Testament (Valley Forge, PA: Trinity Press International, 1994). See also Frank Lentricchia, *After the New Criticism* (Chicago: University of Chicago Press, 1981).

63. Robert Alter and Frank Kermode, eds., *The Literary Guide to the Bible* (Cambridge: Harvard University Press, 1987); Robert Alter, *The Art of Biblical Narrative* (New York: Basic, 1981) and *The Art of Biblical Poetry* (New York: Basic, 1985); Meir Sternberg, *The Poetics of Biblical Narrative: Ideological Literature and the Drama of Reading* (Bloomington: Indiana University Press, 1987).

64. Alter, *The Art of Biblical Narrative*, 189.

65. For the Yale Report, see Richard Hofstadter and Wilson Smith, *American Higher Education: A Documentary History*, 2 vols. (Chicago: University of Chicago Press, 1961), 1:289.

66. For a defense of our "Western canon," see Harold Bloom, *The Western Canon: The Books and School for the Ages* (New York: Harcourt Brace, 1994); and Christian Kopff, *The Devil Knows Latin: Why America Needs the Classical Tradition* (Wilmington, DE: ISI Books, 1999).

67. See interview of Hershel Shanks with Phyllis Trible, "Wrestling with Scripture," *Biblical Archaeology Review* 32, no. 2 (March/April 2006): 49.

68. For a stark illustration of this, see Avalos, "Yahweh Is a Moral Monster," in *The Christian Delusion*, 209–36.

69. See Peter Lamarque and Stein Haugom Olsen, *Truth, Fiction, and Literature: A Philosophical Perspective* (Oxford: Clarendon, 2002).

70. For more demonstrations and discussion of this point, see Avalos, *End of Biblical Studies*, 219–48 (and see 289–342 for a demonstration of the institutional inertia and ignominious commercial interests likewise sustaining biblical studies).

71. For basic historical surveys, see John H. Hayes and Frederick C. Prussner, *Old Testament Theology: Its History and Development* (Atlanta: John Knox, 1985). Also useful is Robert B. Laurin, ed., *Contemporary Old Testament Theologians* (Valley Forge, PA: Judson, 1970).

72. Krister Stendahl, "Biblical Theology, Contemporary," in *The Interpreter's Dictionary of the Bible*, ed. George A. Buttrick, et al. (Nashville: Abingdon, 1962), 1:420. Compare Stendahl's view with that of E. D. Hirsch, *Validity in Interpretation* (New Haven, CT: Yale University Press, 1967), 8: "*Meaning* is that which is represented by a text; it is what the author meant by his use of a particular sign sequence. . . . *Significance*, on the other hand, names a relationship between that meaning and a person. . . ."

73. For the history and philosophical issues surrounding the concept of "authorship" and authorial intentionality, see Jed Wyrick, *The Ascension of Authorship: Attribution and Canon Formation in Jewish, Hellenistic, and Christian Traditions*

(Cambridge, MA: Harvard University Department of Comparative Literature, 2004); Jeff Mitscherling, Tanya DiTommaso, and Aref Nayed, *The Author's Intention* (Lanham, MD: Lexington, 2004).

74. John J. Collins, *Encounters with Biblical Theology* (Minneapolis: Fortress, 2005), 7.

75. For more demonstrations and discussion of this point, see Avalos, *End of Biblical Studies*, 249–88.

CHAPTER 5

1. This chapter is a revised and shortened extract from an argument against the existence of Yahweh in my doctoral dissertation (Jaco Gericke, *Does YHWH Exist? A Philosophical-Critical Reconstruction of the Case against Realism in Old Testament Theology* [PhD thesis, Pretoria, South Africa: University of Pretoria, 2003]), and a full survey of this argument and its evidence was published in J. W. Gericke, "Yahwism and Projection: An A/theological Perspective on Polymorphism in the Old Testament," *Scriptura* 96 (2007): 407–42. The same findings and more are corroborated by the work of Thom Stark, *The Human Faces of God: What Scripture Reveals When It Gets God Wrong (and Why Inerrancy Tries to Hide It)* (Wipf & Stock Publishers, 2011).

2. Friedrich Nietzsche, *Daybreak*, trans. R. J. Hollingdale (Cambridge: Cambridge University Press, 1977), 57.

3. Robert Carroll, *Wolf in the Sheepfold* (London: SPCK 1991), 38.

4. David Clines, *Interested Parties: The Ideology of Readers and Writers of the Hebrew Bible* (Sheffield, England: Sheffield Academic Press, 1995), 190.

5. Quoted in William Harwood, *Mythology's Last Gods: Yahweh and Jesus* (Amherst, NY: Prometheus Books, 1992), 257.

6. For a more thorough discussion of the historical and semantic background behind this recent hemming and hawing over how God is physically described in the Old Testament, see Gericke, "Yahwism and Projection," 407–12.

7. For a humorous exposition, see Alexander Waugh, *God* (London: Headline Books, 2002). For a more detailed survey and discussion of examples of God being understood as working with the parts and limitations of a human body, see Gericke, "Yahwism and Projection," 416–18 (anthropomorphic projection).

8. On this see, William G. Dever, *Did God Have a Wife? Archaeology and Folk Religion in Ancient Israel* (Grand Rapids, MI: William Eerdmans Publishing, 2005).

9. See Michael Coogan, *God and Sex: What the Bible Really Says* (New York: Twelve, 2010), 163–88. [Editor's Note: In the last chapter of this book, Coogan describes the sex life of Yahweh, who had one just like the other gods and goddesses of

that era. Yahweh probably had a consort whose name was Asherah (the "queen of heaven," a counterpart to Yahweh as the "king of heaven"). She was worshipped as part of the folk religion of that day, as well as by kings and officials. In one jar fragment archaeologists have found, Yahweh is pictured with a big phallus and his arm around Asherah! The "sons of god" in Genesis 6:1–4 were their offspring. These "sons of god" became problematic to later monotheists, so they reinterpreted them to be "Watchers" and later as angels. Makes sense. Right? What else are you going to do with obvious mythical divine beings like these, and a divine family, after rejecting your former polytheism to become monotheists?

The really fascinating stuff was how Yahweh treated his unfaithful wives. Yes, he was a polygamist. In the prophet's mind this was an allegory, of course, but the allegory must have a meaning for the people it was spoken to, otherwise it wouldn't make sense to them. The prophets Hosea, Jeremiah, and Ezekiel tell us about their unfaithfulness to Yahweh their husband, and what he did to them as a punishment for their unfaithfulness. Ezekiel 16 and 23 contain "some of the most shocking and sexually explicit language in the Bible" Coogan tells us (183). In this allegory, the unfaithful wives of Samaria and Jerusalem are brutally punished by their divine husband Yahweh. At one point he strips them before a mob. Then comes a warning from Yahweh himself, that he did this so "that all women may be instructed not to act promiscuously as you did" (Ezek. 23:48).]

10. Don Cupitt, *Philosophy's Own Religion* (London: SCM Press, 2001), 65.

11. F. Staal, "Noam Chomsky between the Human and Natural Sciences," *Janus Head: Journal of Interdisciplinary Studies in Literature, Continental Philosophy, Phenomenological Psychology, and the Arts* (Special Supplemental Issue, Winter 2001): 21, 25–66.

12. For more detailed discussion and evidence of this psychomorphic projection, see Gericke, "Yahwism and Projection," 418–22; see also Valerie Tarico's chapter 6 of this book, "Why the Biblical God is Hopelessly Human."

13. This point was succinctly argued by Harwood, *Mythology's Last Gods*.

14. For many more examples of this cosmological ignorance displayed in the Old Testament (corresponding to the very same beliefs coincidentally held by surrounding pagan societies), see Ed Babinski, "The Cosmology of the Bible," *The Christian Delusion*, ed. John Loftus (Amherst, NY: Prometheus Books, 2010): 109–47.

15. On the nonexistence of these characters, see chapter 4 by Hector Avalos, "Why Biblical Studies Must End" (previous), and the discussion and scholarship cited in Paul Tobin, "The Bible and Modern Scholarship," in Loftus, *The Christian Delusion*, 148–80.

16. Don Cupitt, *After God: The Future of Religion* (London: SCM Press, 1997), 45.

17. For an introduction to the "less than perfect being" theology of the Old Tes-

tament, albeit an overoptimistic presentation completely ignoring the dark side of Yahweh, see Terrence E. Fretheim, *The Suffering of God: An Old Testament Perspective* (OBT 14, Philadelphia: Fortress Press, 1984). For twenty-four examples of that overlooked dark side, see "The Will of God" at the *Christian Delusion* companion website: http://sites.google.com/site/thechristiandelusion/Home/the-will-of-god.

18. On how suspiciously similar Yahweh's Old Testament law codes are to the human-made codes of surrounding pagan cultures when the Old Testament was written, see Hector Avalos, "Yahweh Is a Moral Monster," in Loftus, *The Christian Delusion*, 209–36.

19. For more examples and discussion of this kind of sociomorphic projection in the Old Testament, see Gericke, "Yahwism and Projection," 413–15.

20. This point is thoroughly proved by Babinski in "Cosmology of the Bible."

21. See Avalos, "Yahweh Is a Moral Monster," 226–27.

CHAPTER 6

1. Laura Kastner and Jennifer Wyatt, *Getting to Calm: Cool-Headed Strategies for Parenting Tweens + Teens* (Seattle: Parent Map, 2009).

2. Paul Watzlawick, *The Situation Is Hopeless But Not Serious (The Pursuit of Unhappiness)* (New York: W. W. Norton, 1993).

3. Valerie Tarico, "Christian Belief through the Lens of Cognitive Science," a six-part series published online at the *Huffington Post* (http://www.huffingtonpost.com/valerie-tarico, see indexes for May through November of 2009); a summary of the main points made in that series was also published in a companion article of the same title in *The Christian Delusion*, ed. John Loftus (Amherst, NY: Prometheus Books, 2010), 47–64. Likewise, an expanded series on the same topic as the present chapter ("Why the Biblical God Is Hopelessly Human") is also available at the *Huffington Post* (as "God's Emotions," October–September 2010).

4. See R. Schwab and K. U. Petersen, "Religiousness: Its Relation to Loneliness, Neuroticism and Subjective Well-Being," *Journal for the Scientific Study of Religion* 29, no. 3 (1990): 335–45; and Justin Barrett and Frank C. Keil, "Conceptualizing a Nonnatural Entity: Anthropomorphism in God Concepts," *Cognitive Psychology* 31 (1996): 219–47.

5. See P. L. Benson and B. Spilka, "God Image as a Function of Self-Esteem and Locus of Control," *Journal for the Scientific Study of Religion* 12, no. 3 (1973): 297–310; and Barrett, "Conceptualizing a Nonnatural Entity."

6. See Pascal Boyer, *Religion Explained: The Human Instincts That Fashion Gods, Spirits, and Ancestors* (London: Heinemann, 2001).

7. See discussion and sources cited in David Eller, "Christianity Does Not Provide the Basis for Morality," in Loftus, *The Christian Delusion*, 347–67.

8. Arthur D'Adamo, *Science without Bounds: A Synthesis of Science, Religion and Mysticism* (Bloomington, IN: AuthorHouse, 2004), 210. See http://www.adamford.com/swb.

9. Barrett, "Conceptualizing a Nonnatural Entity."

10. "Positive Atheism's Big List of Albert Einstein Quotations" (http://www.positiveatheism.org/hist/quotes/einstein.htm).

11. "Question and Answer with John Shelby Spong," September 16, 2010, http://muzicindi.net/?q=node/41#spong3.

12. Alan Nordstrom, "Reconciliation," *Alan Nordstrom's Blog*, June 1, 2008, http://alan-nordstrom.blogspot.com/2008/06/reconciliation-how-reason-and-emotion.html.

13. Robert Plutchik, *The Emotions: Facts, Theories, and a New Model* (New York: Random House, 1962).

14. Nasir Naqvi, Baba Shiv, and Antoine Bechara, "The Role of Emotion in Decision Making: A Cognitive Neuroscience Perspective," *Current Directions in Psychological Science* 15, no. 5 (2006): 260–64.

15. Antonio Damasio, *Descartes' Error: Emotion, Reason, and the Human Brain* (New York: G. P. Putnam, 1994). Notably Darwin wrote up his own scientific studies of emotion in *The Expression of the Emotions in Man and Animals* (1872), available at http://darwin-online.org.uk. The science of emotion has come a long way since then, and yet many of his observations remain apt.

16. Marlene Winell, *Leaving the Fold: A Guide for Former Fundamentalists and Others Leaving Their Religion* (Oakland, CA: New Harbinger Publications), 177–94.

17. Jeremy Bentham, *An Introduction to the Principles of Morals and Legislation* (1789) [(New York: Hafner, 1948), 1–2].

18. Charles Darwin, *The Descent of Man and Selection in Relation to Sex* (New York: D. Appleton, 1872), 1:79.

19. John Tooby and Leda Cosmides. "The Evolutionary Psychology of the Emotions and Their Relationship to Internal Regulatory Variables," in *Handbook of Emotions*, ed. M. Lewis, J. M. Haviland-Jones, and L. F. Barrett, 3rd ed. (New York: Guilford, 2008), 114–37.

20. See the entry for "triune brain" in Wikipedia (http://en.wikipedia.org/wiki/Triune_brain).

21. Jonathan Edwards, "Sinners in the Hands of an Angry God" (Enfield, CT, July 8, 1741, available in *Christian Classics Ethereal Library*, http://www.ccel.org/ccel/edwards/sermons.sinners.html).

22. M. Lewis, "The Development of Anger and Rage," in *Rage, Power and*

Aggression, ed. R. A. Glick and S. P. Roose (New Haven, CT: Yale University Press, 1993), 18–168.

23. Aaron Sell, John Tooby, and Leda Cosmides, "Formidability and the Logic of Human Anger," *PNAS* [*Proceedings of the National Academy of Sciences*] 106, no. 35 (September 1, 2009): 15073–78, http://www.psych.ucsb.edu/research/cep/papers/angerselltoobycosmides09.pdf.

24. Mary Fairchild, "Children's Morning Prayers: Morning Prayers to Teach Your Christian Child," *About.com*, http://christianity.about.com/od/prayersforspecific needs/qt/morningprayers.htm, accessed October 19, 2010.

25. Larissa Tiedens and Alison Fragale, "Power Moves: Complementarity in Dominant and Submissive Nonverbal Behavior," *Journal of Personality and Social Psychology* 84, no. 3 (2003): 558–68, http://www.unc.edu/~fragales/Tiedens&Fragale JPSP.pdf.

26. See chapter 2 of Keith Johnstone, *Improvisation and the Theatre* (New York: Routledge, 1981), summarized and discussed in Michael Arnzen, "Impro II: Status," June 18, 2005, http://blogs.setonhill.edu/MikeArnzen/009704.html.

27. John Wilkins, "Social Dominance Psychology in Humans," *Evolving Thoughts.net*, July 2, 2009, http://evolvingthoughts.net/2009/07/02/social -dominance-psychology-in-humans.

28. "Primate Behavior," *Primate Info Net*, 28, http://pin.primate.wisc.edu/ av/slidesets/slides_b/Behavior28.html.

29. See Tenzin Gyatso (the current Dalai Lama), "Compassion and the Individual," *DalaiLama.com*, http://www.dalailama.com/messages/compassion.

30. See the Wikipedia entry on "Ahimsa in Jainism," http://en.wikipedia.org/ wiki/Ahimsa_in_Jainism.

31. From Charles Darwin, "Letter to Asa Gray" (May 22, 1860). For a complete account of his reasons for abandoning his faith (which still hold true today), see Francis Darwin, ed., *The Life and Letters of Charles Darwin*, vol. 1 (London: J. Murray, 1887), 175–78 (for the letter of 1860, see 2:311–12).

32. Richard Dawkins, *River Out of Eden: A Darwinian View of Life* (London: Weidenfeld & Nicolson, 1995), 133.

33. See discussion of the psychology of this in "Imaginary Friends with Evan Kidd," La Trobe University, 2009, http://www.latrobe.edu.au/news/articles/2009/ podcasts/imaginary-friends-with-evan-kidd/transcript.

34. Dexter VanDango, "Grumpy Old Dad," http://dextervandango.com/view .do?contentId=260&menuId=260.

PART 3

CHAPTER 7

1. The earliest theory of the atonement was the Ransom Theory (cf. 1 Tim. 2:5–6; 1 Pet. 1:18–19; Eph. 2; Rom. 7 [esp. 7:14, 23–24] and 8:23; Gal. 4; Mk. 10:45; etc.). The basic notion is that sinners were being held captive by Satan and the death of Jesus on the cross was the ransom required to free them. Satan, however, was tricked, and he was not able to keep Jesus dead, and thus the resurrection proved Christ's victory over Satan and his demons ("*Christus Victor*"). This theory dominated Christianity for a thousand years (with a number of variants). In the eleventh century, Anselm developed the Satisfaction Theory of the atonement. This theory said that God's honor had been besmirched by man's sin and that man now owed a debt to God that he could not pay. Thus, God decided to pay it for man. God sent his son, who was both God and man, to pay the debt that man could not pay. The Reformers built upon Anselm's theory and developed the Penal Substitutionary Theory (PST) of the Atonement. Other theories of the atonement include the Moral Influence Theory (developed by Peter Abelard), the Governmental Theory (developed by Hugo Grotius), and the Recapitulation Theory (developed by various Eastern theologians). [Editor's Note: Sufficient critiques of these other atonement theories can be read in Michael Martin's *Case against Christianity* (Philadelphia: Temple University Press, 1991), 252–63; John Hick's *Metaphor of God Incarnate: Christology in a Pluralistic Age* (Louisville, KY: Westminster/John Knox Press, 1993), 112–133; and chapter 19 in my book, John Loftus, *Why I Became an Atheist: A Former Preacher Rejects Christianity* (Amherst, NY: Prometheus Books, 2008), 344–50. But the gist of every critique of them is the same: none of these purposes for the atonement is required for an omnipotent, omnibenevolent deity, leaving no reason for such a deity to heed them, much less fashion his system of salvation out of them.]

2. Blurb in Steve Jeffrey et al., *Pierced for Our Transgressions: Rediscovering the Glory of Penal Substitution* (Crossway, 2007). This book contains forty-one blurbs from leading evangelical theologians covering the first ten pages of the book.

3. Ibid.

4. Ibid.

5. John MacArthur, "Open Theism's Attack on the Atonement," *Master's Seminary Journal*, Vol. 12, no. 1 (Spring 2001), 9.

6. Greg Bahnsen, "Penal Substitution," *Penpoint* 4, no. 2 (March 1993), 1.

7. J. I. Packer, "What Did the Cross Achieve: The Logic of Penal Substitution," Tyndale Biblical Theology Lecture, 1973, available online: http://www.the-highway.com/cross_Packer.html.

8. Anthony Quinton, "On Punishment," in *Philosophical Perspectives on Punishment*, ed. Gertrude Ezorsky (State University of New York Press, 1972), 7.

9. Ibid., 10.

10. Mark Murphy, "Not Penal Substitution but Vicarious Punishment," in *Faith and Philosophy* 26, no. 3 (July 2009), 255–57. Murphy argues for vicarious punishment, by which he means that the guilty are punished by seeing the suffering caused to the innocent. This position has its own problems. See http://formerfundy.blogspot .com/2010/08/mark-murphys-view-of-atonement.html.

11. Paul Bloom, "The Moral Life of Babies," *New York Times*, May 5, 2010.

12. Charles Feinberg, "The Image of God," *Bibliotheca Sacra* 129 (1972): 246.

13. Norman McIlwain, *The Biblical Revelation of the Cross* (Oakwood Publishing, 2006).

14. Charles Hodge, *Systematic Theology* (Charles Scribner, 1872), 2:532.

15. Another problem with trying to detach sin or demerit from guilt and punishment is stated by Stanford Burney:

> But substitutionists reverse this natural order of the relation between crime and punishment, making the removal of the reatus poena antecedent to the removal of the reatus culpae—that is, exemption from punishment is the antecedent of deliverance from criminality. Hence, the sinner was pardoned, released from all liability to penal suffering when Christ became his substitute but was left in his criminal and polluted state; morally corrupted by, but not liable to, the divinely ordained consequence of his corruption! At enmity against God, yet not liable to the consequences of that state of enmity. Such a state of things, it is self-evident, is impossible in the sphere of either physical or moral law. It would be possible only in the sphere of human law, and possible here only because of the inherent weakness of human law. Thus, a man commits a malicious murder, is indicted and tried by the proper court; but, by the bribery or death of witnesses or by corrupting the court, he procures a verdict of acquittal and is set free. This verdict operates as a barrier against subsequent prosecution and punishment. This is exactly the state in which substitutionary satisfaction puts all for whom Christ died. His death absolutely delivers from reatus poena, but leaves them in the meshes of reatus culpae. . . .

Quoted from Stanford Burney, *Atonement Soteriology: The Sacrificial, in Contrast with the Penal, Substitutionary, and Merely Moral or Exemplary Theories of Propitiation* (Cumberland Presbyterian Publishing House, 1888), 113–14.

16. William Joseph McGlothin, "Sacrifice, Human," *The International Standard Bible Encyclopedia*, ed. James Orr (Howard-Severance Company, 1915), 4:2658. For a

thorough study of the practice in the ancient Near East, see A. R. W. Green, *The Role of Human Sacrifice in the Ancient Near East* (Scholars Press for the American Schools of Oriental Research, 1975).

17. "Pass through the fire" in the King James Version is rendered "sacrifice in the fire" in the New International Version and "give to be burned as a sacrifice" in the New Living Translation.

18. David Dilling, "The Atonement and Human Sacrifice," *Grace Theological Journal* 12, no. 2 (Spring 1971): 25. On Yahweh's original endorsement of human sacrifice in the Old Testament, see Hector Avalos, "Yahweh Is a Moral Monster," *The Christian Delusion*, ed. John Loftus (Amherst, NY: Prometheus Books, 2010), 226–27.

19. Dilling, "Atonement and Human Sacrifice," 26–27.

20. Jeffrey et al., *Pierced for Our Transgressions*, 21.

21. I have used sin(ners) because as I understand the Bible, God's wrath is not focused against sin in the abstract but against sin as it manifests itself in human beings, that is: sinners.

22. The Greek word (or its cognate) occurs four times in the New Testament (Rom. 3:25; 1 John 2:2; 1 John 4:10; Heb. 2:17). C. H. Dodd argued that the word is better translated "expiation," but most scholars have sided with Leon Morris in translating it as "propitiation." See C. H. Dodd, *The Bible and the Greeks* (London: Hodder & Stoughton, 1935), 82–95; and Leon Morris, *The Apostolic Preaching of the Cross* (London: Tyndale, 1955), 144–213.

23. See also 1 Peter 2:24; 2 Corinthians 5:21; and 1 John 2:2.

24. John H. Leith, *Creeds of the Church*, 3rd. ed. (Louisiville: Westminster John Knox, 1982), 35–36.

25. Martin Luther, *Select Works of Martin Luther*, trans. Henry Cole (London: Simpkin and Marshall, 1826), 4:365.

26. John Calvin, *Institutes of the Christian Religion*, 2.16.10 [translation by Ford Lewis Battles, in John T. McNeill, ed., *Calvin: Institutes of the Christian Religion* (Philadelphia: Westminster John Knox, 1960)].

27. Hodge, *Systematic Theology*, 2:473.

28. Loraine Boettner, *The Reformed Faith* (Phillipsburg, NJ: P&R, 1983), Section III ("Christ's Atonement"). [Editor's Note: It makes no sense, of course, how a few hours in hell are equal to an eternity in hell. Were that the case, then by definition an eternity in hell would not be necessary to satisfy justice and would therefore be a gratuitous evil for God to allow. So either hell is not eternal (for anyone), or Jesus did not assume the actual punishment for human sin and thus cannot have atoned for any of it, much less all of it.]

29. Jürgen Moltmann, *The Trinity and the Kingdom: The Doctrine of God* (Minneapolis: Fortress Press, 1993), 174–75. Theologians have described the relationship

between the members of the Trinity in terms of *perichoresis*. Moltmann explains: *[T]his concept grasps the circulatory character of the eternal divine life. An eternal life process takes place in the triune God through the exchange of energies. The Father exists in the Son, the Son in the Father, and both of them in the Spirit, just as the Spirit exists in both the Father and the Son. By virtue of their eternal love they live in one another to such an extent, and dwell in one another to such an extent, that they are one. . . . The unity of the triunity lies in the eternal perichoresis of the trinitarian persons.*

30. A. T. B. McGowan, ed., *Always Reforming: Explorations in Systematic Theology* (Downers Grove, IL: InterVarsity, 2006), 199.

31. Rustin Umstattd, "A Trinitarian Crucifixion: The Holy Spirit and Substitutionary Atonement," paper presented at the 2008 annual meeting of the Evangelical Theological Society in Providence, Rhode Island.

32. Some Christians may object that what has been said in this paper does not apply to their view of the atonement. All views of the atonement, however, hold that in some way the suffering and death of an innocent person makes it possible for man to receive salvation. Thus, all views of the atonement share at least some of the problems associated with the PST.

33. Tertullian, "De Carne Christi," in the *Ante-Nicene Christian Library: Translations of the Writings of the Fathers Down to A.D. 325* (Elibron Classics, 2005), 15:173–74.

34. Marlene Winell, *Leaving the Fold: A Guide for Former Fundamentalists and Others Leaving Their Religion* (Oakland, CA: New Harbinger Publications), 75.

CHAPTER 8

1. Stephen Law has done an excellent job of putting his finger on the problems with this kind of response: see "Going Nuclear" in Stephen Law, *Believing Bullshit: How Not to Get Sucked into an Intellectual Black Hole* (Amherst, NY: Prometheus Books, 2011), 97–110.

2. In my forthcoming book *The Case against Christ* I will consider a wide range of challenges that undermine Christian belief. Consider the millions of miracle claims alleged about Lourdes, France. The Catholic Church has officially recognized sixty-seven of them. A rough estimation of the general reliability of human miracle testimony from Lourdes comes out to be a mere .0000167. That is, in general, when humans give miracle testimony, their reliability is orders of magnitude worse than it needs to be for us to even provisionally accept it. This dismal fact alone seriously undermines the acceptability of early Christian reports about the miracles of Jesus.

3. Apparently "arational" is not a commonly recognized word, but it should be.

"Irrational" means contrary to the dictates of reason. By "arational," I mean outside or without reason, and I leave open for the moment whether believing arationally is also irrational.

4. Richard Carrier, "Why the Resurrection Is Unbelievable," in *The Christian Delusion*, ed. John Loftus (Amherst, NY: Prometheus Books, 2010), 291–92.

5. Here's a tiny portion of empirical evidence about the effects of desire on belief formation and evidence gathering, from Jonathan Baron's *Thinking and Deciding* (New York: Cambridge University Press, 1988): E. Babad and Y. Katz, "Wishful Thinking—Against All Odds," *Journal of Applied Social Psychology* 21 (1991): 1921–38; L. A Brenner, D. J. Koehler, and A. Tversky, "On the Evaluation of One-Sided Evidence," *Journal of Behavioral Decision Making* 9 (1996) 59–70; D. Frey, "Recent Research on Selective Exposure to Information," in *Advances in Experimental Social Psychology*, ed. L. Berkowitz, vol. 19 (New York: Academic Press, 1986): 41–80; A. Lowin, "Approach and Avoidance: Alternative Modes of Selective Exposure to Information," *Journal of Personality and Social Psychology* 6 (1967): 1–9; W. J. McGuire, "A Syllogistic Analysis of Cognitive Relationships," in *Attitude Organization and Change*, ed. M. J. Rosenberg et al. (New Haven, CT: Yale University Press, 1960), 65–111; E. Pronin, T. Gilovich, and L. Ross, "Objectivity in the Eye of the Beholder: Divergent Perceptions of Bias in Self versus Others," *Psychological Review* 111, no. 3 (2004): 781–99; N. Weinstein, "Unrealistic Optimism about Future Life Events," *Journal of Personality and Social Psychology* 39 (1980): 806–20; J. C. Weeks et al., "Relationship between Cancer Patients' Predictions of Prognosis and Their Treatment Preferences," *Journal of the American Medical Association* 279 (1998): 1709–14. See also the chapters by Valerie Tarico and Jason Long in Loftus, *The Christian Delusion*.

6. Some of the influential arguments for the historical resurrection can be found in: N. T. Wright, *The Resurrection of the Son of God* (Minneapolis: Fortress, 2003); Richard Swinburne, *The Resurrection of God Incarnate* (New York: Oxford University Press, 2003); Gary Habermas, *The Historical Jesus: Ancient Evidence for the Life of Christ* (Joplin, MO: College Press, 1996); William Lane Craig, "The Bodily Resurrection of Jesus, " in *Gospel Perspectives I*, ed. R. T. France and D. Wenham (Sheffield, England: JSOT, 1980), 47–74; and "The Historicity of the Empty Tomb of Jesus," *New Testament Studies* 31 (1985): 39–67; Tim McGrew and Lydia McGrew, "The Argument from Miracles: A Cumulative Case for the Resurrection of Jesus of Nazareth," in *The Blackwell Companion to Natural Theology*, ed. W. L. Craig and J. P. Moreland (Oxford: Wiley-Blackwell, 2009), 593–662.

7. Gary Habermas, "The Case for Christ's Resurrection," in *To Everyone an Answer: A Case for the Christian World View*, ed. Francis Beckwith, William Lane Craig, and J. P. Moreland (Downers Grove, IL: InterVarsity, 2004), 180–98.

8. Ibid., 194.

9. Ibid., 195.

10. For example: Vaughan Bell, "Ghost Stories: Visits from the Deceased," *Scientific American*, December 2, 2008, at http://www.scientificamerican.com/article .cfm?id=ghost-stories-visits-from-the-deceased; A. Grimby, "Bereavement among Elderly People: Grief Reactions, Postbereavement Hallucinations, and Quality of Life," *Acta Psychiatrica Scandinavica* 87, no. 1 (January 1993): 72–80; W. Dewi Rees, "The Hallucinations of Widowhood," *British Medical Journal* 4 (October 2, 1971): 37–41.

11. For a start, see: C. Chabris and D. Simons, *The Invisible Gorilla and Other Ways Our Intuitions Deceive Us* (New York: Crown, 2010), 45–46; Daniel Greenberg, "President Bush's False 'Flashbulb' Memory of 9/11/01," *Applied Cognitive Psychology* 18 (2004): 363–70; Elizabeth Loftus, *The Myth of Repressed Memory: False Memories and Allegations of Sexual Abuse* (New York: St. Martin's/Griffin, 1994); Ulric Neisser and Nicole Harsch, "Phantom Flashbulbs: False Recollections of Hearing the News about *Challenger*," in *Affect and Accuracy in Recall: Studies of "Flashbulb" Memories,* ed. Eugene Winograd and Ulric Neisser (Cambridge: Cambridge University Press, 1992), 9–31; D. L. M. Sacchi, F. Agnoli, and E. F. Loftus, "Changing History: Doctored Photographs Affect Memory for Past Public Events," *Applied Cognitive Psychology* 21 (2007): 1005–22; J. M. Talarico and D. C. Rubin, "Confidence, Not Consistency, Characterizes Flashbulb Memories," *Psychological Science* 14 (2003): 455–61; K. A. Wade et al., "A Picture Is Worth a Thousand Lies: Using False Photographs to Create False Childhood Memories," *Psychonomic Bulletin and Review* 9 (2002): 597–603; Sam Wang and Sandra Aamodt, *Welcome to Your Brain: Why You Lose Your Car Keys but Never Forget How to Drive and Other Puzzles of Everyday Life* (New York: Bloomsbury, 2008).

12. For example, see http://www.michaeljacksonsightings.com/.

13. N. T. Wright, "Jesus' Resurrection and Christian Origins," *Gregorianum* 83, no. 4 (2002): 615–35.

14. Ibid.

15. Ibid.

16. See Richard Carrier, *Not the Impossible Faith: Why Christianity Didn't Need a Miracle to Succeed* (Raleigh, NC: Lulu, 2009), 85–127; and Jeffery Jay Lowder and Robert M. Price, eds., *The Empty Tomb: Jesus beyond the Grave* (Amherst, NY: Prometheus Books, 2005), 107–18, 142–46.

17. Many of which have been exposed by the points made and scholarship cited in Richard Carrier, "Why the Resurrection Is Unbelievable" in Loftus, *The Christian Delusion*, 291–315, and here in chap. 2; see also Robert Price's chapter in that same volume, "Jesus: Myth and Method" (273–90); and Lowder and Price, *The Empty Tomb*.

18. For just a start, see: Paul Boyer and Stephen Nissenbaum, eds., *Salem-Village Witchcraft: A Documentary Record of Local Conflict in Colonial New England* (Boston:

Northeastern University Press, 1993); Paul Boyer and Stephen Nissenbaum, eds., *The Salem Witchcraft Papers: Verbatim Transcripts of the Legal Documents of the Salem Witchcraft Outbreak of 1692*, 3 vols. (New York: Da Capo, 1976); Richard Weisman, *Witchcraft, Magic, and Religion in 17th Century Massachusetts* (Amherst: University of Massachusetts Amherst Press, 1984).

19. See, for example, the kinds of claims encountered across the world by John Cornwell in *The Hiding Places of God: A Personal Journey into the World of Religious Visions, Holy Objects, and Miracles* (New York: Warner Books, 1991), and again consider the earlier example of the thousands of claims investigated at Lourdes, and by private investigators like James Randi, Joe Nickel, and Massimo Polidoro (who have authored many books on the subject), and documented in such reference collections as *Harper's Encyclopedia of Mystical & Paranormal Experience*, ed. Rosemary Ellen Guiley (San Francisco: HarperSanFrancisco, 1991), Gordon Stein's *The Encyclopedia of the Paranormal* (Amherst, NY: Prometheus Books, 1996), and Patricia Netzley's *The Greenhaven Encyclopedia of Paranormal Phenomena* (Detroit: Greenhaven Press, 2006).

20. As demonstrated in Carrier, "Resurrection Is Unbelievable," 298–99.

CHAPTER 9

1. See John Warwick Montgomery, *History and Christianity* (Downers Grove, IL: InterVarsity Press, 1974), 41–58.

2. By William Lane Craig: *The Son Rises: Historical Evidence for the Resurrection of Jesus* (Chicago: Moody, 1981); *Reasonable Faith: Christian Truth and Apologetics*, rev. ed. (Wheaton, IL: Crossway, 1994); "The Bodily Resurrection of Jesus," in *Gospel Perspectives: Studies of History and Tradition in the Four Gospels*, ed. R. T. France and David Wenham (Sheffield, England: JSOT Press, 1980), 47–74; "The Empty Tomb of Jesus," in *Gospel Perspectives II: Studies of History and Tradition in the Four Gospels*, ed. R. T. France and David Wenham (Sheffield, England: JSOT Press, 1980), 173–200; "Did Jesus Rise from the Dead?" in *Jesus under Fire: Modern Scholarship Reinvents the Historical Jesus*, ed. Michael J. Wilkins and J. P. Moreland (Grand Rapids, MI: Zondervan, 1995), 141–76. Other examples: Gary R. Habermas and Michael Licona, *The Case for the Resurrection of Jesus* (Grand Rapids, MI: Kregel, 2004); Gregory A. Boyd and Paul Rhodes Eddy, *The Jesus Legend: A Case for the Historical Reliability of the Synoptic Jesus* (Grand Rapids, MI: Baker, 2007); Michael Licona, *The Resurrection of Jesus: A New Historiographical Approach* (Downers Grove, IL: IVP Academic, 2010).

3. David Friedrich Strauss, "Death and Resurrection of Jesus" in *The Life of Jesus Critically Examined*, trans. George Eliot and Mary Ann Evans (Philadelphia: Fortress, 1972), 691–744; Willi Marxsen, *The Resurrection of Jesus of Nazareth*, trans. Margaret

Kohl (Philadelphia: Fortress 1970); Reginald H. Fuller, *The Formation of the Resurrection Narratives* (New York: Macmillan, 1971); Norman Perrin, *The Resurrection according to Matthew, Mark, and Luke* (Philadelphia: Fortress 1977); and see discussion and scholarship cited in Richard Carrier, "Why the Resurrection Is Unbelievable," in John Loftus, ed., *The Christian Delusion: Why Faith Fails* (Amherst, NY: Prometheus Books, 2010), 291–315.

4. Their polemics are aimed out into the ambient air, by way of apostrophe ("O Death, where is thy sting?"), to absent opponents, the old Rationalists, but the actual audience/readership is mostly believers looking to quiet their doubts. They, too, are already eager to believe what the narrative says and thus take most of it for granted without even noticing—even when the story itself is at issue. No wonder Evangelicals, especially fellow apologists, purport to find these apologetics cogent!

5. Albert Schweitzer, *The Quest of the Historical Jesus: A Critical Study of Its Progress from Reimarus to Wrede*, trans. W. Montgomery (New York: Macmillan, 1975), 27–67. See chapters 3–6 devoted to the Rationalists, including Heinrich Eberhard Gottlob Paulus, Karl Friedrich Bahrdt, and Karl Heinrich Venturini.

6. Charles H. Talbert, *What Is a Gospel? The Genre of the Canonical Gospels* (Philadelphia: Fortress, 1977); Robert M. Price, "Brand X Easters," in *The Resurrection of Jesus: A Sourcebook*, ed. Bernard Brandon Scott (Santa Rosa, CA: Polebridge, 2008), 49–59.

7. C. S. Lewis, "Myth Became Fact," in C. S. Lewis, *God in the Dock: Essays on Theology and Ethics*, ed. Walter Hooper (Grand Rapids, MI: Eerdmans, 1970), 63–67.

8. Price, "Jesus: Myth and Method," in Loftus, *The Christian Delusion*, 273–90.

9. Robert M. Price, *The Case against the Case for Christ: A New Testament Scholar Refutes the Reverend Lee Strobel* (Cranford, NJ: American Atheist, 2010), 209–10. See the astute "Jesus and Mo" cartoon, on which I am dependent, accompanying the text (from jesusandmo.net, used with permission).

10. R. G. Collingwood, *The Idea of History* (New York: Oxford University Press/Galaxy Books, 1956), 236–39; see Price, *Against the Case for Christ*, 210.

11. David Friedrich Strauss, *The Life of Jesus for the People*, 2nd ed. (London: Williams and Norgate, 1879), 1:412.

12. Yes, yes, I know apologists will blow the whistle here, insisting that there was no time for such textual evolution and no manuscript evidence that it occurred. But the early dating apologists take for granted is simply the dating that would, if true, be most convenient for them. And as for manuscript evidence, there isn't any one way or the other for the tunnel period between the composition of the Gospels and the first copies we possess. We have no alternative to trying to look for internal clues of redaction, and no right simply to assume the Gospels have always read as they do now, say, in the United Bible Societies Greek New Testament.

13. Mumtaz Ahmad Faruqui, *The Crumbling of the Cross* (Lahore, Pakistan:

Ahmadiyya Anjuman Isha'at-i-Islam, 1973), 25. Faruqui already makes this connection, though surely he is speaking for a long polemical/exegetical tradition.

14. "It is certain that the prayer prayed at Gethsemane was accepted." Hazrat Mirza Ghulam Ahmad, *Jesus in India: Being an Account of Jesus' Escape from Death on the Cross and of His Journey to India*, trans. Qazi Abdul Hamid (Rabwah, Pakistan: Ahmadiyya Muslim Foreign Missions Department, 1962), 37.

15. Solomon Schechter, *Some Aspects of Rabbinic Theology* (New York: Macmillan, 1910), 174–75; Shalom Spiegel, *The Last Trial: On the Legends and Lore of the Command to Abraham to Offer Isaac as a Sacrifice: The Akedah*, trans. Judah Goldin (Woodstock, VT: Jewish Lights Classic Reprints, 1993), 41–43. Spiegel is arguing that, in accordance with a persistent and ancient tradition, Jews first told the story with Isaac actually being slain and his death availing for Israel's sin. Then the story was changed out of later disdain for human sacrifice: Isaac's willingness (or Abraham's) must have been enough. Even so, one might infer that the Gospel story originally told of a real death, and that the features I am highlighting were part of a widespread "docetic" rewrite. That may be. It does not tell on my theory one way or the other. It is just that a precanonical, preredactional *Scheintod* version, whether primary or secondary, makes the state of the evidence easily ambiguous enough that the Swoon Theory remains fully plausible, which is the only verdict that can be rendered for any of the theories at this late date in history.

16. Ahmad, *Jesus in India*, 33. This brand of Islam accepts the Koranic assertion that Jesus did not die on the cross (4:157–58), but they believe Jesus came down from the cross still alive, for which, among other things, the followers of the teachings of Ahmad (the Ahmadiyya) are dismissed as heretics by most Muslims.

17. Josephus, *Life* 75 [William Whiston translation].

18. See Josephus, *Life* 1. For apologists it is axiomatic (i.e., an article of faith) that Acts and the Gospel writers cannot have used Josephus, since that would play hell with the too-early dates they prefer for those New Testament books. However, Steve Mason, *Josephus and the New Testament* (Peabody, MA: Hendrickson, 1992), 185–229, tells a very different story, and leading scholars are in agreement, e.g., Richard Pervo, *The Mystery of Acts: Unraveling Its Story* (Santa Rosa, CA: Polebridge, 2008) and *Acts: A Commentary* (Minneapolis: Fortress, 2009). And Theodore J. Weeden, *The Two Jesuses: Jesus of Jerusalem and Jesus of Nazareth* [monograph published as *Forum*, New Series 6, no. 2 (Fall 2003), 137–341] rearranges the furniture on the Titanic but good: the passion narrative turns out to be based on Josephus's account of Jesus ben Ananias (Josephus, *Jewish War* 6.300–9)! This possibility is corroborated in Craig Evans, "Jesus in Non-Christian Sources," in *Studying the Historical Jesus: Evaluations of the State of Current Research,* ed. Bruce Chilton and Craig Evans (Leiden, South Holland: Brill Academic, 1998), 475–77.

19. Krister Stendahl, *The School of St. Matthew and Its Use of the Old Testament* (Philadelphia: Fortress, 1986); Richard Longenecker, *Biblical Exegesis in the Apostolic Period* (Grand Rapids, MI: Eerdmans, 1975), 140–52.

20. 20. B. P. Reardon, ed., *Collected Ancient Greek Novels* (Berkeley: University of California Press, 1989), 29–32 (Chariton, Book 1, Chapters 7–9) and 151–53 (Xenophon, Book 3, Chapters 8–10).

21. Philostratus, *Life of Apollonius of Tyana* 8.12, trans. C. P. Jones, I am not suggesting Luke borrowed the scene from Philostratus or from some earlier source about Apollonius. No, it is just that the one puts the other in a new light: they sound so similar, who's to say Luke is trying to say anything more than Philostratus does?

22. Stephen Fuchs, *Rebellious Prophets: A Study of Messianic Movements in Indian Religions* (New York: Asia Publishing House, 1965), 31, 33, 154, 188, 197, 220.

23. Robert Graves and Joshua Podro, *Jesus in Rome: A Historical Conjecture* (London: Cassell, 1957); J. Duncan and M. Derrett, *The Anastasia: The Resurrection of Jesus as an Historical Event* (Shipston-on-Stour, UK: P. Drinkwater, 1982); Barbara Thiering, *Jesus of the Apocalypse: The Life of Jesus After the Crucifixion* (New York: Doubleday, 1995).

24. See Richard Carrier, "The Plausibility of Theft," in *The Empty Tomb: Jesus beyond the Grave*, ed. Robert M. Price and Jeffery Jay Lowder (Amherst, NY: Prometheus Books, 2005), 358–64.

25. Pilate so describes the brutalized Jesus in Tim Rice, *Jesus Christ Superstar*.

26. See Richard Carrier, "The Burial of Jesus in Light of Jewish Law," Price and Lowder, *The Empty Tomb*, 369–92.

27. Similarly, Matthew's attesting to a widespread report that the body was stolen is evidence it was: see Carrier, "Plausibility of Theft," in Price and Lowder, *The Empty Tomb*, 355–57.

28. Graham Chapman, John Cleese, Terry Gilliam, Eric Idle, Terry Jones, and Michael Palin, *Monty Python's The Life of Brian (of Nazareth)* (New York: Ace, 1979), 99.

29. James M. Robinson, "Jesus from Easter to Valentinus (or to the Apostles Creed)," in *Jesus according to the Earliest Witness*, ed. James M. Robinson (Minneapolis: Fortress, 2007), 38–39.

30. Rudolf Bultmann, *History of the Synoptic Tradition*, trans. John Marsh (New York: Harper and Row, 1972), 259–61.

31. Contrary to contentious but popular modern translations, the text simply reads *kai idontes auton prosekunêsan hoi de edistasan*, "and upon seeing him they worshipped, but they doubted," implying all eleven disciples (the *hoi* of Matt. 28:17 being the same *hoi* of Matt. 28:16, specifically in fact the *hoi endeka mathêtai*, "the eleven disciples").

32. Quoted in Origen, *Contra Celsum*, trans. Henry Chadwick (New York: Cambridge University Press, 1980), 402.

33. Irenaeus, *Against Heresies* 1.23.1, 3.

34. Scott D. Hill, "The Local Hero in Palestine in Comparative Perspective," in *Elijah and Elisha in Socioliterary Perspective*, ed. Robert B. Coote (Atlanta: Scholars Press, 1992), 37–74.

35. Yes, Baal worship! That was the brainchild of the Wildean emperor Heliogabalus; it had already been popular in Roman Syria.

36. Rodney Stark, *The Rise of Christianity: A Sociologist Reconsiders History* (Princeton: Princeton University Press, 1996).

37. Richard Carrier, *Not the Impossible Faith: Why Christianity Didn't Need a Miracle to Succeed* (Raleigh, NC: Lulu, 2009). See Carrier's chapter 2 in the present volume.

38. Leon Festinger, Henry Riecken, and Stanley Schachter, *When Prophecy Fails: A Social and Psychological Study of a Modern Group that Predicted the Destruction of the World* (New York: Harper and Row Torchbooks, 1964).

39. Cognitive dissonance theory is well-established in psychology and has been applied to the origins of Christianity by Adela Collins and others: see Carrier, "Burial of Jesus," 387–88 (with note 55, 392); and Carrier, "Plausibility of Theft," 356–57, for several other examples in the history of religion.

40. Festinger, Riecken, and Schachter, *When Prophecy Fails*, 12.

41. Eric Hoffer, *The True Believer: Thoughts on the Nature of Mass Movements* (New York: Harper and Row, 1951).

CHAPTER 10

1. Quoted in David Quammen, *The Reluctant Mr. Darwin: An Intimate Portrait of Charles Darwin and the Making of His Theory of Evolution* (New York: Atlas Books/Norton, 2006), 245–46.

2. Tertullian, *De Spectaculis* 30, http://www.newadvent.org/fathers/0303.htm, accessed April 19, 2011.

3. Paul Johnson, *A History of Christianity* (New York: Atheneum, 1976), 342.

4. Ibid., 341.

5. James Joyce, *A Portrait of the Artist as a Young Man* (New York: Viking, 1972).

6. Jonathan Edwards, "Sinners in the Hand of an Angry God," http://www.apuritansmind.com/jonathanedwards/JonathanEdwards-Sermons.htm.

7. Johnson, *History of Christianity*, 341.

8. Peter Kreeft and R. K. Tacelli, *Handbook of Christian Apologetics* (Downers Grove, IL: InterVarsity, 1994), 290.

9. Ibid.

10. Rational Christianity, "Hell," http://www.rationalchristianity.net/hell.html, accessed April 19, 2011.

11. *The Catholic Encyclopedia*, "Hell," http://www.newadvent.org/cathen/, accessed April 19, 2011.

12. Various points in this paragraph were inspired by the following remarks from Richard Carrier (personal communication, October 15, 2010), whom I would like to thank for reading a draft of this chapter and making some excellent editorial and substantive suggestions:

> Of course, "infinite authority" is nonsensical. It confuses the word "total" with the word "infinite." God's authority is not "infinite" in any degree, it's just final and complete (and thus by definition *finite*, per the phrase "the buck stops here"). Indeed, the severity of a crime is measured by the amount of harm it does, and surely being infinite and omnipotent God can't be harmed, even in principle, so it doesn't even make sense to say that sinning "against" him causes any harm deserving of any punishment, much less of infinite degree. And God is supposed to be supremely forgiving anyway (otherwise we are superior to him in being more merciful than he), so this idea that he would infinitely punish every crime makes no sense on that account either.

Thanks also to John Beversluis for reading the material on C. S. Lewis and making valuable suggestions.

13. John Beversluis, *C. S. Lewis and the Search for Rational Religion* (Amherst, NY: Prometheus Books, 2007).

14. All quoted material and cited arguments in this rebuttal of C. S. Lewis come from C. S. Lewis, *The Problem of Pain* (New York: Macmillan, 1961), 109–15.

15. Conversely, heaven has many people who did very bad things yet who repented before death. As Eddie Tabash often notes in his debates with religious apologists and theistic philosophers, had Hitler earnestly repented, even he would have made it to heaven. Eddie's mother, on the other hand, an Auschwitz survivor who remained a faithful Jew throughout her life, is presumably in hell.

16. Emma Darwin, Charles's beloved and traditionally pious wife, wrote him an anguished letter about her fears that his loss of faith would mean that they would be separated in the next life. So far as I can tell, traditional Christianity has no answer to Emma Darwin's concern.

17. Dante Alighieri, *The Inferno*, trans. John Ciardi (New York: Signet, 1982), 42.

18. The Athanasian Creed, http://www.ccel.org/creeds/athanasian.creed.html, accessed April 19, 2011.

19. All quoted material and cited arguments in this rebuttal of Jerry Walls come from Jerry L. Walls, *Heaven: The Logic of Eternal Joy* (Oxford: Oxford University Press, 2002), 66, 82, 87.

20. Kreeft and Tacelli, *Christian Apologetics*, 285.

PART 4

CHAPTER 11

1. Francis S. Collins, *The Language of God: A Scientist Presents Evidence for Belief* (New York: Simon & Schuster, 2006).

2. See, for example, John C. Polkinghorne, *The Faith of a Physicist* (Minneapolis: Fortress, 1996); *One World: The Interaction of Science and Theology* (West Conshohocken, PA: Templeton, 2007); *Exploring Reality: The Intertwining of Science and Religion* (New Haven, CT: Yale University Press, 2007); *Quantum Physics and Theology: An Unexpected Kinship* (New Haven, CT: Yale University Press, 2008).

3. Elaine Howard Ecklund, *Science vs. Religion: What Scientists Really Think* (New York: Oxford University Press, 2010).

4. Richard Dawkins, *The God Delusion* (Boston: Houghton Mifflin, 2006).

5. Stephen Jay Gould, *Rock of Ages: Science and Religion in the Fullness of Life* (New York: Ballantine, 1999).

6. Pascal Boyer, *Religion Explained: The Evolutionary Origins of Religious Thought* (New York: Basic, 2001), 94.

7. Émile Durkheim, *The Elementary Forms of the Religious Life* (New York: Free Press, 1965 [1915]), 62.

8. Clifford Geertz, *The Interpretation of Cultures* (New York: Basic, 1973), 90.

9. Mark Pendergrast, *For God, Country, and Coca-Cola: The Unauthorized History of the World's Most Popular Soft Drink* (New York: Charles Scribner's Sons, 1993).

10. E. B. Tylor, *Primitive Culture, Volume I: The Origins of Culture* (New York: Harper and Brothers, 1958 [1871]), 23.

11. Anthony F. C. Wallace, *Religion: An Anthropological View* (New York: Random House, 1966), 52. [Editor's Note: see Dr. Eller's supporting discussion of this definition of religion (and similar difficulties in defining "morality") in David Eller, "Christianity Does Not Provide the Basis for Morality," in *The Christian Delusion*, ed. John Loftus (Amherst, NY: Prometheus Books, 2010), 347–67 (348–50 on defining religion).]

12. Boyer, *Religion Explained*.

13. Scott Atran, *In Gods We Trust: The Evolutionary Landscape of Religion* (Oxford: Oxford University Press, 2002).

14. Stewart Guthrie, *Faces in the Clouds: A New Theory of Religion* (New York: Oxford University Press, 1993).

15. Graham Harvey, *Animism: Respecting the Living World* (New York: Columbia University Press, 2006), xvii.

16. Martin Buber, *I and Thou*, 2nd ed., trans. Ronald Gregor Smith (New York: Charles Scribner's Sons, 1958).

17. Robin Horton, "A Definition of Religion, and Its Uses," *The Journal of the Royal Anthropological Institute of Great Britain and Ireland* 90 (1960): 211.

18. Michael Shermer, *How We Believe: The Search for God in an Age of Science*. (New York: W. H. Freeman and Company, 2000), 129–35.

19. Ian G. Barbour, *Religion and Science: Historical and Contemporary Issues* (New York: HarperCollins Publishers, 1997).

20. Ibid., 98.

21. Massimo Pigliucci, "Science and Religion," *The Skeptic Encyclopedia of Pseudoscience*, ed. Michael Shermer (Santa Barbara, CA: ABC-CLIO, 2002), 443–54.

22. The Discovery Institute can be found at http://www.discovery.org.

23. Hugh Ross and Reasons to Believe can be found at http://www.reasons.org.

24. *Webster's Third New International Dictionary of the English Language Unabridged*, ed. Philip Babcock Gove (Springfield, MA: Merriam-Webster, 1986), s.v. "compatible."

25. Todd Pitock, "Science and Islam," *Discover*, July 2007, 40–41 (see http://discovermagazine.com/2007/jul/science-and-islam/, accessed April 19, 2011).

26. Arun Bala, *The Dialogue of Civilizations in the Birth of Modern Science* (New York: Palgrave Macmillan, 2008), 99.

27. Ibid.

28. Ibid.

29. Thomas Kuhn, *The Structure of Scientific Revolutions*, 2nd ed. (Chicago: University of Chicago Press, 1975).

30. Quoted in Ed L. Miller, ed., *Classical Statements on Faith and Reason* (New York: Random House, 1970), 5.

31. Quoted in Walter Kaufmann, *The Faith of a Heretic* (Garden City, NY: Doubleday, 1961), 75.

CHAPTER 12

1. On Bayes' theorem, see discussion and references in: Richard Carrier, "Bayes' Theorem for Beginners: Formal Logic and Its Relevance to Historical Method," in *Sources of the Jesus Tradition: Separating History from Myth*, ed. R. Joseph Hoffmann (Amherst, NY: Prometheus Books, 2010); and Richard Carrier, *Bayes' Theorem and Historical Method* (tentative title, Amherst, NY: Prometheus Books, 2011).

2. $P(h|e.b) = [P(h|b) \times P(e|h.b)] / [P(e|b)]$, where $P(e|b) = [P(h|b) \times P(e|h.b)] + [P(\sim h|b) \times P(e|\sim h.b)]$.

3. Including: Victor Stenger, *God: The Failed Hypothesis: How Science Shows That God Does Not Exist* (Amherst, NY: Prometheus Books, 2007); and Victor Stenger, *The Comprehensible Cosmos: Where Do the Laws of Physics Come From?* (Amherst, NY: Prometheus Books, 2006); Michael Ikeda and Bill Jefferys, "The Anthropic Principle Does Not Support Supernaturalism," http://www.bayesrules.net/anthropic.html, an earlier version of which appeared in Michael Martin and Ricki Monnier, eds., *The Improbability of God* (Amherst, NY: Prometheus Books, 2006), 150–66; and Elliott Sober, "The Design Argument," http://www.philosophy.wisc.edu/sober/design%20argument%2011%202004.pdf, an earlier version of which appeared in Charles Taliaferro, Paul Draper, and Philip Quinn, eds., *A Companion to Philosophy of Religion* (Cambridge, MA: Wiley-Blackwell, 2004), 117–48. I'll also rely on my previous work: Richard Carrier, "The Argument from Biogenesis: Probabilities against a Natural Origin of Life," *Biology and Philosophy* 19, no. 5 (November 2004): 739–64; and Richard Carrier, "Statistics and Biogenesis," May 1, 2009 at richardcarrier.blogspot.com/2009/05/statistics-biogenesis_01.html; and *Sense and Goodness without God: A Defense of Metaphysical Naturalism* (Bloomington, IN: AuthorHouse, 2005), 71–95, 165–76; and "Naturalism vs. Theism: The Carrier-Wanchick Debate," the Secular Web, 2006, at http://www.infidels.org/library/modern/richard_carrier/carrier-wanchick.

4. In other words, I will assume $P(God|NID) \to 1$.

5. So if $P(God|NID) = 1$, then $P(NID|e.b) = P(God|e.b)$.

6. In other words, $P(NID|b) \to 0$. In William Dembski, *No Free Lunch: Why Specified Complexity Cannot Be Purchased without Intelligence* (Lanham, MD: Rowman and Littlefield, 2002) (much of which is more correct than his critics gave him credit, though not all: see http://www.talkorigins.org/design/faqs/nfl) a reasonable case is made for this prior being around 1 in 10^{150} (which is indeed quite near zero), at least for events inside our known universe (see notes 13 and 31).

7. In other words, it cannot be the case that $P(NID|b) > 25$ percent.

8. Note that I have selected this maximum prior of 0.25 for an additional reason: because no higher prior can be developed even by pure logic (i.e., assuming no information exists in *b* other than bare propositions and logic). Given such zero knowledge there would be no more than a 50-50 chance any self-existent god exists, and a 50–50 chance such a god would be an intelligently designing god (as opposed to one who was not), and $0.5 \times 0.5 = 0.25$, which is therefore the maximum possible probability God can have prior to considering any evidence for or against his existence. This does mean, by the way, that the vast absence of confirmed divine activity that I just surveyed (i.e., the zero frequency of such verified causes in human observation so far) is in this sense evidence "against" God's existence, meaning not contradictory to his existence but lowering its probability. This is precisely because the vast *presence* of divine activity would

have been evidence *for* his existence, greatly *increasing* its probability; therefore not having that evidence must necessarily reduce that probability by exactly as much as having that evidence would increase it.

9. If $P(NID|b) = 0.25$, then $P(\sim NID|b) = 0.75$. Formally, given my prior definitions, no one can rationally deny that $P(God|b) \leq 0.25$ and therefore that $P(\sim God|b) \geq 0.75$. That the infrequency of NID entails the same improbability that God even exists follows from my definition of God as a God that entails NID. Accordingly, if God intelligently did only one thing ever (which would entail $P(God|b) = 1/\text{EVERY-}$ THING), it would be exceedingly hard to ever know he existed. That "one thing" would have to be less likely (than 1/EVERYTHING) on any other explanation before we could be sure it actually was God who did it. Whereas if God did many intelligent things that we all observed, which were each or together very improbable on any other explanation, then their cumulative improbability could eventually exceed any countermanding prior. Hence, with enough evidence we would be warranted in believing there was a God (I give many examples in Carrier, *Sense and Goodness*, 222–23, 257, 273–82). Of course, the difficulty of distinguishing God from 'god' (a *not*-self-existent being, who thus only looks like a god but isn't really) still intervenes. But solving that problem is the theist's burden, not mine (as here I'm just generously assuming that that obstacle doesn't exist).

10. The literature summarizing this evidence is vast beyond imagining, but the very best primers include: Richard Dawkins, *The Greatest Show on Earth: The Evidence for Evolution* (New York: Free Press, 2009); Jerry Coyne, *Why Evolution Is True* (New York: Viking, 2009); Neil Shubin, *Your Inner Fish: A Journey into the 3.5 Billion-Year History of the Human Body* (New York: Pantheon, 2008); Donald Prothero, *Evolution: What the Fossils Say and Why It Matters* (New York: Columbia University Press, 2007); Sean Carroll, *The Making of the Fittest: DNA and the Ultimate Forensic Record of Evolution* (New York: W. W. Norton, 2006); Marc Kirschner and John Gerhart, *The Plausibility of Life: Resolving Darwin's Dilemma* (New Haven, CT: Yale University Press, 2005); and Ernst Mayr, *What Evolution Is* (New York: Basic, 2001). See also discussion and sources in Carrier, *Sense and Goodness*, 165–76.

11. See discussion and references in Dembski, *No Free Lunch*, 239–310. There is of course a vast literature on Behe's argument, which argument has been shown to be wrong on almost every single particular (cf. http://www.talkorigins.org/faqs/behe .html), but Dembski's treatment is sufficient to illustrate Behe's argument, which has not significantly changed.

12. Conceded in Michael Behe, *The Edge of Evolution: The Search for the Limits of Darwinism* (New York: Free Press, 2007).

13. Dembski argues in *No Free Lunch* that any single mutation involving more than five hundred bits of specified information is effectively impossible as a result of

chance (having a probability on a hypothesis of chance less than 1 in 10^{150}), but that any mutation involving a gain in information *less* than that *is* possible as a result of chance and in fact certainly happens (see 18–22, 161, and 314–21; see also 246 and 306, note 57, and cf. 218–19). To date no one has ever found any feature of any life-form on earth that required any mutation involving more than even fifty bits of new specified information, much less five hundred. Every evolutionary theory of every feature of every life-form so far studied posits only individual stepwise advances far smaller than that. Thus there is no evidence of irreducible complexity nor any established need of such a theory to explain any feature of modern life.

14. P(NID|CURRENT LIFE.b) = [P(NID|b) × P(CURRENT LIFE|NID.b)] / [P(NID|b) × P(CURRENT LIFE|NID.b)] + [P(EVOLUTION|b) × P(CURRENT LIFE| EVOLUTION.b)] = [0.25 × 0.5] / [0.25 × 0.5] + [0.75 × 1.0] = 0.125 / (0.125 + 0.75) = 0.125 / 0.875 = 0.143 (rounded) = 14.3 percent, which is less than 15 percent.

15. See Carrier, "Argument from Biogenesis" and "Statistics and Biogenesis" (cited in note 3).

16. See extensive analysis of this point in: Nicholas Everitt, *The Non-Existence of God* (New York: Routledge, 2003), 213–26; and John Loftus, *Why I Became an Atheist: A Former Preacher Rejects Christianity* (Amherst, NY: Prometheus Books, 2008), 95–110.

17. P(NID|ORIGIN OF LIFE.b) = [P(NID|b) × P(ORIGIN OF LIFE|NID.b)] / [P(NID|b) × P(ORIGIN OF LIFE|NID.b)] + [P(~NID|b) × P(ORIGIN OF LIFE| ~NID.b)] = [0.25 × 0.5] / [0.25 × 0.5] + [0.75 × 1.0] = 0.125 / (0.125 + 0.75) = 0.125 / 0.875 = 0.143 (rounded) = 14.3 percent, which is less than 15 percent.

18. For the latest and most extensive presentation of this argument see: Robin Collins, "The Teleological Argument: An Exploration of the Fine-Tuning of the Universe," in *The Blackwell Companion to Natural Theology*, ed. William Lane Craig and J. P. Moreland (Oxford: Wiley-Blackwell, 2009), 202–81.

19. I will not address the factual flaws in Collins's paper, many of which are dispatched by Stenger (see note 3). Collins attempts to respond (222–24), but a comparison of what Stenger actually says with Collins's criticisms reveals a shocking panoply of odd blindspots in Collins's analysis. Collins also ignores other recent findings, for example, Fred Adams, "Stars in Other Universes: Stellar Structure with Different Fundamental Constants," *Journal of Cosmology and Astroparticle Physics* 8 (August 2008). Stenger will refute Collins in more detail in his forthcoming book *The Fallacy of Fine-Tuning: Why the Universe Is Not Designed for Us* (Amherst, NY: Prometheus Books, 2011).

20. Even though that hypothesis has an extremely high prior probability: in our background knowledge *b* we have no knowledge of any law of physics that would prevent there being other universes (and no means of seeing if there are none), so the probability that there are is exactly what that probability would be if the number of

universes that exist were selected at random. Of all the possible conditions that could obtain (no universe; just one universe; two universes; three; four; etc., all the way to infinitely many universes), that there would be only one universe is only one out of infinitely many alternatives. This entails it is effectively 100 percent certain an infinite multiverse exists because the probability of there being only one universe is then $1/\text{INFINITY}$, which is ≈ 0 percent. In fact, for any finite number n of universes, the probability of having only that many or less is $n/\text{INFINITY}$, which is still ≈ 0 percent. If the probability of having any finite number of universes is always ≈ 0 percent, then the probability that there is an infinite multiverse is ≈ 100 percent. This further entails we have no need to explain why there is something rather than nothing: as then nothing (a state of exactly zero universes) also has a probability of $1/\text{INFINITY}$, which is again ≈ 0 percent. The probability that there will be something rather than nothing is therefore ≈ 100 percent. This conclusion can only be averted if something were proved to exist that would change any of these probabilities, thereby making nothing (or only one thing) more likely than any other logical possibility. But we know of no such thing. Therefore, so far as we must conclude given what we actually know, there is an infinite multiverse, and there must necessarily be an infinite multiverse (both to a certainty of ≈ 100 percent). This already entails that $P(\text{LIFE-BEARING UNIVERSE}|\sim\text{NID.b}) \approx 100$ percent. But we don't need this hypothesis, so I will proceed without it.

21. All of this is formally proven, and in fully decisive detail, by Ikeda and Jefferys and by Sober (see note 3).

22. In other words, $P(\text{FINELY TUNED UNIVERSE}|\text{INTELLIGENT OBSERVERS EXIST}) = 1$, so if "intelligent observers exist" is established background knowledge (and it is), then $P(\text{FINELY TUNED UNIVERSE}|\sim\text{NID.b}) = 1$ (see following note).

23. This is undeniable: if only a finely tuned universe can produce life, then by definition $P(\text{FINELY TUNED UNIVERSE}|\text{INTELLIGENT OBSERVERS EXIST}) = 1$, because of (a) the logical fact that "if and only if A, then B" entails "if B, then A" (hence "if and only if a finely tuned universe, then intelligent observers" entails "if intelligent observers, then a finely tuned universe," which is strict entailment, hence true *regardless* of how that fine-tuning came about; by analogy with "if and only if colors exist, then orange is a color" entails "if orange is a color, then colors exist"; note that this is not the fallacy of affirming the consequent because it properly derives from a biconditional), and because of (b) the fact in conditional probability that $P(\text{INTELLIGENT OBSERVERS EXIST}) = 1$ (the probability that we are mistaken about intelligent observers existing is zero, à la Descartes, therefore the probability that they exist is 100 percent) and $P(A \text{ and } B) = P(A|B) \times P(B)$, and $1 \times 1 = 1$. Collins concedes that if we include in b "everything we know about the world, including our existence," then $P(\text{L}|\sim\text{God \&}$ A LIFE-BEARING UNIVERSE IS OBSERVED$) = 100$ percent (Collins, "The Teleological Argument," 207). He thus desperately needs to somehow "not count" such known

facts. That's irrational, and he ought to know it's irrational. He tries anyway (e.g., 241–44), by putting "a life-bearing universe is observed" (his LPU) in e instead of b. But then b still contains "observers exist," which still entails "a life-bearing universe exists," and anything entailed by a 100 percent probability has itself a probability of 100 percent (as proven above). In other words, since the probability of observing ~LPU if ~LPU is zero (since if ~LPU, observers won't exist), it can never be the case that $P(\text{LPU}|\text{~God.b}) < 100$ percent as Collins claims (on 207), because if the probability of ~LPU is zero the probability of LPU is 1 (being the converse), and b contains "observers exist," which entails the probability of ~LPU is zero. If (in even greater desperation) Collins tried putting "observers exist" in e, b would then contain the Cartesian fact "I think, therefore I am," which then entails e. So we're back at 100 percent again. If (in even *greater* desperation) Collins tried putting "I think, therefore I am" in e, his conclusion would only be true for people who aren't observers (since b then contains no observers), and since the probability of there being people who aren't observers is zero, his calculation would be irrelevant (it would be true only for people who don't exist, i.e., any conclusion that is conditional on "there are no observers" is of no interest to observers).

24. See Peter Ward and Donald Brownlee, *Rare Earth: Why Complex Life Is Uncommon in the Universe* (New York: Copernicus, 2000).

25. John Hawley and Katherine Holcomb, *Foundations of Modern Cosmology*, 2nd ed. (Oxford: Oxford University Press, 2005), 158. The factor calculation is mine, based on the fact that Aristotle's cosmos was inhabitable (and inhabited) throughout and thus had a habitability of one part in one, but our universe has a habitability of less than one part in 10^{30} (the volume of the intergalactic void in ratio to the maximum possible volume of planets in an average galaxy summed for all galaxies).

26. Of course, a *compassionate* God would imply even *more* should be the case about the world he would make (see Carrier, *Sense and Goodness*, 273–75 and 256–57). This means it would be even more improbable that we would observe the world we do if a compassionate God exists, in fact $P(\text{THE WORLD WE OBSERVE}|\text{COMPASSIONATE GOD.b})$ must be quite low indeed, whereas $P(\text{THE WORLD WE OBSERVE}|\text{~GOD.b})$ is effectively 100 percent. Both conclusions follow with even more force when considering easily removable evils (ibid., 277–89), but one needn't even consider those to get this larger differential.

27. In other words, $P(\text{L}|\text{~GOD \& OBSERVERS EXIST}) = 1$ (i.e., 1 in 1, not 1 in $10^{1,000,000}$), unless it's not true that "~GOD & OBSERVERS EXIST" only if L, but how else could life exist if there is no God? If there is no God, then life exists only if L (or whatever improbability actually *is* the case, but substituting any L_n for L gives the same result).

28. In other words, even at most, $P(\text{L}|\text{GOD \& OBSERVERS EXIST}) = 1$, the exact same probability you get if ~GOD.

29. P(NID|FINE-TUNED UNIVERSE.b) = [P(NID|b) × P(FINE-TUNED UNI-VERSE|NID.b)] / [P(NID|b) × P(FINE-TUNED UNIVERSE|NID.b)] + [P(~NID|b) × P(FINE-TUNED UNIVERSE|~NID.b)] = [0.25 × 1.0] / [0.25 × 1.0] + [0.75 × 1.0] = 0.25 / (0.25 + 0.75) = 0.25 / 1.0 = 0.25 = 25 percent.

30. Collins, "The Teleological Argument," 276–77; Sober, "The Design Argument," 137–40.

31. At this point one might try to argue that the *prior probability* (for the universe case) should be based this time on a narrower reference class of "super improbable" events, such as the set of all things William Dembski quantifies with his probability threshold of 1 in 10^{150} (see notes 6 and 13 above), based on the assumption that the ratio of designed-to-chance causes *within that set* should strongly favor design. But even if this could get us to any actual ratio of NID to ~NID (see discussion of prior probability earlier on why, for lack of data, it probably can't), it is still inapplicable to the universe's *origin* because that threshold was based on the size and age of the universe *itself*. We are talking about an event beyond that limiting sphere, and thus must calculate a threshold relative to a larger total set of opportunities, which is precisely what we don't know anything about. For instance, if the universe in some form will continue to exist for $10^{1,000,000}$ years, then it could easily contain an event as improbable, and that event would as likely be its origin as anything else. In fact, since quantum mechanics entails that a big bang of any size and initial entropy always has some (albeit absurdly small) probability of spontaneously occurring at any time, and since on any long enough timeline any nonzero probability approaches 100 percent no matter how singularly improbable, it could easily be that this has been going on for untold ages, our big bang merely being just one late in the chain. We could be at year $10^{1,000,000}$ right now, and as this conclusion follows from established facts and there is no known fact to contradict it, it's no more unlikely than the existence of a god (and arguably a great deal more likely). Since we therefore don't know what the applicable probability threshold is, we can't use one (other than by circular logic). To infer design we simply need the result to have features more expected on design than chance, and features that are necessary for observers even to exist will never be such (because those features will appear in both outcomes 100 percent of the time). Dembski's threshold may pertain to events now *in* the universe, however, precisely because those outcomes are *not* necessary. For example, if the total probability of terrestrial biogenesis were 1 in $10^{1,000,000}$ every fourteen billion years, then we would expect to find ourselves much later in the history of the universe—it would not necessarily be the case that we would observe ourselves only fourteen billion years after the big bang; whereas it *would* necessarily be the case that the universe came to exist with the right properties for us to be observing it at all. Hence the two problems are not commensurate.

32. Note that P(e|b) in this case equals 1 for both *h* (DESIGN) and ~*h* (CHANCE)

because $P(\sim e|b) = 0$ for both h and $\sim h$ (i.e., you can only ever observe instances of survival, as otherwise you will be dead). On why this matters, see following note.

33. These scenarios differ from the poker analogy, in which less amazing outcomes *can* be observed (unlike with the strange bullet machine or the universe: see previous note), thus the previously stipulated rate of amazing hands being rigged of 1 in 1,000 entails a prior probability of rigged hands equal to 1 in 100,000,000, when "amazing hand" is defined as having a probability of 1 in 100,000 absent design. By analogy, if 1 in 4 life-bearing universes (and no lifeless universes) are designed, and all others are the products of chance, then if fine-tuning had a probability of 1 in 100,000 absent design, then the prior probability of *design* is necessarily equal to 1 in 400,000 universes (of course if the probability of fine-tuning is less, then this prior probability is likewise less, in direct proportion). Since most of those 400,000 universes are lifeless (and thus we would never have observed ourselves being in one), *that* prior probability is not applicable to our calculation—instead, the only relevant prior probability is the original 1 in 4 (because our only applicable reference class is life-bearing universes, since our probability of seeing any of the others is zero).

34. P(NID|OBSERVED UNIVERSE.b) = [P(NID|b) × P(OBSERVED UNIVERSE| NID.b)] / [P(NID|b) × P(OBSERVED UNIVERSE|NID.b)] + [P(~NID|b) × P(OBSERVED UNIVERSE|~NID.b)] = [0.25 × 0.5] / [0.25 × 0.5] + [0.75 × 1.0] = 0.125 / (0.125 + 0.75) = 0.125 / 0.875 = 0.143 (rounded) = 14.3 percent, which is less than 15 percent.

35. In addition to the summary provided in Carrier, *Sense and Goodness*, 135–57 (and the next chapter by Victor Stenger, "Life after Death: Examining the Evidence"), see: V. S. Ramachandran, *A Brief Tour of Human Consciousness: From Impostor Poodles to Purple Numbers* (New York: Pi Press, 2004), *Encyclopedia of the Human Brain* (San Diego: Academic, 2002), and *Phantoms in the Brain: Probing the Mysteries of the Human Mind* (New York: William Morrow, 1998); Stanislas Dehaene, *Reading in the Brain: The Science and Evolution of a Human Invention* (New York: Viking, 2009) and *The Number Sense* (New York: Oxford University Press, 1999); Gary Marcus, *Kluge: The Haphazard Construction of the Human Mind* (Boston: Houghton Mifflin, 2008); David Linden, *The Accidental Mind: How Brain Evolution Has Given Us Love, Memory, Dreams, and God* (London: Belknap, 2008); Cordelia Fine, *A Mind of Its Own: How Your Brain Distorts and Deceives* (New York: W. W. Norton, 2006); Keith Devlin, *The Math Instinct: Why You're a Mathematical Genius (Along with Lobsters, Birds, Cats, and Dogs)* (New York: Thunder's Mouth, 2005); Gerald Edelman, *Wider than the Sky: The Phenomenal Gift of Consciousness* (New Haven, CT: Yale University Press, 2004); Steven Johnson, *Mind Wide Open: Your Brain and the Neuroscience of Everyday Life* (New York: Scribner, 2004); Jeff Hawkins and Sandra Blakeslee, *On Intelligence: How a New Understanding of the Brain Will Lead to the Creation of Truly*

Intelligent Machines (New York: Owl, 2005); Christof Koch, *The Quest for Consciousness: A Neurobiological Approach* (Denver: Roberts, 2004); Susan Blackmore, *Consciousness: An Introduction* (New York: Oxford University Press, 2004); Joseph Ledoux, *Synaptic Self: How Our Brains Become Who We Are* (New York: Viking, 2002); John Ratey, *A User's Guide to the Brain: Perception, Attention and the Four Theaters of the Brain* (New York: Pantheon, 2001); Bernard Baars and James Newman, eds., *Essential Sources in the Scientific Study of Consciousness* (Cambridge, MA: MIT Press, 2003); Gerald Woerlee, *Mortal Minds: A Biology of the Soul and the Dying Experience* (Utrecht: De Tijdstroom, 2003); Frederick Schiffer, *Of Two Minds: The Revolutionary Science of Dual-Brain Psychology* (New York: Free Press, 1998); Oliver Sacks, *The Man Who Mistook His Wife for a Hat, and Other Clinical Tales* (New York: Summit, 1985). I could go on.

36. For summary of this and other evidence, see Carrier, *Sense and Goodness*, 150–60.

37. In other words, $P(\text{OUR BRAIN-BASED MIND}|\sim\text{NID}.b) = 1$ (= 100 percent), whereas $P(\text{OUR BRAIN-BASED MIND}|\text{NID}.b) \leq 0.5$.

38. $P(\text{NID}|\text{OUR BRAIN-BASED MIND}.b) = [P(\text{NID}|b) \times P(\text{OUR BRAIN-BASED MIND}|\text{NID}.b)] / [P(\text{NID}|b) \times P(\text{OUR BRAIN-BASED MIND}|\text{NID}.b)] + [P(\sim\text{NID}|b) \times P(\text{OUR BRAIN-BASED MIND}|\sim\text{NID}.b)] = [0.25 \times 0.5] / [0.25 \times 0.5] + [0.75 \times 1.0] = 0.125 / (0.125 + 0.75) = 0.125 / 0.875 = 0.143$ (rounded) = 14.3 percent, which is less than 15 percent. On whether such naturally evolved brains can be expected to be able to reason, see following discussion of the argument from intelligibility (and with it note 47).

39. Contrary to the argument in J. P. Moreland, "The Argument from Consciousness," in *The Blackwell Companion to Natural Theology*, ed. W. L. Craig and J. P. Moreland (Oxford: Wiley-Blackwell, 2009), 282–343.

40. In which case, $P(\text{QUALIA}|\sim\text{NID}.b) = 1$.

41. See Carrier, *Sense and Goodness*, 146–48, esp. with Allin Cottrell's "Sniffing the Camembert: On the Conceivability of Zombies," *Journal of Consciousness Studies* 6.1 (1999): 4–12. Moreland illogically considers scientific naturalism the only alternative to NID as if Taoism and other godless supernaturalisms were impossible, but even on scientific naturalism alone we do not know what $P(\text{QUALIA}|\sim\text{NID}.b)$ is.

42. See note 46 (and references in note 35).

43. In other words, $P(\text{QUALIA}|\sim\text{NID}.b) = 0.5$.

44. In other words, either $P(\text{NID \& QUALIA}|b) = 0.25 \times 0.5 = 0.125$ (to account for the prior probability of other gods existing instead of the one particular kind of God we are presuming) or $P(\text{QUALIA}|\text{NID}.b) = 0.5$ (since we don't have confirmed knowledge of god's nature or desires in this respect) and 0.25 (our generic prior probability) $\times 0.5 = 0.125$.

45. $P(\text{NID}|\text{QUALIA}.b) = [P(\text{NID}|b) \times P(\text{QUALIA}|\text{NID}.b)] / [P(\text{NID}|b) \times P(\text{QUALIA}|\text{NID}.b)] + [P(\sim\text{NID}|b) \times P(\text{QUALIA}|\sim\text{NID}.b)]$ = at best either $\{[0.25 \times 0.5] / [0.25 \times 0.5] + [0.75 \times 0.5] = 0.125 / (0.125 + 0.375) = 0.125 / 0.5 = 0.25\}$ or $\{[0.125 \times 1] / [0.125 \times 1] + [0.75 \times 0.5] = 0.125 / (0.125 + 0.375) = 0.125 / 0.5 = 0.25\}$, hence the same either way (which is simply the prior probability of NID).

46. See Carrier, *Sense and Goodness*, 349–66. Also: Paul Bloom, *How Pleasure Works: The New Science of Why We Like What We Like* (New York: W. W. Norton, 2010); Daniel Levitin, *This Is Your Brain on Music: The Science of a Human Obsession* (New York: Dutton, 2006) and Oliver Sacks, *Musicophilia* (New York: Alfred A. Knopf, 2007); Rachel Herz, *The Scent of Desire: Discovering Our Enigmatic Sense of Smell* (New York: William Morrow, 2007); Robert Provine, *Laughter: A Scientific Investigation* (New York: Viking, 2000); Stephen Palmer, *Vision Science: Photons to Phenomenology* (Cambridge, MA: MIT Press, 1999); and the relevant sections of the *Skeptical Inquirer* 30, no. 6 (November–December 2006).

47. See Carrier, *Sense and Goodness*, 177–208, along with Richard Carrier, "Critical Review of Victor Reppert's Defense of the Argument from Reason," *Secular Web*, 2004, at http://www.infidels.org/library/modern/richard_carrier/reppert.html, as well as "Our Mathematical Universe" (October 5, 2007) at http://richardcarrier .blogspot.com/2007/10/our-mathematical-universe.html, and "Fundamental Flaws in Mark Steiner's Challenge to Naturalism in *The Applicability of Mathematics as a Philosophical Problem*," *Secular Web*, 2003, at http://www.infidels.org/library/modern/ richard_carrier/steiner.html. These together constitute a refutation of Victor Reppert, "The Argument from Reason," in Craig and Moreland, *The Blackwell Companion to Natural Theology*, 344–90 (as well as refuting the related claim that the "applicability" of mathematics in describing the universe entails NID—languages are designed *by us* to be applicable to the universe, not the other way around).

48. Therefore, in other words, $P(\text{ACTUAL INTELLIGIBILITY}|\sim\text{NID}.b) = 1$ but $P(\text{ACTUAL INTELLIGIBILITY}|\text{NID}.b) \leq 0.50$.

49. $P(\text{NID}|\text{ACTUAL INTELLIGIBILITY}.b) = [P(\text{NID}|b) \times P(\text{ACTUAL INTELLIGIBILITY}|\text{NID}.b)] / [P(\text{NID}|b) \times P(\text{ACTUAL INTELLIGIBILITY}|\text{NID}.b)] + [P(\sim\text{NID}|b) \times P(\text{ACTUAL INTELLIGIBILITY}|\sim\text{NID}.b)] = [0.25 \times 0.5] / [0.25 \times 0.5] + [0.75 \times 1.0] = 0.125 / (0.125 + 0.75) = 0.125 / 0.875 = 0.143$ (rounded) = 14.3 percent, which is less than 15 percent.

50. I needn't prove how making excuses for why the evidence doesn't conform to expectation on NID makes no mathematical difference to this conclusion: any such tactic halves the prior probability or more (thus losing all the ground the excuse was supposed to gain). At best, all the excuses in the world can only ever get $P(e|\text{NID}.b)$ up to 100 percent, which leaves every conclusion at 25 percent—still not enough to make NID probable. Collins demonstrates these points himself: cf. "The Teleological Argument," 206 (Groodal example) and 209–11 (ad hoc theory enhancement).

CHAPTER 13

1. Dinesh D'Souza, *What's So Great about Christianity* (Washington, DC: Regnery, 2007).

2. Dinesh D'Souza, *Life After Death: The Evidence* (Washington, DC: Regenery, 2009).

3. Ibid., 18.

4. Ibid., 17.

5. Ibid., 22–23.

6. See scholarship and examples cited in Paul Tobin, "The Bible and Modern Scholarship," in *The Christian Delusion*, ed. John Loftus (Amherst, NY: Prometheus Books, 2010), 148–80; and Hector Avalos, "Why Biblical Studies Must End," chapter 4 in the present book.

7. D'Souza, *Life After Death*, 24.

8. Francis Crick, *The Astonishing Hypothesis: The Scientific Search for the Soul* (New York: Scribner Maxwell Macmillan International, 1994), 258.

9. D'Souza, *Life After Death*, 24.

10. Ibid.

11. Victor J. Stenger, *Physics and Psychics: The Search for a World beyond the Senses* (Amherst, NY: Prometheus Books, 1995), 150–59.

12. D'Souza, *Life After Death*, 25.

13. Ibid., 27.

14. Ibid., 37–38.

15. Ibid., 18, 36.

16. Alan F. Segal, *Life After Death: A History of the Afterlife in the Religions of the West* (New York: Doubleday, 2004).

17. D'Souza, *Life After Death*, 42.

18. Most experts agree the pagan Zoroastrians introduced this idea to the Jews. See Segal, *Life After Death*, 173–203; and discussion and sources in Richard Carrier, *Not the Impossible Faith: Why Christianity Didn't Need a Miracle to Succeed* (Raleigh, NC: Lulu, 2009), 85–86, 90–99.

19. D'Souza, *Life After Death*, 46.

20. Ibid., 47–48.

21. Ibid., 48.

22. Ibid., 51.

23. Ibid., 50–51.

24. Ibid., 51.

25. Ibid.

26. See my discussion of ancient Eastern thinking in Victor Stenger, *The New*

Atheism: Taking a Stand for Science and Reason (Amherst, NY: Prometheus Books, 2009), 201–10.

27. See: J. M. Bering, "The Folk Psychology of Souls," *Behavioral and Brain Sciences* 29 (2006): 453–98; Paul Bloom, *Descartes' Baby: How the Science of Child Development Explains What Makes Us Human* (New York: Basic, 2004), 189–229.

28. Stenger, *Physics and Psychics*; and Victor Stenger, *Has Science Found God? The Latest Results in the Search for Purpose in the Universe* (Amherst, NY: Prometheus Books, 2003), 276–305.

29. It's also probably unacceptable in any science: Tom Siegfried, "Odds Are, It's Wrong: Science Fails to Face the Shortcomings of Statistics," *Science News* 177, no. 7 (March 27, 2010): 26–29.

30. Dean I. Radin, *The Conscious Universe: The Scientific Truth of Psychic Phenomena* (New York: HarperEdge, 1997).

31. I. J. Good, "Where Has the Billion Trillion Gone?" *Nature* 389, no. 6653 (1997): 806–807; Douglas M. Stokes, "The Shrinking Filedrawer: On the Validity of Statistical Meta-Analysis in Parapsychology," *Skeptical Inquirer* 35, no. 3 (2001): 22–25.

32. Morey Bernstein, *The Search for Bridey Murphy* (Garden City, NY: Doubleday, 1956).

33. Terence Hines, *Pseudoscience and the Paranormal: A Critical Examination of the Evidence* (Amherst, NY: Prometheus Books, 1988); Martin Gardner, *Fads and Fallacies in the Name of Science* (New York: Dover, 1957); James Alcock, "Psychology and Near-Death Experiences," *Skeptical Inquirer* 3, no. 3 (1978): 25–41.

34. Deepak Chopra, *Life After Death: The Burden of Proof* (New York: Harmony Books, 2006), 72–73.

35. Ian Stevenson, *Twenty Cases Suggestive of Reincarnation*, 2nd ed. (Charlottesville: University Press of Virginia, 1974).

36. Leonard Angel, "Reincarnation and Biology (Book Review)," *Skeptic* 9, no. 3 (2002): 86–90. (A review of Ian Stevenson, *Reincarnation and Biology: A Contribution to the Etiology of Birthmarks and Birth Defects* (Westport, CT: Praeger, 1997).)

37. D'Souza, *Life After Death*, 60.

38. Paul Edwards, *Reincarnation: A Critical Examination* (Amherst, NY: Prometheus Books, 2002).

39. Janice Minor Holden, Bruce Greyson, and Debbie James, eds. *The Handbook of Near-Death Experiences: Thirty Years of Investigation* (Santa Barbara, CA: Praeger, 2009), 1–16.

40. Raymond A. Moody, *Life After Life: The Investigation of a Phenomenon—Survival of Bodily Death* (Harrisburg, PA: Stackpole, 1976).

41. Susan J. Blackmore, *Dying to Live: Near-Death Experiences* (Amherst, NY: Prometheus Books, 1993).

42. Gerald Woerlee, *Mortal Minds: The Biology of Near Death Experiences* (Amherst, NY: Prometheus Books, 2003).

43. Holden, Greyson, and James, *Handbook of Near-Death Experiences*, 16.

44. Ibid., 27.

45. Ibid., 186.

46. Ibid.

47. Ibid., 209.

48. Ibid., 210.

49. D'Souza, *Life After Death*, 64.

50. Kimberly Clark, "Clinical Interventions with NDEs," in Bruce Greyson and Charles P. Flynn, eds., *The Near-Death Experience: Problems, Prospects, Perspectives* (Springfield, IL: C. C. Thomas, 1984), 242–55.

51. Hayden Ebbern, Sean Mulligan, and Barry Beyerstein, "Maria's Near-Death Experience: Waiting for the Other Shoe to Drop," *Skeptical Inquirer* 20, no. 4 (1996): 27–33. See discussion of this incident and these claims by Keith Augustine and others in the *Journal of Near-Death Studies* 25, no. 1, and 26, nos. 1 and 2 (see note 62).

52. Stenger, *Has Science Found God?* 297.

53. Jeffrey P. Bishop and Victor J. Stenger, "Retroactive Prayer: Lots of History, Not Much Mystery, No Science," *British Medical Journal* 329 (2004): 1444–46.

54. Larry Dossey, *Recovering the Soul: A Scientific and Spiritual Search* (New York: Bantam, 1989).

55. Kenneth Ring and Sharon Cooper, *Mindsight: Near-Death and Out-of-Body Experiences in the Blind* (Palo Alto, CA: William James Center for Consciousness Studies, 1999).

56. Blackmore, *Dying to Live*, 131–32.

57. Ring and Cooper, *Mindsight*, 9.

58. Jeffrey Long and Paul Perry, *Evidence of the Afterlife: The Science of Near-Death Experiences* (New York: HarperCollins, 2010).

59. Ibid., 44.

60. Mark Fox, *Religion, Spirituality and the Near-Death Experience* (New York: Routledge, 2003).

61. Internet Infidels (accessed December 11, 2009).

62. Keith Augustine, "Does Paranormal Perception Occur in Near-Death Experiences?" *Journal of Near-Death Studies* 25, no. 4 (2007): 203–36; "Near-Death Experiences with Hallucinatory Features," *Journal of Near-Death Studies* 26, no. 1 (2007): 3–31; "Psychophysiological and Cultural Correlates Undermining a Survivalist Interpretation of Near-Death Experiences," *Journal of Near-Death Studies* 26, no. 2 (2007): 89–125. See the papers following in each volume, which present criticisms and Augustine's responses to them.

63. Keith Augustine, "Halluncinatory Near-Death Experiences," *Secular Web*, http://www.infidels.org/library/modern/keith_augustine/HNDEs.html (accessed December 7, 2009).

64. Dannion Brinkley and Paul Perry, *Saved By the Light: The True Story of a Man Who Died Twice and the Profound Revelations He Received* (New York: Villard, 1994).

65. *Wikipedia* (accessed December 9, 2009).

66. D'Souza, *Life After Death*, 167.

67. Ibid.

68. Ibid., 168.

69. Ibid., 171.

70. Ibid., 172.

71. Ruth Miller, Larry S. Miller, and Mary R. Langenbrunner, "Religiosity and Child Sexual Abuse: A Risk Factor Assessment," *Journal of Child Sexual Abuse* 6, issue 4 (1997): 14–34; Michael Franklin and Marian Hetherly, "How Fundamentalism Affects Society," *Humanist* 57 (September–October 1997): 25. And there may be other evidence supporting this conclusion: see Richard Carrier's next chapter on morality in the present volume.

72. D'Souza, *Life After Death*, 172.

73. Many other pressures will have had the same effect (e.g., sexual selection; differential advantages of cooperating over noncooperating groups; etc.). See recent surveys of the evidence in Walter Sinnott-Armstrong, ed., *Moral Psychology, Volume 1: The Evolution of Morality: Adaptations and Innateness* (Cambridge, MA: MIT Press, 2008).

74. Richard Dawkins, *The Selfish Gene* (New York: Oxford University Press, 1976).

75. Robert Trivers, "The Evolution of Reciprocal Altruism," *Quarterly Review of Biology* 46 (1971): 35–57.

76. D'Souza, *Life After Death*, 176.

77. Ibid., 177.

78. Michael Shermer, *The Science of Good and Evil: Why People Cheat, Gossip, Care, Share, and Follow the Golden Rule* (New York: Times Books, 2004), 235–36. See related discussion and notes in Richard Carrier's next chapter, "Moral Facts."

79. Dawkins, *The Selfish Gene*, 3, 201.

80. D'Souza, *Life After Death*, 181.

81. Ibid., 195.

82. Ibid., 199.

83. Ibid., 204.

84. Ibid.

85. Ibid., 203.

86. Ibid., 206.

87. Friedrich Nietzsche, *Twilight of the Idols* (New York: Penguin, 1990), 80–81.

88. D'Souza, *Life After Death*, 208.

89. Shermer, *Science of Good and Evil*, 25–26. For a thorough survey of the history and cross-cultural evidence for this, see Jeffrey Wattles, *The Golden Rule* (New York: Oxford University Press, 1996); see also David Eller, "Christianity Does Not Provide the Basis for Morality," in Loftus, *The Christian Delusion*, 347–67.

90. See, for example, Richard Carrier, "The End of Pascal's Wager: Only Non-theists Go to Heaven," *Secular Web*, 2002, at http://www.infidels.org/library/modern/richard_carrier/heaven.html.

91. This is especially noticeable in India, where the most wretched people blame themselves; that is, their previous lives, for their wretchedness rather than rising up against their oppressors.

92. Yoichi Chida, Andrew Steptoe, and Lynda H. Powell, "Religiosity/Spirituality and Mortality," *Psychotherapy and Psychosomatics* 78, no. 2 (2009): 81–90.

93. For this very reason Chida, Steptoe, and Powell warn, "[T]he presence of publication biases indicates that results [like this] should be interpreted with caution," ibid., 81. Note that the reliability of the methods and some of the results of the Chida study group have been seriously challenged (illustrating many of the problems inherent in meta-analyses generally): James C. Coyne and Howard Tennen, "Positive Psychology in Cancer Care: Bad Science, Exaggerated Claims, and Unproven Medicine," *Annals of Behavioral Medicine* 39, no. 1 (February 2010): 16–26.

94. Yoichi Chida and Andrew Steptoe, "Positive Psychological Well-Being and Mortality: A Quantitative Review of Prospective Observational Studies," *Psychosomatic Medicine* 70, no. 7 (2008): 741–56 (though see previous note). [Editor's Note: a more recent study similarly found that previous studies showing life satisfaction increases with religious belief were only finding that friendmaking and social networking, not the belief itself, generate the effect: Chaeyoon Lim and Robert Putnam, "Religion, Social Networks, and Life Satisfaction," *American Sociological Review* 75, no. 6 (2010): 914–33. Lim and Putnam concluded that "religious belonging, rather than religious meaning, is central to the religion–life satisfaction nexus" (926), which means atheists who feel they belong to a group or movement and participate therein will probably see the same benefits, and given the findings of the Chida study group, this is as likely to be true for health and mortality).]

95. D'Souza, *Life After Death*, 220.

96. Ibid., 171

97. Ibid., 220.

98. Ibid.

CHAPTER 14

1. This chapter was peer reviewed by several professors of philosophy who did not always agree with my conclusions but nevertheless approved its publication, including Erik Wielenberg, Matt McCormick, John Shook, and Evan Fales. Their criticisms and advice led to numerous improvements, many unfortunately having to be relegated to the endnotes. I am very grateful for their input. This chapter formalizes the case made in greater detail in Richard Carrier, *Sense and Goodness without God: A Defense of Metaphysical Naturalism* (Bloomington, IN: AuthorHouse, 2005), 291–348. Note that the hypertechnical style of this chapter was made necessary to meet the peer-review standards of logical precision and validity.

2. Hereafter by "imperatives" I will not mean sentences in the imperative grammatical mood but propositions making a factual claim on our obedience (so that we should think of such "imperatives as statements to the effect that something ought to be done" and not merely as "injunctions expressed in the imperative mood." Quoted from Philippa Foot, "Morality as a System of Hypothetical Imperatives," in *Moral Discourse and Practice: Some Philosophical Approaches,* ed. Stephen Darwall, Allan Gibbard, and Peter Railton (Oxford: Oxford University Press, 1997) 313; cf. note 6 below).

3. By "science" I shall mean any empirical inquiry employing a logically sound and valid methodology. Thus I include methodologically sound history and journalism in this term, as well as any personal inquiry conducted scientifically. But the sciences as ordinarily conceived produce far more reliable conclusions and thus still carry primary authority.

4. In this chapter I shall only ever mean by "desire" and "want" (and all equivalent terminology) any actual preferring of one thing to another (for whatever reason and in whatever way); though in other contexts the same terms can denote other things (such as in cognitive science, an emotional state of perturbation cognitively and causally associated with a particular relieving outcome).

5. I will demonstrate the *logical* connection between these two facts in the next section.

6. A collection of the most famous essays arguing it can be found in Darwall, Allan, and Railton, *Moral Discourse and Practice* (see note 2); a recent demonstration using modern game theory is provided in Gary Drescher, *Good and Real: Demystifying Paradoxes from Physics to Ethics* (Cambridge, MA: MIT Press, 2006), 273–320. Noted philosophers who have espoused the view that moral facts are (at least in principle) empirically discoverable by science include Richard Boyd, Stephen Darwall, Allan Gibbard, Peter Railton, Philippa Foot, and many others, past and present. In fact, contrary to modern myth, even David Hume declared that imperatives not only do, but can *only*

derive from the facts of nature, and are therefore proper objects of scientific inquiry: David Hume, "Of Morals," in *Treatise on Human Nature* (1739), § 3.1.2, more fully expounded in *An Enquiry Concerning the Principles of Morals* (1751); see note 17 below. Modern scientists who study normative ethics are approaching agreement on this point (and old-guard philosophers just haven't gotten the memo), cf., e.g., Jeff Schweitzer and Giuseppe Notarbartolo-Di-Sciara, *Beyond Cosmic Dice: Moral Life in a Random World* (Los Angeles: Jacquie Jordan, 2009); Walter Sinnott-Armstrong, *Moral Psychology*, 3 vols. (Cambridge, MA: MIT Press, 2008); Owen Flanagan, *The Really Hard Problem: Meaning in a Material World* (Cambridge, MA: MIT Press, 2007); William Casebeer, *Natural Ethical Facts: Evolution, Connectionism, and Moral Cognition* (Cambridge, MA: MIT Press, 2003); and now most recently Sam Harris, *The Moral Landscape: How Science Can Determine Human Values* (New York: Free Press, 2010).

7. For a survey of all the reasons Christian philosopher J. P. Moreland could think of (which are pretty nearly all the credible reasons there are to be had), see Carrier, *Sense and Goodness*, 293–311.

8. By rational I mean nothing more than deriving conclusions from premises with logical validity (i.e., without fallacy). And by irrational I shall mean nothing more than not rational.

9. Despite fallacious or empirically groundless claims to the contrary, as demonstrated in *The Christian Delusion*, and works cited therein, and in other chapters in the present volume.

10. That is, when all measures are compared, there is no significant net difference between comparable societies (e.g., burglary rates in Australia are higher than in the United States but the crime rate in Australia overall is much lower; and the crime rate in Russia is higher than in the United States but the social conditions aren't equal). See: Gregory Paul, "The Chronic Dependence of Popular Religiosity upon Dysfunctional Psychosociological Conditions," *Evolutionary Psychology* 7, no. 3 (2009): 398–441, and "Cross-National Correlations of Quantifiable Societal Health with Popular Religiosity and Secularism in the Prosperous Democracies: A First Look," *Journal of Religion and Society* 7 (2005): http://moses.creighton.edu/JRS/2005/2005-11.html; Phil Zuckerman, *Society without God: What the Least Religious Nations Can Tell Us about Contentment* (New York: New York University Press, 2008); Pippa Norris and Ronald Inglehart, *Sacred and Secular: Religion and Politics Worldwide* (Cambridge: Cambridge University Press, 2004); Michael Shermer, *The Science of Good and Evil* (New York: Times Books, 2004), 235–36. Claims to the contrary are generally bogus, cf., e.g., Carrier, *Sense and Goodness*, 303–308.

11. For example see Ronald Inglehart, Roberto Foa, Christopher Peterson, and Christian Welzel, "Development, Freedom, and Rising Happiness," *Perspectives on Psy-*

chological Science 3, no. 4 (2008): 264–85. When combined with the evidence surveyed in the previous note, this study establishes there is no evidence rising atheism
leads to any decline in morality or happiness.

12. This is inherently obvious to any informed observer of modern Christianity
(and its history), as well as all other religions (which employ the exact same threats and
promises to ground their own moralities), but for Christianity this is well enough
proven in *The Christian Delusion* by several chapters collectively: David Eller, "The
Cultures of Christianities," 25–46, and "Christianity Does Not Provide the Basis for
Morality," 347–67; John Loftus, "What We've Got Here Is a Failure to Communicate,"
181–206; and Hector Avalos, "Yahweh Is a Moral Monster," 209–36 (with Richard
Carrier, "The Will of God" at http://sites.google.com/site/thechristiandelusion/
Home/the-will-of-god).

13. Hector Avalos, "Atheism Was Not the Cause of the Holocaust," in *The Christian Delusion*, ed. John Loftus (Amherst, NY: Prometheus: 2010), 368–95.

14. See, for example: Monika Keller, Wolfgang Edelstein, Christine Schmid, Fu-
xi Fang, Ge Fang, "Reasoning about Responsibilities and Obligations in Close Relationships: A Comparison across Two Cultures," *Developmental Psychology* 34, no. 4
(1998): 731–41; Nancy Eisenberg, Klaus Boehnke, Petra Schuler, Rainer K. Sil-
bereisen, "The Development of Prosocial Behavior and Cognitions in German
Children," *Journal of Cross-Cultural Psychology* 16, no. 1 (March 1985): 69–82; and
discussion and sources in Sinnott-Armstrong, *Moral Psychology*, 3:297–370. That hell-
centered moral theories actually correlate with societal dysfunction, see Gary Jensen,
"Religious Cosmologies and Homicide Rates among Nations: A Closer Look," *Journal
of Religion and Society* 8 (2006): http://moses.creighton.edu/JRS/2006/2006-7.html.

15. This is amusingly but accurately lampooned by "The Gospel of Supply Side
Jesus" in Al Franken, *Lies and the Lying Liars Who Tell Them: A Fair and Balanced
Look at the Right* (New York: Dutton, 2003), 313–23 (cf. 213–16). Some prominent
devout Christians (including both Catholics and Evangelicals) have documented the
same facts with sadness: Ronald Sider, *The Scandal of the Evangelical Conscience*
(Grand Rapids, MI: Baker, 2005); Garry Wills, *What Jesus Meant* (New York: Viking,
2006); Gregory Boyd, *The Myth of a Christian Nation* (Grand Rapids, MI: Zondervan, 2007); and Robin Meyers, *Why the Christian Right Is Wrong* (San Francisco:
Jossey-Bass, 2008).

16. Other respects in which Christianity harms moral progress include its central
doctrines that humans are innately sinful and thus incapable of their own moral reform
(so nothing they do of themselves will make them better people) and that through a
mere faith claim they will be forgiven all crimes no matter what they do (thus negating
all the moral incentives Christianity is supposed to have provided in the first place): see
Evan Fales, "Satanic Verses: Moral Chaos in Holy Writ," in *Divine Evil? The Moral*

Character of the God of Abraham, ed. Michael Bergmann, Michael Murray, and Michael Rea (Oxford: Oxford University Press, 2011).

17. David Hume, "Of Morals," in *Treatise on Human Nature* (1739), § 3.1.1, where he only declares that "vulgar systems of morality" have failed to establish that connection, not that no system ever could; to the contrary, in the very next section he argues he *can*—so, even if you believe his specific moral theory is incorrect, it's still wrong to claim he declared a reduction of values to facts to be *impossible*.

18. First extensively demonstrated by Immanual Kant in his *Groundwork of the Metaphysic of Morals* (1785); subsequently modernized by Philippa Foot, "Morality as a System of Hypothetical Imperatives," reproduced in *Moral Discourse and Practice: Some Philosophical Approaches,* ed. Stephen Darwall, Allan Gibbard, and Peter Railton (Oxford: Oxford University Press, 1997) 313–22; and others. See Carrier, *Sense and Goodness*, 331–35.

19. Immanuel Kant, *Groundwork of the Metaphysic of Morals* or *Grundlegung zur Metaphysik der Sitten* (1785) § 3.4 (Kant's arrangement) or § 4.454 (Royal Prussian Academy edition), 112–13 in Kant's 2nd German ed. (1786), or 122 of H. J. Paton's English translation (New York: Harper Torchbooks, 1964); see also Robert Wolff, *The Autonomy of Reason: A Commentary on Kant's Groundwork of the Metaphysic of Morals* (New York: Harper & Row, 1973), 211 (§ 3.5). Psychology has since verified and revised Kant's claim considerably: see Carrier, *Sense and Goodness*, 313–27.

20. Hence one might attempt to patch up Kant by proposing other reasons to obey K (e.g., such as from game theory: that it's contrary to your interest to promote, by example, actions the universalization of which would bring you to harm), but if that is factually true and sufficiently motivating, then it's simply M; and insofar as it *isn't* true or sufficiently motivating, then it's overridden by M. Either way, we're left with M as the only relevantly true moral system. Similarly, in Philippa Foot, *Natural Goodness* (New York: Oxford University Press, 2001), she revised her earlier work by proposing instead that a system of hypothetical moral imperatives follows from desiring most to be a rational person (thus allowing irrational people could never be persuaded), but just as with Kant, even that is still at root a hypothetical imperative (see note 36 below).

21. This is effectively argued by Stephen Darwall in his own demonstration that Kant's categorical imperatives either necessarily reduce to hypothetical imperatives (as I have also shown) or else have no motivating truth value: Stephen Darwall, "Kantian Practical Reason Defended," *Ethics* 96, no. 1 (October 1985): 89–99. From the principles assumed therein it's obvious that the same reduction can be performed on *any* moral system. Conversely, through a covering law, all true hypothetical imperatives reduce to a categorical: R. S. Downie, "The Hypothetical Imperative," *Mind* 93 (October 1984): 481–90. But that categorical is tautologically also a hypothetical (that we be rational and informed: see note 36).

22. Note that any such proposed *M*-defeating alternative need not be verified *empirically*, it need only be verified as true by any means that's sufficiently motivating (thus I am not presupposing only empirically verified imperatives can warrant our overriding obedience—although I seriously doubt anything else can, it's not necessary to assume it can't).

23. Bernard Williams, "Internal and External Reasons," in *Moral Discourse and Practice*, 363–71. Supported in *Moral Psychology*, 3:173–90 and 217–25. In effect, externalism reduces to descriptive, not prescriptive ethics.

24. For the formal proof of this, see Argument 1 in the appendix to this chapter (on p. 359). See also following note.

25. For the formal proof of this, see Argument 2 in the appendix to this chapter (on pp. 360–61). See also the upcoming section of this chapter, "That There Are Moral Facts to Discover."

26. Carrier, *Sense and Goodness*, 291–348; Drescher, *Good and Real*, 273–320; also Casebeer, *Natural Ethical Facts*; Flanagan, *Really Hard Problem*; and now most recently Harris, *Moral Landscape*. As my statement implies, a virtue theory of ethics has the most scientific support (see, for example, *Moral Psychology* 1:209–67, 2:207–11; modern social contract theory still explains the evolution of most human moral reasoning, e.g., *Moral Psychology*, 1:53–119, 143–64, but such reasoning still assumes the primacy of associated virtues), and is thus what I defend elsewhere, but virtue theories still reduce to a system of foundational imperatives (e.g., "you ought to develop and cultivate the virtue of compassion"), from which follows a system of occasional imperatives (e.g., "if you are compassionate, then you ought to x in circumstance z"); hence in *Sense and Goodness*, I present a unification of teleological, deontological, and virtue ethics (see 345–48), and I further unify cognitivism and intuitionism (see 339–41, with 178–80, 192). A theory that can unify all competing theories under one umbrella (and thereby explain and justify them all) has a strong claim to being true.

27. That moral truth must derive from rationally informed motives, not the actual motives of the moment, is demonstrated in Stephen Darwall, "Reasons, Motives, and the Demands of Morality: An Introduction," in *Moral Discourse and Practice*, 305–12. I give an important example of this in Loftus, *The Christian Delusion*, 100–101.

28. In the absence of perfect knowledge, approximate knowledge is optimal, a fact we accept in all domains (e.g., we needn't know exactly what's in an atom to make successful predictions from approximately what's in an atom; for a broad defense of this principle, see Kees van Deemter, *Not Exactly: In Praise of Vagueness* [New York: Oxford University Press: 2010]). Thus if we do not know (because due to our limitations we cannot know) what the best thing is, we can still know what the best thing is *so far as we know*, which will always be better than any other thing we know (see dis-

cussion in Sinnott-Armstrong, *Moral Psychology*, 1:1–46). It may still be the case that something is better, and thus we will be obligated to find out what that is as soon as we are able, but when we are unable, we are not obligated (see note 34).

29. See Carrier, *Sense and Goodness*, 316–24, 341–42.

30. This is not the only unsettling conclusion game theory entails a rationally informed slavemaster must live with. The complete analysis (for all morally asymmetrical relationships) is provided in Drescher, *Good and Real*, 273–320. See also Ken Binmore, *Game Theory and the Social Contract* (Cambridge, MA: MIT Press: Vol. 1, 1994; Vol. 2, 1998).

31. Many examples of this, even in the very field of moral psychology, are discussed in contributions to the volumes of Sinnott-Armstrong's *Moral Psychology*, and examples in the study of differential happiness are even more numerous: besides the many references provided in Carrier, *Sense and Goodness*, 322–23, including most notably (but not only) Martin Seligman, *Authentic Happiness* (New York: Free Press, 2002), more recent summaries include: Daniel Pink, *Drive: The Surprising Truth about What Motivates Us* (New York: Riverhead, 2009); Sonja Lyubomirsky, *The How of Happiness* (New York: Penguin, 2008); Eric Weiner, *The Geography of Bliss* (New York: Twelve, 2008); Eduardo Punset, *The Happiness Trip* (White River Junction, VT: Sciencewriters, 2007); Daniel Todd Gilbert, *Stumbling on Happiness* (New York: Alfred A. Knopf, 2006); and P. R. G. Layard, *Happiness: Lessons from a New Science* (New York: Penguin, 2005); and an important *earlier* example I had missed is Martha Nussbaum and Amartya Sen, eds., *The Quality of Life* (New York: Oxford University Press, 1993).

32. Harris, *Moral Landscape*, deals with both issues deftly and in detail (how scientific methods can answer these questions, and why unknowable truths are still nevertheless true facts of the world).

33. Of course someone may ask what to do if there are conflicting moral imperatives: well, either (a) one will be the more imperative and thus supersede or (b) neither will be the more imperative, in which case there will be no truth of the matter as to which should be preferred (i.e., doing either will be exactly as moral as doing the other—though still to the exclusion of everything else). If any sound and valid argument can be made to the contrary of (b), then that argument necessarily entails that (a) (i.e., that one is the more imperative than the other, and therefore (b) is not true).

34. Things we want that are unachievable are of course out of account precisely because there is no action we can take to obtain them and therefore no true imperative fact upon us in the matter. But this distinction can only pertain to the absolutely unachievable (e.g., stopping a bullet with your hand), not the contingently unachievable (e.g., failing to take cover when cover was obtainable in principle). Free will is thus not an issue. The distinction is between defects of calculation and defects beyond any

calculation to overcome (which are different states, regardless of free will)—because (a) improved calculation can correct the one but not the other, and (b) the one is a causal product of the character we wish to evaluate while the other is not (see Carrier, *Sense and Goodness*, 97–117).

35. Given the formal proofs in the appendix, this entails moral facts are such that: "*S* morally ought to do *A*" means "If *S*'s desires were rationally deduced from as many facts as *S* can reasonably obtain at that time (about *S*'s preferences and the outcomes of *S*'s available alternatives in *S*'s circumstances), then *S* would prefer *A* over all the available alternative courses of action (at that time and in those circumstances)." This definition does mean willful irrationality is immoral, but not irrationality born of (a) unalterable mental defect (because unachievable ends can never be imperative for *S*— see note 34) or (b) inaccessible information (because then *S* has properly acted on all information reasonably obtainable at that time—see note 28). Nevertheless, though irrationality *itself* can be morally excusable on either case, irrational *actions* can still be morally blameworthy even for such people, insofar as they know what they are doing is nevertheless wrong, or they had reasonable access to facts that would have informed them that it was (even given their irrationality), as then the moral end (and knowledge thereof) was obtainable and still neglected (hence a failure of calculation, not of calculability). Nevertheless, excusability exists in principle, so we can sometimes acknowledge people as "acting morally" yet who could have done better had they known better (see note 28 on optimal moral knowledge). Conversely, we have greater emotional and institutional interest in actions by others whose generalization or continuance can put ourselves or people we care about at risk of harm (and thus we often voice "moral outrage" at only such acts), but that certain moral failures are of greater concern to us does not mean acts of lesser concern are not also moral failures. A similar logic makes supererogatory acts possible (acts that are not morally obligatory but nevertheless praiseworthy). Praise and blame thus only report what we like and dislike, not necessarily what's right and wrong (although there will still be a right and wrong about what to praise or blame).

36. Someone may object that perhaps we ought to be irrational and uninformed, but still the conclusion would follow that *when* we are rational and informed we would want *x*. Only if *x* were then "to be irrational and/or uninformed in circumstance *z*" would it then be true that we ought to be irrational and uninformed, and yet even that conclusion can only follow if we are rational and informed when we arrive at it. Because for an imperative to pursue *x* to be *true*, whatever we want most must *in fact* be best achieved by obeying *x*, yet it's unlikely that we will arrive at that conclusion by being irrational and uninformed. Such an approach is very unlikely to light upon the truth of what best achieves our desires (as if it could do so by accident). Therefore, any conclusion arrived at regarding what *x* is must be either rational and informed or prob-

ably false. Ergo, to achieve anything we desire, we ought to endeavor to be rational and informed.

37. "Weakness of will" is therefore merely an irrational preference for one thing over another (e.g., preferring instant gratification to long-term well-being). That we call it a weakness simply expresses our acknowledgment that such a preference is irrational.

38. For the formal proof of this, see Argument 3 in the appendix to this chapter (on pp. 361–62).

39. I believe science has established a Humean account of motivation more than amply (Carrier, *Sense and Goodness*, 193–97, for discussion and scientific bibliography), and all philosophical objections to it have been ably dispatched by Neil Sinhababu, "The Humean Theory of Motivation Reformulated and Defended," *Philosophical Review* 118, no. 4 (2009): 465–500 (though he occasionally confuses the phenomenology of desire with the logical mechanics of desire, this only interferes with his ability to unify internalism and cognitivism, the rest of his argument remains correct even using my definition of desire in note 4). Nevertheless, my moral theory as stated here is compatible with either Humean or non-Humean accounts of moral motivation (e.g., "When rational and sufficiently informed, you will want x more than $\sim x$" does not presuppose where this desire for x comes from, only that it will survive rational review).

40. On innate and learned theories of mind and their role in autism, see Simon Baron-Cohen, *Mindblindness: An Essay on Autism and Theory of Mind* (Cambridge, MA: MIT Press, 1995).

41. See discussion and sources in Carrier, *Sense and Goodness*, 342–44; and in Sinnott-Armstrong, *Moral Psychology*, 1:390, 3:119–296, 363–66, 381–82. Their insanity does not mean psychopaths have an excuse, however, because when they act immorally they usually still know what they are doing is wrong (see note 35). And even when they don't, like schizophrenics, we still have to contain them and protect ourselves from them.

42. For the formal proof of what has just been argued see Argument 4 in the appendix to this chapter (on pp. 362–64); and for the formal proof that these moral facts are ascertainable scientifically see Argument 5 (on p. 364).

43. Do not mistake me for saying that moral facts consist of evolutionary strategies for increasing differential reproductive success. Such strategies have evolved. But they carry no imperative authority when we want something else more. We (as persons making moral decisions) are minds, not genomes. We prefer things like happiness to differential reproductive success (and I predict this will be commonplace among civilized species). The latter can at best only be instrumental to the former—for us, that is; whereas for our genes, obviously, it was the other way around, which is how we got that way, but we're running the show now, not our genes: see Keith Stanovich, *The Robot's*

Rebellion: Finding Meaning in the Age of Darwin (Chicago: University of Chicago Press, 2004), and related remarks in Victor Stenger's chapter in the present volume.

44. This is a very important consequence of my analysis, as this being the case, we need to be extremely careful in any endeavor to develop AI of any kind, genetically or digitally, as its recognition of moral facts will be dependent on what nature we engineer it to have (or fail to engineer it to have). This danger has been aptly illustrated, for example, in the films *Dark Star* (1974) and *2010* (1984).

45. There is no relevant difference here between propositional knowledge ("I know how to swim") and nonpropositional knowledge (actually knowing how to swim). The same conclusions follow for either (the latter merely consisting of subconsciously assimilated information, like Trinity's "uploading" of piloting skills in *The Matrix* [1999]).

46. Hence the conclusions of Jonathan Haidt and Fredrik Bjorklund in Sinnott-Armstrong, *Moral Psychology*, 2:213–16 (with 250–54).

47. This has the added consequence of refuting the Moral Argument for God, e.g., Mark Linville, "The Moral Argument," in *The Blackwell Companion to Natural Theology*, ed. W. L. Craig and J. P. Moreland (Wiley-Blackwell, 2009), 391–448. If I'm wrong, of course, that still does not entail the moral argument succeeds (if there are no moral facts, then there are no moral facts—atheism is not thereby refuted). But as I have demonstrated that moral facts must necessarily exist regardless of whether God exists or any religion is true, the existence of moral facts cannot argue for the existence of God or the truth of any religion. Linville's counter-argument, that deriving moral facts from the evolved facts of human biology commits a genetic fallacy, is self-defeating if true, as then deriving moral facts from the creative acts of God commits a genetic fallacy, too (for we cannot conclude that what God wants is best except by appeal to the nature God already gave us, which becomes a circular argument). Either way, the question remains what we ought most to do, which is still entailed by what we want most to happen. It doesn't matter how we got that way (though it will matter when we become the creators of intelligent beings). Even if Linville were to argue that he wished he were different than evolution made him, he would be contradicting himself—as he cannot have wished for anything but what (ultimately) evolution gave him the desire to wish for, and whether he can change to satisfy that desire will depend on his actual nature, which is a matter of fact that remains the same whether evolution made us or God, so if Linville wishes he were different but cannot satisfy that wish, then he is as much objecting to how God made him as evolution did—whereas if he can satisfy that wish, then his complaint is groundless, as he would then no longer have to be different than he wished to be.

48. I present the formal deductive proof of these conclusions in an appendix to this chapter (pp. 359–64), such that you cannot rationally disagree unless you can

rationally reject one of the premises therein; as otherwise my conclusions necessarily follow from them, and it is irrational to disagree with a conclusion that necessarily follows from premises you cannot rationally reject. I note this because my arguments are rejected by some atheists of my acquaintance, but for no rational reason I can ascertain. They consistently fail to identify any premise that they can rationally reject in the formal arguments in this appendix. Thus their rejection of the conclusions is simply irrational.

LIST OF CONTRIBUTORS

HECTOR AVALOS, PHD, is professor of religious studies, Iowa State University, and author of *Slavery, Abolitionism, and the Ethics of Biblical Scholarship* (Sheffield, England: Sheffield Phoenix Press, 2011), *Fighting Words: The Origin of Religious Violence* (Amherst, NY: Prometheus Books, 2005), *The End of Biblical Studies* (Amherst, NY: Prometheus Books, 2007), and a chapter in *The Christian Delusion: Why Faith Fails*, edited by John W. Loftus (Amherst, NY: Prometheus Books, 2010).

RICHARD CARRIER, PHD, is a published philosopher and historian of antiquity and author of *Sense and Goodness without God: A Defense of Metaphysical Naturalism* (Bloomington, IN: AuthorHouse, 2005); *Not the Impossible Faith: Why Christianity Didn't Need a Miracle to Succeed* (Raleigh, NC: Lulu, 2009); *Why I Am Not a Christian: Four Conclusive Reasons to Reject the Faith* (Richmond, CA: Philosophy Press, 2011); of three chapters for the book *The Empty Tomb: Jesus beyond the Grave*, edited by Robert Price and Jeffery Lowder (Amherst, NY: Prometheus Books, 2005); and two chapters in *The Christian Delusion: Why Faith Fails*, edited by John W. Loftus (Amherst, NY: Prometheus Books, 2010). You can find his website at http://www.richard carrier.info.

DAVID ELLER, PHD, is assistant professor of anthropology at the Community College of Denver. He has written the books *Natural Atheism* (Cranford, NJ: American Atheist, 2004); *Atheism Advanced: Further Thoughts of a Freethinker* (Cranford, NJ: American Atheist, 2007); a college textbook, *Introducing Anthropology of Religion: Culture to the Ultimate* (New York: Routledge, 2007); *Cruel Creeds, Virtuous Violence: Religious Violence across Culture and*

History (Amherst, NY: Prometheus Books, 2010), and two chapters in *The Christian Delusion: Why Faith Fails*, edited by John W. Loftus (Amherst, NY: Prometheus Books, 2010).

JACO GERICKE, PHD, is an Old Testament biblical scholar and philosopher of religion, North-West University, South Africa.

JOHN W. LOFTUS, MA, MDIV, THM, is the author of the book *Why I Became an Atheist: A Former Preacher Rejects Christianity* (Amherst, NY: Prometheus Books, 2008); editor of *The Christian Delusion: Why Faith Fails* (Amherst, NY: Prometheus Books, 2010); and founder of http://debunkingchristianity.blogspot.com.

MATT MCCORMICK, PHD, professor of philosophy, California State University, Sacramento, California.

KEITH PARSONS, PHD, professor of philosophy, University of Houston, and author of the books *God and the Burden of Proof* (Amherst, NY: Prometheus Books, 1989) and *Rational Episodes: Logic for the Intermittently Reasonable* (Amherst, NY: Prometheus Books, 2009).

ROBERT PRICE, PHD, is a member of the Jesus Seminar and author of several books including *Deconstructing Jesus* (Amherst, NY: Prometheus Books, 2000); *The Incredible Shrinking Son of Man: How Reliable Is the Gospel Tradition?* (Amherst, NY: Prometheus Books, 2003); coeditor of *The Empty Tomb: Jesus beyond the Grave* (Amherst, NY: Prometheus Books, 2005); *Inerrant the Wind: The Evangelical Crisis of Biblical Authority* (Amherst, NY: Prometheus Books, 2009); and a chapter in *The Christian Delusion: Why Faith Fails* (Amherst, NY: Prometheus Books, 2010), edited by John W. Loftus.

KEN PULLIAM, PHD, earned his doctorate from Bob Jones University in 1986. Then, for nine years, Ken taught New Testament Greek, systematic theology, and apologetics at the International Baptist College in Tempe, Arizona, before becoming an agnostic atheist. At the time of his untimely death in October of 2010, he was writing a book that would surely have been a tour de force on the various atonement theories. His story can be read here: http://www.bible interp.com/articles/funding357924.shtml.

VICTOR STENGER, PhD, is adjunct professor of philosophy at the University of Colorado and emeritus professor of physics at the University of Hawaii. He spent forty years doing research in elementary particle physics and astrophysics before retiring in 2000. He is the author of ten books including the 2007 *New York Times* bestseller *God: The Failed Hypothesis* (Amherst, NY: Prometheus Books, 2007), and *The Fallacy of Fine-Tuning: Why the Universe Is Not Designed for Us* (Amherst, NY: Prometheus Books, 2011).

VALERIE TARICO, PhD, is a psychologist and former director of the Children's Behavior and Learning Clinic in Bellevue, Washington. She is the author of the book *The Dark Side: How Evangelical Teachings Corrupt Love and Truth* (Seattle: Dea, 2006), revised and republished as *Trusting Doubt: A Former Evangelical Looks at Old Beliefs in a New Light* (Hamilton, VA: Oracle Institute, 2010); and a chapter in *The Christian Delusion: Why Faith Fails*, edited by John W. Loftus (Amherst, NY: Prometheus Books, 2010). Her website can be found at http://www.valerietarico.com.

COMMITMENT PAGE

Date_____

I _____, having read this book and/or the series as a whole, do hereby state for the record that I no longer believe. I am a non-believer. As a result, I commit myself to doing some or all of the following actions for the cause of unbelief:

- ❏ I will tell the people in my life at the appropriate moments that I no longer believe. I will set specific dates by which I plan on accomplishing this goal with specific people. We need more and more people to do this. There is power in numbers.
- ❏ I will tell others about this book and/or this series of books. Christians won't be convinced with sound bites. We must create within them enough doubt that they will want to read entire books like these rather than avoiding them.

I will get involved to help end Christianity in the following way(s):

- ❏ I will seek out and become involved in a local freethought group.
- ❏ I will get active in online forums and blogs.
- ❏ I will donate money to good secular causes, or to humanitarian causes in the name of secularism.
- ❏ I will get an education for the express purpose of making a difference on behalf of reason and science.
- ❏ I will become politically active on behalf of the separation of church and state, or even run for an elected office.